LONG-RUN EFFECTS OF SHORT-RUN STABILIZATION POLICY

During the last decade, the Western economies have been exposed to unusually severe macroeconomic problems: inflation, unemployment, slow growth, current account imbalances and structural maladjustments. Shocks have been of a new type, originating on the supply side in the form of both raw material price shocks (mainly oil) and wage disturbances. In this situation, traditional stabilization policies have been inadequate. They have also often had negative effects on resource allocation and on future macroeconomic performance. This book analyzes different types of such long-run effects on the size of various production sectors, on the current account and the allocation of consumption over time, on investment and growth, and on future wage-setting behaviour of trade unions. An important feature of the book is the careful integration of micro and macro theory.

The book contains the following contributions: 'The Current Account in the Macroeconomic Adjustment Process' by Jeffrey Sachs; 'Global Effects of National Stabilization Policies under Fixed and Floating Exchange Rates' by Torsten Persson; 'Adjustment and Structural Change under Supply Shocks' by Michael Bruno; 'Sectoral Shocks in a Dependent Economy: Long-run Adjustment and Short-run Accommodation' by J. Peter Neary and Douglas D. Purvis; 'Stabilization, Allocation and the 1970s Oil Price Shocks' by John F. Helliwell, Paul M. Boothe and Robert N. McRae; 'Inflation, Tax Rules and the Accumulation of Residential and Nonresidential Capital' by Martin Feldstein; 'Profitability and Growth' by Pentti J. K. Kouri; and 'Employment Policies, Wage Formation and Trade Union Behaviour in a Small Open Economy' by Lars Calmfors.

In the same series

Edited by Peter Bohm and Allen V. Kneese
THE ECONOMICS OF ENVIRONMENT

Edited by Jan Herin, Assar Lindbeck and Johan Myhrman
FLEXIBLE EXCHANGE RATES AND STABILIZATION POLICY

Edited by Steinar Strøm and Lars Werin
TOPICS IN DISEQUILIBRIUM ECONOMICS

Edited by Steinar Strøm and Björn Thalberg
THE THEORETICAL CONTRIBUTIONS OF KNUT WICKSELL

Edited by Steinar Strøm
MEASUREMENT IN PUBLIC CHOICE

Edited by Lars Matthiessen and Steinar Strøm
UNEMPLOYMENT: MACRO AND MICRO-ECONOMIC EXPLANATIONS

Edited by Lars Matthiessen
THE IMPACT OF RISING OIL PRICES ON THE WORLD ECONOMY

LONG-RUN EFFECTS OF SHORT-RUN STABILIZATION POLICY

Edited by

Lars Calmfors
Institute for International Economic Studies
Stockholm, Sweden

M

This collection was originally published in *The Scandinavian Journal of Economics*, Vol. 84, 1982, No. 2

First published in book form 1983 by
THE MACMILLAN PRESS LTD
London and Basingstoke
Companies and representatives throughout the world

ISBN 978-1-349-06351-2 ISBN 978-1-349-06349-9 (eBook)
DOI 10.1007/978-1-349-06349-9

Contents

Preface

This volume contains the proceedings of a conference on 'Long-run Effects of Short-run Stabilization Policy', held at Saltsjöbaden, Stockholm, 31 August–2 September 1981. The conference was organized by the Institute for International Economic Studies at the University of Stockholm and the Marcus Wallenberg Foundation for International Cooperation in Science. The conference was planned by a committee consisting of Assar Lindbeck, Erik Dahmén, Hans Munck, Johan Myhrman, Hans Tson Söderström and Lars Calmfors. The administrative responsibility was carried by Lars Calmfors, who also served as editor. Birgitta Eliason of the IIES took care of the practical arrangements. These proceedings were originally published in *The Scandinavian Journal of Economics*, Vol. 84, 1982, No. 2.

Stockholm, July 1982 *Assar Lindbeck* *Erik Dahmén*

Notes on the Contributors

Paul M. Boothe	Bank of Canada, Ottawa, ON, Canada
Michael Bruno	Professor of Economics, Hebrew University of Jerusalem, Israel
Lars Calmfors	Researcher, Institute for International Economic Studies, Stockholm, Sweden
Martin Feldstein	Professor of Economics, Harvard University, Cambridge, MA, USA, and Director of the National Bureau of Economic Research, Cambridge, MA, and New York, NY, USA
John Flemming	Professor of Economics, Oxford University, Oxford, England, and associated with the Bank of England
Hans Genberg	Professor of Economics, Graduate Institute of International Studies, Geneva, Switzerland
Nils Gottfries	Researcher, Department of Economics, University of Stockholm, Sweden
Thorvaldur Gylfason	Researcher, Institute for International Economic Studies, Stockholm, Sweden
John Helliwell	Professor of Economics, University of British Columbia, Vancouver, BC, Canada
Michael Hoel	Professor of Economics, University of Oslo, Norway
Pentti J. K. Kouri	Professor of Economics, New York University, NY, USA, and Helsinki University, Finland
R. C. O. Matthews	Master of Clare College; Professor of Economics, Cambridge University, England
Robert N. McRae	Professor of Economics, University of Calgary, Alberta, Canada
Johan Myhrman	Professor of Economics, Stockholm School of Economics, Sweden
J. Peter Neary	Professor of Economics, University College, Dublin, Republic of Ireland
Torsten Persson	Researcher, Institute for International Economic Studies, Stockholm, Sweden

Douglas D. Purvis	Professor of Economics, Queen's University, Kingston, ON, Canada
Assaf Razin	Professor of Economics, Tel-Aviv University, Israel
Jeffrey D. Sachs	Associate Professor of Economics, Harvard University, Cambridge, MA, USA
Lars Svensson	Researcher, Institute for International Economic Studies, Stockholm, Sweden
Hans Tson Söderström	Assistant Director and Researcher, Institute for International Economic Studies, Stockholm, Sweden
Staffan Viotti	Associate Professor of Economics, Stockholm School of Economics, Sweden

Long-run Effects of Short-run Stabilization Policy—An Introduction

*Lars Calmfors**

Institute for International Economic Studies, Stockholm, Sweden

Against the background of the failures of stabilization policies in most developed countries during the 1970s, it seems natural that a more critical attitude towards such policies has gradually evolved. The skepticism has usually focused on the *long-run effects of stabilization policy,* which is the theme of this conference.

There appear to be two lines along which this critical reevaluation has been pursued. The *first* emphasizes the effects of short-run stabilization policies on the long-run *allocation of resources*. The *second* stresses the consequences for *future macroeconomic performance*.

Turning first to the *long-run allocation effects,* an obvious starting point is the new type of shocks which the developed countries have been exposed to during the last decade. Traditional Keynesian stabilization policies were designed to smoothen the cyclical swings of aggregate demand around a full-employment growth path. They were not designed to cope with disturbances originating on the supply side of the economy such as oil (or other raw material) shocks and wage disturbances. Given such supply shocks, traditional expenditure policies are faced with a dilemma: expenditure-increasing policies may prevent unemployment but exacerbate inflation, expenditure-reducing policies reduce inflation but exacerbate unemployment.

The supply shocks of the 1970s have to a large degree been permanent real shocks that require real readjustments. These must be preceded by appropriate changes in relative prices and real wages. To the extent that traditional expenditure policies prevent or slow down these price adjustments, the long-run allocation of resources will be affected adversely. In order to evaluate the welfare effects of stabilization policy, these long-run allocational losses must be weighed against short-run gains.

* I would like to thank Erik Dahmén, Thorvaldur Gylfason, Assar Lindbeck, Torsten Persson, Michael Schmid and Staffan Viotti for helpful comments.

The other line of criticism stresses instead the conflict between *short-run and long-run macroeconomic policy goals*. This has been a major theme in the theoretical macroeconomic discussion throughout the 1970s. In its weakest form, this line of thought emphasizes how expansionary stabilization policy will have output and employment effects in the short run but only affect the price level in the long run. In its strongest form (the new classical macroeconomics), it even questions the possibility of affecting output and employment in the short run. This is based on the well-known argument that economic agents are likely to learn to take all systematic policy rules into account when setting wages and prices.

Both of the above approaches to stabilization policy are pursued in this volume. The themes of the papers can, of course, be structured in many ways. This introduction is organized around the following topics: (1) the nature of the shocks discussed; (2) resource allocation effects; (3) effects on future macroeconomic performance ; (4) policy conclusions; and (5) questions for future research.

As a starting point it is worth noting that a common characteristic of the papers is the careful integration of micro and macro theory. This integration is natural in those papers which stress the links between stabilization policy and the long-run structure of production and demand and those which focus on the importance of intertemporal choices with respect to saving and investment. But more careful micro foundations can also be important for e.g. the analysis of wage formation. The policy problems of today no longer make it possible to maintain the old dichotomy between micro and macro theory; on the contrary a rigorous analysis of stabilization policy requires a careful integration.

I. The Nature of Shocks

The last decade has shown the need for a careful distinction between various types of shocks. The effects on the economy differ crucially, depending on whether the shocks are *real* or *monetary,* whether they originate on the *supply* or *demand* side of the economy and whether they are *temporary* or *permanent*.

A common theme in most of the papers seems to be the emphasis on *real shocks* originating on the *supply side*. The papers stress both *raw material shocks* and *wage disturbances*.

Raw Material Shocks

The effects of raw material price increases are highlighted from different angles in the papers by Bruno, Neary–Purvis, and Helliwell–Boothe–

McRae. A main theme is to explain the "deindustrialization" that has occurred in many developed countries. Here it is important to distinguish between *wealth* and *input* effects.

For *net exporters* of raw materials (such as Canada, the Netherlands or Norway in the case of oil and natural gas), a raw material price increase —whether permanent, temporary or anticipated—means increased *wealth* (= the discounted value of present and future income). Such a wealth increase could also arise because of a new resource discovery (such as North Sea oil). It is discussed in all of the above-mentioned papers, but is stressed the most by Neary–Purvis. A wealth increase causes increased spending, which—since the foreign-currency price of tradables is exogenously given in the world market for a small economy—drives up the relative price of nontradables and the product real wage in the tradables (manufacturing) sector. The result is an instantaneous shift of labor away from the tradables sector to the other sectors of the economy. If the raw material price increase is permanent, the fall in profitability in the tradables sector (and the rise in the resource sector) will also induce a gradual shift of capital from the tradables to the resource sector, where the exact time path of the adjustment depends on the degree of price flexibility. As stressed by Bruno, the resource shifts due to the wealth increase may very well start before the shock actually takes place. Anticipation of a raw material price increase (or a resource discovery) already represents a wealth increase, which will cause spending to increase and make it profitable to start shifting resources from the tradables sector into the other sectors.

In addition to the wealth effects, Bruno also discusses the effects of raw material price increases that work via the *input side*. In the short run, the return to capital falls and unemployment emerges if real wages are sticky. In the long run—when the capital stock has adjusted so as to equalize the domestic return to capital with the world rate of interest—the adjustment will involve a fall in both the real wage and the capital intensity of production. But the long-run structure of the economy is also affected. Resources will shift from raw material-intensive activities to less intensive ones. If the production of tradables (manufactured goods) is raw material-intensive, a relative price increase for raw materials can thus serve as one explanation for deindustrialization.

Supply shocks of this type also raise the possibility of "new" types of stabilization policy directed against these shocks. In their empirical paper, Helliwell–Boothe–McRae discuss the Canadian case where one method of maintaining aggregate demand after the first oil price shock was to delay the response of domestic energy prices. Such a policy obviously causes serious conflicts with the goals of an efficient long-run allocation of resources. But in the Canadian case the welfare losses for domestic citizens were small because of the large share of nonresidence ownership of the oil and gas industry, which meant that the policy of holding down domestic energy prices became a method of restricting windfall profits to foreigners.

Wage Formation

The supply side can also enter the analysis via *wage formation*. A common characteristic of the papers is that when unemployment is discussed, it is not regarded, in the terminology of Malinvaud,[1] as Keynesian but as classical instead, resulting from excessively high real wages. The papers differ, however, in their assumptions on whether it is the *real* wage or the *money* wage that is *sticky*. This distinction is crucial, since an overly high real wage can be inflated away in the latter case but not in the former.

Both types of wage stickiness play an important role in the papers dealing with raw material shocks. Bruno sketches an inflexible real wage as a cause of short-run unemployment. Neary–Purvis argue that a sticky *real* wage will cause excess demand for labor and may result in a cyclical adjustment path in the case of a resource boom. A sticky *money* wage and a sticky *money* price of nontradables may, in the same situation, cause an increase in the real wage resulting in temporary unemployment. The reason is that the increased demand for money due to the increase in real income from a resource boom causes a Dornbusch-type overshooting of the nominal exchange rate.[2]

But the supply side disturbances may, of course, also *originate* on the wage side. Such disturbances play an important role in the papers by Persson, Kouri and Calmfors. In Persson's paper, an exogenously determined money wage that is too high in relation to the price of goods is seen as the reason for unemployment and motivates stabilization policies which inflate the price level or reduce employers' wage costs. The reason for the excessively high money wage is presumably that price increases during the period of the wage contract have been overestimated. According to Kouri, an exogenously fixed too high real wage causes not only (classical) unemployment but serves as a restriction on investment and growth as well.

Calmfors analyzes explicitly the reasons for overly high real wages. This is done within a framework where the wage rate is determined by an all-encompassing trade union that maximizes the utility of its members. It may then be optimal for the trade union to obtain such a high real wage that some of its members are left unemployed.

---

[1] Malinvaud, Edmond, *The Theory of Unemployment Reconsidered*, Basil Blackwell, Oxford, 1977.

[2] Cf. e.g. Dornbusch, Rudiger, "Expectations and exchange rate dynamics", *Journal of Political Economy* 1976.

II. Resource Allocation Effects

Another way of structuring the themes of the conference is according to which types of effects of shocks and policies are discussed. Although there is a great deal of overlapping between different papers, the following resource allocation effects can be discerned: (1) allocation of consumption over time and determination of the current account; (2) determination of investment and growth and (3) allocation of resources among different production sectors (tradables/nontradables/government and resource sectors).

The Allocation of Consumption over Time

A first type of issue concerns the allocation of *consumption over time* and the determination of the *current account.* Sachs is the one who focuses most heavily on these issues, although they receive similar treatment by Persson and Bruno and are illustrated empirically for Canada by Helliwell–Boothe–McRae.

The starting point is that macroeconomic adjustment to various shocks depends on the *intertemporal* choices of economic agents and that a more complete analysis of various shocks and government policies requires a full-fledged intertemporal optimization framework. This allows an explicit analysis of how the present is affected by expectations about the future and how transitory disturbances may have permanent effects. These considerations are especially important with respect to the current account, which represents a country's net accumulation of financial claims on the rest of the world.

Sachs highlights these issues by neglecting investment and focusing exclusively on the current account as a way of redistributing consumption over time. One reason for current account imbalances in this framework is a possible discrepancy between the domestic rate of time preference and the world rate of interest, which may make it optimal to tilt the consumption stream in one direction or the other. But the main emphasis is on the current account as a *shock absorber,* smoothing the path of consumption over time in the event of disturbances.

The distinction between *temporary, permanent* and *future* (anticipated) shocks becomes crucial in this context. Take e.g. the case of a *temporary* fall in income due to a temporary fall in world demand for domestic products. In the absence of an international capital market, this would necessarily result in an immediate reduction in consumption. But with access to foreign borrowing, the effect on consumption will be smoothened. Indeed, if the temporary fall in income leaves *permanent income* unchanged, consumption will not fall at all. The temporary discrepancy between consumption and income will be made up by a current account deficit.

But if there is a *permanent* fall in income (e.g. due to a permanent fall in world demand for domestic products), the current account has no consumption-smoothing role to play. Instead consumption immediately falls.[3]

Similar considerations apply to fiscal policy. Take e.g. the case of a *temporary* increase in government expenditure, which is expected to be met by a future expenditure decrease so that the discounted value of taxes is left unchanged. Then the discounted value of private real disposable income and thus also private consumption will remain unchanged. Such a temporary government budget deficit results in a discrepancy between *total* current domestic absorption and domestic current income, i.e. a deficit on the current account. But a *permanent* increase in government expenditure financed by present and/or future taxes will lower the discounted value of private real disposable income and therefore lead to an immediate reduction in private consumption. The immediate fall in private consumption in this case completely offsets the increase in government expenditure, so that the current account remains unchanged.

The consumption-smoothing role of the current account also appears in the models by Persson and Bruno, who both perform their intertemporal analysis within a two-period framework. Persson uses a two-country model and discusses how the *world real rate of interest* is affected by stabilization policy in various countries. One key conclusion is that although flexible exchange rates may insulate prices and employment abroad from domestic disturbances, they will still fail to insulate foreign consumption, because the world real rate of interest will change.

In Bruno's model there is no longer the same simple link between consumption smoothing and the current account as above, since he also considers investment in real capital. The current account is then determined by the difference between savings and investment, so that the investment motive may dominate the consumption-reallocation motive in the determination of the current account.

This analysis clearly illustrates the dangers of governments pursuing short-term *targets* for the current account. In the extreme case where current account deficits are the result of a full-fledged intertemporal optimization by individuals with infinite lifetime under conditions of perfect foresight and perfect price flexibility, there will be no scope whatsoever for stabilization policies to affect the current account. Indeed, attempts at reaching current account targets that are not consistent with the outcome of

[3] We then abstract from the possibility of differences between the domestic rate of time preference and the world rate of interest and concentrate on the consumption-smoothing aspect of the current account.

private individual maximizing behavior will impose rigidities on the system and reduce welfare. Although these conclusions are drawn from a model with extreme and rather unrealistic assumptions (discussed further below), they serve to emphasize that current account imbalances *may* be socially desirable.

It is also clear, however, from the theoretical papers by Sachs, Persson and Bruno, that expansionary employment-promoting policies may conflict with the goal of an optimal long-run path for consumption; the foreign indebtedness resulting from current account deficits today may lower future consumption possibilities to such an extent that the net welfare effects are negative. An empirical illustration of how increased foreign indebtedness drives a wedge between future output and national income and thus reduces the scope for future employment policies is given by Helliwell–Boothe–McRae. They show how more expansionary fiscal policies in Canada than in the rest of the world during the 1974–75 world recession initially had positive output and employment effects. But these effects were reversed over time to a large extent because increasing debt-service payments caused an increasing discrepancy between GDP and GNP (the inflation generated by the short-run increase in aggregate demand, of course, also played a role).

Investment and Growth

A second type of intertemporal effect concerns the extent to which savings are channeled into investment in physical business capital. This is the main topic in the papers by Feldstein and Kouri, but is also dealt with by Bruno.

Feldstein stresses how *inflation* affects the allocation of savings between investment in *real business capital* and investment in *real housing capital*. This is an issue which, despite its large practical importance, has not received adequate attention in the theoretical literature. The usual conclusion that fully anticipated inflation will have small or zero real effects does not recognize that existing tax laws in most countries do not take proper account of inflation.

It is a widespread belief that the deductability of nominal interest rates *per se* is responsible for the increase in the relative profitability of investment in owner-occupied housing in relation to business investment. Feldstein shows that it is instead the differential tax treatment of firms and housing that produces this result. Both business and housing investments benefit from nominal interest deductions, but the latter benefit more because the inflationary gains on housing are virtually untaxed, whereas inflationary gains in firms are taxed to a large extent in most countries.[4]

[4] Another reason, which is emphasized less by Feldstein, is that personal marginal tax rates may be higher than the marginal corporate tax rate.

Within the framework of a monetary equilibrium growth model, Feldstein shows how inflation in the U.S. reduces the after-tax profitability of business investment. This in turn lowers the real net rate of return to providers of business capital, which in his model is equal to the implicit rental cost of owner-occupied housing. Investment in housing capital will therefore increase and crowd out investment in business capital. The equilibrium amount of business capital per employee is reduced and this results in a lower real income per capita than with zero inflation or a fully indexed tax system.

Kouri analyzes capital formation from another point of view. He treats the problem of the importance of *profitability* for capital formation and growth. Using the cost-of-adjustment approach, he elaborates a model of stagflation that is reminiscent of labor-excess-supply models for developing economies; an excessively high real wage not only causes classical unemployment in the short run, but the resulting lower return to capital also depresses investment, growth and employment over time. The size of the capital stock is thus seen as a major constraint for output and labor demand.

In Kouri's analysis of investment, the distinction between temporary, permanent and future shocks is again important. Although a real wage increase that is perceived to be temporary will have weaker effects on investment than a permanent increase, the analysis illustrates that significant long-run effects will arise. After such a temporary real wage increase, the economy cannot immediately return to its old growth path; the temporary fall in capital formation will have permanent output effects. Furthermore, Kouri illustrates how future anticipated shocks, e.g. an increase in the real wage, will have immediate effects. As soon as the new information is received, the shadow price of capital and investment falls. Because the event has been fully discounted in advance, there will be no discontinuity in investment when the disturbance actually occurs.

The Allocation of Production Resources

A third type of effect concerns the allocation of resources among production sectors. The effects of supply shocks on the relative sizes of the resource, tradables and nontradables sectors in the papers by Neary–Purvis and Bruno have already been commented on. The role of *fiscal policies* for the allocation of resources is, however, also discussed in several of the papers, including those by Sachs, Bruno and Calmfors.

Both Sachs and Bruno stress how short-run fiscal policies are likely to have long-run effects on resource allocation. Take the case of a temporary increase in government expenditure on non-tradables that is financed by present and future taxes. The result is a reduction in private wealth, which causes a fall in both present and future private consumption and a temporary current account deficit. In the short run, the net effect of decreased private consumption and increased public expenditure on the nontradables market is unclear, but in the long run the result is an unambiguous fall in the demand for nontradables and thus also a fall in output of these goods. Given full employment, this must be matched by expansion of the tradables sector, which is necessary to service the increased debt resulting from the temporary current account deficit. If this is foreseen by producers, the paradoxical result may even be that the increased government expenditure causes increased investment in the tradables sector and decreased investment in the nontradables sector today, as discussed by Bruno. Needless to say, these conclusions presuppose that the increase in government expenditure *is* indeed temporary. As illustrated by recent experience in many countries, "temporary" increases in government spending have a strong tendency to become permanent, in which case the shift of resources back to the tradables sector never comes about.

Similarly, the effect of future anticipated changes in government expenditure—e.g. a Reagan-type announcement of a future cut in government spending—can be analyzed by means of intertemporal models. An anticipated future cut in government spending that is expected to result in lower taxes, increases private wealth and therefore causes increased private consumption both today and in the future. Today the unambiguous result is an increase in demand and thus also in output of nontradables (and a decrease in output of tradables given full employment). Tomorrow, when the cut in government spending actually takes place, the net effect of decreased government spending and increased private consumption on output of nontradables (and thus also on output of tradables) is again unclear.

Bruno and Sachs discuss the resource allocation effects of fiscal policies mainly within a full-employment model, where the reasons for stabilization policy are not made explicit. In his model of an economy with a trade-union determined wage, Calmfors neglects the intertemporal links and concentrates instead on the links between unemployment, stabilization policy and the allocation of resources. Policy-makers will be strong tempted to increase government expenditure—purchases of labor for use in the public sector in his model—if such a policy increases employment in the short run when *money* wages are fixed by existing wage contracts. In the long run, when the trade union can adjust the money wage, increased government purchases of labor will cause the real wage (in terms of a consumption basket) to increase. This will entail an increase in the product real wage in the tradables sector as well and thus a contraction of this sector. If the increase in government expenditure is permanent, the contraction of the tradables sector also becomes permanent. In order to evaluate stabilization policies which lead to such results, the initial positive employment effects have to be weighed against the long-run change in relative sector sizes.

III. Future Macroeconomic Performance

The next question concerns how short-run stabilization policy affects *future* possibilities of attaining the macroeconomic goals of output, national income and employment. This theme has already been discussed to some extent in connection with the papers on the current account and investment.

Another important channel through which present 'stabilization policies may affect the attainment of future macroeconomic goals is through the effects on future *price and wage setting behavior*. The rational expectations school has stressed how economic agents will gradually learn about systematic stabilization policy rules and take them into account in future wage and price setting. The well-known conclusion is that monetary policy will lose its effect on employment, if the private sector has access to the same information as policy makers. A money supply change will then change all money prices and money wages equiproportionally, leaving relative prices and real wages unchanged.

The usual rational expectations scenario, however, assumes *atomistic* markets; the *individual* price or wage setter has no reason to believe that his *individual* decision will influence government policy action. But the situation is different if there is e.g. a limited number of wage setters, as is the case in many small European countries where wages are determined in centralized negotiations between only a few trade unions and employer federations. Then a *game situation* exists, where wage setters may expect their wage decisions to trigger accommodating government responses that it will pay to take into account when the original wage decision is made. Such a game situation is treated in Calmfors' model, where *one* omnipotent trade union sets the wage.

When discussing the link between wage setting and government responses, it is worthwhile to distinguish between *monetary* and *real* accommodation. In the case of *monetary* accommodation, the government responds to a money wage increase by inflating the economy, thereby maintaining the initial level of employment by restoring the initial real wage. The economy is thus moved back *along* the labor demand schedule. The risk is that such a policy results in runaway inflation, if the government and the trade union have incompatible real wage objectives.

Another possibility is that the government adheres to a policy of *real* accommodation and makes systematic use of fiscal policy—government purchases of labor in Calmfors' model—in order to prevent employment from falling below a target value in the case of money wage disturbances.

Such a real policy *shifts* the labor demand schedule and thus increases employment at each given real wage. It is shown that such a real accommodation policy will raise the real wage. Indeed, the increase in the real wage may be so large that the employment stabilization rule actually reduces employment. The reason for this *perverse* employment effect is that the "price" of higher real wages in terms of lost employment is reduced, which may induce a utility-maximizing trade union to choose a higher real wage at the expense of lower employment. Therefore, in the long run, accommodating Keynesian policies may result in lower employment than a policy of nonaccommodation.

IV. Policy Conclusions

Although a number of policy conclusions have already been discussed, it may be worthwhile to summarize the lessons that emerge. The general attitude towards stabilization policy in the conference papers is undoubtedly critical. But such policies are in no way ruled out. On the contrary, most of the papers assume sticky *money wages* in the short run, which even assigns a role to pure monetary policy in order to counter unanticipated shocks unforeseen in wage contracts. The power of stabilization policy is reduced in the medium and long run, because various types of *real wage* and *relative price* stickiness then become crucial. But various types of fiscal policy will still be able to affect employment.

The main theme of the conference is that short-run stabilization policies have long-run *costs*, and that the benefits have to be weighed against these costs. The costs analyzed differ depending on varying definitions of "the long run". One definition is a time period of such length that intertemporal substitution in consumption between subperiods becomes possible (Sachs, Persson). Other definitions are that reallocations of the existing capital stock can be made among sectors (Neary–Purvis) or that investment in new capital stock can be undertaken (Bruno, Feldstein, Kouri). A more narrow macroeconomic definition is that price and wage setting behavior can be affected (Calmfors).

The main effects of stabilization policy that have been discussed are: (1) effects on future consumption possibilities because of current account imbalances; (2) effects on investment in real business capital and thus on future growth; (3) effects on the long-run production structure; (4) effects on future price and wage setting behavior.

To these risks could be added the dangers of policy confusion, because policy-makers fail to identify the source of a disturbance correctly. Neary–Purvis discuss how confusion of *real* and *monetary* shocks may lead to policies that are inappropriate also in the short run.

The above conclusions thus emphasize the need for welfare evaluations of stabilization policy. The paper by Persson is an example of how this can be achieved. One conclusion seems to be that there is a serious danger that the costs of employment policies dominate, at least when they take the form of general expenditure-increasing policies.

The papers also question some conventional truths about stabilization policy.

(1) One such conventional wisdom has been that easy monetary policies stimulate investment and growth. But if the long-run effect is an increase in inflation, such policies will (as discussed by Feldstein) have *perverse* effects on growth and investment in business capital because of asymmetries in the tax system. A possible conclusion is that it may be better to assign monetary policy to the target of price stability and change tax rules in order to promote investment and growth.

(2) In the same way, expansive fiscal policies may also have negative effects on investment, growth and long-run employment. If such policies cause an increase in both employment and real wages, it follows from Kouri's analysis that there may be a serious conflict between short-run employment and future output and employment. Contrary to conventional wisdom, it may be that temporary unemployment reducing real wages and thus increasing profitability in the tradables sector is a necessary prerequisite for capital formation and future growth in output and employment.

(3) In the long run, a strict policy of nonaccommodation may (as shown by Calmfors) result in *higher* employment than active policies aimed at stabilizing employment.

The papers also point to conflicts between different considerations. *On one hand,* a strict policy of government nonintervention and nonaccommodation will eliminate the negative effects of stabilization policy that we have discussed. *On the other hand,* since current unemployment seems to be caused mainly by sticky relative prices and sticky real wages, one could argue in favor of government intervention in order to increase relative-price and real-wage flexibility. If real wages are sticky because wage-earners defend targets of real after-tax wages, changes in direct and indirect taxes may be powerful tools for changing real pretax wages. And employers' real wage costs can be reduced by lowering payroll taxes. But such measures may conflict with principles of nonaccommodation. Although relative prices and real wages can be moved in the right direction in the *short run,* learning about such accommodation policies may reinforce the *long-run* stickiness of real wages and relative prices, since the need for private-sector adjustment is reduced. Any decision on this type of government relative-price policy would, therefore, have to be based on a clear perception of the character of the present economic crisis. To what extent has it been caused by *unusually severe shocks* and to what extent has it been caused by *decreased flexibility* in the private sector in response to increased government intervention?

V. Questions for Future Research

As always, the conference papers point to a number of questions that we know too little about, and where further research is needed. It may be worthwhile to end with a short list of such questions:

(1) One question concerns the applicability of the models of *intertemporal* optimization. As in the monetary approach to the balance of payments ten years ago, there is a risk for overemphasis. The extreme assumptions made in most cases should be kept in mind: no role for money, perfect capital markets, perfect foresight, households of infinite lifetime. These assumptions should be relaxed in a more realistic analysis. Introducing *money* permits capital movements to occur not only as the financial counterpart of current account imbalances, but also as a way of adjusting cash balances (cf. Persson). Taking *capital market imperfections* into account would require an explicit analysis of liquidity constraints. Allowing for *imperfect information* would introduce the possibilities that permanent shocks are mistaken for temporary ones and that households do not fully realize the extent of future tax burdens due to current government budget deficits. Allowing for *households of finite lifetime* raises the problem of how welfare should be distributed across generations. Although the intergenerational allocation of resources will be Pareto optimal, when an optimizing private sector is left to itself under conditions of perfect competition, perfect foresight and perfect international capital markets, an important role for economic policy would still be to transfer income across generations according to some social welfare function. The hypothesis would then presumably be that governments have a longer time horizon than individuals, in which case government policy actions would serve the interests of future generations. Such a presumption, however, raises the *positive* question of *why* individuals, when acting as a collective, should be more farsighted than the same individuals when acting on their own.[5] Indeed, practical experience would rather tend to support the opposite view, i.e. that through the political process, present generations manage to expand their budget constraint by taxing future generations via government budget deficits (and thus deficits in the current account).

(2) A second question concerns the *rigidities* of prices and wages that play such an important role in most of the papers. Obviously, we still know too little about the reasons for such rigidities. To what extent are they the

---

[5] Cf. Genberg's comment to Sachs' paper.

10–824815

outcome of rational optimizing behavior in a comprehensive model with information costs, uncertainty and costs of price and wage changes.[6] A related point concerns the relation between various types of rigidities and *government policies*. To what extent are the private sector's responses affected by expectations of government policies that may serve as substitutes for private adjustments? This question is crucial for the problem of accommodation versus nonaccommodation. How likely is it that a change from traditional Keynesian employment policies to a policy of nonaccommodation will cause the economy to end up in a game situation with excessively high real wages and heavy unemployment, where trade unions wait for the government to abandon its nonaccommodation policy and the government waits for the trade unions to reduce real wages? How long can such situations persist? Which side is likely to bend first, trade unions or the government?

(3) The above points carry over to the determinants of *government behavior*. There is a striking contrast in most of the papers between elaborate modelling of the private sector's behavior and rather simple-minded modelling of government behavior. Of course, there is great value in analyzing how the private sector responds to the effects of various exogenously stipulated policy actions and policy rules. But when it comes to understanding actual developments, a more careful modelling of government behavior seems necessary. This would be important when modelling e.g. the relations between governments and trade unions as discussed above. Governments and trade unions should, of course, be expected to take the likely responses of the other agent into account when making their decisions. In the same way the behavior of governments becomes important in the analysis of determination of the current account.

A *final* conclusion seems to be that we need not only theoretical research based on the paradigm of private optimizing behavior, but also more institutional knowledge. We also need to subject our theoretical conclusions to more *empirical testing*. How long does it take for changes in policy rules to affect private behavior? Do the models of intertemporal optimization explain actual developments better than models with myopic behavior? Can the long-run costs of stabilization policy discussed here be quantified? Future research along these lines would seem to be more urgent than further elaborations of complex theoretical model structures.

---

[6] Cf. e.g. Okun, Arthur M., *Prices and Quantities: A Macroeconomic Analysis*, Basil Blackwell, Oxford, 1981.

The Current Account in the Macroeconomic Adjustment Process

*Jeffrey Sachs**

Harvard University, Cambridge, MA, USA

Abstract

Macroeconomic adjustments to changes in the economic environment are to a large extent conditioned by the intertemporal choices of economic agents. When agents face an intertemporal budget constraint, a decision to alter current indebtedness implies changes in future consumption possibilities and will be based on expectations of the entire future path of key variables and not only current variables. A formal model to show how today's current account is a function of both current and future economic variables is presented. The determination of the current account under classical assumptions of market clearing and continuous full employment is emphasized.

I. Introduction

Macroeconomic adjustments to changes in the economic environment are importantly conditioned by the intertemporal choices of economic agents. Purely transitory disturbances, for example, can have persistent effects when they cause agents to recalculate plans over an extended planning horizon. For an open economy linked to a world market, one important aspect of intertemporal plans is the time path of net indebtedness of domestic agents to the rest of the world. When agents face an intertemporal budget constraint, a decision to alter current indebtedness implies changes in future consumption possibilities, and so will be based on expectations of the entire future path of key variables, and not just today's variables. For this reason, an economy's current account, which measures changes in national net indebtedness, depends as much on future economic trends as on the current economic environment.

In the first section of this paper, I present a formal model to show how today's current account is a function of both current and future economic variables. A given shift in fiscal policy, for example, will have one effect on the current account if it is perceived to be temporary and another if it is seen to be permanent. Moreover, when temporary disturbances alter the current account today, they also affect the future values of consumption,

---

* I would like to thank Michael Bruno for his many helpful comments on this version, and Paul Krugman, Torsten Persson and Lars Svensson for earlier comments.

prices and output, as agents adjust future spending in line with changing indebtedness. These future changes are often neglected in analyses of the effects of a policy change. As a side point, it will be clear that "external balance" or a zero current account position is not, in general, a valid policy target. Household welfare is improved by the possibility of running current account surpluses and deficits in response to exogenous shocks.

This paper stresses the determination of the current account under classical assumptions of market clearing and continuous full employment. Without doubt, the impact of various disturbances on the current account will be different under Keynesian, or non-market clearing conditions. But even in the Keynesian case, the importance of the intertemporal dimension in current account determination will remain unchanged.

II. The Nature of Current Account Determination

The current account measures the extent of an economy's net borrowing or lending vis-à-vis the rest of the world in a given period, and thus is the outcome of savings and investment decisions. Static models that write the current account as a function of export and import demand often blur the intertemporal considerations inherent in savings and investment behavior. I will approach the current account from the other extreme, modelling it as an outcome of behavior of far-sighted, intertemporally optimizing households and firms.

The intertemporal choices reflect, of course, the interaction of intertemporal budget constraints and tastes. The budget constraints can be stated two ways, and each is insightful. From a national perspective, financial claims on the rest of the world B change according to the relationship.

$$B = \mathrm{CA} = Q + r^*B - C - G \qquad (1)$$

Here CA stands for current account, Q is gross domestic product (hence $Q+r^*B$ is gross national product), C is household consumption and G is government fiscal expenditure. (I ignore investment until the concluding section.) When $B>0$, the country is a creditor, and when $B<0$, it is a debtor. For simplicity, we suppose that all financial assets are short-term, with an instantaneous fixed real yield (in terms of numeraire commodity) r^*.

One way to impose an intertemporal budget constraint is to posit that in the long run, the country is neither a creditor nor debtor in present value terms:

$$\lim_{t\to\infty} e^{-r^*t}B = 0.$$

That is, claims or debt vis-à-vis the rest of the world must grow more slowly than the rate of interest. Imposing this condition on (1) yields immediately:[1]

$$\int_0^\infty e^{-r^*t}(C+G)\,dt = B(0)+\int_0^\infty e^{-r^*t}Q\,dt. \tag{2}$$

Thus, the discounted value of domestic absorption must equal the sum of initial net claims on the rest of the world and the discounted value of demestic production. Note that by transposing G in (2), we have the budget constraint for household spending:

$$\int_0^\infty e^{-r^*t}C\,dt = B(0)+\int_0^\infty e^{-r^*t}(Q-G)\,dt = W(0). \tag{3}$$

Here, $W(0)$ is initial household human and financial wealth. If an infinite-lived household takes (3) as its budget constraint, its consumption possibilities are affected by the present value of guvernment expenditures, but not by the *paths* of government expenditure and taxes.[2] For this reason, a "Ricardian equivalence proposition" will apply in the models that follow, so that consumer expenditure, the trade balance and current account will be invariant to the path of taxes and government deficits, given the path of government expenditure, $\{G(t)\}$.[3] (I use the notation $\{x(t)\}$ to signify the time path of x.)

If we rearrange (2) once again, we get a second way to view the intertemporal budget constraint:

$$\int_0^\infty e^{-r^*t}(Q-G-C)\,dt = -B(0). \tag{4}$$

According to this expression, which is stressed by Krugman (1981), the discounted value of trade surpluses $(Q-C-G)$ must exactly balance the

---

[1] Solving (1), we have that

$$B(t) = B(0)\cdot e^{r^*t}+e^{r^*t}\cdot\int_0^t e^{-r^*\tau}[Q(\tau)-C(\tau)-G(\tau)]d\tau.$$

Multiplying both sides of this expression by e^{-r^*t}, and taking limits, we have

$$0 = B(0)+\int_0^\infty e^{-r^*\tau}[Q(\tau)-C(\tau)-G(\tau)]d\tau.$$

From this, (2) is immediate.

[2] Of course, the government's budget constraint implies that the discounted value of taxes equals the discounted value of government expenditures net of initial government claims on the private sector and the rest of the world.

[3] See Barro (1974) for a discussion of this doctrine. In addition to the assumption of infinite-lived households, the equivalence proposition requires that taxes be non-distorting, as is assumed in this model.

initial net indebtedness of the economy, $-B(0)$. Trade deficits in early years, for example, must be matched in present value terms by surpluses in later years, if $B(0)=0$. Policies which increase borrowing in early years imply a fall in absorption relative to output in later years.

It is convenient to define the "permanent" or "perpetuity equivalent" of a variable X, which we will denote $X^P(t)$, by the relationship:

$$\int_t^{\infty} e^{-r^*(\tau-t)} X^P(t)\, d\tau = \int_t^{\infty} e^{-r^*(\tau-t)} X(\tau)\, d\tau \tag{5}$$

or $X^P(t)=r^* \int_t^{\infty} e^{-r^*(\tau-t)} X(\tau)\, d\tau$. With this definition, the household constraint becomes:

$$\int_0^{\infty} e^{-r^*t} C(t)\, dt = B(0)+[Q^P(0)-G^P(0)]/r^* \tag{6}$$

or

$$C^P(t) = r^* W(t). \tag{6'}$$

Also, with the trade balance $Q-C-G$ denoted as TB, we have $TB^P(0)= -r^*B(0)=Q^P(0)-C^P(0)-G^P(0)$.

This last expression suggests the following approach to trade balance and current account determination.[4] Since $TB=Q-C-G$ and $TB^P= Q^P-C^P-G^P$, we know that $TB-TB^P=(Q-Q^P)-(C-C^P)-(G-G^P)$. The intertemporal budget constraint implies $TB^P=-r^*B$, and since $CA= TB+r^*B$, we can write $CA=(Q-Q^P)-(C-C^P)-(G-G^P)$. In the model that follows, $C-C^P$ results from the consumer's intertemporal allocation problem. The basic result of the consumer decision is that consumption is *smoothed* relative to income, as in the permanent income model. In the extreme case of smoothing, $C\equiv C^P$, so $CA=(Q-Q^P)-(G-G^P)$. More generally, $C-C^P$ will depend on wealth, the interest rate, and the rate of time preference, $(C-C^P)=(\delta-r)\,W$, so that $CA=(Q-Q^P)+(r^*-\delta)W-(G-G^P)$.

From this simple expression for CA, we see that at least three phenomena give rise to current account deficits, all related to household preferences for certain consumption paths and to the intertemporal budget constraint.

First, when current income is low relative to permanent income, $(Q-Q^P)<0$, households dissave in order to maintain consumption. Absorption remains higher than temporarily-depressed income, and a deficit results. Thus, a *temporary* deline in world demand for home goods that

[4] I thank Michael Bruno for suggesting this simplified approach for deriving the current account equation.

reduces the terms of trade, or a *temporary* decline in domestic productivity that reduces real income tends to give rise to trade and current account deficits. *Permanent* demand or supply shocks, on the contrary, need not induce a deficit, if both current and permanent income are reduced in equal proportion by the shocks. Household consumption drops by the extent of the reduction in (permanent) real income.

Second a divergence of the rate of return to savings and the rate of time preference may give rise to an external imbalance, $(r^*-\delta)W$. Even with a flat real income profile, households may have an incentive to tilt their consumption streams relative to income streams because of the rewards or costs of postponing consumption.

Third, when fiscal expenditure is high relative to its permanent level, the current account will tend to be in deficit, by $(G-G^P)$. Note that in (6), the household budget constraint is a negative function of G^P, but for a given G^P is unaffected by the path of G. Thus, farsighted households will adjust consumption downward according to the permanent level of government spending, not the current level.[5] When $G>G^P$, total absorption $C+G$ will also tend to be above average, so that a current temporary fiscal expansion will tend to cause trade deficits now and surpluses in the future.

III. A Formal Model of the Current Account

Now I turn to a model of the current account and dynamic responses to supply and demand shocks. In general, dynamic models with optimizing agents are not easily solved analytically, and recourse to simulations is often necessary. To facilitate the discussion, then, I focus on a specific model that *can* be analytically solved, and describe how various modifications would affect key results.

National output Q is assumed to be the sum of outputs of two productive sectors, a pure traded good sector, producing Q^T, and a semi-tradeable sector, producing Q^S. The pure traded good is in perfectly elastic supply on the world market, and is taken as *numéraire*. The semi-tradeable good is exported on the world market subject to an export demand schedule that is downward sloping in its relative price $\pi(t)$. For simplicity, the instantaneous demand schedule is assumed to be $W^*(t)/\pi(t)$, where W^* is an external and exogenous foreign demand-shift variable. (The unitary elasticity helps to preserve linearity in the model.)

Households consume both goods, in amounts C^T and C^S. The value of total consumption in traded goods units is $C=C^T+\pi C^S$. The government also consumes both goods with $G=G^T+\pi G^S$. For simplicity, I assume that

---

[5] The complete independence of C and G, for given G^P, depends on the assumption that the household utility from G and C is strongly separable.

G is divided in fixed proportion among the two goods, with $\pi G^S = \lambda G$, $G^T = (1-\lambda)G$. Equilibrium in the S-market requires:

$$Q^S(t) = C^S(t) + G^S(t) + W^*(t)/\pi(t). \tag{7}$$

Household demands are derived from an intertemporal optimization problem of the form:

$$\max_{C^T, C^S} \int_0^\infty e^{-\delta t} U(C^T, C^S)\, dt, \tag{8}$$

subject to the budget constraint in (4). Here, utility is additively separable, with the important implication (and simplification) that households can use a two-step procedure: first select $C(t)$, and then divide $C(t)$ among $C^T(t)$ and $C^S(s)$ as a function of $\pi(t)$. I also assume that δ, the pure rate of time preference, is fixed.

To get a tractable model it is useful to specialize utility further, by writing $U(C^T, C^S)$ as $\log(C^{T(1-\alpha)} C^{S\alpha})$. This form has a number of helpful features. First, total expenditure $C(t)$ is linear in household wealth $W(t)$. This linearity is a property of a class of "intertemporally homothetic" utility functions, of which $\log(\cdot)$ is a member.[6,7] Second, $C(t)$ is divided in constant expenditure shares on πC^S and C^T, respectively.

When this assumption is maximized subject to (4), the optimal consumption path is governed by the relationships:

$$\dot{C}_T = (r^* - \delta)\, C_T$$

$$\pi C^S = [\alpha/(1-\alpha)] C_T$$

and the budget constraint

$$\int_0^\infty e^{-r^* t}[C_T + \pi C^S]\, dt = W(0). \tag{9}$$

Solving the differential equation in (9), it is easy to show that

$$C^T(t) = (1-\alpha)\,\delta W(t)$$

$$\pi(t) C^S(t) = \alpha \delta W(t)$$

$$W(t) = e^{(r^* - \delta)t} W(0)$$

$$C(t) = e^{(r^* - \delta)t} C(0). \tag{10}$$

---

[6] See Lipton & Sachs (1981) for a formal derivation of the optimal consumption program under the assumptions of this paper.

[7] Specifically, the constant relative risk aversion function $U(C) = (C^{1-\phi})/(1-\phi)$ results in $C(t)$ linear in $W(t)$. Only in the case of $\log(\cdot)$, with $\phi = 1$ is the constant of proportionality between $C(t)$ and $W(t)$ invariant to the future path of interest rates. For a useful discussion of the utility function in current account behavior, see Svensson & Razin (1981).

Thus, both wealth and consumption expenditure rise according to the divergence of r^* and δ, with households accumulating wealth whenever the rate of return exceeds the rate of time preference. Expenditures are linear in wealth, as noted above, with a constant of proportionality δ. Note that in (10) the consumption function is not a reduced form since W depends on $Q(=Q^T+\pi Q^S)$, which in turn depends on other variables as shown below.

To complete the model, the supply side must be further laid out. I chose a convenient production possibility frontier of the form:[8]

$$Q^S=(\gamma(t)L-Q^T)^\beta. \tag{11}$$

Here $\gamma(t)$ represents an exogenous productivity shift variable, and L is exogenous (and fixed) labor supply. With perfect competition $-dQ^T/dQ^S=\pi(t)$, which implies that $Q^T=\gamma(t)L-\beta\pi Q^S$. Since $Q=Q^T+\pi Q^S$, we have

$$Q=\gamma(t)L+(1-\beta)\pi Q^S. \tag{12}$$

To solve the model, we first find $W(0)$. The trick here is that the value of production itself depends on demand through demand effects on the relative price π. We know from the definition of W that:

$$W(0)=[Q^P(0)-G^P(0)]/r^*+B(0). \tag{13}$$

Now, $Q^P(0)=[\gamma L+(1-\beta)\pi Q^S]^P$, by equation (12), and the definition of the P-operator, defined in equation (5). By market clearing $\pi Q^S=\alpha\delta W+\lambda G+W^*$, which we can substitute into the expression for $Q^P(0)$. Note also that the perpetuity-equivalent of wealth, $W^P(0)$, equals $r^*W(0)/\delta$.[9] Using the linearity of the P-operator, and the definition of $Q^P(0)$, we can rewrite (13) as

$$W(0)=r^{*-1}[1-\alpha(1-\beta)]^{-1}\{L\gamma^P(0)+(1-\beta)W^{*P}(0)$$
$$-[1-(1-\beta)\lambda]G^P(0)+r^*B(0)\}. \tag{14}$$

Equation (14) also holds for all t.

Now from the consumer demand equations, C^T and $\pi(t)C^S(t)$ depend only on wealth, and not on current values of any variables, with $C^T(t)=\delta(1-\alpha)W(t)=\delta e^{(r^*-\delta)t}(1-\alpha)W(0)$, and $W(0)$ given in (14). $\pi(t)C^S(t)$ is similarly found.

We can summarize current account behavior in two ways. First,

---

[8] The PPF can be derived from sectoral production functions of the form:
$Q^T=\gamma(t)L^T$, $Q^S=(\gamma(t)L^S)^\beta$, $L^T+L^S=L$.

[9] By (5), $W^P(0)=r^*\int_0^\infty e^{-r^*\tau}W(\tau)\,d\tau$. Since $W(t)=W(0)e^{(r^*-\delta)t}$, we find by direct substitution that $W^P(0)=r^*W(0)/\delta$.

$CA(0)=Q(0)+r^*B(0)-G(0)-C(0)$. Substituting $\gamma L+(1-\beta)\pi Q^S(0)$ for $Q(0)$, invoking market clearing, and using (10) in the consumer demand expression, we find:

$$CA(0)=(r^*-\delta)[1-\alpha(1-\beta)]W(0)+(1-\beta)[W^*(0)-W^{*P}(0)] \\ -[1-\lambda(1-\beta)][G(0)-G^P(0)]+L[\gamma(0)-\gamma^P(0)]. \quad (15)$$

This is the general equilibrium version of the CA equation that was motivated heuristically in the first section. It differs from the earlier formula by allowing for the general equilibrium feedbacks of W^* and G on Q. Once again, we see a *time-preference* motive in the first RHS term in (15) and a *consumption-smoothing* motive in the next three terms. When r^* exceeds the rate of time preference, households accumulate wealth. Next, when world demand is above its permanent level, or productivity is above its permanent level, then households also accumulate. Finally, when G exceeds G^P, total absorption is temporarily high and the country runs a deficit. As before, equation (15) holds for any time t.

A related way to summarize current account behavior is to measure the cummulative deficits between 0 and t. Since $CA=\dot{B}$, we have that

$$B(t)-B(0)=\int_0^t CA(\tau)\,d\tau.$$

To find $B(t)$, we may use the differential equation (1). Thus

$$B(t)=e^{r^*t}B(0)+e^{r^*t}\int_0^t (Q-C-G)\,e^{-r^*\tau}d\tau.$$

Now we substitute δW for C, and $\gamma L+(1-\beta)\pi Q^S$ for Q. After tedious manipulation, we end up with the expression:

$$\int_0^t CA(\tau)\,d\tau=B(t)-B(0)$$

$$=[e^{(r^*-\delta)t}-1]W(0)+Le^{r^*t}\int_0^t e^{-r^*\tau}[\gamma(\tau)-\gamma^P(0)]d\tau$$

$$+(1-\beta)\,e^{r^*t}\int_0^t e^{-r^*\tau}[W^*(\tau)-W^{*P}(0)]\,d\tau$$

$$-[1-(1-\beta)\,\lambda]e^{-r^*t}\int_0^t e^{-r^*\tau}[G(\tau)-G^P(0)]d\tau. \quad (16)$$

The *cumulative* current account deficit between 0 and t is thus: (1) proportional to $W(0)$ with a positive dependence if and only if $r^*>\delta$, (2) increasing in the discounted cumulative deviations of γ and W^* from $\gamma^P(0)$ and $W^*(0)$, and (3) decreasing in the discounted cumulative deviation of $G(\tau)$ from $G^P(0)$. Once again, cumulative deficits depend on the average deviations of actual from permanent income over the interval.

To some extent, these results depend on the specific household utility function that we are examining. Obstfeld (1980, 1981) among others has recently modelled the current account under the Uzawa formulation that the households' rate of time preperence varies according to the level of instantaneous utility, with $\delta'[U(\cdot)]>0$. When this alternative assumption is made, the level of $W(0)$ has the additional role of influencing the magnitude of δ along an adjustment path. A high value of initial wealth $W(0)$, by itself, will tend to induce current account deficits, by raising $\delta[U(C(0))]$ relative to r^*.

Finally, let us now turn to some comparative dynamic exercises. Consider three types of perturbations:

(a) a *temporary* shock:
$x(t)$ becomes $x(t)+\Theta \quad 0\leq t\leq T$
$x(t) \quad T<t$

(b) a *permanent* shock:
$x(t)$ become $x(t)+\Theta \quad 0\leq t\leq\infty$

(c) an *anticipated future* shock:
$x(t)$ becomes $x(t) \quad 0\leq t\leq T$
$x(t)+\Theta \quad T<t.$

Such shocks to W^*, γ, or G affect the current account both through the wealth term in (16), and the consumption-smoothing terms. In general, a temporary rise in γ, or W^*, or fall in G, will lead to a rise in CA, unless δ is much greater than r^*. In the latter case, the positive wealth effect following such a shock leads households to borrow even more against their now higher wealth, causing deficits to rise.[10] A permanent shock that raises wealth improves the current account if and only if $r^*>\delta$. An anticipated shock that raises wealth typically worsens the current account, and does so necessarily if $r^*<\delta$.

Perhaps more interesting are the comparative dynamic effects of various perturbations on $\pi(t)$, $Q^T(t)$, and $Q^S(t)$. Here we find explicit expressions for the long-run effects of temporary disturbances in G, γ and W^*. First, note from the market equilibrium conditions that:

$$\pi Q^S(t) = \alpha\delta W(t)+\lambda G(t)+W^*(t)$$
$$Q^S(t) = K_0[\alpha\delta W(t)+\lambda G(t)+W^*(t)]^\beta$$

[10] From (15), $\Delta CA(0)=(r^*-\delta)\,\Delta W(0)$+consumption smoothing terms. For $\delta>>r^*$ the positive wealth effect may dominate the consumption-smoothing effect.

$$\pi(t) \quad = K_1[\alpha\delta W(t)+\lambda G(t)+W^*(t)]^{1-\beta}$$

$$Q^T(t) \;= \gamma(t)L-\beta\alpha\delta W(t)-\beta\lambda G(t)-\beta W^*(t) \tag{17}$$

where K_0, K_1 are constants.

We see that semi-tradeable production and its relative price are increasing function of $W(t)$, $W^*(t)$, and $G(t)$. $Q^T(t)$ is, in turn, a declining function of Q^S. From (17), it is clear that production and prices at time $t>T$, are affected by temporary shocks during $0\leq t\leq T$ according to the effects of these shocks on $W(t)$. Since $W(t)=e^{(r^*-\delta)t}W(0)$, any temporary shock which reduces $W(0)$ will lead, after time T, to a lower profile of $Q^S(t)$, $\pi(t)$, and a higher profile of $Q^T(t)$.

As an example, consider a temporary fiscal expansion. The change in $G^P(0)$ is given by:

$$-r^*\int_0^T e^{-r^*\tau}\Theta d\tau = -(1-e^{-r^*T})\,\Theta.$$

Thus, according to (14), $\Delta W(0)$ is given by $-r^{*-1}[1-\alpha(1-\beta)]^{-1}(1-\beta)$ $(1-e^{-r^*T})\Theta$. Since $W(t)$ is given by $e^{(r^*-\delta)t}W(0)$, we have:

$$\Delta W(t) = -r^{*-1}[1-\alpha(1-\beta)]^{-1}[1-(1-\beta)\lambda](1-e^{-r^*T})\,e^{(r^*-\delta)t}\Theta, \quad \text{for all } t. \tag{18}$$

Thus, $W(t)$ is necessarily reduced. Since $G(t)$ is unchanged for $t>T$, it is clear from (18) that the temporary fiscal expansion unambiguously reduces $\pi(t)$ $Q^S(t)$, and raises $Q^T(t)$, for $t>T$. The effects on production and relative prices before time T depend on two offsetting effects. Demand for Q^S, at given π, rises by $\lambda\Theta$, while household demand falls by $\alpha\delta\Delta W(t)$. The relative magnitude of these offsetting effects depends on: (1) the marginal propensities to consume Q^S out of G and C, and (2) the duration of the temporary expansion. If the expansion is very short ($T\simeq 0$), then $\Delta W(0)$ is also small, and $\pi(t)$ and $Q^S(t)$ are positively affected. In the benchmark case $r^*=\delta$, we find that $\Delta Q^S\geq 0$ and $\Delta\pi\geq 0$ for $t<T$ if and only if $\lambda>(1-e^{-r^*T})\,\alpha$.

It is useful to remember how these results differ in the case of no capital mobility. With a zero current account balance, $\Delta C(t)=-\Theta$for $t\leq T$ and $\Delta C(t)=0$ for $t>T$, rather than $\Delta C(t)=-\delta e^{(r^*-\delta)t}\Delta W(0)$. That is, the fiscal expansion crowds out consumption one-for-one. The general expressions for πQ^S, π, Q^S, and Q^T become:

$$\pi(t)Q^S(t) = (1-\alpha\beta)^{-1}[\alpha\gamma(t)L+(\lambda-\alpha)\,G(t)+W^*(t)]$$

$$Q^S(t) \quad = \varepsilon_0[\alpha\gamma(t)\,L+(\lambda-\alpha)\,G(t)+W^*(t)]^{\beta}$$

$$\pi(t) \quad = \varepsilon_1[\alpha\gamma(t)\,L+(\lambda-\alpha)\,G(t)+W^*(t)]^{(1-\beta)}$$

$$Q^T(t) \quad = (1-\alpha\beta)^{-1}[(1-\alpha)\,\gamma(t)\,L-\beta(\lambda-\alpha)\,G-\beta W^*(t)] \tag{19}$$

where $\varepsilon_0, \varepsilon_1$ are constants.

First, notice that temporary shocks during $t \leq T$ have *no* effect on resource allocation for $t > T$. Households, in the aggregate, cannot reallocate their consumption streams to smooth the effects of ΔG. If they try, the *domestic interest rates adjust* until households are satisfied with the path governed by $\Delta C(t) = -\Delta G(t)$. Second, notice that the direction of the fiscal effect is now given by $\lambda - \alpha$, rather than $\lambda - \alpha(1 - e^{-r^*T})$. This difference again reflects the fact that with no capital mobility the drop in consumption is the opposite of the rise in G.

As a final exercise, let us examine the current account and resource allocational effects of a "Reagan-type" announcement of future cuts in government spending. (Remember that in our analysis, announced *tax* cuts have no effect unless they presage cuts in government spending.) To simplify the illustration, we set $r^* = \delta$. Then:

$$\Delta W(0) = \Delta W(t) = r^{*-1}[1 - \alpha(1-\beta)^{-1}] \left[\int_T^\infty e^{-r^*\tau} \Theta d\tau \right] [1 - (1-\beta)\lambda].$$

We see that $\Delta C(t)$, which equals $\delta \Delta W(t)$, is necessarily positive, with the implication that for $t < T$, $\pi(t)$ rises along with $Q^S(t)$, while $Q^T(t)$ falls. The trade balance and current account deteriorate initially. After time T, the change in the current account is zero, while the trade balance improves to support an increased service account deficit. Note that $\Delta\pi(t)$ is either positive or negative for $t > T$, with the sign again depending on the relative magnitudes of α and λ. Specifically, for $t > T$, $\Delta\pi(t) > 0$ if and only if $\lambda < \alpha e^{-r^*T}$. For large T, the long-run effect is almost surely a fall in π.

IV. Extensions and Conclusions

Some of the intertemporal aspects of current account determination and the role of the current account in macroeconomic adjustment are illustrated in this paper. Given the difficulties inherent in working with intertemporal optimizing models, the paper relies heavily on a simple framework, and a specific set of functional forms. The principle that farsighted behavior by householders and firms makes the current account a function of current and future expected variables is certainly robust to changes in model specification. So too is the notion that temporary disturbances have long-run effects through their impact on the optimal intertemporal consumption path of households.

Certain key results do, however, depend on the specific assumptions laid out in the model. I have already mentioned how the introduction of a time-varying discount factor in the utility function can change the likelihood of surpluses and deficits following shocks to real income. A second type of modification, in which households have a finite rather than infinite planning horizon, has even stronger effects on some of our conclusions.[11] In this case, government *tax* and debt policy can have important effects on the level of the current account balance and the path of resource allocation. Government can reallocate welfare between alternative generations (defined by their planning horizons), raising the possibility of an optimal current account policy that maximizes an intergenerational social welfare function.

Perhaps the most important deficiency of the simple model is the absence of investment in physical capital. Shifts in investment opportunities over time give rise to strong current account effects in theoretical models, and empirical work seems to confirm the strong, even dominant, role of investment in cross-country current account behavior; cf. Sachs (1981 *a*, 1981 *b*). Investment is important because under perfect capital mobility all domestic investment are undertaken that exceed the world cost of capital, regardless of domestic savings rates. If new domestic investment opportunities arise that just meet the world market rate of return, the domestic current account worsens one-for-one with the rise in investment.

Adding optimal investment plans to an intertemporal model enormously complicates the algebra, and typically forces a retreat to simulations; cf. Sachs (1980, 1982). The simulation exercises point to the following conclusions. First, permanent increases in world demand are likely to induce *deficits* initially, as the demand increases spur domestic capital formation and hence foreign capital inflows. Similarly, a fall in world demand can actually result in surpluses. Second, the resource allocational effects of temporary disturbances tend to be magnified when capital accumulation is permitted, since the long-run supply elasticities of the various sectors are raised by the possibility of sectoral capital accumulation.

References

Barro, Robert: Are government bonds net wealth? *Journal of Political Economy 82* (6), November/December 1974.

Buiter, Willem H.: Time preferences and international lending and borrowing in an overlapping generations model. *Journal of Political Economy 4* (4), August 1981.

Krugman, Paul: Real and financial determinants of the real exchange rate. Unpublished manuscript, MIT, July 1981.

Lipton, David & Sachs, Jeffrey: Accumulation and growth in a two-country model: A simulation approach. NBER Working Paper No. 572, October 1980.

Obstfeld, Maurice: Macroeconomic policy, exchange-rate dynamics, and optimal asset accumulation. NBER Working Paper No. 599, December 1980.

Obstfeld, Maurice: Intermediate imports, the terms of trade, and the dynamics of the exchange rate and current account. NBER Working Paper No. 599, December 1980.

Sachs, Jeffrey: The current account and macroeconomic adjustment in the 1970s.

[11] See Buiter (1981) for an example of such a model, using the overlapping generations framework.

Brookings Papers on Economic Activity, 1981: 1.

Sachs, Jeffrey: Aspects of the current account behavior of OECD economies. Presented at the Fifth International Conference of the University of Paris-Dauphine on Monetary and International Monetary Problems, June 1981.

Sachs, Jeffrey: Energy and growth under flexible exchange rates. Forthcoming in *The International Transmission of Economic Disturbances* (ed. Bondain and Putnam). MIT Press, 1982.

Svensson, Lars & Razin, Assaf: The terms of trade, spending, and the current account. Seminar Paper No. 170, Institute for International Economic Studies, University of Stockholm, March 1981.

Comment on J. D. Sachs, "The Current Account in the Macroeconomic Adjustment Process"

Hans Genberg

Graduate Institute of International Studies, Geneva, Switzerland

I would like to take up two issues raised in Jeff Sachs' paper which are of particular relevance for the theme of the conference. The first concerns the long-run effects of temporary government expenditure policies; the second relates to the question of government attitudes towards foreign borrowing and the concept of an optimum current account policy.

One major advantage of studying current account movements in an explicitly intertemporal framework is that the long-run consequences of current disturbances and policies are automatically brought out in the open. The fact that the current account is equal to the change in the net debtor position of the country in question implies that a shock or policy which alters the current account will lead to a change in the foreign debt, and hence to a change in future debt service payments and future consumption possibilities. This argument suggests that temporary government expenditure changes undertaken, for example, for short-run macroeconomic stabilization purposes might influence the allocation of resources in the long run. This implication is discussed in Sachs' paper where it is shown that a temporary expansion of government expenditures will lead to a future deterioration in the terms of trade, a future shift in resources from the import-competing sector and a reduction in future aggregate consumption. These results can be established intuitively by the following reasoning. A temporary increase in current government expenditures will induce a contemporaneous current account deficit which, as noted above, will lead to increased foreign indebtedness. Even if government expenditures subsequently return to their normal level the larger foreign debt implies a continued deficit on current account as a result of debt service payments. In order to return to balance, the trade balance will have to improve which in turn requires an expansion of the export sector, a possible deterioration of the terms of trade, and a reduction in aggregate absorption.

These intertemporal consequences of current stabilization policy raise a number of important issues for the conduct of such policies. First of all, the analysis suggests that it is not in general possible to divorce short-run stabilization policy from (long-run) structural policies. To apply the former without regard to its long-run consequences for resource allocation may lead to substantial and undesired structural changes. Second, current temporary stabilization policies affect the welfare of future generations. A current expansion financed by foreign borrowing makes future generations worse off. In deciding on the desirability of such a policy, the burden it puts on future generations should thus be taken into account. Third, and related to the previous point, since changes in current government expenditures affect the level of foreign indebtedness, conflicts may arise between policies aimed at stabilization in the short run and policies which are aimed at achieving an optimal path for foreign debt and future consumption possibilities, i.e. policies which are aimed at achieving an "optimum current account balance" to borrow a term from Sachs' paper. None of these issues can be discussed in models of the current account which do not explicitly treat it in an intertemporal setting. The model set out in Sachs' paper on the other hand offers a convenient framework for doing so, and is thus particularly appropriate for the theme of the conference.

I now turn to some comments on the concept of an optimum current account balance and what role there might be for governments in designing policies to achieve a particular path for the current account over time. It is clear from Sachs' analysis that there is no particular virtue in a balanced current account. In a model where agents optimize over extended horizons, the current account will reflect optimal savings (and investment) plans. These will in general depend on both the types and expected duration of shocks that disturb the economy and expectations concerning future values of relevant economic variables. In each given situation therefore, the optimum response of savings and investment will typically imply a non-zero current account, and any attempt to balance it would result in a suboptimal path of consumption. This conclusion holds exactly when the economy is free from distortions and when savings plans take appropriate account of future generations. In this case there is no role for the government in trying to modify the resulting current account balance or level of foreign debt. What are then the conditions which would provide a case for an explicit government policy in order to reach an optimum current account path? I argue that the specific distortions which are most frequently brought up in this context are either not likely to be rectified by government policy aimed at the current account or imply that other measures are going to be more efficient.

In Section IV, Sachs suggests that his model might imply a case for government policy to redistribute income between generations in a situation where agents do not optimize over infinite horizons. However, unless we have some knowledge of the reason behind the less than infinite planning horizon, it is difficult to make a case for government intervention. Of course, it might merely be stated that agents simply do not take appropriate account of future generations and derive an optimal policy accordingly. But then it seems difficult to argue that governments (especially if they are chosen by a democratic political process) could be any more farsighted given that they have to respond to the desires of the electorate. At a practical level it would rather seem that governments are typically more *short-sighted* than the private sector.

This then leaves only the possibility that distortions associated with foreign borrowing and foreign debt holdings provide a case for government intervention to achieve a particular current account balance. The distortions which have been mentioned most often in this context are restrictions on private capital movements, limited access of the private sector to the international capital market, and more complete information available to the government compared to the private sector. While all three of these distortions would lead to suboptimal private decisions and hence provide an opportunity for welfare-improving government interventions, it is easily demonstrated that the first-best policy is not one which would attempt to modify the current account balance directly. The argument is most straightforward for the second and third types of distortion. If the private sector does not have access to the international capital market on the same terms as the government, then there is a divergence between the private marginal cost and the social marginal cost of international credit. Applying the principle that a policy should be directed as closely as possible to the source of divergence between social and private costs, the appropriate policy in this situation would be to provide a subsidy to domestic private borrowing in the international capital market. This subsidy could take the form of either a direct interest rate subsidy or a partial guarantee by the government of the loan. Either of these policies would be superior to a tax policy aimed at modifying directly the amount of savings and investment undertaken domestically. In the situation where the government receives more accurate information about the nature of current shocks or about future developments, there will again be a difference between privately chosen savings and investment plans and socially optimal plans. It is difficult to conceive of situations where the best policy to follow in this situation would not simply be to make the additional information in the government's possession available to the private sector.

Concerning the appropriate policy to follow when there are restrictions imposed by the government on private capital flows, the analysis is less straightforward. To the extent that these restrictions were imposed in order to reduce the amount of private net foreign indebtedness, then it does of course not make sense to *encourage* such indebtedness by modifying tax rates to achieve a different current account. To the extent that the restrictions were imposed for some other reason, it is imperative to take this other reason into account in order to determine whether a "current account policy" is appropriate or whether some other policy(ies) might be more efficient in correcting the distortion brought about by the restriction on capital flows. My guess is that in most cases more efficient policies do in fact exist, and I therefore conclude that the case in favor of the government actively seeking to establish an optimum current account balance is a weak one. The related proposition that the government should not strive for current account balance, continues, of course, to be valid.

Global Effects of National Stabilization Policies under Fixed and Floating Exchange Rates

*Torsten Persson**

Institute for International Economic Studies, Stockholm, Sweden

Abstract

This paper deals with international effects of two types of stabilization policies: monetary expansion directed towards the demand side and a reduction in payroll taxes directed towards the supply side. The analysis focuses on employment, relative prices and welfare issues. It rests on a simple intertemporal general equilibrium model of two countries that includes a specific micro theory of money. Under floating exchange rates, a country's employment is insulated from both policies abroad, but its consumption generally changes. Under fixed exchange rates, no such insulation prevails; while monetary expansion is generally expansionary, reduced payroll taxes constitute a beggar-thy-neighbor policy. In both systems, the welfare of a country may decrease although its employment increases—an "immiserizing expansion" may occur.

I. Introduction

This paper deals with international effects of national stabilization policies under fixed and floating exchange rates. Earlier discussions of this issue in the literature have mostly been concerned with a two-country framework in the Mundell-Fleming tradition.[1] Such analyses are confined to aggregate production in each of the two countries. As in the case of most conventional income-expenditure models, they can be criticized from a methodological point of view, for assuming sticky prices, while neglecting to analyze agents' quantity-constrained choice in a satisfactory way.

We propose a more ambitious treatment. For this purpose, we use a simple, but fully specified general equilibrium model of two countries. The two countries may be interpreted either literally as two large countries or as two groups of countries which each pursue similar policies. This model, which enables us to combine elements of international monetary and trade theory, is used to study the effects of expansionary policies in one of the countries. In addition to the effects on employment and production at home

---

* I would like to thank participants in the conference and in a seminar at the I.I.E.S. Discussions with Lars Calmfors, J. Peter Neary, Assaf Razin and Lars E. O. Svensson were particularly helpful. Financial support from The Jacob Wallenberg Research Foundation is gratefully acknowledged.

[1] See Dornbusch (1980, Ch. 10 and 11) for a summary of the main arguments.

and abroad, we also consider welfare and resource allocation effects via changes in relative prices.

We are concerned with a situation of unemployment that motivates the government in one of the countries to engage in expansionary policies. The unemployment is caused by excessively high wages. These wages can, for example, be thought of as having been determined by long-term contracts which fix the money wage for a certain period. The labor market thus clears via rationing of households' supply. By contrast, all other markets are assumed to clear via price adjustment. For analytical convenience, the situation in the other country is assumed to be similar.

The government actions analyzed are probably best viewed as alternative responses to some unexpected disturbance (not dealt with explicity here) which has caused the economy to deviate from full employment at the fixed nominal wage. We study two types of expansionary policies: *monetary expansion* via an increase in the budget deficit and a *reduction in payroll taxes*. The latter is interesting in the sense that it has seldom been treated in the theoretical macroeconomic literature, although it is quite often discussed in the policy debate.[2] Moreover, it represents a measure directed towards the supply side of the economy.

Given this point of departure, the theory of temporary equilibrium with rationing and, in particular, its application to open economies as in Dixit (1978) offer a useful approach. To the best of our knowledge this approach has not previously been applied to international equilibria, except in the recent textbook by Dixit & Norman (1980, ch. 9). Our model is considerably richer, however, as it includes a government budget, financial capital mobility and an important role for intertemporal considerations.

The structure of each of the two economies is very reminiscient of the form in Dixit's (1976) closed economy model. Some aspects, such as the treatment of firms' choices, are simpler and the battery of policy tools is much more restricted. On the other hand, unlike Dixit's analysis, this study incorporates both bonds and money. Also, the role of money as a means of transactions is explicitly modelled.

The specification of the monetary mechanism, including the modelling of international monetary arrangements, owes a great deal of its inspiration to the recent work by Helpman (1981).[3] One of the advantages of this type of framework is that it clearly illustrates the importance of the precise structure of such arrangements. It also offers a possibility of consistently introducing money and other assets into the analysis in a simple way, without

---

[2] Argy & Salop (1979), Rødseth (1979) and some of the papers in Okun & Perry (1978) are among the few exceptions.

[3] Subsequent work by Helpman & Razin (1981 and 1982) relies on the same type of framework. Similar approaches have also been used in recent studies by Lucas (1981), Stockman (1980) and Persson (1982).

modelling uncertainty or transactions costs explicitly. However, some readers might find the assumptions about the monetary mechanism and the underlying transactions structure rather specific. Indeed, as commented on below, some (although far from all) of the results hinge on these assumptions.

The basic structure of the model is outlined in Section II. In Section III we introduce the institutional peculiarities in the system of floating rates and analyze the effects of the two alternative expansionary policies. Section IV deals with fixed exchange rates. Section V offers a summary of the main results and some suggestions for further research.

II. The Analytical Framework

Assume that the world consists of two countries, the home country and the foreign country. There is a representative household, a representative firm and a government in each of them. These agents interact on markets that are open in the beginning of each time period. All markets are spot markets, but agents' plans are also concerned with the future, so their actions are contingent on their expectations. There is a temporary equilibrium in each period, which guarantees that current actions are mutually consistent. We impose certain consistency requirements on expectations, but do not always require them to be correct, so that future planned actions are not always consistent. We also assume that expectations are held with subjective certainty (point expectations). For simplicity the analysis is restricted to an economy with two periods. In Appendix I (which should be read after this section), we show that with not very restrictive assumptions about preferences and expectations, essentially the same analysis may be extended to a multi-period, infinite-horizon framework.

As an institutional fact, we assume a *monetary* economy. This means that money has to be one side of each transaction, regardless of whether it concerns factors, goods, tax payments or financial assets. Each country has its own currency and foreign goods or assets have to be purchased with foreign money. The assumption that payments for goods are made in the seller's currency is important for some of the results; see Section III.

Factors are confined within borders and traded on national markets only, but the markets for goods and financial assets are completely integrated internationally. Financial assets are traded on a foreign exchange market and a bond market. Bonds are issued in the first period and mature in the next. They can be issued in either currency.

The timing of actual transactions differs between contracts in different markets. Financial assets are transacted instantaneously, in the beginning of periods when markets are open. Payments for goods are made during periods, since production and consumption take place successively over time. Actual payments according to contracts in factor markets are distributed at the end of periods. This transaction structure has the convenient property that it yields a well-defined (transactions) demand for money.

We also make some additional assumptions, which could be dispensed with, but facilitate the analysis considerably. *First,* there is only one perishable good. This means that the only relative goods price is intertemporal. Furthermore, there can be no intertemporal links in production, since the good cannot be stored. *Second,* this good is produced with decreasing returns to scale by one factor, labor. *Third,* while all other markets clear via price adjustment, labor markets clear via rationing. Nominal wages are assumed fixed at a level such that households always perceive a binding constraint on their supply. In addition, this unemployment regime is expected to extend into the second period. *Fourth,* there is no debt outstanding when agents enter the first period and *fifth,* the interest rate on bonds denominated in both currencies is strictly positive.

To begin with, consider the *government* in the home country. (The treatment of the foreign country is symmetric throughout the analysis.) It has three policy variables: (1) *Government purchases* of goods g; (2) a *lump-sum tax* T, which the households pay in the beginning of each period; and (3) a *payroll tax* t, per unit of labor l, that firms pay at the end of periods.[4]

We assume that the government sets g, t and T and that the resulting deficit D is always financed via money creation. Since an increased deficit financed by bonds would have no expansionary effects on employment in this model, the assumption is crucial. Hence, the first period's budget deficit, which coincides with (domestic) money creation, may be written as

$$p_1 g_1 - T_1 = D_1, \tag{1}$$

where D_1, to save on notation, includes the money receipts from payroll taxes in the previous period $t_0 l_0$. (Numerical subscripts denote periods when attached to variables and partial derivatives when attached to functional operators.) Current payroll taxes appear with a lag in the second-period budget

$$p_2 g_2 - t_1 l_1 - T_2 = D_2.$$

Since money creation is the source of finance, there are no interest payments and the two budgets are not directly interdependent. If there were

[4] A lump-sum tax is simpler to analyze than an income tax. Furthermore, only the income effect of the tax is important (incentive effects do not matter since households are rationed). The effects of an income tax would not coincide with those of the payroll tax, since the labor market is in a state of rationing rather than competitive equilibrium.

bond financing, the government would face an intertemporal budget constraint, similar to the constraint described below with respect to the household.

As mentioned in the introduction, we consider two types of expansionary policies. The first has its impact on the demand side via an increase in D_1. We look at decreases in T_1, rather than increases in g_1, because changes in g_1 raise problems as to the household's valuation of government expenditure. The main impact of the second policy, a decrease in t_1, is on the supply side, due to its direct effect on firms' labor costs. Since firms pay their taxes with a lag, the effects via the budget deficit do not appear until the second period. Agents' current decisions may change anyway as a result of these effects because of changed expectations about the variables in the second period.

Nevertheless, our assumption about the lag in tax payments introduces an asymmetry between the policies. This assumption is convenient analytically since firms accumulate money from sales of current production successively and make their payments to the government and the factor owners at the same time, at the end of the period. One way of incorporating payroll taxes into the current budget would be to let firms borrow the necessary amount on the bond market and, similar to the households, pay their taxes in the beginning of the period. This would increase complexity and would not change the main results (except possibly in one case—see Section IV).[5]

We now turn to the *household*. It comes to the market with a given wealth endowment $\bar{M}$. Since there is no debt outstanding, this is in the form of money from the preceding period's wage and profit income and hoarding. Prior to contracting in the markets, the household pays its taxes T to the government. Its supply of labor, at the given money wage w, is rationed by the firm's demand, but in the goods and financial markets the household contracts freely at given market prices. The decision problem is to choose consumption c in the two periods, net borrowing B and money hoarding, given the household's known factor incomes and its expectations about the future. We may aggregate the domestic and foreign components of c and B, since goods and bonds in different denominations can be treated as perfect substitutes (see below). Moreover, because expectations are subjectively certain and nominal interest rates are strictly positive, bonds dominate money as a store of value. Therefore there will be no hoarding and money will be used only for transactions; see Helpman (1981) for a fuller treatment of this issue.

---

[5] In this alternative case, firms would maximize an expression that included the nominal interest rate. This would eliminate the useful recursivity of the present model; see Section III.

Formally, the household maximizes a well-behaved utility function $u=U(c_1, c_2, l_1, l_2)$, where the evaluation of g_1 and g_2 is buried in U. It has to obey the liquidity and nonnegativity constraints

$$p_1 c_1 - B \leqslant \bar{M} - T_1,$$

$$p_2 c_2 \leqslant w_1 l_1 + \pi_1 - (1+r) B - T_2 \tag{2}$$

and

$$c_1, c_2 > 0.$$

Since there are no sign restrictions on B, the liquidity constraints may be collapsed into a single intertemporal budget constraint

$$p_1 c_1 + \beta p_2 c_2 + \leqslant (\bar{M} - T_1) + \beta(w_1 l_1 + \pi_1 - T_2),$$

where $\beta \equiv 1/(1+r)$. It is convenient to describe household behavior by means of the constrained (or restricted) *expenditure function*[6]

$$E(p_1, \beta p_2, l_1, l_2, u) \equiv \min \{p_1 c_1 + \beta p_2 c_2 | U(\cdot) \geqslant u\}.$$

$E(\cdot)$ is homogeneous of degree one in prices and its derivatives with respect to the first two arguments are the Hicksian compensated demands for current and future consumption. We may then describe the household's equilibrium by

$$E(1, \mu, l_1, l_2, u) = (\bar{M} - T_1)/p_1 + \beta(w_1 l_1 + \pi_1 - T_2)/p_1, \tag{3}$$

$$c_1 = E_1(1, \mu, l_1, l_2, u) \tag{4}$$

and

$$B = p_1 c_1 - (\bar{M} - T_1) \tag{5}$$

where $\mu \equiv \beta p_2 / p_1$, and π_1 is the value of dividends distributed by the firm. (Equation (5) follows from the first equation in (2).) When c_1 involves foreign goods and/or B involves bonds denominated in foreign currency, the household must acquire foreign money. These holdings, as well as the holdings of domestic transactions balances, are omitted from the formal

---

[6] Our formulation is the same as in Dixit (1976). See Cornes (1979) and Neary & Roberts (1980) for a general treatment of the constrained expenditure function.

treatment for expositary reasons (see, however, the beginning of the next section).[7,8]

The variables p_2, l_2 and T_2 are all expected values. Specific consistency assumptions about these expectations are made below. At this stage, we assume that the point expectations about all variables are shared by agents in both countries. This does not mean that p_2 and p_2^*, for example, cannot differ, but it requires that all agents agree on how they differ. Furthermore, we take expected variables to be differentiable functions, with the exogenous variables in the model as arguments.

As for the *firm*, there are no intertemporal links in production according to our assumptions, so it maximizes after-tax profits in each period separately, subject to a strictly concave production function $x=f(l)$. We describe its choices by the *profit function*

$$\Pi(p, w+t) \equiv \max \{px-(w+t)l \,|\, f(l) \geqslant x\};$$

see e.g. Varian (1978, Ch. 1). The firm's supply of goods and demand for labor in the first period obviously depend on the real after-tax wage. Formally (by Hotelling's Lemma), we have

$$x_1 = \Pi_1(p_1, w_1+t_1) \tag{6}$$

and

$$l_1 = -\Pi_2(p_1, w_1+t_1) \tag{7}$$

where both Π_1 and Π_2 are homogeneous of degree zero. Furthermore, $\Pi(\cdot)$ is strictly convex in both of its arguments, so we know that $\Pi_{11}>0$, $\Pi_{22}>0$. By homogeneity, it also follows that $\Pi_{12}=\Pi_{21}<0$. These properties will be of use in the comparative statics.

Hence, the firm contracts according to (6) and (7) at the beginning of the first period, produces and sells its output accordingly during the period and accumulates the money it receives. It distributes wage income plus profits and pays taxes at the end of the period. All profits are distributed, so dividends and actual profits coincide:

$$\pi_1 = p_1 x_1 - (w_1+t_1) l_1. \tag{8}$$

---

[7] Helpman (1981) provides a formal treatment of these decisions.

[8] The careful reader might wonder why the household would work at all in the second and last period when there is no opportunity of spending the income. This problem is a consequence of the simplified two-period structure; it disappears in an infinite horizon framework. The choices in an infinite horizon decision problem would, under certain conditions (see Appendix I), coincide with those represented by eqs. (3)–(5). Note, however, that the r.h.s. of (3) indeed contains factor incomes from two periods, namely 0 and 1.

Thus payments of wages, taxes and dividends completely exhaust the money that the firm has accumulated from its sales during the first period.

A *temporary equilibrium* in the first period occurs when agents act as described by (1)–(8) and all markets clear. The market for foreign exchange and equilibrium conditions for national money stocks are different under fixed and floating exchange rates, but the other markets remain the same. Since households are rationed on the labor markets in both countries, actual employment is determined by firms' demands, given by (7). We also have clearing conditions for the goods market (the superscript * denotes foreign variables)

$$c_1+c_1^*+g_1+g_1^*-x_1-x_1^*=0, \tag{9}$$

and for the bond market

$$B+e_1B^*=0, \tag{10}$$

where e is the exchange rate measured as the home currency price of foreign exchange.

So as to eliminate possibilities of arbitrage, the goods must sell at the same price in both currencies in equilibrium. In other words, the law of one prince

$$p_1=e_1p_1^* \tag{11}$$

must hold. As a first consistency requirement on expectations, we impose $p_2=e_2p_2^*$, that is agents' expectations about future prices and exchange rates must be consistent with the law of one price. Then, recalling that price expectations are common to agents in both countries, differences in returns (in terms of consumption) to savings in bonds of different denominations must be ruled out so agents face the same intertemporal relative prices of goods in terms of both currencies

$$\beta p_2/p_1=\beta^*p_2^*/p_1^*=\mu. \qquad 12)$$

It is easy to verify that (12) can also be written in the form $(1+r)=(1+r^*)e_2/e_1$, the standard nominal interest rate parity relation. The common value of the intertemporal terms of trade, μ, is a key variable in the analysis. However, some readers might find it easier to view changes in μ in terms of changes in a real interest rate ϱ, defined by $1/(1+\varrho)\equiv\mu$. Indeed, agents in the two economies observe changes in the intertemporal terms of trade via changes in nominal interest rates above (or below) changes in the expected increase in (spot) prices.[9]

---

[9] According to the definition of ϱ in the text, it follows from (12) that

$$r=\varrho+\frac{p_2-p_1}{p_1}+\varrho\left(\frac{p_2-p_1}{p_1}\right),$$

that is, the nominal interest rates faced by households satisfy the Fisher equation.

III. Flexible Exchange Rates

The system of floating exchange rates is distinguished by the fact that neither of the two governments intervenes in the foreign exchange market. The foreign exchange market in the economy studied here is in equilibrium when the balance-of-payments (b-o-p) surplus is zero in both countries. For the home country, define the current account surplus $s \equiv p_1[x_1-(c_1+g_1)]$, which is simply the trade surplus, since interest payments are absent due to our assumption of no outstanding debts. The capital account surplus simply equals net borrowing $B=p_1 c_1-(\bar{M}-T_1)$. Adding s and B and setting the sum equal to zero, we have the following equilibrium requirement

$$p_1 x_1-(\bar{M}-T_1+p_1 g_1)=0. \tag{13}$$

A similar expression holds for the foreign country.

Another way of justifying this equilibrium condition is as follows. There are no official interventions, so the amount of each country's money in circulation in each period must equal the given inherited money balances plus the amount of money created to finance the government's deficit. Since r, $r^*>0$, each country's total money holdings constitute a transactions demand. It is derived from the planned purchases of the country's goods, which in equilibrium must equal the total value of production. Therefore, the condition that the excess demand for the home country's money in the beginning of the first period is zero can be expressed as $p_1 x_1-(\bar{M}+D_1)=0$. This is (13) in the light of (1). In this model then, requirements of stock and flow equilibrium coincide.

We observe that (13) is in effect a particularly simple version of the quantity equation, where the unitary velocity derives from the transactions structure in the model.

The addition of (13) to the equilibrium conditions closes the model. We can then define an equilibrium under a floating exchange rate by the joint fulfillment of (1), (3) and (6)–(13), where it is understood that for country-specific equations, corresponding equations apply to the foreign country. The model is recursive. Let us briefly outline the stepwise solution.

First, given $\bar{M}$, w_1 and the government policy parameters, we can solve (7) and (13) for l_1 and p_1. This immediately gives x_1 from (6); in fact, because $x_1=f(l_1)$, it is immaterial whether we choose to solve (6) or (7). Then we can also determine D_1 from (1), π_1 from (8) and e_1 from (11). Next, we want to determine μ from the remaining equilibrium conditions (9) and (10). One of them is redundant, so we skip explicit treatment of the bond market. Given the point expectations of future variables, we now have the value of the r.h.s. of the household's budget constraint, call it y. We then use (3) to derive an expression for u in terms of y. Substituting this into the demand function $c_1=E_1(\cdot)$ and similarly for the foreign country, we may thus solve for μ, from (9) alone.[10] Finally, we can go backwards to determine u and use (12) to get β and hence r.

Before turning to the comparative statics, we make some further assumptions about expectations. In the sequel, expectations about those future variables which enter the agents' decision problems must be consistent with future market clearing. In other words, we use the ingredient in rational expectations models that agents' forecasts are consistent with the structure of the model. Although we treat the perfect foresight case in the welfare discussion below, we do not assume it *à priori*. That is, at this stage agents are allowed to make errors in their expectations about the exogenous variables in the second period. Turnovsky (1977) has labeled this weak form of rational expectations "structural" expectations. This consistency assumption is for convenience; the treatment of inconsistent expectations is no more difficult but somewhat messier; cf. Persson (1982, Ch. III).

Formally then, expectations about p_2, l_2 and T_2 have to be consistent with the second-period analogues to (6), (7) and (13), i.e.

$$x_2 = \Pi_1(p_2, w_2+t_2), \tag{14}$$

$$l_2 = -\Pi_2(p_2, w_2+t_2), \tag{15}$$

and

$$p_2 x_2 = M_1 + D_2 = M_1 + p_2 g_2 - t_1 l_1 - T_2, \tag{16}$$

where $M_1 \equiv \bar{M} + D_1$.

The household budget constraint can now be expressed in a simple form. By simple substitutions from (8), (11), (13) and (16) we have $y=(\bar{M}-T_1)/p_1+\beta(w_1 l_1+\pi_1-T_2)/p_1=(x_1-g_1)+\mu(x_2-g_2)$. Thus, the intertemporal resource constraint can be expressed entirely in terms of real variables.[11]

The starting point for the *comparative statics* is that the government in the home country wants to lower unemployment. Consider first the situation where the government chooses to do this through a decrease in household taxes, that is $dT_1<0$. This, by assumption, increases the budget deficit.

---

[10] We proceed in an analogous way in the comparative statics (cf. Appendix I). Note that $u=V(\mu, l_1, l_2, y)$, where V is an indirect utility function. Substituting $V(\cdot)$ into $E_i(1, \mu, l_1, l_2, u)$, we get the ordinary uncompensated demand function.

[11] Had we assumed Walrasian market clearing throughout, this would have been sufficient to ensure that all real variables in the model were independent of monetary conditions; see Persson (1982, Ch. III) for an elaboration.

We begin by looking at the effects on employment and current prices. Differentiating (7) and (13), and using the fact that $p_1 \Pi_{11} + (w_1 + t_1) \Pi_{12} = 0$ from the homogeneity of $\Pi(\cdot)$, we get

$$dp_1 = -\Delta_1^{-1} dT_1 > 0$$

and

$$dl_1 = \Delta_1^{-1} \Pi_{12}(\cdot) dT_1 > 0,$$

where $\Delta_1 \equiv (x_1 - g_1) - \Pi_{12}(\cdot)(w_1 + t_1) > 0$. In other words, the expansionary policy raises prices, thereby lowering real labor costs to the firm in the home country. The result, of course, is an increase in employment and production.[12]

Next, from (11) we have

$$de_1/e_1 = dp_1/p_1 > 0;$$

that is, the exchange rate depreciates to maintain the law of one price. Thus, the foreign country's price level is fully insulated from the price effects and consequently x_1^* and l_1^* are unaffected. But this does not mean that the foreign country is completely insulated because the intertemporal relative prices will be constant only by accident (see below).

The reader is cautioned, however, that the insulation of p_1^* and l_1^* hinges on the particular monetary mechanism which we have adopted. With a conventional specification of interest-sensitive money demands, insulation would not, in general, occur, although the direction of the change in foreign employment is uncertain.[13] However, insulation would also break down if the present framework had instead used the alternative assumption that payments for foreign goods were made in the *buyer's*, instead of the *seller's* currency; see Helpman & Razin (1981) for a discussion of the two systems.

---

[12] The monetary effects of the budget expansion are instrumental. A bond-financed tax cut would not change the money stock in circulation, so p_1 and then l_1 would remain constant. The effects would be limited to changes in intertemporal relative prices.

[13] Assume, for example, that within the present framework only a share α (where α was a positive function of the nominal interest rate) of each country's currency was spent by households and that the rest was hoarded. The expression corresponding to (13) for the foreign country would then read $p_1^* x_1^* - \alpha^*(r^*)[\bar{M}^* - T_1^*] - p_1^* g_1^* = 0$. With this (*ad hoc*) specification, x_1^* and l_1^* would be positively related to r^*. Therefore, whether l_1^* would expand or contract would then depend on the combined effect of the changes in ϱ and $(p_2^* - p_1^*)/p_1^*$ on r^* (see footnote 9). Neither of these changes can be signed à priori ($d\varrho$ has a sign opposite to $d\mu$—see below—and $d[(p_2^* - p_1^*)/p_1^*]$ depends on 'the elasticity of expectations''—in our model ultimately on the expectations of the exogenous variables).

In this case the result regarding foreign employment would also be ambiguous.[14]

We should also point out that the changes in p_1 and e_1 themselves could have had real effects on the foreign country, had we not assumed that there was no debt outstanding at the outset. If debt had been denominated in *home* currency, there would have been a redistribution of wealth, whose direction would have depended on the net position; for a detailed discussion of such redistributions, see Helpman & Razin (1982).

Let us now, after this detour, return to our model. Since x_1 goes up, there is an increase in the world supply of goods, but because of the generated change in y, there is also a change in the home household's demand. The relative price μ rises or falls according to whether there is excess supply or demand at its old value. In Appendix II we show that this condition can be expressed in the following form

$$d\mu = S^{-1}\left[\left(\frac{w_1+t_1}{p_1} - A_1\right)dl_1 - A_2\,dl_2\right], \tag{17}$$

where S is the derivative of world consumption $(c_1+c_1^*)$ with respect to μ, which is assumed to be positive. This amounts to assuming stability of the world goods market.

Therefore, if the expression within brackets is positive, μ rises and vice versa. We know from above that dl_1 is positive and, as is shown below, dl_2 is likely to be positive as well. The terms A_1 and A_2 consist of income and substitution effects. They are discussed more closely in Appendix II, where we conclude that if the first-period good and leisure are strong complements, then $A_1<0$. If the same applies to first-period goods and second-period leisure, $A_2<0$. Then c_1 decreases, when l_1 and l_2 increase, because of the complementarity in demand. The result is excess supply of goods, so that $d\mu>0$ (the real interest rate falls). On the other hand, if the first-period good and leisure in the two periods are net substitutes, this guarantees A_1, $A_2>0$. When substitutability is strong, the results is excess demand and $d\mu<0$. However, if it is not too strong (or there is weak complementarity), $0<A_1<(w_1+t_1)/p_1$. This assumption may seem quite reasonable since we are dealing with one aggregate good. As the size (and sign) of dl_2 becomes crucial in this case, it should be scrutinized further.

The general expression for dl_2 can be derived from (15) and (16) as

$$dl_2 = -\Delta_2^{-1}[\Pi_{12}(\cdot)(dM_1 - d(t_1 l_1) - dT_2) + \Pi_{22}(\cdot)(x_2-g_2)\,d(t_2+w_2)], \tag{18}$$

---

[14] In this case, the analogue to (13) would be $p_1^*\ (c_1^*+g_1^*)-(\bar{M}^*-T_1^*+p_1^*g_1)=0$. Here l_1^* would (through p_1^*) be negatively related to c_1^*. Hence, the sign of $d\mu$ would determine whether l_1^* would rise or fall. This case and the one discussed in footnote 13 would be more complicated to analyze than the case treated in the text, since the model would no longer be recursive.

where $\Delta_2 \equiv (x_2 - g_2) - \Pi_{12}(\cdot)(w_2 + t_2) > 0$. The rationally expected change in l_2 depends partly on the (known) changes in the money stock which spill over from the current period and partly on the expected changes in exogenous variables. Suppose now that, in the present case, agents expect all future exogenous variables except T_2 to be constant. Then, in view of our earlier results, (18) reduces to

$$dl_2 = \Delta_2^{-1}\Pi_{12}(\cdot)\left[-dT_1\left(1+\frac{(g_1+t_1\Pi_{12}(\cdot))}{\Delta_1}\right)-dT_2\right]$$

Because the first term in brackets is always positive, l_2 is expected to rise, unless agents expect the current expansion to be followed by a considerably more contractionary policy than before ($dT_2 > 0$). If agents believe that the tax cut is "temporary" ($dT_2 = 0$), dl_2 is unambiguously positive and if they believe it to be "permanent" ($dT_2 = dT_1$), it is even more strongly so.[15] Hence, we have the appealing result that the more expansionary the expected future policy, the more likely a state of excess demand today, that is, a fall in μ (a rise in the real rate of interest).[16]

In all cases where μ changes, consumption in the foreign country does not remain the same. For example, if $d\mu < 0$, c_1^* falls to accomodate an initial excess demand for goods. Or, savings increase in the foreign country as a response to a higher real interest rate; the increased savings take the form of increased net loans to the home country.

Now, consider the situation where the home government instead lowers payroll taxes, $dt_1 < 0$. From (7) and (13) we get

$$dp_1 = \Delta_1^{-1}(w_1+t_1)\Pi_{22}(\cdot)\,dt_1 < 0,$$

and

$$dl_1 = \Delta_1^{-1}(x_1-g_1)\Pi_{22}(\cdot)\,dt_1 > 0.$$

Employment and production indeed increase, as expected, but since the money stock is kept constant, this leads to a fall in prices, which in turn curbs the initial fall in firms' labor costs and the rise in employment somewhat.

---

[15] It would be interesting to analyze a case where agents took current expansion as evidence of a government policy rule and formed their expectations accordingly. Also, if wages were set by long-term contracts, expectations about second-period variables should be reflected in w_2 (unless, of course, contracts lasted for two periods). However, these extensions are outside the scope of this paper.

[16] The influence of rationally expected optimism about the future on current decision-making is reminiscient of the way it enters the analysis of Neary & Stiglitz (1982). The "bootstraps" equilibria they considered do not arise here, however, since output is entirely supply determined.

The exchange rate again changes proportionally, but since prices fall, the result this time is an appreciation. However, as before, p_1^* and hence x_1^* and l_1^* are not affected, so it is again through changes in intertemporal relative prices that foreign consumers experience expansion in the home country. The change in μ is again decided by (17), our general condition, and most of the earlier discussion also applies here.[17]

We have thus shown that although the foreign country's employment is insulated from the effects of expansionary policies in the home country, its consumption generally changes as a response to the change in intertemporal relative prices. In order to determine the direction of this change we need restrictions on preferences and/or expectations. It should be clear that had we not chosen to abstract from intertemporal links in production, then investment and production decisions of foreign, as well as domestic, firms would also have been affected.

What are the *welfare implications* of the policies in question? This is a difficult aspect, as long as we do not restrict agents' expectations to be correct. Households maximize their utility given expectations that may turn out to be wrong, in which case *ex ante* and *ex post* evaluations of welfare changes will differ.

We therefore assume that agents' expectations are not only consistent with market clearing, but also that their expectations about the exogenous variables are correct, i.e. that there is *perfect foresight*. The model then lends itself to welfare evaluations (we do assume away certain problems, however, by discussing a representative household that is "partly" unemployed). Actually, we have already derived an expression (A 3), showing the change in welfare of the home-country household. Applying a similar expression to the foreign country, we have the following welfare effects of either of the two expansionary policies

$$du = \frac{1}{E_5}\left[(x_2-g_2-c_2)\,d\mu + \left(\frac{w_1+t_1}{p_1} - E_3\right) dl_1 + \left(\beta\frac{w_2+t_2}{p_1} - E_4\right) dl_2\right]$$

and

$$du^* = \frac{1}{E_5^*}(x_2^*-g_2^*-c_2^*)\,d\mu.$$

Consider du^* first. Since $E^*(\cdot)$ is increasing in u^*, E_5^* is positive, so the sign of du^* hinges on the sign of $(x_2^*-g_2^*-c_2^*)\,d\mu$. Therefore, we arrive at a conclusion, which is analogous to a result in the standard analysis of

[17] The implications for dl_2 are slightly different, however. This is because the effects on the budget deficit are ambiguous. Therefore, we cannot conclude that perception of the policy change as temporary ($dt_2=0$) implies $dl_2>0$ without further restrictions.

atemporal terms-of-trade changes. If the foreign country is a net exporter in the second period, its welfare increases if the intertemporal terms of trade rise—$d\mu > 0$, while it decreases if they fall. Another way to express this is, of course, that the welfare of a net debtor country increases if the real interest rate falls and vice versa.

What about the welfare implications for the home country? Let us suppose that the (perfectly foreseen) policies in the second period are such that $dl_2 > 0$. From the discussion in Appendix II, we know that the coefficients on dl_1 and dl_2 can be interpreted as the wedges between (real) demand and supply prices of labor in the two periods and that they are both positive. Is this then sufficient to conclude that $du > 0$? Clearly not, since the converse is true if the terms-of-trade effects is negative and sufficiently strong. The possibility of such an *immiserizing expansion* suggests that it may be premature to judge the desirability of a given policy exclusively on the basis of its employment effects. In an extended version of the model, incorporating for example two goods in each period, we would (provided, of course, that both goods were traded) in general get additional atemporal terms-of-trade effects in the formulas for du and du^*.[18] In other words, if we allow for terms-of-trade changes, a preoccupation solely with aggregate production and employment in the analysis of stabilization policies may, in certain cases, be misleading.

IV. Fixed Exchange Rates

We now discuss a situation where the exchange rate between the two countries is kept fixed by government interventions. The anatomy of these interventions has to be specified precisely, since the results depend on what assumptions are made. The formal analysis here agrees with the recent modelling of fixed exchange rates in the well-known "monetary approach". It is also in accordance with our earlier assumption that governments finance deficits in their current activities solely by money creation. An alternative formulation in which the interventions are instead financed on the bond market, thereby approximating a case with interest-bearing reserves, is not treated explicitly, but the implications of adopting it are discussed at the end of this section.

Under fixed exchange rates, the excess demand for the *sum* of the two countries' monies must be zero in equilibrium. But either of the two countries may have a currency in excess demand which, according to the arguments in the preceding section, corresponds to a surplus in the b-o-p.

---

[18] The reason for the caveat "in general" is that cases where one of the countries exported both goods in the first period are conceivable. Then the notion of atemporal terms of trade would be meaningless.

Obviously, there must then be an excess supply of the other currency, that is, a deficit in the other country's b-o-p. In such a situation it is necessary to support the fixed exchange rate. We assume that the two governments have agreed to support a particular exchange rate $\bar{e}$, by *joint* intervention, as follows. The government in the surplus country issues new money to cover the excess demand at $\bar{e}$. This money is handed over to the other government which sells it and keeps the receipts.

Although these stabilization operations are reminiscent of a swap agreement, the monetary effects are the same as if $\bar{e}$ had been stabilized by currency reserves or as those which would occur under a gold standard. All settings lead to an injection of the surplus country's money and a withdrawal of the same amount of the deficit country' money, but the world money stock is kept constant. An advantage of this formulation is simplicity in the sense that reserve holdings do not have to be considered explicitly; see Persson (1982, Ch. V) for a treatment of these and other stabilization schemes.

We simplify matters by assuming that all agents believe the stabilization operations will also be successful in the future. Therefore, $e_1=e_2=\bar{e}$. For convenience, choose units so that $\bar{e}=1$. Then current, as well as expected, prices in terms of both currencies must coincide. Let p denote these common prices. We may then summarize the above paragraphs in the following equilibrium conditions:

$$p_1(x_1+x_1^*) = \bar{M}-T_1+p_1 g_1+\bar{M}^*-T_1^*+p_1 g_1^*, \tag{19}$$

$$-X_1 = p_1 x_1-(\bar{M}-T_1+p_1 g_1) \quad \text{and} \quad -X_1^* = p_1 x_1^*-(\bar{M}^*-T_1^*+p_1 g_1^*), \tag{20}$$

where X_1 and X_1^* are the withdrawals of money brought about by the interventions. Obviously, from (19), X and X^* are equal in size but opposite in sign. In this system then, the quantity equation holds for the world economy as a whole but not for each country separately.

Replacing (13) by (19) and (20), we get our definition of an equilibrium under fixed exchange rates. Consequently, we solve for p_1, X_1 and X_1^* instead of p_1, p_1^* and e_1, but otherwise the same algorithm as in the solution under floating rates may be applied, so we need not repeat it here.[19]

We maintain our earlier consistency requirement on expectations, but it has to be reformulated in the light of the peculiarities of the system. We have to assume that expectations about l_2, p_2 and T_2 are consistent with (14), (15),

$$p_2(x_2+x_2^*) = M_1+D_2+M_1^*+D_2^*, \tag{21}$$

[19] It is easy to see from (12) that in any equilibrium under fixed exchange rates $r=r^*$, since p_1 and p_2 are common to both countries.

$$-X_2 = p_2 x_2 - (M_1 - X_1 + D_2) \quad \text{and} \quad -X_2^* = p_2 x_2^* - (M_1^* - X_1^* + D_2^*), \tag{22}$$

where M_1, M_1^*, D_2 and D_2^* are defined as above.

Substitutions from (8), (11), (20) and (22) and some rearrangements then give us $y=(x_1-g_1)+\mu(x_2-g_2)+(X_1/p_1+\mu X_2/p_2)$. The difference between this expression and the one derived under floating is the inclusion of the final term. It measures the present value to home consumers of the accumulated deficits in the b-o-p.

The analogous expression for the foreign country is $y^*=(x_1^*-g_1^*)+\mu(x_2^*-g_2^*)+(X_1^*/p_1+\mu X_2^*/p_2)=(x_1^*-g_1^*)+\mu(x_2^*-g_2^*)-(X_1/p_1+\mu X_2/p_2)$, where the last equality follows from (19) and (21). There is thus a potential redistribution of purchasing power inherent in this type of exchange rate arrangement; see Helpman (1981) for a more detailed discussion. A redistribution is also inherent in a gold standard and a system with currency reserves; see Persson (1982, Ch. V).

Let us now study the effects of the expansionary policies. First, take the case of lower lump-sum taxes in the home country, that is $dT_1<0$. Employment and production abroad are no longer insulated, since there is now a common world price level. Therefore we have to determine the effects on p_1, l_1 and l_1^* simultaneously. Differentiating (7), a similar expression for the foreign country, and (19), we obtain

$$dp_1 = -\bar{\Delta}^{-1} dT_1 > 0,$$

$$dl_1 = \bar{\Delta}^{-1} \Pi_{12}(\cdot)\, dT_1 > 0$$

and

$$dl_1^* = \bar{\Delta}^{-1} \Pi_{12}^*(\cdot)\, dT_1 > 0,$$

where $\bar{\Delta} \equiv [(x_1-g_1)+(x_1^*-g_1^*)-\Pi_{12}(\cdot)(w_1+t_1)-\Pi_{12}^*(\cdot)(w_1^*+t_1^*)] > 0.$

So we find that employment expands both at home and abroad. The reason is, of course, that the increase in p_1 brings about a decrease in real wages in both countries which makes it profitable to expand production. We note, however, that the expansionary effects arise because the home country is large enough to influence p_1. Such a policy would not have been successful for a small country in the present framework.

The exchange rate does not change, by assumption, but from (20) we can derive

$$dX_1 = -dX_1^* = p_1\, dx_1^* + x_1^*\, dp_1 > 0$$

and

$$d(X_1/p_1) = -d(X_1^*/p_1) = dx_1^* + \left(\frac{\bar{M}^* - T_1^*}{p_1}\frac{dp_1}{p_1}\right) > 0,$$

so there is an increased excess supply of home currency at the going exchange rate and the governments must invervene to support it. We also have a redistribution of wealth towards the home country in the first period.

The results with respect to the change in the intertemporal terms of trade are less clear-cut. In Appendix III, we show that the general expression for $d\mu$ in this regime is

$$d\mu = \bar{S}^{-1}\Bigg[\left(\frac{w_1+t_1}{p_1} - A_1\right)dl_1 + \left(\frac{w_1^*+t_1^*}{p_1} - A_1^*\right)dl_1^* - A_2\,dl_2$$
$$- A_2^*\,dl_2^* - ((C_y - C_y^*)(d(X_1/p_1) + \mu d(X_2/p_2)))\Bigg], \qquad (23)$$

where the A-terms are the same as under floating, $\bar{S}>0$ if we maintain our stability assumption and $C_y \equiv \partial c_1/\partial y$. The condition is interpreted as before. Extra complications arise in this regime, since we have to take supply and demand effects in both countries into account. There is also an additional term (the last in (23)) which reflects the change in demand that ensues from the reallocation of purchasing power, to the extent that marginal propensities to consume are different. It is therefore impossible to indicate the sign of $d\mu$ without specific restrictions on preferences and/or expectations. The exploration of different cases is left to the reader.

What then, are the effects of lowered payroll taxes under fixed exchange rates? We find first

$$dp_1 = \bar{\Delta}^{-1}\Pi_{22}(\cdot)(w_1+t_1)\,dt_1 < 0,$$

$$dl_1 = \bar{\Delta}^{-1}[\Pi_{22}(\cdot)(x_1 - g_1 + x_1^* - g_1^*) - \Pi_{12}^*(\cdot)\Pi_{22}(\cdot)(w_1^*+t_1^*)]\,dt_1 > 0$$

and

$$dl_1^* = \bar{\Delta}^{-1}\Pi_{12}^*(\cdot)\Pi_{22}(\cdot)(w_1+t_1)\,dt_1 < 0.$$

Employment is stimulated in the home country, but depressed in the foreign country. It is easy to understand that $dl_1>0$, since the lower payroll taxes decrease labor costs directly, but what about $dl_1^*<0$? The explanation is that prices fall because the world money stock has not been altered. This raises labor costs abroad and depresses employment and production, which in turn mitigates somewhat the fall in prices and the associated cushioning effect on home employment.[20] It is clear that world production increases;

[20] In this case there is a possibility that introducing budget effects of the tax cut in the first period would change the results. If demand for l_1 is inelastic, tax revenue would fall as a result of the cut in t_1. If the fall were very sharp, p_1 might actually rise, which would lead to an increase in l_1^*.

the world money stock is constant and since $dp_1<0, (x_1+x_1^*)$ must increase to fulfill (19). But the effect on world employment is uncertain. It is likely to be positive though, unless technologies in the two countries are very different.

From (20) we find that $dX_1<0$ and $d(X_1/p_1)<0$. In contrast to the demand expansion, this policy thus generates an increase in the home country's first-period b-o-p surplus and corresponding interventions to support the foreign currency.[21] There is also a redistribution of purchasing power towards the foreign country.

As for the effect on intertemporal relative prices, our general expression (23) still applies. But since dl_1 and dl_1^* now enter with different signs, the effect is even more uncertain than previously and we have to resort to quite restrictive assumptions to get unambiguous results. As an example, let us assume (i) there is no disutility of work, and (ii) in the second period agents expect the home government to raise t to its previous level and adjust T to neutralize the monetary effects of dt_1. Then (23) reduces to

$$d\mu = \bar{S}^{-1}[dx_1(1-C_y)+dx_1^*(1-C_y^*)-(C_y-C_y^*)\,d(X_1/p_1)].$$

It can be shown that, as long as both goods are normal (that is $0<C_y$ and $C_y^*<1$), this expression is always positive. Hence, if the particular conditions (i) and (ii) are satisfied, we know that $d\mu>0$. But it is not difficult to find equally plausible (or implausible) sets of assumptions that would yield the opposite result.

As for welfare evaluations of the two policies, we again assume perfect foresight. The expressions for changes in household utility (derived in Appendix III) are:

$$du = \frac{1}{E_5}\left[\left(x_2+\frac{X_2}{p_2}-g_2-c_2\right)d\mu+\left(\frac{w_1+t_1}{p_1}-E_3\right)dl_1 + \left(\beta\frac{w_2+t_2}{p_1}-E_4\right)dl_2+dX\right]$$

and

$$du^* = \frac{1}{E_5^*}\left[\left(x_2^*+\frac{X_2^*}{p_2^*}-g_2^*-c_2^*\right)d\mu+\left(\frac{w_1^*+t_1^*}{p_1}-E_3^*\right)dl_1^* + \left(\beta\frac{w_2^*+t_2^*}{p_1}-E_4^*\right)dl_2^*-dX\right],$$

[21] This difference between the two policies corresponds to the difference between depreciation and appreciation we found under floating.

where $dX \equiv d(X_1/p_1) + \mu d(X_2/p_2)$. For the home country this is essentially the same expression as under floating, except for the last term which captures the effect of the wealth redistribution. The same term, but with an opposite sign, also appears in the expression for du^*, which now, of course, also encompasses the effects of changes in foreign employment and income.

In the same way as under floating, these expressions serve to qualify hasty conclusions about benefits of the policies based on employment effects alone. Consider the demand expansion. Assume that the policies are such that dl_2 and $dl_2^* > 0$. It should be clear that in spite of an increase in both home and foreign employment in both periods, there is no guarantee that welfare improves in both countries, although this may be likely. Not only the terms-of-trade effect (the first term), but also the redistribution effect (the last term) can counteract the favorable effect of improved employment. Welfare must clearly increase in at least one country, however.[22]

Similarly, the fact that the supply-led expansion is a beggar-thy-neighbor policy from an employment point of view does not necessarily mean that $du^* < 0$. If the other effects are favorable to the foreign country, welfare may increase although dl_1^*, $dl_2^* < 0$.

We conclude this section by commenting on the implications of changing the assumptions about how the inverventions in the foreign exchange market are financed. Assume instead that one of the countries took a one-sided decision to stabilize e and to finance its interventions on the bond market. Helpman (1981) calls this a one-sided peg regime. One crucial difference between this regime and ours is that in the alternative system, the world money stock does not remain constant when there are b-o-p adjustments.[23] As a consequence, the results derived earlier would change. A more comprehensive guide can be found in Persson (1982, Ch. IV and V), so we merely state the differences here.

In the alternative system it would no longer be immaterial in which of the two countries the expansionary policies were pursued. Suppose that the *home* country maintained the parity by its interventions. Then the effects of both types of policies, as long as they originated in the *foreign* country, would be similar to those in our model (but would not involve the same kind of redistribution). A monetary expansion in the *home* country, on the other hand, would not affect either l_1 or l_1^*. In the case of lower payroll taxes at home, there would be an increase in l_1 but no fall in l_1^*.

---

[22] If we add $E_5 du + E_5^* du^*$, terms in $d\mu$ and dX cancel out and we end up with only positive terms on the r.h.s. Since E_5 and E_5^* are positive, du and du^* cannot both be negative.

[23] As Helpman shows, the two regimes generally differ from a welfare point of view, even with perfect foresight and Walrasian market clearing throughout.

V. Concluding Comments

We have studied the international effects of two kinds of national expansionary employment policies: lowered lump-sum taxes resulting in an increased money-financed budget deficit and a reduction in firms' labor costs via lower payroll taxes.

Under flexible exchange rates, the foreign country's production and employment levels were insulated in the case of both policies in the home country. However, there were still real effects abroad via a change in the real rate of interest—the intertemporal terms of trade—the direction of which was shown to depend on preferences in the home country and the change in expectations about future policies. From our welfare analysis we concluded that this terms-of-trade change could benefit or hurt the foreign country, depending on its direction and whether it was a debtor or a creditor. We were also cautioned that conclusions regarding the benefits of increased employment had to be qualified, because of the possibility of an immiserizing expansion.

In the fixed exchange rate system, the foreign country's employment was also affected. The monetary expansion was shown to generate an expansion of employment in both countries, while the supply-directed tax decrease was a beggar-thy-neighbor policy from an employment point of view. The welfare discussion revealed that not only terms-of-trade changes, but also the redistribution of purchasing power inherent in the system, could work in a direction opposite to the employment effects.

As we have already emphasized, some of our particular results, for example the insulation of foreign employment under floating rates, hinge on the particular assumptions underlying the model. However, it should also be stressed that some parts of the analysis, the welfare discussion in particular, are perfectly general and would apply to any properly specified model.

Our model offers a consistent framework for analyzing international effects of stabilization policies, but it clearly has its limitations. The reason for unemployment (and indirectly for the expansionary policies in the model) is that nominal wages are fixed at an excessively high level. This explanation is somewhat controversial, but even if it is accepted, one would really like to endogenize the wage setting rather than assume a sticky wage. Of course, varying degrees of "wage indexation" could also be analyzed. This would undoubtedly change some results. In the opposite polar case of *real* wage rigidity, for example, employment would not be affected by changes in the lump-sum tax. Obviously, there are also other explanations of low employment that would be worth considering.

It may also be of interest to consider the implications of asymmetry in the initial conditions in the two countries. One could easily think of alternative situations. There could, for instance, be full employment or unemployment due to deficient demand in one of the countries.

Another point which is treated unsatisfactorily is the government's policy objectives.[24] These are not only interesting in themselves, but, as mentioned in Section III, there might be close links between wage setting and government behavior.[25]

It would also be worthwhile to look at other available policy instruments. Dixit's (1976) analysis of a closed economy offers a number of suggestions. An analysis of exchange-rate policies would also be interesting, particularly since such policies and changed payroll taxes are often suggested as alternatives in the policy debate in many countries. A full analysis is outside the scope of this paper, but the effects of a devaluation of the home currency on production in the two countries are derived in Appendix IV. Production is shown to increase unambiguously at home, but whether it rises or falls abroad is uncertain. Hence, unlike the lowering of payroll taxes, devaluation is not necessarily a beggar-thy-neighbor policy in our model. It should be pointed out that the framework in this paper ignores aspects of exchange-rate changes because there are no atemporal relative goods prices. In order to discuss reallocation between sectors in the two countries, the model would have to be extended by adding at least one more good. An extension to more than one traded good would also give rise to additional welfare effects via changes in the atemporal terms of trade.

Another extension would be a world with more than two countries where there were blocks of countries with internally fixed exchange rates. Indeed, the international monetary system has developed in this direction since the breakdown of the Bretton Woods Agreement. Some aspects of the global functioning of such *intermediate* exchange rate systems have been analyzed elsewhere by this author. If one country on floating rates were added to the two countries on fixed rates, the discussion in Persson (1982, Ch. III and IV) indicates that the global effects of, at least supply-oriented, expansionary policies in one of the two block countries would often be quite asymmetric. Then, looking at the welfare implications as we did above for example, welfare in the two other countries would often move in different directions.

Appendix I

We show sufficient conditions for the choices of c_1 and c_2 by a household that faces an infinite horizon maximization problem and a household that

---

[24] In this framework the government could always bring the economy to full employment in the first period by a sufficient monetary expansion. In order to explain why governments do not exploit this possibility, it would have to be argued that such policies have certain costs. But as it now stands, the model does not allow for a discussion of these issues.

[25] Calmfors (1982) suggests how these links can be modelled.

faces the two-period problem in the text to coincide. For simplicity, we treat the case where there is no disutility of work.

Let the household face the problem

$$\max u = U(c_1, c_2, c_3 \ldots)$$

$$\text{s.t. } p_1 c_1 + \beta_1 p_2 c_2 + \beta_2 p_3 c_3 \ldots = M_1 + \beta_1 M_2 + \beta_2 M_3 \ldots = Y,$$

where β_1, β_2 ... are discount factors and M_1, M_2 ... are the money endowments available in the beginning of each period.

We then want to show sufficient conditions for representing the household's equilibrium by

$$E(p_1, \beta_1 p_2, v) = k(M_1 + \beta_1 M_2),$$

where k is some positive constant.

(i) Assume weakly separable preferences, viz.

$$u = U(F(c_1, c_2), G(c_3 \ldots)).$$

(ii) Assume that U is homothetic and that F and G are homogenous of degree one. Using these two assumptions it can be shown that

$$\tilde{E}(p_1, \beta_1 p_2, \beta_2 p_3, \ldots, u) = \tilde{E}(\psi_1(p_1, \beta_1 p_2), \psi_2(\beta_2 p_3, \ldots))\, g(u),$$

where ψ_1 and ψ_2 are well-defined price indices. The budget constraint can be written as

$$\tilde{E}(\psi_1(\cdot), \psi_2(\cdot))\, g(u) = Y$$

or, since $\tilde{E}(\cdot)$ is homogeneous of degree one

$$\tilde{E}(1, \psi_2/\psi_1)\, g(u) = Y/\psi_1 \equiv y.$$

If we define spending levels $Z_1 \equiv p_1 c_1 + \beta_1 p_2 c_2$, $Z_2 \equiv \beta_2 p_3 c_3 + \ldots$, we also have "real" spending levels; cf. Svensson & Razin (1983).

$$z_1 = Z_1/\psi_1 = \tilde{E}_1(1, \psi_2/\psi_1)\, g(u)$$

$$z_2 = Z_2/\psi_2 = \tilde{E}_2(1, \psi_2/\psi_1)\, g(u);$$

Consequently the ratio between Z_1 and Y is

$$\frac{Z_1}{Y} = \frac{\psi_1 z_1}{\psi_1 y} = \frac{\psi_1 \tilde{E}_1(1, \psi_2/\psi_1)\, g(u)}{\psi_1 \tilde{E}(1, \psi_2/\psi_1)\, g(u)} = \frac{\tilde{E}_1(1, \psi_2/\psi_1)}{\tilde{E}(1, \psi_2/\psi_1)} = \gamma(\psi_2/\psi_1).$$

(iii) Assume that ψ_2/ψ_1 is constant; that is, expectations about (present value) prices in the "distant future" are unit elastic with respect to prices "today and in the near future".

Then $Z_1 = \bar{\gamma} Y$.

(iv) Define $Y_1 \equiv M_1 + \beta_1 M_2$ and $Y_2 \equiv \beta_2 M_3 + \ldots$ Assume that Y_2/Y_1 is constant, which is an assumption similar to (iii) but on "distant future income".

When (iv) holds, we have $Y = (1+\alpha) Y_1$, where $\alpha = Y_2/Y_1$. Now, putting the pieces together

$$Z_1 = \bar{\gamma} Y = \bar{\gamma}(1+\alpha) Y_1,$$

or, if we set $\bar{\gamma}(1+\alpha) \equiv k$,

$$p_1 c_1 + \beta_1 p_2 c_2 = k Y_1 = k(M_1 + \beta_1 M_2).$$

Hence, the household's equilibrium can be represented by

$$E(p_1, \beta_1 p_2, v) = \bar{E}(p_1, \beta_1 p_2)\, v = k(M_1 + \beta_1 M_2),$$

where $v = V(p_1, \beta_1 p_2, kY_1)$ is an indirect utility function. □

If we are instead willing to assume a particular from of additive separability, for example

$$u = \log(F(c_1, c_2)) + \delta \log(G(c_3 \ldots)),$$

where F and G as before are homogeneous of degree one, we can skip assumption (iii) and it is sufficient that (iv) holds for a similar conclusion.

Appendix II

First, we want to derive a general formula for the change in the intertemporal terms of trade, when there is a policy change in the home country under floating exchange rates.

First differentiate (3) totally, denoting the r.h.s. by y

$$E_2\, d\mu + E_3\, dl_1 + E_4\, dl_2 + E_5\, du = dy. \qquad \text{(A 1)}$$

Use the result that, with our restrictions on expectations, $y = (x_1 - g_1) + \mu(x_2 - g_2)$ and our assumption that $dg_1 = dg_2 = 0$ to derive

$$dy = dx_1 + \mu dx_2 + (x_2 - g_2)\, d\mu.$$

Since $x_1 = f(l_1)$ and $f_1(l) = (w_1 + t_1)/p_1$, we must have $dx_1 = (w_1 + t_1)\, dl_1/p_1$. Applying a similar argument to dx_2 and using $\mu = \beta p_2/p_1$, we can write

$$dy=\frac{w_1+t_1}{p_1}\,dl_1+\beta\frac{w_2+t_2}{p_1}\,dl_2+(x_2-g_2)\,d\mu. \tag{A 2}$$

Substitution of (A 2) into (A 1) and some rearrangement gives

$$du=\frac{1}{E_5}\left[(x_2-g_2-E_2)\,d\mu+\left(\frac{w_1+t_1}{p_1}-E_3\right)dl_1+\left(\beta\frac{w_2+t_2}{p_1}-E_4\right)dl_2\right], \tag{A 3}$$

which is a general expression for the change in home welfare.

After this intermediate step, differentiate (4) to get

$$dc_1=E_{12}\,d\mu+E_{13}\,dl_1+E_{14}\,dl_2+E_{15}\,du. \tag{A 4}$$

Then differentiate (9), the goods market equilibrium condition

$$dc_1+dc_1^*+dg_1+dg_1^*-dx_1-dx_1^*=0. \tag{A 5}$$

Finally, take into account that for both dt_1 and dT_1 we can set dg_1, dg_1^*,dx_1^*, dl_1^*, $dl_2^*=0$, and substitute from (A 3) and (A 4) and the similar expressions that apply to the foreign country to obtain

$$d\mu=S^{-1}\left[\left(\frac{w_1+t_1}{p_1}-\left(E_{13}+\frac{E_{15}}{E_5}\left(\frac{w_1+t_1}{p_1}-E_3\right)\right)dl_1\right)\right.$$
$$\left.-\left(E_{14}+\frac{E_{15}}{E_5}\left(\beta\frac{w_2+t_2}{p_1}-E_4\right)\right)dl_2\right],$$

where $S\equiv\left[E_{12}+\frac{E_{15}}{E_5}(x_2-g_2-E_2)+E_{12}^*+\frac{E_{15}^*}{E_5^*}(x_2^*-g_2^*-E_2^*)\right]$,

and we have substituted for dx_1 in the same way as above.

This expression equals (17) if we define

$$A_1\equiv E_{13}+\frac{E_{15}}{E_5}\left(\frac{w_1+t_1}{p_1}-E_3\right), A_2\equiv E_{14}+\frac{E_{15}}{E_5}\left(\beta\frac{w_2+t_2}{p_1}-E_4\right).$$

Next, we interpet S, A_1 and A_2 and discuss the assumptions which have to be made in order to determine their signs.

Consider S first. It si the partial derivative of total first-period consumption with respect to intertemporal relative prices. From the properties of $E(\cdot)$, E_{12} is the compensated (cross) substitution effect, $E_{15}/E_5=\partial c_1/\partial y\equiv C_y$ the marginal propensity to consume and $E_2=c_2$ in equilibrium. The interpretation of the starred terms is analogous. We assume $S>0$, since this ensures stability. Since $(x_2-g_2-c_2)=-(x_2^*-g_2^*-c_2^*)$ (agents expectations are consistent with market clearing) it is clear that, if C_y and C_y^* are not too different, it is sufficient that goods in the two periods are net substitutes in both countries, that is $E_{12}, E_{12}^*>0$.

Then look at $A_1=\partial c_1/\partial l_1$. The term $C_y(w_1+t_1)/p_1$ measures the "Keynesian" income effect of a change in employment, while $-C_y E_3$ is the "ordinary" income effect, since E_3 is in fact the supply price of labor (in terms of first-period goods). But because the home household is rationed in the labor market, it must be that $w_1/p_1>E_3$ and thus we may conclude that the second term in A_1 is positive. the remaining effect, E_{13}, is the compensated substitution effect of a change in current employment on current consumption. It is positive if goods and leisure are substitutes and negative if they are complements. Hence we get the results: if c_1 and l_1 are strong complements $A_1<0$, if they are weak complements or substitutes $0<A_1<(w_1+t_1)/p_1$ and if they are strong substitutes $A_1>(w_1+t_1)/p_1$. A similar discussion applies to A_2.

Appendix III

We now derive the general expression for $d\mu$ when there is a policy change under fixed exchange rates. We use the sama approach as in Appendix II.

Use the fact that, with our assumptions about expectations, we have $y=(x_1-g_1+\mu(x_2-g_2)+(X_1/p_1+\mu X_2/p_2)$ to derive

$$dy = dx_1+\mu dx_2+(x_2-g_2)\, d\mu+d(X_2/p_2)+(X_2/p_2)\, d\mu.$$

This can be expressed in terms of dl_1 and dl_2 as in Appendix II. Substituting the resulting expression into (A 1) and rearranging, we get

$$du = \frac{1}{E_5}\left[\left(x_2+\frac{X_2}{p_2}-g_2-E_2\right) d\mu+\left(\frac{w_1+t_1}{p_1}-E_3\right) dl_1 + \left(\beta\frac{w_2+t_2}{p_1}-E_4\right) dl_2+dX\right], \tag{A 6}$$

where $dX=d(X_1/p_1)+\mu d(X_2/p_2)$.

Then set $dg_1=dg_1^*=0$ and substitute from (A 4) and (A 6) and similar expressions for the foreign country into (A 5). This yields

$$d\mu=\bar{S}^{-1}\left[\left(\frac{w_1+t_1}{p_1}-A_1\right) dl_1+\left(\frac{w_1^*+t_1^*}{p_1}-A_1^*\right) dl_1^*-A_2\, dl_2 -A_2^*\, dl_2^*-(C_y-C_y^*)\, dX\right],$$

where $\bar{S}\equiv S+(C_y-C_y^*)X_2/p_2$, and A_1, A_2 are defined as previously and A_1^*, A_2^* in an analogous way.

Therefore, we may have to make somewhat stronger assumptions than before to ensure that $\bar{S}>0$. As far as the A-terms are concerned, the same comments as in Appendix II apply.

Appendix IV

We want to analyze the effects of a "devaluation", $d\bar{e}>0$ say, on x_1 and x_1^*. First, we express (6) and (19) in foreign currency. Let p_1^* denote foreign prices and set $g_1=g_1^*=0$ for simplicity. Then

$$p_1^*(x_1+x_1^*) = \bar{e}(\bar{M}-T_1)+\bar{M}^*-T_1^*,$$

$$x_1 = \Pi_1(w_1+t_1))$$

and

$$x_1^* = \Pi_1^*(p_1^*, (w_1^*+t_1^*)).$$

Differentiate and set the changes in all exogeneous variables except $d\bar{e}$ equal to zero. Then solve for dp_1, dx_1, dx_1^* to get

$$dp_1^* = \Delta^{-1}((\bar{M}-T_1)-p_1^*\Pi_{11}p_1^*)\,d\bar{e},$$

$$dx_1 = \Delta^{-1}[p_1^*\Pi_{11}p_1^*\Pi_{11}^*+p_1^*\Pi_{11}(x_1+x_1^*)+\bar{e}\Pi_{11}(\bar{M}-T_1)]\,d\bar{e}$$

and

$$dx_1^* = \Delta^{-1}[\Pi_{11}^*((\bar{M}-T_1)-p_1^*\Pi_{11}p_1^*)]\,d\bar{e} = \Pi_{11}^*\,dp_1^*,$$

where $\Delta \equiv (x_1+x_1^*)+p_1\Pi_{11}^*+\bar{e}p_1^*\Pi_{11}>0.$

The upshot is that $dx_1>0$, but dp_1^* and $dx_1^* \gtreqless 0$. Whether dx_1^* is negative or not depends essentially on the size of $\Pi_{11}(\cdot)$, that is, on the slope of the home supply curve.

References

Argy, Victor & Salop, Joanne: Price and output effects of monetary and fiscal policy under flexible exchange rates. *IMF Staff Papers 26*, 224–256, 1979.

Calmfors, Lars: Employment policies, wage formation and trade union behavior in a small open economy. *Scandinavian Journal of Economics 84*, this issue, 345–373, 1982.

Cornes, Richard: Duality, quantity constraints and consumer behaviour. *Warwick Economic Research Papers*, No. 149, 1979.

Dixit, Avinash K. Public finance in a Keynesian temporary equilibrium. *Journal of Economic Theory 12*, 242–258, 1976.

Dixit, Avinash K: The balance of trade in a model of temporary equilibrium with rationing. *Review of Economic Studies 45*, 393–404, 1978.

Dixit, Avinash K: & Norman, Victor: *Theory of international trade*. Nisbet-Cambridge, London, 1980.

Dornbusch, Rudiger: *Open economy macroeconomics*. Basic Books Inc., New York, 1980.

Helpman, Elhanan: An exploration in the theory of exchange rate regimes. *Journal of Political Economy 89*, 865–890, 1981.

Helpman, Elhanan & Razin, Assaf: The role of saving and investment in exchange rate determination under alternative monetary mechanisms. Seminar Paper No. 181, Institute for International Economic Studies, University of Stockholm, 1981.

Helpman, Elhanan & Razin, Assaf: Dynamics of a floating exchange rate regime. *Journal of Political Economy 90*, forthcoming, 1982.

Lucas, Robert E.: Interest rates and currency prices in a two-country world. University of Chicago (mimeo), 1981.

Neary, J. Peter & Stiglitz, Joseph: Towards a Reconstruction of Keynesian Economics: Expectations and Constrained Equilibria", *Quarterly Journal of Economics 97*, forthcoming, 1982.

Neary, J. Peter & Roberts, Kevin W.S.: The theory of household behaviour under rationing. *Eureopean Economic Review 13*, 25–42, 1980.

Okun, Arthur M. & Perry, George L. (eds.) *Curing chronic inflation*. Brookings Institution, Washington, 1978.

Persson, Torsten: *Studies of alternative exchange rate systems. An intertemporal general equilibrium approach*. Monograph No. 13, Institute for International Economic Studies, Stockholm, 1982.

Rødseth, Asbjørn: Macroeconomic policy in a small open economy. *The Scandinavian Journal of Economics 5*, 48–59, 1979.

Stockman, Alan C.: A theory of exchange rate determination. *Journal of Political Economy 88*, 673–698, 1980.

Svensson, Lars E. O. & Razin, Assaf: The terms-of-trade, spending, and the current account: The Harberger-Laursen-Metzler effect. *Journal of Political Economy 91*, forthcoming, 1983.

Turnovsky, Stephen J.: Structural expectations and the effectiveness of government policy in a short-run macroeconomic model. *American Economic Review 67*, 851–866, 1977.

Varian, Hal R.: *Microeconomic analysis*. Norton, New York 1978.

Comment on T. Persson, "Global Effects of National Stabilization Policies under Fixed and Floating Exchange Rates"

Assaf Razin

Tel-Aviv University, Ramat-Aviv, Israel

The main concern of Persson's paper is the effects of stabilization policies on employment in a two-country framework and under alternative exchange rate systems. This familiar issue has been a major preoccupation in the open economy macroeconomics litterature for many years. The analysis in this paper, however, is carried out in a new framework. The framework is based on a general equilibrium approach with optimizing consumers. The advantages of such an approach are that it enables us (a) to isolate the effects of policies, expectations, payment arrangements, exchange rate systems, etc. in a consistent manner; and (b) to carry out welfare evaluations. These evaluations are based on the same objective functions from which individual behavior is derived. This approach provides a departure from the more commonly used—but rather vague—notion of economic stabilization.

However, the paper's approach to the key issue of wage setting is rather *ad hoc*. It is assumed that nominal wages are exogenously fixed. Thus it does not deal with the interaction between wage contracts and, for example, monetary changes, tax changes and expectations.

My interpretation is that nominal wage contracts are determined prior to the period in which they become effective. I regard the monetary changes considered in this paper as monetary *disturbances*. They are unanticipated by the private sector and cannot be controlled by the monetary authorities. If the monetary changes were anticipated, they would have been reflected in the wage contracts. Therefore, here, as in the Sargent-Wallace argument, anticipated monetary changes cannot explain fluctuations in employment.[1] If the monetary changes were perfectly controllable by the monetary authorities, then the unanticipated monetary changes could be used to prevent unemployment altogether. For example, it wages are to high, the money supply can be increased to raise prices and increase employment. This can

[1] Cf. e.g. Sargent and Wallace (1975).

be done once or twice but not repeatedly, since a systematic unemployment policy must eventually be anticipated. However, a stochastic framework that specifies the form of wage contracts and the process of money creation is called for in order to deal with these matters.

The nature of wage contracts is crucial to the results of the paper. Consider, for example, an alternative arrangement, in which wages are fully linked to prices. In this case employment levels do not depend on monetary disturbances and domestic employment is completely insulated from foreign disturbances.

Let me summarize the main argument of the paper and provide some extensions. There are two countries, H, and F. Nominal wages are fixed. Thus, the level of output X is an increasing function of the price level P in each country.

$$X_H = X_H[P_H] \tag{1a}$$

$$X_F = X_F[P_F], \tag{1b}$$

where the derivatives $X'_H[\cdot]$ and $X'_F[\cdot]$ are positive. Purchases of goods are institutionally restricted to be paid in the seller's currency. Thus, domestic goods are purchased in domestic currency and foreign goods are purchased in foreign currency. In the presence of interest-bearing assets (as long as the interest rate is positive), monies are spent on goods and not used for store of value purposes. Therefore the equilibrium demand for a country's money must be equal to the value of the country's output, in terms of its currency:

$$M_H = P_H X_H[P_H] \tag{2a}$$

$$M_F = P_F X_F[P_F], \tag{2b}$$

where M_j is the money supply of country j, $j = H, F$.

It is clear from (2) that the level of output, and hence the employment level, depend only on the money supply.

Under a flexible exchange rate regime, monetary changes in a country are independent of monetary changes in the other country. Thus, domestic employment is completely insulated from foreign disturbances.

The fixed exchange rate regime in this paper is a cooperative peg. In the cooperative peg regime, countries cooperate by providing each other with monies required for stabilizing the exchange rate. This means, for example, that in the presence of an excess demand for foreign currency, the foreign government provides the domestic government with the currency needed to stabilize the exchange rate, and vice versa in the case of an excess supply of foreign currency. Consider now a decrease in the foreign money supply which lowers foreign prices and the level of foreign employment; see (2b).

The smaller amount of foreign money creates an excess demand for foreign money which, via the cooperative peg arrangements, requires the domestic government to sell foreign currency to the private sector. The implied absorption of domestic currency lowers domestic prices, thereby reducing the level of domestic employment. Therefore, under the cooperative peg, monetary disturbances generate a positive correlation between home employment and foreign employment.

To sum up, the paper describes a dichotomy: under the flexible exchange rate domestic employment is insulated from foreign disturbances, while under the cooperative peg employment is positively associated with foreign monetary changes.

The insulation property shown under the flexible exchange rate regime is, however, very special. If there are several traded goods it will not hold. Foreign monetary disturbances and the resulting changes in the foreign output bundle will generate changes in the terms of trade as well. Terms of trade changes, in turn, generate changes in the composition of domestic output and hence in domestic employment. However, the direction of the change in employment is not clear.

The insulation property also depends crucially on the payment arrangement, as shown in the following extension. Suppose that purchasers of goods are institutionally restricted to be performed with the buyer's currency rather than the seller's currency as in Persson's paper.[2] Consider a simple example: the marginal propensity to spend out of wealth, β, is constant and $0<\beta<1$;[3] nominal wages are fixed in the first period (the short run) but are completely flexible in the second period (the long run). Denote output at full employment by $\bar{X}$ and, with obvious notation, the equilibrium conditions are:

$$M_{H1} = \beta_H P_H W_H \quad \text{(Home Money)} \tag{3a}$$

$$M_{F1} = \beta_F P_{F1} W_F \quad \text{(Foreign Money)} \tag{3b}$$

$$\beta_H W_H + \beta_F W_F = X_H[P_{H1}] + X_F[P_{F1}] \quad \text{(Traded Good)} \tag{3c}$$

where W_k is country k's wealth, which is equal to the present value of output $X_k[P_{k1}]+\mu\bar{X}_k$, where $k=H, F$ and μ=the real interest factor. The subscript 1 denotes period one variables.

Differentiating (3) we obtain:

$$\frac{dP_{H1}}{dM_{F1}} = -\frac{P_{H1}\bar{X}_H(1-\beta_F)X'_F[P_{F1}]}{\Delta} < 0$$

[2] See Helpman and Razin (1981) for a description of this payment arrangement.

[3] This means that the utility function is logarithmic. We assume that tax policies are used to ensure that the real interest rate is equal in both countries. See Helpman and Razin (1981) for a discussion of distortions under this payment arrangement.

where

$$\Delta = (W_H + P_{H1} X'_H[P_{H1}])\,(W_F + P_{F1} X'_F[P_{F1}])\,(\beta_H P_{H1} \bar{X}_H + \beta_F P_{F1} \bar{X}_F)$$
$$+ (1-\beta_F) P_{F1} X'_F\,[P_{F1}]\,\bar{X}_F)$$
$$+ (1-\beta_H) P_{H1} X'_H\,[P_{H1}]\bar{X}_H (W_F + P_{F1} X'_F\,[P_{F1}]) > 0.$$

Thus, the increase in the foreign money supply pushes domestic prices down and hence the domestic employment level falls.

An economic explanation is as follows. The increase in the foreign money supply pushes foreign prices up and hence the foreign output level increases. The increase in world output creates an excess in *world* savings. Thus the real interest rate falls, thereby inducing an increase in domestic consumption. Since the real demand for domestic money is equal to real domestic consumption, this creates a situation of excess demand for domestic money and hence leads to a fall in domestic prices. Thus, the domestic employment level also falls. In this example monetary disturbances generate a negative correlation between domestic employment and foreign employment.

Turing back to the fixed exchange rate regime, consider a one-sided peg regime as an alternative to the cooperative peg. Let the home country one-sidedly peg the exchange rate of its currency in terms of foreign currency. This means that the home country will borrow foreign currency from the private sector in a situation of excess demand for foreign currency, and vice versa in a situation of excess supply of foreign currency. The foreign money supply does not change with stabilization of the exchange rate because the stabilizing transactions take place strictly between the domestic government and the private sector. From (2b), then, it is clear that foreign employment is completely insulated from domestic monetary disturbances. However, the domestic employment level is negatively associated with foreign monetary disturbances.

This discussion shows that the association between domestic employment and foreign emplyment depends on: (a) the payment system, i.e. whether purchases of goods are paid with the seller's or the buyer's currency; and (b) the exchange rate regime. Essentially this means that with sticky nominal wages, inter-country correlations in employment levels are very sensitive to the specification of the demand for as well as the supply of money.

Finally, Persson's paper makes a welfare evaluation which is based on three elements: (a) changes in the level of employment; (b) changes in the real interest rate which amount to changes in the intertemporal terms of trade; and (c) the redistribution of purchasing power between countries associated with the cooperative peg regime.

However, it seems that the tradeoffs between these components in the welfare evaluation depend crucially on the specification of wage contracts, money supply and the stochastic nature of the economy. Since this model is deterministic, we cannot assess the significance of these tradeoffs.

A great deal can be learned from reconsidering existing propositions using the general equilibrium approach. This paper makes a useful contribution in its presentation of new issues concerning the interactions between the monetary structure and employment.

References

Helpman, Elhanan & Razin, Assaf: The role of saving and investment in exchange rate determination and alternative monetary mechanisms. Working Paper No. 32–81, The Foerder Institute for Economic Research, Tel Aviv University, August 1981.

Sargent, T. J. & Wallace N.: Rational expectations, the optimal monetary instrument, and the optimal money supply rate. *Journal of Political Economy*, April, 1975.

Adjustment and Structural Change under Supply Shocks

*Michael Bruno**

Hebrew University, Jerusalem, Israel

Abstract

The resource boom effect and the input price effect of raw material price changes are analyzed within a two-period, two-sector (plus resource industry), open economy framework. Diagrammatic exposition is used to study the "Dutch disease", and in particular the distinction between the short-term wealth effects (causing a real appreciation and a movement of variable factors from tradeable to nontradeable industries) and the long-run effects on total investment, its sectoral allocation and its finance by foreign borrowing. The framework further enables analysis of the different allocational effects of temporary versus permanent raw material price increases, when the two sectors differ in material use. The effects of changes in the world interest rate on factor allocation and foreign borrowing, and the allocational effects of government intervention in the case of temporary real wage rigidity are also discussed.

I. Introduction

Macroeconomic adjustment and long-term structural changes are often closely related, yet they are usually kept in separate analytical boxes. Nowhere is the inadequacy of such a dichotomy more apparent than in the understanding of the developments of individual countries after the supply shocks of the 1970s. Raw material price increases played a major role in the ensuing stagflation, which could be perceived as a short-term macroeconomic adjustment problem. However, as time progressed, it became more and more clear that the longer-run implications of these shocks on productivity and profitability are at least as important.

There are two different aspects of raw material price effects which have been discussed under separate headings. One is the resource boom effect analyzed by e.g. Corden & Neary (1980). If a country is a net exporter of a

---

* This paper is part of a project on Structural Adjustment in Open Economies, conducted with Jeffrey Sachs, at the National Bureau for Economic Research in Cambridge, MA and at the Falk Institute for Economic Research, Jerusalem. Financial support from the National Science Foundation and the Ford Foundation is gratefully acknowledged.

I have benefited from discussions with Jeffrey Sachs in the preparation of this paper. Likewise, I am indebted to Lars Svensson, Lars Calmfors and other participants at the 1981 Saltsjöbaden conference for helpful comments on an earlier draft. Svensson (1981) has independently worked out several of the propositions analyzed here.

raw material whose price has increased, there will be a short run increase in the relative price of nontradeable goods (or a real appreciation) and a shift in variable factors out of existing tradeable goods such as manufacturing and into, say, services. Relative profitability will further affect today's investment and therefore future production and allocation of capital. This, however, is only one example of a pure wealth effect, which could also take place when an oil discovery is announced or, in a completely different context, when a country receives an unexpected foreign currency transfer (much like the old "transfer problem"). The analysis of this type of problem is best conceived in a framework where international capital mobility is allowed for, because a wealth change affects the country's borrowing.

Another, probably more important, aspect is the role of raw materials as a major input into the productive system. This may hit both net importers and net exporters of such material and would tend to shift resources away from a raw-material-intensive activity into less intensive ones. This, too, might cause "de-industrialization" but for a different reason. In this context, it is important to distinguish between temporary and permanent change in raw material prices. The former may have wealth effects but need not cause long-run changes in relative prices. It is mainly the latter that affects investment behavior.

In this paper, an earlier factor-price frontier analysis of mine (1981) is extended to a two-sector framework (Sections II and III). The above issues are then analyzed in a two-period dynamic framework which is a stripped-down version of a model previously used for simulation experiments in Sachs (1980) and Bruno & Sachs (1981).[1]

After specifying the ingredients of the model in terms of production (III), household behavior (IV), investment and the current account (V), diagrammatic exposition is used to show the effects of pure wealth and public expenditure changes (VI), temporary and permanent change in raw material prices (VII) and the effect of changes in world interest rates and alternative current account objectives (VIII). The paper ends with a brief discussion of the effect of short-term real wage rigidity and the related policy response.

II. The Factor-Price Frontier, Raw Material Prices and Dynamic Adjustment

The effect of raw material prices on the supply side of an open economy is best illustrated within the framework of the factor-price frontier, which is reiterated here only in summary form. Assume first that the economy consists of a single sector and let $Q=Q(L, K, N)$ be a well-behaved constant

---

[1] Louis Dicks-Mireaux is presently applying a similar framework for the U.K.

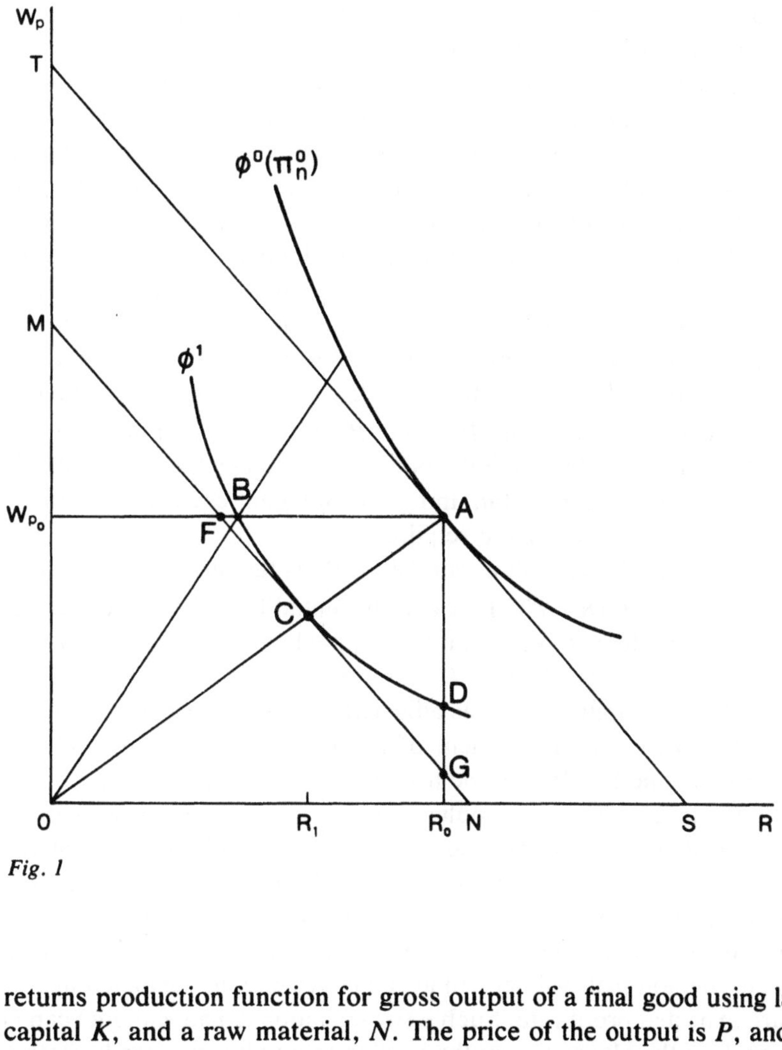

Fig. 1

returns production function for gross output of a final good using labor, L, capital K, and a raw material, N. The price of the output is P, and that of the raw material is P_n. For the time being, assume that the relative price $\Pi_n = P_n/P$ is given (as is the case if both N and Q are tradeable goods in a small open economy). Let Y be the real income derived, $Y = Q - \Pi_n N$, and assume optimal use of N such that $\partial Q/\partial N = \Pi_n$. Denote the real returns (marginal products) to labor and capital by W_p and R, respectively.

The factor-price frontier (FPF) summarizes the information about the technology in terms of maximal combinations of the three marginal factor products, $\phi(W_p, R, \Pi_n) = 0$. The curve ϕ^0 is drawn in $W_p - R$ space (Figure 1) for a given relative raw material price Π_n^0, is downward sloping and convex to the origin. The slope of the tangent at point A measures the capital/labor ratio that corresponds to the pair of factor prices (R^0, W_p^0) and its intercept on the W_p axis (OT) measures Y/L. Likewise, the intercept on the R axis (OS) measures Y/K. The elasticity of FPF at point $A = SA/TA$ measures the relative shares of capital and labor in Y.

Weak separability of the production function, i.e., $Q = Q[V(L, K), N]$, implies weak separability of the dual FPF, i.e., ϕ takes the form $\phi[f(W_p, R), \Pi_n] = 0$. A raw material price increase, like Hicks-neutral technical regress, is represented by a homothetic inward shift of the FPF from ϕ^0 to ϕ^1. The capital/labor ratio will be the same as at A only at point C on the new FPF, on a ray OA. C is thus a full-employment point, in the *short run* (when $K = \bar{K}, L = \bar{L}$). Both real factor rewards at C must fall at the same rate from their original level at A. Total real income per unit of labor (Y/L) falls likewise by the same proportion from OT to OM (and Y/K from OS to ON). The case of real wage rigidity at W_p^0, which may occur in the *very short run*, is represented by point B, where R and Y/K must of necessity fall by more than at C and the capital/labor ratio is higher than at C. At the initial/capital stock $\bar{K}$, L must fall and unemployment emerges, as long as the real wage does not fall by the required amount.[2]

The polar case to the very short run ($W_p = W_p^0$) is that of an imposed long-run real rate of return ($R = R^0$). This is represented by point D, termed the *long run*, at which the real wage and the capital/labor ratio are below their levels at C. In contrast to C, point D may represent an equilibrium steady-state level after the capital stock has adjusted downward to a given real rate of return, R^0. With full employment of labor, both the capital stock and output (gross and net) at D must be lower than at the initial point A.

The short-run and long-run implications of a permanent raw material price shock within this framework are revealed by considering some simple dynamics in terms of two key variables, the real wage and the capital stock. The real wage can be assumed to change as a function of unemployment, in a Phillips curve fashion. The capital stock can be assumed to adjust via an investment function that will depend in some measure on the instantaneous and future expected profit rate. Such a two-equation dynamic model can be used to analyze the alternative paths leading to an ultimate steady state at point D.[3] An alternate procedure, adopted in the more detailed two-sector

[2] In the putty-clay case where the capital/labor ratio cannot immediately adjust to the new factor prices, the various solutions are given along the line FCG, i.e. in the rigid real wage, rigid capital/labor ratio case, the economy will be at F and not at B, as the rate of profit falls by more than at B, and L remains constant. Note also that under alternative technological assumptions, the FPF need not shift homothetically; cf. Bruno (1981).

[3] It should be kept in mind that a growing economy will usually also exhibit pure technical progress. In order to avoid the need of having the FPF simultaneously shift outward when there is technical progress, factor products may instead be redefined to be measured in intensity units. Thus in the empirically relevant case of Harrod neutral (or labor-augmenting) technical progress, the real wage (W_p) must be reinterpreted as being measured relative to its long-run trend. Another implication of this is that when we talk of a fall in capital/labor ratios, we then imply only a fall relative to what it would be in the absence of the exogenous shock.

discussion below, is to think of the horizon as consisting of two periods: the short run, where the capital stock is fixed, and the long run, where first-period investment may affect long-run capital in place. In this way today's investment is uniquely determined by the expected future rate of profit, which in turn depends on the assumptions about future factor prices and the extent of international capital mobility.

III. A Two-Period Model of Production and Factor Allocation

There are a number of interesting issues, related to the role of raw materials, which are of necessity ignored when considering a single-sector economy.[4] So far, demand has not been accounted for. Also, no role was assigned to endogenous changes in relative commodity prices leading to compositional shifts within the economy. In the context of raw materials, compositional shifts may be of great importance in more than one respect. A mineral boom leads to the so-called "Dutch disease", whereby an existing tradable goods industry may be squeezed out by real appreciation of the exchange rate, while a domestic service industry may expand, as discussed by Corden & Neary (1981), Neary & Purvis (1981) and van Wijnbergen (1981). A more direct effect of a rise in the price of raw materials might be to contract the industry that is relatively intensive in raw-material use, while a less raw-material intensive industry might contract less or even expand.[5] In both cases, it is important to distinguish between short-run and long-run effects of the exogenous changes. In the short run, only variable factors (e.g. labor) may be free to move from one sector to the other. Relative profitability changes, however, may induce long-run changes in capital investment patterns. Whether the latter will in fact take place depends in turn on the extent to which the exogenous changes (e.g. in mineral prices) are perceived to be temporary or permanent. These considerations lead to a multisectoral as well as intertemporal framework.

A natural extension would be a model in which another nontradeable goods sector is added on, in true Scandinavian tradition. However, its extension to an infinite horizon framework becomes analytically intractable, as the number of state variables jumps to three or more. One way out is to run computer simulations which can be made as complex as one wishes.[6]

---

[4] The single-sector formulation can, however, be usefully applied to the empirical analysis of a single large tradable goods sector such as manufacturing.

[5] If the country is a producer of both the raw material and the raw material using final tradeable goods, such as most manufactures, deindustrialization may thus occur for both reasons, as is the case in the U.K.

[6] Cf. Sachs (1980) or Bruno & Sachs (1981).

Useful as these are, however, they do have the drawback that it is often hard to ascertain how particular results depend on specific numerical assumptions.

In order to obtain relative analytical simplicity, we sacrifice the full-fledged long-term horizon. Much of what is relevant in the distinction between the short and the long run can be seen from two-period simplifications of the world. Even a rational expectations view of investment, based on future prices, can be expressed in this way, without having to bring in explicitly Tobin's q or "costs of adjustment". The view of the balance of payments in its intertemporal allocation aspects can be fitted well into this scheme.[7]

Consider a two-commodity framework, tradeables (or the "foreign" sector with subscript f) and domestic nontradeables (with subscript d) within a two-period horizon (using superscript $t=1,2$).

Production of tradeables $Q_f=Q_f(L_f, \bar{K}_f, N)$ uses inputs of labor (L_f), fixed initial capital ($\bar{K}_f$) and raw materials (N).[8] Tradeables can be used for private consumption (C_f), investment (I) and net exports (X). The latter may be negative (net imports). The domestic price of tradeables (P_f) equals the world price (p^*) times the exchange rate (e). The nontradeable goods sector is assumed to use only labor and capital, $Q_d=Q_d(L_d, \bar{K}_d)$ and to supply goods only for private (C_d) and public consumption (G). The respective sector specialization in the production of exports, investment goods and public consumption and in the use of raw materials is not essential, but simplifies the analysis. There is a third sector in the economy that produces a fixed quantity of tradeable raw materials (H^1, H^2), for which the fixed inputs will not be separately accounted. The country may be a net importer or net exporter of raw materials which command a given world price p_n^*.

While the total labor supply is fixed in both periods ($L_d^t+L_f^t=\bar{L}^t$), capital in each sector in the second period is augmented or contracted by the amount of investments made in each sector in the first period ($K_d^2-\bar{K}_d+K_f^2-\bar{K}_f=I^1$). For simplicity we assume no depreciation, but allow for negative I^1. No new investment goods have to be produced in the second period since this represents the "long run" where K_d^2, K_f^2 remain for posterity.

The main distinction between the two periods is that in the first, the short

[7] A multisectoral, intertemporal view of foreign trade and investment allocation was very popular in the trade and development literature of the 1960s, which was mostly based on empirical development programming models, but also included some theoretical contributions; see e.g. Bardhan (1966) or Bruno (1967). However, the associated short-term adjustment problem was usually discussed in a separate box. For recent two-period formulations of investment and the balance of payments, see Razin (1980) or Sachs (1981).

[8] We assume separability $Q_f=Q_f[V_f(L_f, K_f), N]$ as before, and constant returns.

run, capital is held fixed and is sector specific, while in the second, the long run, it is malleable. On the production side, this model has its antecedents in the work of Mayer (1974) and others. The earlier model is extended here to take investment, wealth and the role of raw materials into account.

Production and factor rewards are obtained from firm maximization of discounted cash flow. If the relative price of domestic over foreign goods is denoted by $\pi = p_d/p_f$,[9] that of raw materials by $\pi_n = p_n/p_f$, the real wage in foreign good units is w_f and the own rate of interest on foreign goods is r, firms maximize

$$(Q_f^1 + \pi^1 Q_d^1 - w_f^1 L^1 - \pi_n^1 N^1 - I^1) + (1+r)^{-1}(Q_f^2 + \pi^2 Q_d^2 - w_f^2 L^2 - \pi_n^2 N^2)$$

subject to the labor and production constraints.

The usual first-order conditions are obtained for both periods:

$$\pi^t \partial Q_d^t / \partial L_d^t = \partial Q_f^t / \partial L_f^t = w_f^t; \quad \partial Q_f^t / \partial N^t = \pi_n^t. \tag{1}$$

For capital in the second period we get:

$$R = \pi^2 \partial Q_d^2 / \partial K_d^2 = \partial Q_f^2 / \partial K_f^2 = 1 + r. \tag{2}$$

(First-period equality of marginal products at the inital point $\bar{K}_d, \bar{K}_f$ is assumed.)

Equations (1) give the conventional static optimal allocations of variable factors of production in each period. They simply say that for profit maximization, factors which are mobile should be allocated in each period so as to equate the marginal products in both sectors, subject to proper accounting of relative output prices (π).

Equation (2), on the other hand, represents the intertemporal arbitrage condition. It says that investment in the first period and its allocation to capital growth (or contraction) in each sector must be such that the marginal products of capital by the second period in each sector will be equal to the given foreign real interest factor ($R = 1 + r$).

We can now use these conditions to return to a factor-price frontier framework, this time looking at both sectors in the same diagram.

While the factor-price frontier for the f good is $\phi_f(w_f, R, \pi_n) = 0$ (see curve ϕ_f^0 in Figure 2), that of the d good can be represented in the same diagram if written in the form $\phi_d(w_f/\pi, R/\pi) = 0$. The curve ϕ_d^0 in Figure 2 represents the FPF for the initial relative price π^0. It is drawn here under the assumption that d are more capital intensive than f goods. An increase in the relative price π (a real appreciation) will shift this curve homothetically outwards, while a decrease in π (a real depreciation) will shift it inwards.

Consider now the case where the real rate of interest is given exogenous-

---

[9] The reciprocal of $\pi(p_f/p_d = e \cdot p^*/p_d)$ is often termed the *real exchange rate*.

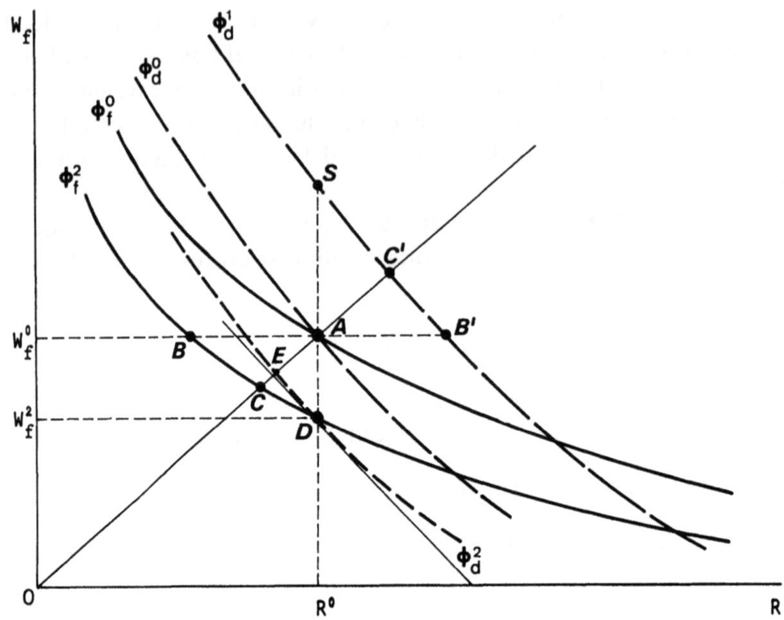

Fig. 2

ly, $R=R^0$, as would be the case under free international capital mobility and consider the case of a once-and-for-all increase in the relative price of raw materials, moving ϕ_f^0 to ϕ_f^2. The "long run" (i.e. second period) solution must entail a shift of ϕ_d^0 to ϕ_d^2 passing through the long-run point D. We can thus immediately deduce a number of important properties:

(1) The given marginal product of capital R^0 $(=1+r^*)$ fixes the long-run real wage w_f^2 as well as the relative price π^2 uniquely.

(2) We know that with an increase in raw material prices affecting only the f sector, π^2 must in this case *fall* in the second period, i.e. $\pi^2<\pi^0$.

(3) From the geometry of Figure 2, we can deduce that the capital/labor ratio in the d sector must fall (as it does in f) in the long run. This follows from the fact that the tangent at D has lower slope than at E, which in turn is the same as at A (on ϕ_d^0)

We have thus established that a permanent rise in relative raw material prices, at given real rates of return to capital, must cause a long-run fall in the real wage and the capital intensities in both sectors as well as a real depreciation, on the assumption that the traded goods sector is the raw-material-intensive industry. What is left open is the composition of output. Here demand must naturally play an important role.

IV. Consumption, Wealth and Short-run Equilibrium

We assume that households decide on their consumption basket by maximizing discounted utility subject to a given net wealth constraint:

$$C_f^1+\pi^1 C_d^1+R^{-1}(C_f^2+\pi^2 C_d^2) = \Omega. \tag{3}$$

Net household wealth (Ω) equals discounted real income in all sectors (Y_f, Y_d, H), net of taxes (T) and minus physical investment (I^1):

$$\Omega = (Y_f^1+\pi^1 Y_d^1)+R^{-1}(Y_f^2+\pi^2 Y_d^2)+H-T-I^1$$

where $Y_f^t=Q_f^t-\pi_n^t N^t$, $Y_d^t=Q_d^t$, are real incomes derived in the two sectors and $H=\pi_n^1 H^1+R^{-1}\pi_n^2 H^2=$ the value of raw material production. $T=T^1+R^{-1}T^2=\pi^1 G^1+R^{-1}\pi^2 G^2=$ total cumulative government tax revenues and expenditure (in f units).

By making use of the fact that real incomes equal real factor products and that in the d-sector $C_d^t+G^t=Y_d^t=Q_d^t$, net wealth can be rewritten in the following simplified form:

$$\Omega = Y_f^1(\pi^1,\pi_n^1)+\pi^1 C_d^1+[R^{-1}W_f^2\bar{L}^2-R^{-1}\pi^2 G^2+\bar{K}_d+\bar{K}_f+H]. \tag{4}$$

The expression in brackets in (4) is only a function of exogenous variables and does not involve first-period investment, which has been netted out (under firm optimal behavior). Y_f^1, on the other hand, can be expressed as a function of the relevant first-period variables.

In the case of a flexible labor market, with which we deal most of the time, the first period's net output of tradeables ($Y_f^1=Q_f^1-\pi_n^1 N^1$) can be written as a negative function of π^1, which equals the marginal rate of substitution on the short-run production possibility curve. It will also be a negative function of the exogenous π_n^1 (we ignore the fixed factors here).[10]

For households, we introduce the simplification of a linear logarithmic utility function as in Sachs (1981), which implies that consumption of each good in each period is a fixed proportion of total net wealth:

$$\beta C_f^1 = \pi^1 C_d^1 = (1+\delta)R^{-1}\pi^2 C_d^2 = \beta(1+\delta)R^{-1}C_f^2 = b\Omega \tag{5}$$

where $\delta=$the pure discount rate and β, b depend on the utility parameters.[11]

Although this particular specification of the utility function is not required for most of the qualitative results, its very simple implications for

---

[10] When real wages are slow to adjust (see below), the economy may not be on its PPC and we must instead use the supply function $Y_f^1=Y_f^1(w_f^1,\pi_n^1)<Y_f^1(\pi^1,\pi_n^1)$.

[11] If the utility function is $U(C_d^1, C_f^1)+(1+\delta)^{-1}U(C_d^2, C_f^2)$ with $U(C_d, C_f)=\alpha\log C_d+(1-\alpha)\times\log C_f$, we have: $\beta=\alpha/(1-\alpha)$ and $b=(2+\delta)^{-1}(1+\delta)\alpha$.

consumption behavior enable a convenient diagrammatic representation of the model.

When we combine $\pi^1 C_d^1 = b\Omega$ from (5) with the expression for net wealth (4), we can relate the present consumption of the domestic good expressed in foreign good units, $\pi^1 C_d^1$, to its relative price and to the main exogenous variables determining the value of net wealth:

$$\pi^1 C_d^1 = b\Omega\left[\underset{-}{\pi^1}; \underset{\pm}{\pi_n^t}, \underset{+}{H^t}, \underset{-}{R}, \underset{-}{G^2}\right] \tag{6}$$

where $t=1,2$.

The curve marked $b\Omega$ in the first quadrant of Figure 3 gives a downward sloping demand curve for consumption of the domestic good.[12] It will shift upward or downward depending on the exogenous increases or decreases in wealth. Private net wealth increases with the size of raw material deposits (H^t) and falls with the rate of interest (R) and the expected future government expenditure (G^2). The signs on the effect of raw material prices for each period depend on whether the economy is a net exporter or net importer of the raw material, i.e., on whether $H^t - N^t \gtreqless 0$.[13] We use this property in analyzing the effect of temporary or permanent increases in raw material prices.

All we need to obtain the first-period equilibrium is to add a supply schedule for domestic consumer goods:

$$C_d^1 = \underset{+}{Q_d^1(\pi^1)} - G^1 \tag{7}$$

In order to achieve conformity with the variables in the diagram, we multiply both sides of equation (7) by the relative price π^1. This curve is upward sloping and shifts downward and to the right with increases in G^1.

Even before turning to investment and second-period equilibrium, we can already deduce that any factor which increases wealth (in units of the f good) will cause an increase in present consumption and a real appreciation in the short run. The latter in turn implies a shift of labor and production from tradeable goods to nontradeable goods, e.g. from manufacturing into services. This is a manifestation of de-industrialization in the short run. An increase in wealth may be caused by a variety of reasons, including the news that a North Sea oil discovery is expected in the long run (i.e. H^2

---

[12] Since C_f is proportional to πC_d, it also represents consumption of the foreign good and total first-period consumption. Note that C_d in physical units is represented in this diagram by the slope of a ray from the origin.

[13] Strictly speaking we have $\partial\Omega/\partial\pi_n^1 = H^1 - N^1$, $\partial\Omega/\partial\pi_n^2 = H^2 - N^2 -$(positive term). The additional term in period 2 comes from the fact that R is held constant and not π^2.

rises). Likewise we get the usual result that a temporary fiscal expansion (G^1 rises but G^2 stays constant) crowds out private consumption and causes a real appreciation, if public expenditure is centered on domestic goods. More relevant in the present context, however, are the long-run effects of such expansion. We appropriately turn to investment and second-period equilibrium.

V. Investment, Foreign Borrowing and Long-run Production

Having shown how future factor prices and first-period equilibrium are determined, all that is left to complete the solution of the system is to show how the future composition of output and capital stock are determined. This will tell us what today's investment is which in turn determines the current account.

With constant returns to scale, output and labor demands can be written as proportions of capital stocks in each sector. Since future relative prices are uniquely determined, we can write the second-period supply equation for the domestic consumption good as a linear function of the capital stock:

$$C_d^2 = K_d^2 g_d^2(w_f^2/\pi^2) - G^2 \tag{8}$$

where g_d is output per unit of capital in the domestic goods industry. (This is measured in Figure 2 by the R-intercept of the tangent to the point D.) Multiplying both sides of (8) by the second-period relative price, we can draw (8) as an upward sloping supply curve in the $\pi^2 C_d^2$ and K_d^2 space (see quadrant II of Figure 3). The use of the common vertical axis for the consumption good of both periods is justified by our simplifying assumption on consumption behavior (5), since the two are proportional to each other as long as interest rates do not change.[14]

Since consumption in the two periods is proportional, eq. (8) and the curve marked $(\pi^2 Q_d^2)$ in Figure 3 uniquely determine the amount to be invested in the domestic industry (K_d^2), as given, for example, at point A_2.

The system is closed by assuming full employment and labor-market clearing in the second period:

$$K_d^2 \lambda_d^2(\underset{-}{w_f^2/\pi^2}) + K_f^2 \lambda_f^2(\underset{-}{w_f^2}, \underset{-}{\pi_n^2}) = \bar{L}^2. \tag{9}$$

Equation (9) is represented by the line marked $\bar{L}^2$ in quadrant III of Figure 3 in which the two axes represent the two capital stocks, respectively. Its slope equals the capital/labor ratios $(\lambda_d^2/\lambda_f^2)$ in the two sectors. The

[14] By intertemporal optimality (5), we have $\pi^2 C_d^2/\pi^1 C_d^1 = (1+r)/(1+\delta)$.

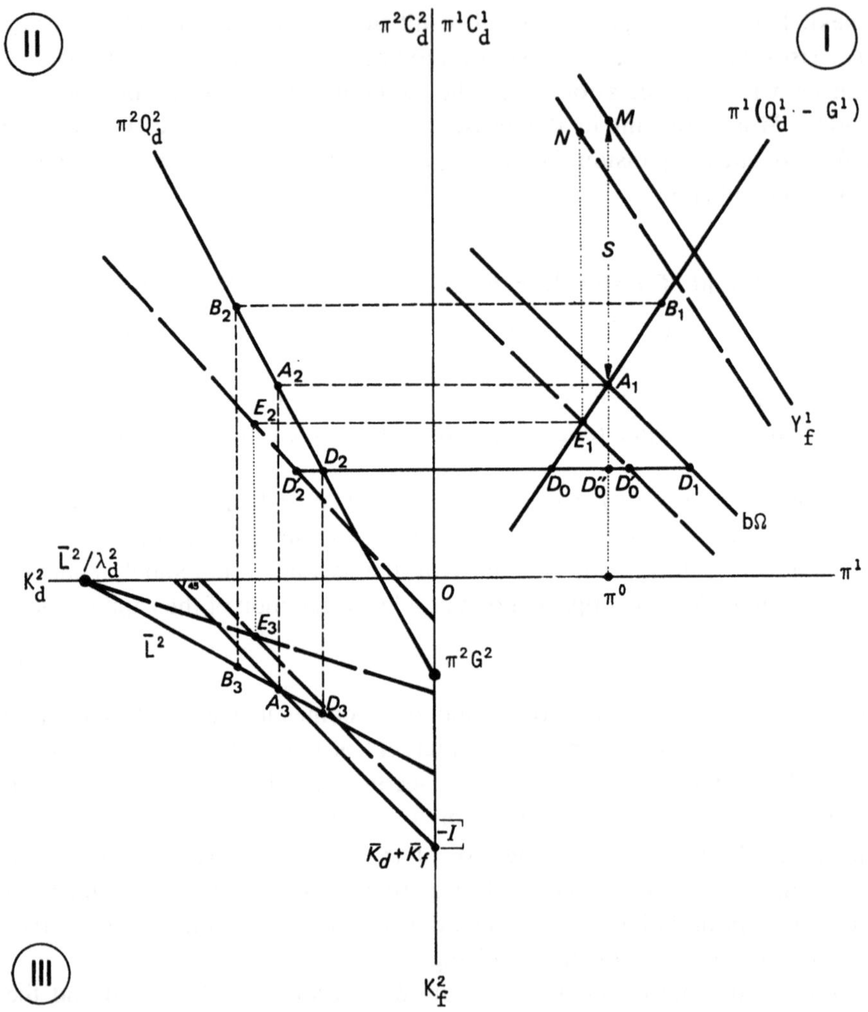

Fig. 3

way the line has been drawn here, relative to a 45° line, assumes that the *d* sector is the more capital-intensive one. In the reverse capital intensity case, the $\bar{L}^2$ line must cut the 45° line in the other direction. As we shall see, relative intensities will matter as far as total investment requirements are concerned. The distance of the intercepts of the respective 45° lines through the initial (A_3) and any post-shock equilibrium (e.g. B_3 or D_3) will measure total investment requirements $I^1 = (K_d^2 + K_f^2) - (\bar{K}_d + \bar{K}_f)$.

Equations (6)–(9) and the corresponding four curves of Figure 3 uniquely determine the equilibrium of the system in terms of the relevant endogenous variables.[15]

Before we turn to the analysis of the response to various kinds of exogenous shocks, we should look at the implications for the current account.

The current account in f units (F^t) can be written as follows ($t=1,2$):

$$F^t = Q_f^t - \pi_n^t N^t + \pi_n^t H^t - C_f^t - I^t = Y_f^t + \pi_n^t H^t - C_f^t - I^t \tag{10}$$

where $I^2=0$ and $C_f^2=(1+\delta)^{-1}RC_f^1$ by (3).

For each period $(Y_f+\pi_n H)$ is total net production of foreign exchange (including raw materials), while $(Y_f+\pi_n H-C_f)$ must by definition equal total domestic savings $(S)^1$, which is $I+F$.[16] The line marked Y_f^1 in quadrant I of Figure 3 describes $\beta[Y_f^1(\pi^1,\pi_n^1)+\pi_n^1 H_n^1]$. Its vertical distance from the Ω line (whose coordinate is $\pi^1 C_d^1=\beta C_f^1$) is proportional to savings[17] in the first period (S^1). The Y_f^1 line is of necessity steeper than Ω so that *ceteris paribus* S^1 falls with π^1. The difference (S^1-I^1) measures the current account surplus (F^1).

We mainly consider the case of free international capital mobility in which borrowing and lending take place at a given world interest rate r^*. In this case, we must have $R^0=(1+r^*)$ and the balance of payments constraint takes the form

$$F^1+(1+r^*)^{-1}F^2=0. \tag{11}$$

It is readily established that, upon substitution of (10), equations (11) and (3) become the same budget constraint for $R=1+r^*$. In fact, the whole pattern of resource allocation and pricing described above could be obtained from the solution of an optimal growth problem in which society is assumed to maximize discounted utility, as above, subject to the various production and supply constraints in the two periods plus the intertemporal capital mobility condition (11).

---

[15] When the first-period labor market clears, there will be a fifth equation to determine the first-period real wage.

[16] Another way of looking at this is to note that

$S=Y_f+\pi_n H+\pi Q_d-(\pi C_d+C_f)-\pi G=Y_f+\pi_n H-C_f,$

since $Q_d=C_d+G$.

[17] This vertical distance depends on $(\beta-b)\,Y_f^1(\pi^1)$ which is a negative function of π^1, since $\beta>b$.

VI. The Implications of Pure Wealth and Expenditure Effects

For the time being, we stick to the assumption that the long-run real interest rate is given and therefore, once the future price of raw materials is set, all future relative prices are known. Since investors are assumed to behave rationally and look only at future relative prices, factor proportions in each sector are known. Future intersectional allocation of capital, labor and output may still be affected by changes in wealth or relative demand for different goods today. We begin with another look at pure wealth shifts and changes in government expenditure.

Consider again the effect of an exogenous change in total wealth. A relevant example in the present context would be the discovery of North Sea oil, raising H on the r.h.s. of equation (6). An alternative (not unheard of in Israel) would be a large foreign exchange transfer. In terms of Figure 3, this appears as an upward shift in the curve Ω in quadrant I with equilibrium taking place at points B_1, B_2, B_3, respectively, in the various quadrants. Consumption goes up (in all goods and periods), the relative price π^1 today rises, but only temporarily (the second period's π^2 remains unchanged). This induces investment in the nontradeables sector in the next period, whereas the capital stock in the tradeables sector decreases. Since capital/labor ratios are unchanged, this also implies a long-run movement of labor out of f and into d, a clear manifestation of long-run de-industrialization.

As we have seen before, this intersectoral movement of labor already starts in the first period, as the relative price π^1 rises and capital is still frozen at its initial levels. The FPF framework can be used to show how the FPF for d moves temporarily in an outward direction (the move from ϕ_d^0 to ϕ_d^1 in Figure 2). At the inital real wage w_f^0, the rate of return in the d sector rises and $\bar{K}_d/L_d$ falls through the absorption of labor that is moving out of d and into f. At the same time, w_f will be rising to balance the labor market. Eventually π falls back to the predetermined long-run level (which is assumed here to be the same as the initial relative price), and so does the real wage in both f units (w_f) and d units (w_f/π), while the adjustment of capital stocks takes place. The production possibility curve will have a shift biased towards the Q_d axis. In the case where $\lambda_d^2 < \lambda_f^2$, as depicted in Figure 3, total net investment in the first period will be positive (compare the 45° lines through A_3 and B_3). It is easy to see that under reverse relative capital intensities, this intersectoral shift will take place together with a *fall* in total net investment.

There is an interesting point related to savings and current account behavior which can be read off the diagram. Suppose the wealth shift comes only from the *expectation* of future oil finds (i.e., only H^2 rises, while H^1 does not change). In this case, the curve Y_f stays put while Ω

moves up. Savings today thus fall in expectation of greater riches (note the vertical distance between B_1 and the Y_f^1 curve). If I^1 rises (in the case $\lambda_d^2 < \lambda_f^2$), these developments can be unambiguously associated with a decrease in today's current account surplus (or increase in the deficit).[18]

Consider again an increase in government expenditure, which is confined here to d goods, coupled with an equivalent increase in taxes. As we have seen, this must crowd out private consumption expenditure. In Figure 3, it will appear as a downward shift of curve Q_d^1 in quadrant I, with Ω staying put and equilibrium now taking place at D_1, D_2, and D_3, respectively. Consumption falls, π rises temporarily, S falls, K_d^2 falls and K_f^2 rises. Total investment falls if d is more capital intensive than f. Total investment goes up (and the current account falls) in the reverse capital-intensity case. d-biased increase in public consumption today in this case thus induces a shift into f goods production tomorrow. This seemingly counterintuitive result comes from the reduction in savings and the current account today. Production for net exports in the second period will thus have to increase (in the first period Q_f^1 falls with the temporary rise in π^1).

VII. Temporary or Permanent Increases in Raw Material Prices[19]

Suppose now that π_n^1 goes up, but π_n^2 is expected to stay put. This would be the case if, say, a real oil-price increase is expected to be only temporary. The crucial question is what happens to net wealth. If the country is not self-sufficient today ($N^1 > H^1$), the Ω curve shifts downward causing a fall in consumption, and in π^1, a fall in K_d^2 (as well as L_d^2, Q_d^2) and a rise in K_f^2 (as well as L_f^2, Q_f^2). Again this seemingly paradoxical result comes from the demand side, and it depends crucially on the assumed *temporary* nature of the raw material price increase.

Suppose now that both present and future prices of raw materials (π_n^1, π_n^2) increase at the same rate. Again the Ω curve could shift upward or downward, depending on the effect on private wealth. If I^1 does not vary much, the analysis suggests a corresponding multiperiod self-sufficiency condition. For a country that is a net importer, we would anyway expect a downward shift in the Ω curve. This time, however, the other curves in quadrants II and III shift as well. Consider first the supply curve Q_d^2. Since the future relative price of (π^2) now also goes down, the intercept on the consumption axis ($-\pi^2 G^2$) is reduced. The slope of the Q_d^2 curve, on the

[18] If one were to allow for investment in the H-industry, this point would be further strengthened.

[19] For a very similar analysis of raw material price shocks within a two-period model, as well as the welfare implications, see Svensson (1981).

other hand, depends on what happens to the output/capital ratio in the d sector (R-axis intercept of the tangent to ϕ_d^2 in Figure 3). If, as is likely, it falls, the curve Q_d^2 rotates leftward. In Figure 3, equilibrium is at the point E_2 which, relative to A_2, shows an increase in capital requirements in the d sector (K_d^2). Similarly the curve $\bar{L}^2$ in quadrant III now shifts inward with equilibrium taking place at E_3. K_f^2 thus falls while K_d^2 increases. In the case described in Figure 3, total investment goes down. These results generally seem to agree quite well with the quantitative estimates obtained from the much more detailed empirical simulation model in Bruno & Sachs (1981). However, inspection of the figure indicates that there is a variety of possible outcomes depending on relative shifts in the constituent curves.[20]

A better idea of the various possible outcomes may be obtained by considering the comparative statics of the model in more explicit analytical form. This is done in the Appendix, where we show the quantitative long-run effect of a change in raw material prices and the rate of interest (R) on the real wage (w_f), the relative price of nontradeables (π) and the sectoral allocation of labor, capital and output. Specifically, the following statements can be made:

1. The fall in π due to a rise in π_n will be further strengthened or mitigated, by a concomitant long-run fall in R, according to whether the d-sector is more or less capital intensive than the f-sector.

2. The output/capital ratio in the d-sector will fall as π_n rises as long as the elasticity of substitution between labor and capital in d is less than 1.

3. There is a strong presumption that L_d^2 and Q_d^2 rise, while L_f^2, K_f^2 and Q_f^2 fall. K_d^2 may rise but need not necessarily do so. The latter ambiguity arises from conflicting income and substitution effects.

VIII. World Equilibrium, Changes in the Rate of Interest and the Current Account

So far we have conducted the analysis under the assumption that the world rate r^* remains constant. This is very convenient since it appropriately fixes the long-run factor prices and factor proportions. Of course, this particular small economy assumption need not hold if the implications of an increase in raw material prices are thought of as hitting all industrial countries at the same time. In the short and medium run, as experience has also shown, a shift in the world savings schedule and an investment shortfall may drive the real rate down, although it is not clear why this should be sustained for

---

[20] E.g., both capital goods could fall, if Q_d^2 rotates less to the left, or an extreme case could be conceived of where K_f^2 increases, although this seems relatively unlikely.

a very long period.[21] In any case, the implication of an exogenous change may be considered for a single country within the above model. Specifically let us consider a drop in r^* on top of a permanent increase in π_n.

A fall in r^* causes a rise in w_f^2 (or rather mitigates the fall in w_f^2). If d is more capital intensive than f, there will be a further fall in π^2. The same analysis also shows that Q_d^2/K_d^2 as well as $\pi^2 Q_d^2/K_d^2$ fall relatively to their previous long-run solution. The fall in r raises the present value of wealth (Ω), and thus shifts the curve Ω upward in Figure 3, leading to a relative increase in consumption π^1 and Q_d^1, and a relative fall in Q_f^1. Since the curve Y_f^1 stays the same, saving (S^1) must fall in the process, as one would expect.

The outcome in the second period depends on what happens to consumption demand for nontradeables, which in turn involves both a positive wealth effect and a negative substitution effect. There is also the question of whether the resulting relative fall in demand for nontradeables can outweigh the effect of rising per unit capital requirements. As is shown in the Appendix, the elasticity of K_d^2 and L_d^2 with respect to R is in general ambiguous, but is very likely to be negative for K_d^2 and positive for L_d^2. Thus a fall in R is likely to increase K_d and mitigate the increase in L_d^2.

If the fall in the rate of interest reduces L_d^2, it certainly increases L_f^2. With the relative increase in K_f^2/L_f^2, the capital stock as well as the output of f in the second period must be higher than otherwise. With the fall in $C_f^2=(1+r)\,C_f^1$, it turns out that the current account in the second period (F^2) must improve and therefore F^1 in the first period must worsen.[22]

The final upshot, which makes intuitive sense, is that an exogenous fall in the interest rate makes for more net foreign borrowing (or reduction in capital outflow) today at the expense of the future. This has a counterpart in the structure of production and consumption; i.e., less production and more consumption (by imports) of tradeables today and more production (less consumption) in the next period. Correspondingly the relative price π falls less today (a smaller real depreciation) and more tomorrow.[23]

This monotonic relationship between r and the current account can also be used to consider the case where we do not assume free capital mobility. Suppose the government sets a target for the current account which involves a smaller deficit (or larger surplus) than would be obtained as an

---

[21] This will hold as long as the weighted marginal propensity to save out of wealth of the net exporters of raw materials outweighs the marginal propensity to save of the net importers.

[22] This would immediately follow if total investment (I^1) rises; savings (S^1), as we have seen, certainly fall. The rise in investments is probable but not certain, while the fall in the difference ($F^1=S^1-I^1$) is ambiguous.

[23] Again this is not unfamiliar from the trade and development literature (op. cit.).

endogenous solution of the system.[24] This implies government intervention in the form of fiscal and real exchange rate policy that implicitly involves an *increase* in the domestic real rate of interest. The implications for the structure of production and consumption in both periods will be exactly the reverse of that found in the case previously considered. In other words, there will now be an increase in savings and net production of f today at the expense of less of the same tomorrow, with all the concomitant effects on patterns of investment and labor use.

The converse may also take place. A government may decide to run a larger deficit than would otherwise be obtained for reasons of supporting price stability or full employment. These questions are discussed briefly in the next section.

IX. Real Wage Rigidity and Other Modifications

So far we have assumed wage and peice flexibility and automatic clearing of all markets. Under a raw material price shock, unemployment may arise when real wages are temporarily downward rigid; see Bruno & Sachs (1979). For simplicity, consider such rigidity in terms of this period's wage in f units (w_f).[25] In the extreme case where w_f is held fixed at its initial level ($w_f = w_f^0$ in the "very short run"), a raw material price increase will now appear as a greater reduction in real wealth since net output of $f(Y_f^1)$, for a given w_f, falls by more than it otherwise would fall.[26] Wealth (Ω) will no longer depend directly on π, and the Ω curve in Figure 3 (quadrant I) will now be replaced by a line parallel to the π axis which shifts downward as π_n increases to a position like the line passing through points D_0 and D_1 in the figure. If π were also downward rigid—say the nominal exchange rate were fixed and the price of $d(p_d)$ is downward rigid—the economy would momentarily stay at point D_0'', where there is excess supply in the commodity market (the demand for C_d^1 is less than $Q_d^1 - G^1$), as well as unemployment. If commodity prices are free to adjust, π^1 will fall and C_d^1 will rise to point D_0, where the d market clears but labor does not. Full employment could be

[24] We implicitly assume that only the government now conducts foreign borrowing or lending, with the budget absorbing the difference in interest rates.

[25] More realistically, the consumption wage should be expressed in terms of an average of w_f and w_f/π. Real wage rigidity may thus imply a constraint on the relationship between w_f and π, rather than on w_f alone.

[26] Formally, this can be seen by showing that

$$\partial Y_f / \partial \pi_n |_\pi = -N,$$

while

$$(\partial Y_f / \partial \pi_n)|_{w_f} = -N - \text{positive term}).$$

reached, with a rigid real wage, at point D_0'. This corresponds to the case where government expenditure is increased to ensure full employment (the line Q_d^2 shifts to pass exactly through D_0'), while taxes are suitably adjusted and domestic consumption of d falls.

Since consumption along with private wealth must be lower than in the flexible wage case (which corresponds to point E_1, E_2, etc.), the effect in the second period is to reduce K_d^2, L_d^2 and Q_d^2 (point D_2' in quadrant II) and increase K_f^2, L_f^2 and Q_f^2 relative to what they would be otherwise. This solution correspondingly implies that there will be a larger surplus (or smaller deficit) in the current account in the second period at the expense of the first period where both domestic savings and the current account must fall.

The above analysis may appear somewhat mechanistic since we have fixed the real wage independently of the state of the labor market, in which case the size of public expenditure does not seem to have any quantitative effects in the future. This could easily be modified by assuming, in Phillips curve fashion, that w_f changes smoothly as a negative function of the unemployment rate. In this case, this period's changes in G will directly affect the size of the structural changes in the second period.[27]

As long as nominal money has not been incorporated in the model, inflation and the role of monetary policy cannot be analyzed explicitly. While this can be remedied formally by introducing money demand/supply and a nominal interest rate, the likely role of money can be guessed even without its explicit introduction. Money may have a real long-term effect in this model if there is short-term nonneutrality. As in similar models, some nominal price (p_d, p_f or w) must be temporarily rigid, in which case real private wealth (as well as π and w_f) may change as a result of monetary policy, thus affecting the next period's factor allocations in a way similar to that analyzed before.

We conclude our discussion by noting again that, with one exception, we have stuck to the simplification that only the second period's quantities are affected by today's disturbances, while relative prices were assumed to remain invariant. A more general approach should also allow for induced changes in long-run relative prices. One example where this may occur is if we relax the assumption that the f good is a perfect substitute for the world final good and assume instead that the individual country faces a downward sloping demand curve for its product (priced p_f), which is an imperfect

[27] Note that the increase in G^1 is assumed to be financed by increased taxes. Had we assumed instead that it is financed by a decrease in next period's G^2 (i.e., by debt) the intertemporal link would also show directly (by an upward shift in the Q_d^2 line in quadrant II of Figure 3).

substitute for the world final good (whose domestic price is $e \cdot p^* \neq p_f$). In that case the final goods terms of trade (p_f/ep^*) become an additional endogenous relative price, which may now move the final position of the FPF for f (the curve ϕ_f^2 in Figure 2), since the relative price of the raw material will also become endogenous[28] [$\pi_n = ep_n^*/p_f = (p_n^*/p^*)(ep^*/p_f)$]. This implies that the present period's stabilization policies may affect the next period's Π^2 and w_f^2 even though r^* is given. Once we introduce these and additional complications, however, there remains less advantage in considering an analytical model over simulations with a more realistically complex empirical framework. After all, we set out with the objective of showing that considerable insight into some of the issues can be gained by looking at a stripped-down version of such a model.

Let us reiterate the main theme of the analysis of the response to supply shocks. The two-period horizon enabled a distinction to be made between short-run rigidities coming from sector specificity of capital, or real wage rigidity, and long-run flexibility in capital investment and labor-market adjustment. It has also helped to draw the distinction between temporary and permanent changes in raw material prices. An added dimension of flexibility in the model comes from assumptions on the degree of international capital mobility which allows smoothening of consumption and investment over time through variations in the current account. In virtually all of the issues discussed here, the close link between short-run macroeconomic adjustment and long-run structural change is of paramount importance.

Appendix to Sections VII and VIII: The Effects of Permanent Changes in π_n (and R)

Consider first a general two-sector three-factor model. Let us denote the factor shares for labor, materials and capital in the two sectors by $\alpha_i, \beta_i, \gamma_i$ ($i = d, f$; $\alpha_i + \beta_i + \gamma_i = 1$). The two factor-price frontiers tell us that the rates of change (denoted by ^) in marginal factor products must obey the following equations:

$$TR: \alpha_f \hat{w}_f + \beta_f \hat{\pi}_n + \gamma_f \hat{R} = 0 \tag{12}$$

$$NT: \alpha_d(\hat{w}_f - \hat{\pi}) + \beta_d(\hat{\pi}_n - \hat{\pi}) + \gamma_d(\hat{R} - \hat{\pi}) = 0. \tag{13}$$

It follows that for a given $\hat{\pi}_n$ and $\hat{R}$, the shifts in the real wage and the relative price of NT are uniquely determined as follows:

---

[28] In a medium-term context, such an argument explains why in face of the same external price shock (in terms of p_n^*/p^*), a country like Germany suffered a smaller internal increase in π_n in the 1970s, compared to Japan or the U.K. The implications for the differential productivity performance in manufacturing are discussed in Bruno (1981).

$$\hat{w}_f = -\alpha_f^{-1}(\beta_f\hat{\pi}_n + \gamma_f\hat{R}) \tag{14}$$

$$\hat{\pi} = \alpha_d\hat{w}_f + \beta_d\hat{\pi}_n + \gamma_d\hat{R} = \alpha_d[(\beta_d/\alpha_d - \beta_f/\alpha_f)\hat{\pi}_n + (\gamma_d/\alpha_d - \gamma_f/\alpha_f)\hat{R}]. \tag{15}$$

Equation (15) shows that π will fall with an increase in π_n as long as the ratio of the raw-material to labor input in the f-sector is higher than in the d-sector (which is identical with the statement that $\beta_d/\alpha_d < \beta_f\alpha_f$). This trivially holds for the case analyzed in the paper ($\beta_d=0$). It also gives the elasticity of long-run change in π for given R. Next, equation (15) shows that π falls further with a *fall* in R as long as d is more capital intensive than $f(\gamma_d/\alpha_d > \gamma_f/\alpha_f)$, which is a statement made in Section VII.

Now consider the production side. Denoting the elasticities of substitution between labor and capital by σ_i $(i=d,f)$, we have:

$$\hat{K}_i - \hat{L}_i = \sigma_i(\hat{w}_f - \hat{R}) = -\sigma_i\alpha_f^{-1}[\beta_f\hat{\pi}_n + (1-\beta_f)\hat{R}]. \tag{16}$$

A fall in R will mitigate the negative substitution effect of π_n on the capital/labor ratios. In principle, it could even reverse it, but with reasonable orders of magnitude this is unlikely to happen. E.g., with $\hat{\pi}_n=0.4$, $\beta_f=0.4$, $R=1+r$ would have to fall by more than 25%, which is highly unlikely as it involves a highly negative r. For the d sector we find (substituting from (14) and assuming $\beta_d=0$):

$$\hat{Q}_d - \hat{L}_d = \gamma_d(\hat{K}_d - \hat{L}_d) = -\alpha_f^{-1}\gamma_d\sigma_d[\beta_f\hat{\pi}_n + (1-\beta_f)\hat{R}] \tag{17}$$

$$\hat{Q}_d - \hat{K}_d = -\alpha_d(\hat{K}_d - \hat{L}_d) = \alpha_f^{-1}\alpha_d\sigma_d[\beta_f\hat{\pi}_n + (1-\beta_f)\hat{R}] \tag{18}$$

and for $\hat{R}=0$

$$(\hat{\pi}g_d) = \hat{\pi} + \hat{Q}_d - \hat{K}_d = -\alpha_f^{-1}\alpha_d(1-\sigma_d)\beta_f\hat{\pi}_n. \tag{19}$$

Equation (19) shows that the output/capital ratio must fall, with a rise in π_n, and likewise the slope of the Q_d^2 line in Figure 3, as long as the elasticity of substitution between labor and capital in d is less than 1. It is interesting to note that in the special Cobb–Douglas case ($\sigma=1$), it will stay put. We have thus justified the analysis of the change in quadrant II of Figure 3 in Section VII.

What can we explicitly say about the changes in the capital stocks and labor inputs as a result of a permanent increase in raw material prices or a fall in the interest rate? Ignoring the superscript notation for period 2 we have, using equations (17) and (18):

$$\hat{K}_d = \hat{Q}_d - (\hat{Q}_d - \hat{K}_d) = c\hat{C}_d - \alpha_f^{-1}\alpha_d\sigma_d[\beta_f\hat{\pi}_n + (1-\beta_f)\hat{R}]$$

$$\hat{L}_d = \hat{Q}_d - (\hat{Q}_d - \hat{L}_d) = c\hat{C}_d + \alpha_f^{-1}\gamma_d\sigma_d[\beta_f\hat{\pi}_n + (1-\beta_f)\hat{R}]$$

where $c=C_d/Q_d$ [since $\dot{Q}_d=\dot{C}_d$ and $\hat{Q}_d=(C_d/Q_d)\hat{C}_d$]. The total response cannot be deduced without further specification of the demand side (which affects $\hat{C}_d$). With the assumptions made in the paper [see eq. (8)], we can write $\hat{C}_d=\hat{\Omega}-\hat{\pi}+\hat{R}$.

Next we can substitute for $\hat{\pi}$ from equation (15) and write $\hat{\Omega}=\theta_n\hat{\pi}_n+\theta_r\hat{R}$, where θ_n is the elasticity[29] of total wealth with respect to a permanent raw material price change ($\pi_n^1=\pi_n^2$), and θ_r is the elasticity with respect to R ($\theta_r<0$); we get:

$$\hat{K}_d=[\alpha_f^{-1}\alpha_d\beta_f(c-\sigma_d)+c\theta_n]\hat{\pi}_n+[\alpha_f^{-1}\alpha_d(1-\beta_f)(c-\sigma_d)+c\theta_r]\hat{R} \quad (20)$$

$$\hat{L}_d=[\alpha_f^{-1}\beta_f(c\alpha_d+\sigma_d\gamma_d)+c\theta_n]\hat{\pi}_n+[\alpha_f^{-1}(1-\beta_f)(c\alpha_d+\sigma_d\gamma_d)+c\theta_r]\hat{R} \quad (21)$$

Consider first the case $\hat{R}=0$. Looking at signs and orders of magnitude of parameters, there is a strong presumption that $\hat{L}_d>0$ and $\hat{Q}_d>0$, while $\hat{K}_d$ may be positive but need not necessarily be so. The ambiguity arises from the fact that the wealth effect ($c\theta_n$) is negative for a net importer while in (20) the consumption and production substitution effect involving ($c-\sigma_d$) may or may not be positive, but is anyway likely to be small. Here is a numerical example (with realistic orders of magnitude): $\alpha_d=0.6$, $\alpha_f=0.4$, $\beta_f=0.4$, $\sigma_d=0.7$, $c=0.8$, $\theta_n=-0.05$. We get (per 1% of $\hat{\pi}_n$): $\hat{K}_d=0.02$, $\hat{L}_d=0.72$, $\hat{Q}_d=0.44$ (percent). If $\theta_n=-0.10$, $\hat{K}_d=-0.02$, $\hat{L}_d=0.68$, $\hat{Q}_d=0.40$ (percent). In both cases, $\hat{\pi}=-0.7$, $\hat{w}_f=-1.0$.

If L_d rises, then by construction L_f must fall, and since K_f/L_f is known to fall in response to a π_n increase, K_f must be falling and so do Q_f and Y_f.

We can thus state as an upshot that there is a strong presumption that employment, output and capital in the f industry will fall and that employment and output (and maybe capital) in the d industry will rise.

Consider now changes in R (discussed in Section VIII). The coefficients of $\hat{R}$ in (20) and (21) may in principle take any sign. θ_r is negative and is likely to be sizable (on the order of, say, between $\frac{1}{2}$ and 1). With the numerical magnitudes given above, there is a strong presumption that K_d will rise with a fall in R and that L_d may fall, i.e., its increase due to π_n will be mitigated. Correspondingly, K_f/L_f rises with a fall in R and there is a strong presumption that both K_f and L_f rise (i.e., their fall due to π_n is mitigated).

References

Bardhan, P.: Optimal foreign borrowing. In K. Shell (ed.), *Essays in the theory of optimal growth*, The MIT Press, 1966.

Berndt, E. R. & Wood, D. O.: Engineering and econometric interpretation of energy–capital complementarity. *American Economic Review*, June 1979.

Bruno, M.: Optimal patterns of trade and development. *The Review of Economics and Statistics*, November 1967.

[29] θ_n can be roughly approximated by the ratio to wealth of the total self-sufficiency measure: $[H^1-N^1+(1+r)^{-1}(H^2-N^2)]/\Omega$. For a net importer $\theta_n<0$.

Bruno, M.: Raw materials, profits and the productivity slowdown. Discussion Paper No. 812, Falk Institute, Jerusalem, April 1981. (Also appeared as NBER Working Paper No. 660.)

Bruno, M. & Sachs, J.: Supply versus demand approaches to the problem of stagflation. NBER Working Paper No. 382, August 1979. (Appeared in *Macroeconomic Policies for Growth and Stability*, Institut für Weltwirtschaft, Kiel, 1981.)

Bruno, M. & Sachs, J.: Input prices shocks and the slowdown in economic growth: Estimates for U.K. Manufacturing, presented at the Conference on Unemployment, Newnham College, Cambridge, July 1981.

Corden, W. M. & Neary, J. P.: Booming sector and de-industrialization in a small open economy. Mimeo, 1980.

Mayer, W.: Short-run and long-run equilibrium for a small open economy. *Journal of Political Economy,* September/October 1974.

Neary, J. P. & Purvis, D. D.: Sectoral shocks in a dependent economy: Short-run accomodation and long-run adjustment. Mimeo, 1981.

Razin, A.: Capital movements, intersectoral resource shifts, and the trade balance. Seminar Paper No. 159, Institute for International Economic Studies, University of Stockholm, October 1980.

Sachs, J.: Energy and growth under flexible exchange rates. NBER Working Paper No. 582, November 1980; also forthcoming in Bhandari and Putnam (eds.), *The international transmission of economic disturbances under flexible exchange rates* (forthcoming). MIT Press, 1982.

Sachs, J.: Aspects of the current account behavior of OECD economies. Presented at the V International Conference of the University of Paris-Dauphine on Money and International Monetary Problems, June 1981.

Svensson, L. E. O.: Oil prices and a small oil-importing economy's welfare and trade balance: An intertemporal approach. Institute for International Economic Studies, University of Stockholm, October 1981.

van Wijnbergen, S.: Optimal investment and exchange rate management in oil exporting countries: A normative analysis of the Dutch disease. Mimeo, Development Research Center, World Bank, Washington, 1981.

Comment on M. Bruno, "Adjustment and Structural Change under Supply Shocks"

Lars E. O. Svensson

Institute for International Economic Studies and University of Stockholm, Sweden

Bruno analyzes short-run and long-run allocational effects of temporary and permanent increases in the prices of imported raw materials, a decrease in the world rate of interest, and several other kinds of disturbances. More precisely, the effects on production and consumption of traded and non-traded final goods, investment and the trade balance are considered.

A general equilibrium analysis of a small open economy is developed. The analysis has many attractive properties. It is explicitly microeconomic, thus rigorously founded on optimizing behavior. Moreover, it is explicitly intertemporal, in the sense that savings and investment behavior is derived from well-specified intertemporal maximization. In particular, the effects of oil price increases on investment and the role of investment in determining the trade balance response is carefully treated. The paper fits together very well with several recent papers describing various aspects of allocation and the current account in an intertemporal setting; see e.g. Obstfeld (1980), Razin (1980), Sachs (1981 *a, b*), and Svensson and Razin (1981).

With regard to the techniques applied in the analysis of these and similar issues, I am personally very much in favor of using the increasingly popular so-called dual approach, which is characterized by a consistent use of dual functions, such as expenditure and revenue functions, to express budget constraints, behavioral functions, and equilibrium conditions. The approach makes for easily derived, yet easily interpreted results.[1] However, Bruno's more traditional analysis in terms of utility and production functions, marginal conditions, etc., has the advantage of still being more familiar and, perhaps, closer to the intuitive thinking of most readers.

As a complement to the rather formal analysis in the paper, I intend to give a more intuitive presentation of the effects of an increase in raw material prices on production, investment and the trade balance. We recall that traded and nontraded goods are produced in the two periods, using capital and labor. Production of traded goods also requires input of raw materials. Raw materials are produced in fixed quantities in both periods.

---

[1] Cf. e.g. Svensson (1981).

They are traded at given prices, and we assume that there is net import of raw materials in both periods. Capital is sector-specific in the first period and mobile in the second period. Traded goods can be invested in the first period, which augments the capital stock in the second period. There is perfect international (financial) capital mobility, and the country faces a given rate of interest. Here we consider only the case of flexible wages and full employment in both periods.

There are constant returns to scale in the production of both goods. This, combined with the assumption of a given rate of interest, simplifies the treatment of investment considerably, as was noted in Razin (1980). For a given (relative) price of raw materials, the standard properties of the two-by-two production model (the Stolper–Samuelson relations) implies that the rate of interest uniquely determines the (relative) price of nontraded goods in period 2. Furthermore, the capital/labor ratios in the traded and nontraded goods sectors are determined and there is a Rybczynski relation between the capital stock in period 2 (and hence investment) and the production of traded and nontraded goods. Bruno assumes that nontraded goods are relatively capital intensive, hence nontraded goods output in period 2 increases with investment in period 1.

In order to understand the effect of raw materials price increases, we first examine the effect of a pure wealth decrease, as would occur if domestic production of oil should diminish. At constant nontraded goods prices and investment, demand for nontraded goods falls in both periods. Hence there is exccss supply, and at constant invcstment, the price of nontraded goods falls in both periods, and there is a fall in the output of nontraded goods. But then the price of nontraded goods in period 2 has fallen below its (long-run) equilibrium given by the Stolper–Samuelson relation. Hence, period 2 output of nontraded goods and period 1 investment fall until the price of nontraded goods is back to its initial level. Thus production of nontraded goods unambiguously decreases in both periods.

The trade balance in period 1 is the difference between the sum of value added in the traded goods sector and the domestic raw materials sector, and the sum of consumption and investment in traded goods. Value added in the traded goods sector is increased, whereas raw materials output, traded goods consumption and investment have decreased. The net outcome is in general ambiguous. For a temporary (future) decrease in oil production, however, it is easy to show that the trade balance is likely to deteriorate (improve).

Consider now a permanent increase in raw materials prices. If the country is a net importer, this corresponds to a decrease in wealth, which decreases demand and leads to exactly the same consequences as we have discussed above for a pure wealth decrease. However, in addition to these effects that are transmitted via an initial *demand* decrease, the raw materials price also has an initial *supply* effect. By assumption, only traded goods production requires raw materials. Then a raw materials price increase leads to a fall in traded goods output and a rise in nontraded goods production, in both periods. This creates an additional excess supply of nontraded goods. Hence at a constant investment level, prices of nontraded goods fall more than after a pure wealth decrease, whereas the net effect on output of nontraded goods seems ambiguous and depends on the specific parameters. The effect on investment is also ambiguous. For since only traded goods production requires raw materials, and traded goods are capital intensive, the long-run price of nontraded goods has also fallen along with the raw materials price increase. If the fall in the period 2 price of nontraded goods at a constant investment level is larger than the fall in the long-run price, investment will decrease. Otherwise it will increase.

The effect on the trade balance is again ambiguous. However, for a *temporary* raw materials price increase in period 1 only, the period 1 trade balance deteriorates. There is no decrease in the long-run price of nontraded goods, so investment definitely falls. Hence output of nontraded goods falls in perid 2 and the period 2 output value added of traded goods unambiguously rises. Consumption of traded goods unambiguously falls, because of the wealth effect and the fall in nontraded goods prices in period 1 (the price in period 2 is constant). Then the change in the trade balance in period 2, being the difference between the change in value added and in consumption of traded goods (there is no investment in period 2) is positive. The trade balance in period 1 is the negative of the present value of the period 2 trade balance. Hence, it must unambiguously deteriorate.

Similarly, it can be argued that an anticipated future raw materials price increase improves the period 1 trade balance.

In this way, Bruno's other results can also be explained intuitively. I shall not do this here, but point instead to the two crucial assumptions that traded goods production is oil dependent and that nontraded goods are relatively capital intensive. It is obvious that some of the effects mentioned above may change signs if either of these assumptions is changed. Another crucial assumption is that of constant returns to scale. Only then does the simple investment theory result. Indeed, the result about the given long-run price of nontraded goods is an example of the general conclusion that trade in factors of production (or rather, here, the given rate of interest which fixes the return to capital) can be a perfect substitute for trade in goods. Thus capital mobility makes the distinction between traded and nontraded goods inessential, in that the price of nontraded goods will be determined by factors exogenous to the country.

Another necessary assumption for the simple investment theory and the given long-run price of nontraded goods is that investment consists of traded goods only. Marion (1981) deals with the case where nontraded goods are used for investment purposes. We also realize that the implicit assumption that domestic raw material production does not require any capital is restrictive; if capital is used in the raw material sector, a raw material price increase would trigger an investment boom there.

Finally, let me round off with some general remarks on the intertemporal emphasis of the paper. Bruno's analysis and the other recent work mentioned above clearly demonstrate the fruitfulness and perhaps even the necessity of an explicitly intertemporal approach to these and similar problems. It seems safe to say that the current account, which constitutes the difference between savings and investment, is inherently dynamic in nature, and that theories which treat this aspect lightly, say by using savings and investment functions that are not founded on maximizing behavior, could be misleading. The intertemporal approach points, for instance, to the crucial role of expectations of future variables for saving and investment decisions. Bruno's results on the differences between temporary and permanent disturbances illustrate this. Of course, the perfect foresight assumption implicit or explicit in most recent work of this kind, including Bruno's, should only be taken as a first step towards more elaborate analysis of the role of expectations.

As for the more technical choice between continuous and discrete time, finite vs. infinite horizon, etc., the discrete two-period model chosen by Bruno is clearly the simplest possible intertemporal framework. Yet it allows for rich results. Nevertheless, there are, of course, problems for which a simple binary distinction between the present and the future, or the short run and the long run, etc., is not sufficient. For instance, suppose we want to analyze the consequences of the possibility, mentioned by Bruno, that the fall in the world interest rate, after a raw material price shock, is temporary rather than permanent. Then we clearly need at least three periods, say the present, the near future and the distant future.

In summary, Bruno has presented us with a competent analysis of a relevant problem which adds to our understanding of the allocational effects of raw material price increases.

References

Marion, N. P.: Anticipated and unanticipated oil price increases and the current account. NBER Working Paper, No. 759, 1981.

Obstfeld, M.: Intermediate inputs, the terms of trade, and the dynamics of the exchange rate and the current account. *Journal of International Economics 10*, 461–480, 1980.

Razin, A.: Capital movements, intersectoral resource shifts, and the trade balance. Seminar Paper No. 159, Institute for International Economic Studies, University of Stockholm, 1980.

Sachs, J.: The current account and macroeconomic adjustment in the 1970's. *Brookings Papers on Economics Activity 1*, 201–268, 1981 *a*.

Sachs, J.: The current account in the macroeconomic adjustment process. This volume, 1981 *b*.

Svensson, L. E. O.: Oil prices and a small oil-importing economy's welfare and trade balance: An intertemporal approach. Seminar Paper No. 184, Institute for International Economic Studies, University of Stockholm, 1981.

Svensson, L. E. O. & Razin, A.: The terms of trade, spending and the current account: The Harberger-Laursen-Metzler effect. Seminar Paper No. 170, Institute for International Economic Studies, University of Stockholm, 1981 and forthcoming in *Journal of Political Economy*.

Sectoral Shocks in a Dependent Economy: Long-run Adjustment and Short-run Accommodation

J. Peter Neary

University College, Dublin, Ireland

*Douglas D. Purvis**

Queen's University, Kingston, Ontario, Canada

Abstract

This paper examines the allocation and stabilization consequences of a resource boom in a small open economy. Both the intersectoral allocation of capital and the price of non-traded goods adjust sluggishly; in contrast the nominal exchange rate adjusts instantaneously to ensure that the conditions for uncovered interest parity in the presence of rational exchange rate expectations are always met. The ability of monetary policy to stabilize the economy is examined, and it is shown that, even when intervention is justified in principle, policy errors which arise from confusing real and monetary shocks may worsen macroeconomic performance.

I. Introduction

Despite, or perhaps because of, the large amount of research devoted to the study of macroeconomic stabilization policy, the 1970s failed to produce anything like a consensus on the subject. Much of the recent literature has focussed on providing explanations for deviations from the classical norm of perpetual full employment, and on analysing the robustness of various policy prescriptions under alternative rationales for the use of such policy. While proponents of the "new Classical macroeconomics" have put forward an equilibrium interpretation of the business cycle in which no constructive role exists for "Keynesian" demand management, others have invoked wage–price stickiness as a justification for policy activism.

However, this focus on short-run demand management has distracted attention from the longer-run implications of intervention through its effects on investment and resource allocation. This paper attempts to redress the balance by exploring the interactions between exogenous shocks, short-run stabilization policy, and long-run resource allocation in a model which

---

* We are grateful to our discussant, John Flemming, to other conference participants, and to Neil Bruce, Willem Buiter, Lars Calmfors and Slobodan Djajic for helpful comments. This research was supported, in part, by the Committee for Social Science Research in Ireland.

combines a rich production structure with an explicit treatment of money-market equilibrium and rational exchange-rate expectations. The model was introduced in Neary & Purvis (1981) where it was shown that the real adjustment of the economy arising from sluggish intersectoral reallocation of resources implies that the nominal exchange rate may overshoot its new long-run value following an exogenous real shock, even when all wages and prices are perfectly flexible. In the present paper we relax this last assumption and thus are able to examine the interaction between the macroeconomic dynamics resulting from sticky prices and the Marshallian dynamics arising from sluggish factor reallocation.

While our focus is on the long-run effects of stabilization policy, we do not conceive of intervention as taking place in a vacuum but rather as evolving in response to specific exogenous disturbances. The dynamic response of the economy thus reflects both the "natural" response following the shock and the "induced" response to the policy. Although policy is characterized as intending to mitigate the effects of the disturbances, the analysis suggests ways in which it might actually exacerbate such effects.

Our procedure is to analyse two different exogenous shocks which have similar short-run effects but different long-run implications for resource allocation. Policies which are appropriate for one may not be appropriate for the other. Yet, since the impact effects are similar, the two may be hard to distinguish if the shocks themselves are not directly observable; this leads us to a discussion of policy errors. Of the two shocks we consider, the first is a purely monetary disturbance in the form of an equal percentage increase in all foreign prices. The second is a "resource boom" which alters the long-run allocation of resources; this focus on a "resource boom" underlies the specifics of the real model.

The allocation and stabilization consequences of resource booms have been analysed elsewhere. Corden & Neary (1982) use a three-sector model —resources, manufactures, and non-traded services—to investigate the channels whereby a resource boom can lead to a reduction of output in the manufacturing sector, a phenomenon often labelled "de-industrialization" or the "Dutch disease". Two main channels are identified: a *resource-movement effect,* whereby the booming sector directly or indirectly bids resources away from the manufacturing sector, and a *spending effect* which squeezes profitability in manufacturing by raising the demand for services and so lowering the real exchange rate (the relative price of traded to non-traded goods). Buiter & Purvis (1981) argue that de-industrialization in many countries is not associated with a significant movement of labour into the booming sector and instead stress the real appreciation arising from the resource boom in conjunction with sticky domestic prices. In their model resources and manufacturing do not compete directly for factors of production since resource output is taken as exogenous; hence no labour-market pressures emerge, and deindustrialization occurs instead through the foreign exchange market.[1]

The model used in this paper retains the three-sector framework of Corden & Neary but modifies the underlying structure to reflect the Buiter & Purvis view that the direct labour-market effects arising from expansion of the resource sector are minimal. Production of the resource is assumed to require a specific factor in addition to capital, but *not labour*. Manufactured goods are produced using capital and labour while services are produced using only labour. Labour is freely mobile between the two sectors in which it is used, manufacturing and services. In contrast, the allocation of capital between the sectors in which it is used, benzine and manufacturing, is fixed in the short run and variable only in the long run. This production structure is combined with the assumption that the economy is "dependent" in the sense that it is a price taker in the markets for both traded goods; hence the domestic demand repercussions of the exogenous shocks have direct influence only in the services sector.

The plan of the paper is as follows. Section II sketches the details of the real model and analyses its short- and long-run responses to a resource boom. Section III extends the analysis to incorporate slow adjustment in the relative price of services, while Section IV introduces a macroeconomic framework and examines the dynamics that arise when both the price of services and the allocation of capital are slow to adjust while the nominal exchange rate is allowed to float. Section V then focusses on the key policy issues and Section VI presents some conclusions.

II. Resource Allocation and Marshallian Adjustment in a Dependent Economy

In this section we introduce the basic production and consumption relationships of the real part of our model, and illustrate the responses of output and resource allocation to structural shocks. We examine both short- and long-run responses in the Marshallian sense that some factors of production are fixed in the short run but variable in the long run. However, in this section we abstract from the macroeconomic distinction between short and long run that arises in the presence of *nominal* price stickiness by assuming perfect price flexibility.

The Model

The model is characterized by three sectors; the economy produces one non-traded good (services) and two traded goods (manufactures and the

---

[1] A third approach is to emphasize the intermediate goods aspect of resources, as is done, for example, by Bruno & Sachs (1979) and Djajic (1980). However, this cannot be central to the case treated here where a boom results from a domestic discovery of a traded resource.

resource good, benzine). We assume that the economy is small in terms of world markets so that it takes the foreign currency prices of the two traded goods, and hence their relative price, as given.

The assumptions concerning the technology of production are intended to reflect the stylized facts that non-traded services are highly labour-intensive while resource-extractive sectors use very little labour. Accordingly, the output of services, X_S, is presumed to require *only* labour, and by appropriate choice of units the input–output coefficient is set equal to unity.[2]

$$X_S = L_S \tag{1}$$

This means that the domestic price of services may be identified throughout with the wage rate:

$$P_S = W \tag{2}$$

Labour is also used in conjunction with capital to produce manufactured goods:

$$X_M = X_M(K_M, L_M) \tag{3}$$

Finally, benzine is produced using capital and a specific factor, V:

$$X_B = X_B(K_B, V) \tag{4}$$

We assume that labour is in fixed supply and instantaneously mobile between the services and manufacturing sectors. In this section we also assume that the full employment condition given by equation (5) is always satisfied.[3]

$$L_M + L_S = L \tag{5}$$

While the services and manufacturing sectors thus compete directly for labour, there is no such direct link between the services and resource sectors since the latter does not use labour. There are, of course, *indirect* links between services and benzine through the market for capital, which is used in the production of both benzine and manufactures. However, capital is a fixed input in the short run, and can only be adjusted slowly through time in response to changes in its perceived return. Details of this adjustment mechanism are postponed until later.

The demand side of the model is straightforward. Since the country is a price-taker in world markets for manufactured goods and benzine, domestic

---

[2] See Kouri (1979) for an earlier use of this assumption.

[3] In Section III we replace this assumption with one specifying a "natural level" of employment about which actual employment can fluctuate.

demand for these goods plays no role in determining their prices or output. In contrast, price and quantity in the market for services are influenced by domestic demand. Domestic demand for services, C_S, depends upon prices and real income Y as shown in equation (6) where the signs of the partial derivatives are as shown:

$$C_S = C_S(\underset{-}{P_S}, \underset{?}{P_M}, \underset{?}{P_B}, \underset{+}{Y}) \tag{6}$$

If services are net substitutes for manufactures and benzine, the two uncertain signs will be positive; for concreteness we assume henceforward that this is the case.

In later sections we will examine macroeconomic phenomena using a framework in which nominal prices are determined. However, we confine our attention in this section and the next to "real" variables. Hence only relative prices are determined; national income and expenditure are always equal, implying a zero trade balance at all times. For the present we choose manufactured goods as numeraire, and define the real exchange rate, π, as the relative price of manufactures in terms of services:

$$\pi \equiv P_M/P_S = P_M/W \tag{7}$$

Movements in the real exchange rate are simply the inverse of movements in the relative price of services or, equivalently, in the real wage rate faced by the manufacturing sector.

We wish to examine how the output of the three goods and the allocation of factors respond to a resource boom in the form of an exogenous increase in either the world price of benzine or in the available supply of V, the specific factor used in the production of benzine. To do so, we first examine the determination of equilibrium and then see how that equilibrium is perturbed by a resource boom. (Technical details and derivations may be found in the Appendix.)

Labour Market Equilibrium

In Fig. 1 the combinations of the real exchange rate and the sectoral allocation of capital consistent with labour market equilibrium are depicted by the curve LL. An increase in π, which is a fall in the manufacturing real wage, increases the demand for labour in the manufacturing sector. A rise in π is equivalent to a fall in P_S so that the demand for services, and hence for labour in the services sector, rises as well. An increase in π leads, therefore, to an unambiguous increase in the demand for labour. A reduction in the capital stock in the manufacturing sector would, at a given wage, lead to a reduction in the demand for labour in the manufacturing sector. Hence the labour market equilibrium locus LL is negatively sloped as

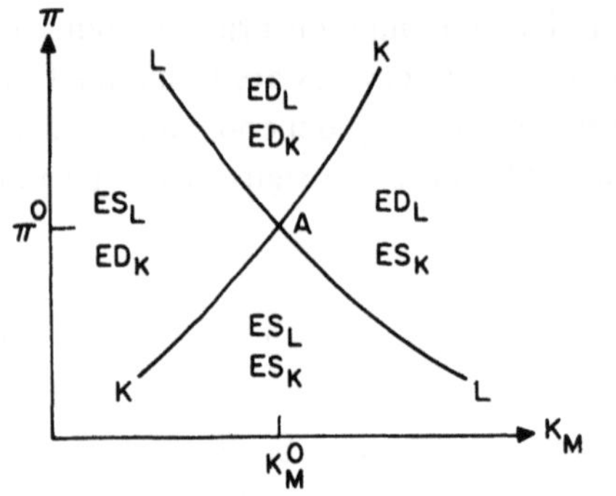

Fig. 1. Factor market equilibrium.

shown in Fig. 1; points above the locus correspond to excess demand for labour and points below to excess supply. Note that *LL* also depicts equilibrium in the market for services.

Capital Market Equilibrium

While at any moment of time the capital stock in both the manufacturing and resources sectors is predetermined, in the long run the capital stocks in both sectors adjust so as to equalize their rates of return. In this paper we consider the case where the total stock of capital in the economy is fixed so that the capital stock adjustment process involves reallocating capital from one sector to the other:

$$K_M + K_B = K \tag{8}$$

This of course follows the tradition of the Heckscher–Ohlin model of international trade. In postulating slow, costly adjustment we follow earlier work by Mayer (1974), Mussa (1974, 1978) and Neary (1978).[4]

Consider the implications of a permanent increase in the real exchange rate for the long-run allocation of capital. An increase in π raises profitability in manufacturing and so raises the long-run return to capital in that sector. If capital market equilibrium is to be restored the return to capital in the benzine sector must also rise, which requires that capital allocated to that sector must decrease. Hence the capital market equilibrium locus, *KK*, is positively sloped as depicted in Fig. 1, with points above the line corresponding to excess demand for capital in manufacturing, and conversely for points below.

[4] In Neary & Purvis (1981) we also examine the case where physical capital is mobile internationally so that the total stock of capital in the country is endogenous.

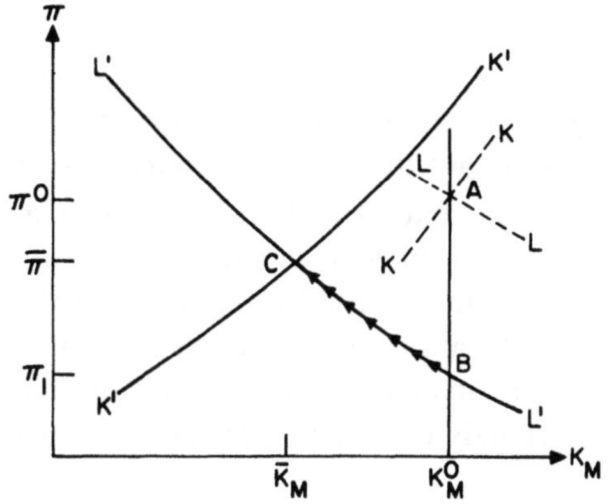

Fig. 2. Comparative statics and Marshallian dynamics.

Long-Run Comparative Statics

Consider now the effects of a "resource boom" due to either a "discovery" of new stocks of the specific factor V or an increase in the price of benzine, P_B.[5] Since real income rises, there is an increased demand for services which amounts to an increased demand for labour in the services sector. To equilibrate the labour market, the demand for labour in manufacturing must fall; at a given real exchange rate and hence at given factor proportions, this is accomplished through a reduction in capital in the manufacturing sector. The LL curve therefore shifts left, reflecting the spending effect of the boom. In addition, the boom raises the rate of return to capital in the benzine sector calling for a long-run reallocation of capital away from manufacturing towards benzine. Hence the KK curve also shifts left, reflecting the resource-movement effect of the boom.

This is illustrated in Fig. 2 where the dashed lines LL and KK replicate the initial equilibrium loci from Fig. 1 and the solid lines $L'L'$ and $K'K'$ are the new loci following the boom. The stock of capital in manufacturing unambiguously falls. The real exchange rate may rise or fall depending on whether the KK or LL curve shifts more; in the figure we illustrate the intuitively more plausible case where the spending effect dominates and so the new long-run equilibrium at C is characterized by a real appreciation.

---

[5] An increase in the foreign relative price of benzine can be identified with a boom only if the country is a net exporter of benzine, so that an increase in its price amounts to an improvement in the terms of trade. Such a price increase also has a cross-price effect on the demand for services, which is positive if and only if benzine and services are net substitutes in demand. For ease of exposition we assume throughout the paper that both these effects are positive, although our results are easily modified to allow for alternative assumptions. See equations (A.1) and (A.4) in the Appendix for further details.

Marshallian Dynamics

While the long-run equilibrium following a resource boom involves a reduced capital stock in manufacturing, in the short run the capital stock is fixed at its initial value, K_M^0. Hence on impact there is no resource-movement effect and the economy moves from A to B in Fig. 2. There is an unambiguous real appreciation, while the return to capital rises in the resource sector and falls in the manufacturing sector.[6] It is clear that this gives rise to an incentive for capital reallocation; we postulate the simple mechanism whereby the capital stock in manufacturing adjusts through time in response to differences in the rentals earned by capital in the two sectors:[7]

$$\dot{K}_M = \Phi(r_M/r_B) \quad \Phi(1) = 0, \ \Phi' > 0 \tag{9}$$

This completely describes the capital adjustment process since, by equation (8), a change in the capital stock in the resource sector is matched by an equal and opposite change in the capital stock in manufacturing.

Since the labour market clears continually, the dynamic adjustment after the jump appreciation to B takes place along the $L'L'$ curve. The economy therefore follows a monotonic path along which K_M steadily declines accompanied by continuous real depreciation, as indicated by the arrows in Fig. 2. Note that there is "overshooting" of the real exchange rate in that it falls immediately to π_1 and then rises continually thereafter until it reaches its new equilibrium value $\bar{\pi}$. This overshooting is of the *real* exchange rate in response to a *real* disturbance; it occurs due to a *real* rigidity—the short-run fixity of the capital stock. Initially, with the capital stock fixed, the brunt of the adjustment is borne by the relative price; in the longer run the adjustment in the capital stock mitigates the required adjustment in price. This, of course, is exactly the Marshallian analysis of short- and long-run adjustment to a change in demand.

In the figure, both π_1 and $\bar{\pi}$ are below the initial exchange rate π^0 so that the initial change is in the right direction but exceeds in magnitude the long-run change. If, however, the resource-movement effect is large relative to the spending effect, so that there is a real *depreciation* in the long run, then rather than overshooting, in the short run the real exchange rate, by falling, moves in the "wrong" direction.

---

[6] The latter occurs since on impact labour moves from manufacturing to services so the capital–labour ratio in manufacturing rises.

[7] Mussa (1978) postulates a more satisfactory but more complicated process whereby the rate of capital movement depends on the present value of expected future rents less the costs incurred in reallocating capital.

III. Marshallian Adjustment with Relative Price Rigidities

In the previous section, following Neary & Purvis (1981), we considered the short- and long-run adjustment to a sectoral shock under the assumption that domestic prices are instantaneously flexible. In the present section we allow for the possibility that the relative price of services adjusts sluggishly in response to imbalances between supply and demand. Recalling that an increase in the real exchange rate, π, is equivalent to a fall in the relative price of services, we may write:

$$\dot{\pi} = \Psi(X_S/C_S) \quad \Psi(1) = 0, \ \Psi' > 0 \tag{10}$$

Since labour is the only factor used in the services sector, equation (10) may be interpreted as either a labour-market or a services-market adjustment mechanism.[8] Thus the presence of non-market clearing in the services market is equivalent to a departure from full employment with the wage rate adjusting slowly to eliminate under- or over-full employment. The parameter L in equation (5) in the last section should therefore now be interpreted as the "natural" rate of full employment rather than as a binding constraint which cannot be exceeded in the short run. In order to simplify the analysis we ignore the fact that departures from this "natural" level may cause either firms or households to face quantity constraints, forcing them to recalculate their decisions on other markets in the manner familiar from Clower's "dual-decision hypothesis". Hence our analysis is strictly applicable only in the neighbourhood of full employment, although for the issues on which we wish to focus this omission is not a crucial one.[9]

While in the present section we allow for sluggish relative price adjustment, the model is still a real one in which nominal magnitudes are not determined. The dynamic evolution of the system can therefore be illustrated in Fig. 3, whose essential features are identical to those of Fig. 2. However, the economy is no longer constrained to lie on the labour-market equilibrium locus $L'L'$. Recall that points above this locus correspond to excess demand for services and hence to upward pressure on their price, and conversely for points below the locus; the resulting tendencies for the real exchange rate to adjust are indicated by the vertical arrows in the diagram. As shown in the Appendix (see equation A.20), the system is globally stable; whether or not it generates cyclical adjustment paths de-

---

[8] The implications of sluggish price adjustment have been studied in open-economy models by, among others, Dornbusch (1976) in the context of goods-market adjustment and Noman & Jones (1980) in the context of labour-market adjustment.

[9] This amounts to ignoring the income effects on the demand for services and money caused by departures from full-employment. The consequences of "disequilibrium" spillovers in open economies have been explored by Dixit (1978), Liviatan (1979) and Neary (1980).

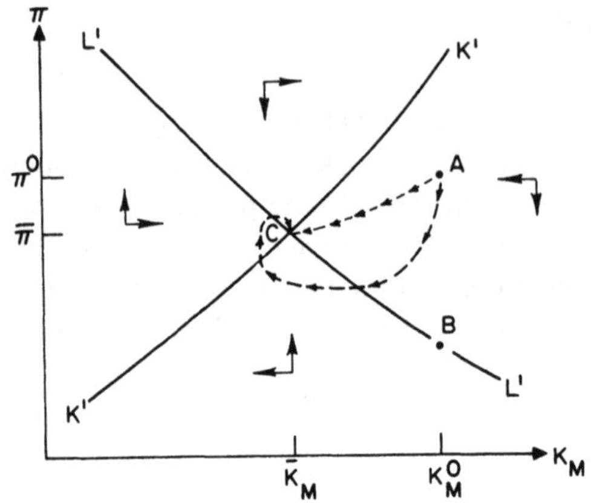

Fig. 3. Simultaneous adjustment of the capital stock and the real exchange rate.

pends on both the parameters of the long-run model and on the relative adjustment speeds embodied in the adjustment equations (9) and (10).

The response of the economy to a boom is now easily determined from Fig. 3. Starting in initial long-run equilibrium at point *A*, the boom gives rise to excess demand for services and an incentive to reallocate capital out of the manufacturing sector. However, unlike the flex-price case analysed in the previous section, the economy does not shift immediately to point *B*. Rather, the economy starts off on a continuous path to the south-west of *A*. Sluggish price adjustment therefore mitigates the extent to which the real exchange rate overshoots its long-run value.

When both the labour and capital markets adjust gradually, the economy may move directly from *A* to *C* as in the dotted path in Fig. 3, or cyclically as in the dashed path. The slower is the speed of price adjustment relative to the speed of capital reallocation, the more likely is the direct path. Hence in contrast to the Dornbusch (1976) analysis of nominal overshooting in response to monetary disturbances, sticky relative prices provide a "stabilizing" influence on the (real) exchange rate.[10]

IV. Macroeconomic Adjustment to Monetary and Real Shocks

In the previous section we postulated a sluggish adjustment mechanism for the real exchange rate, π. However no account was taken of the fact that changes in this variable reflect changes in both the nominal price of serv-

[10] We have restricted our discussion to the "plausible" case of long-run appreciation. If instead, the long-run effect is a rise in π, then inevitably there must be at least one turning point in π during the adjustment.

ices, P_S, and the nominal exchange rate, E, and that the determinants of these two components are likely to be very different. Thus, instead of (7) we may write:

$$\pi \equiv EP_M^f/P_S \tag{11}$$

where P_M^f is the price of manufactures in foreign currency, assumed to be exogenously determined. Following Dornbusch (1976), we assume that the nominal price of domestic goods moves slowly to eliminate imbalances between supply and demand. Hence (10) is replaced by:

$$\dot{P}_S = \Psi(C_S/X_S); \quad \Psi(1) = 0, \ \Psi' > 0 \tag{12}$$

By contrast, the nominal exchange rate is assumed to be determined by the requirement of stock equilibrium in the market for foreign exchange, in an environment where exchange-rate expectations are formed rationally and domestic and foreign interest-bearing assets are perfect substitutes. The latter assumption implies that domestic and foreign nominal interest rates are linked by the uncovered interest parity condition given by equation (13).

$$i = i^f + \hat{E} \tag{13}$$

$\hat{E}$ is the expected proportionate rate of change of the nominal exchange rate which, given the assumption of rational expectations, equals the actual rate of change. Equation (13) thus shows that the domestic interest rate can exceed the foreign rate only if there is an expected depreciation of the domestic currency.

The demand for real balances depends on real income and the domestic nominal interest rate:

$$M/P = l_D(Y, i) \tag{14}$$

The price level P is a linearly homogeneous function of all final-goods prices and hence increases with the nominal exchange rate. An increase in the nominal exchange rate thus gives rise to a fall in real balances; this must be accompanied by a rise in i or a fall in Y in order for monetary equilibrium to be maintained. The values of i and E which are consistent with monetary equilibrium for given values of M, P_S and Y are thus depicted by the positively sloped locus MM in Fig. 4. In the long run the ratio of E to P_S is determined by the conditions for real equilibrium outlined in Section I and so, for a given M and with real income at its full-employment level (contingent on given values of the exogenous variables), the value of P_S adjusts to ensure that equilibrium of the real and nominal sectors is simultaneously attained. Such a long-run equilibrium is illustrated by point Z in Fig. 4: the

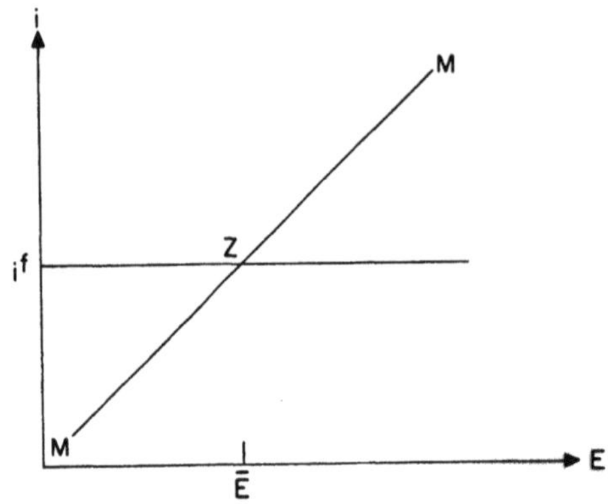

Fig. 4. Long run equilibrium determination of the interest rate and the nominal exchange rate.

domestic interest rate equals the foreign interest rate so the expected and actual change in the exchange rate are zero, and the actual exchange rate is equal to the long-run rate E.

Notice finally that, unlike the real models of Sections I and II, the current account need not be in balance except in long-run equilibrium. Hence the level of domestically-held wealth changes throughout the adjustment period and national expenditure and income are not equal. However, rather than complicating the model further in order to consider these issues, we follow earlier work in omitting them from consideration. We now examine the dynamic responses of the full model following a monetary shock and a resource boom, respectively.

A Monetary Shock

Consider first an unanticipated once-and-for-all reduction in the domestic money supply.[11] In the long run this shock is neutral; the nominal exchange rate and the domestic price of services fall in proportion to the reduction in the money supply. In Fig. 5 the new long-run equilibrium occurs at $\bar{Z}$, with the nominal exchange rate equal to $\bar{E}$, where $(\bar{E}-E_0)/E_0$ equals the percentage fall in the money supply. On impact there is excess demand for money at the initial equilibrium Z_0 so MM shifts leftwards. Moreover MM must shift leftwards by *more* than the extent of the reduction in the money supply, since with a sticky nominal price of services, the nominal exchange rate must fall more than proportionately in order to restore money-market equilibrium for given values of Y and i. With P_S

[11] Throughout the paper, monetary shocks are modelled as changes in the *level* of foreign prices or the domestic money supply, but the model may easily be extended to consider the effects of changes in the *rate* of foreign inflation or domestic monetary growth, along the lines of Buiter & Purvis (1982) or Buiter & Miller (1981).

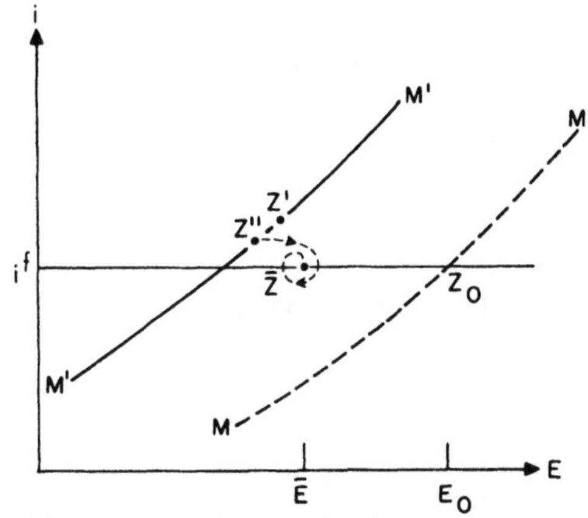

Fig. 5. Short-run equilibrium and exchange-rate dynamics following monetary deflation.

given at its initial value, the money-market equilibrium locus $M'M'$ must therefore cut the horizontal line i^f to the *left* of $\bar{Z}$, as shown in Fig. 5.

While the equilibrium values of E and i immediately following the monetary contraction must therefore lie along $M'M'$, the determination of their precise location requires a more detailed analysis. If the price of services is the only variable which adjusts sluggishly then, as shown by Dornbusch (1976), the new short-run equilibrium must lie at a point such as Z', implying a rise in the domestic interest rate and an overshooting by the nominal exchange rate of its new long-run value. From the condition for uncovered interest parity, equation (13), a higher interest rate is possible only if there is expected depreciation. Speculators therefore set the current spot exchange rate below its long-run value so that the actual adjustment of the exchange rate is consistent with these expectations, and the exchange rate rises monotonically during the adjustment period until it reaches its new long-run equilibrium value. Note that this is a case of overshooting of the *nominal* exchange rate in response to a *monetary* shock and caused by a *nominal* rigidity, in sharp contrast to the real overshooting discussed in Section II.

However when *both* the price of services *and* the allocation of capital adjust slowly, the analysis of the model is considerably more complicated. There is still a presumption that the nominal exchange rate overshoots its long-run value but the adjustment path which it follows need not be monotonic, as shown in the Appendix. One possible path is illustrated by the dashed line from Z'' in Fig. 5. If the adjustment path is cyclical then it must converge in a clockwise fashion as shown, since from equation (13) phases of depreciation must be associated with values of the domestic interest rate which are above the return available on foreign securities.

Corresponding to the adjustment of nominal variables illustrated in Fig.

5, real variables are also adjusting, since with a sticky domestic price of services the initial monetary deflation has real effects. At Z'' the relative price of services has risen, giving rise to excess supply in that sector. According to equation (12) the price of services starts to fall; this in turn tends to raise real balances and to reduce the domestic interest rate. Corresponding to the higher relative price of services is a rise in the real wage. Hence there is an incentive to reallocate capital from the labour-using manufacturing sector to the resource sector, and during the initial stage of the adjustment process X_M falls below its steady-state level.

A Resource Boom

The long-run real effects of a resource boom were analysed in Section II where we saw that the spending effect of the boom tends to reduce the real exchange rate whereas the resource-movement effect tends to raise it. There is an additional effect working on the nominal exchange rate through the money-market equilibrium condition (14); this we call the *liquidity effect*. By raising real income, the boom requires a fall in the domestic price level in the long run which, with a constant real exchange rate, implies a nominal appreciation. Hence we take this to be the "expected" outcome, although as the full expression for the change in E (equation (A.25) in the Appendix) shows, whether or not this actually ensues depends on the parameters of the model.

Confining attention to the case of nominal and real appreciation in the long run, the induced changes in nominal variables may again be illustrated with the aid of Fig. 5. When the price of services adjusts instantaneously, Neary & Purvis (1981) show that the nominal exchange rate may overshoot its long-run value followed by a steady depreciation as capital is reallocated out of the manufacturing sector. This possibility is illustrated by the short-run equilibrium at Z' in Fig. 5 where, on impact, the domestic interest rate has risen. But from the interest parity condition this can occur only if there is a simultaneous expectation of depreciation of the domestic currency. Rational speculators will therefore set the current exchange rate below its long-run value; if the long-run exchange rate itself falls then there must be short-run overshooting. When both the price of services and the capital stock adjust sluggishly, initial overshooting of both the real and nominal exchange rates is again a possibility, with subsequent cyclical or monotonic movement towards the new long-run equilibrium.

V. Interactions between Sectoral Adjustment and Macroeconomic Policy

So far our objective has been to develop the complete model in the absence of intervention. In the present section we turn to the question of how policy

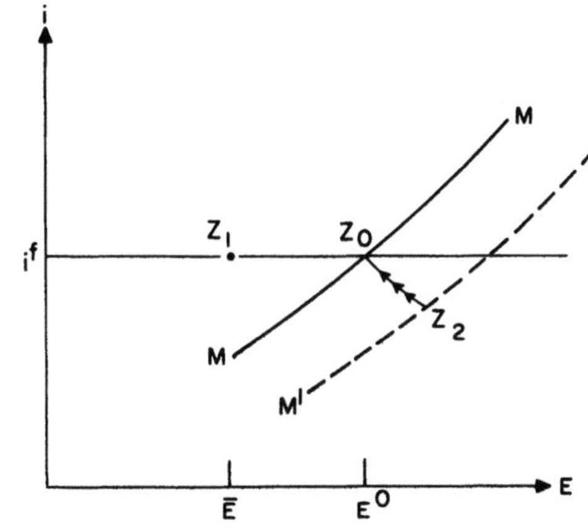

Fig. 6. Inappropriate response to a foreign price shock.

rules intended to stabilize the economy in the short run may affect its longer-run adjustment.

Inappropriate Responses to Nominal Exchange Rate Movements

We begin by considering a foreign price disturbance which if properly perceived requires no response from the authorities. Starting in initial long-run equilibrium at Z_0 in Fig. 6, suppose that the world prices of both traded goods increase by an equi-proportional amount. If there were no policy response, the new long-run equilibrium at Z_1, with a proportionate fall in the exchange rate to E_1, would be attained *instantaneously*. There would be no real changes even in the short run, and the domestic currency prices of all three goods would remain unchanged. Since no change in P_S is required, no dynamics are elicited.[12]

However the nominal appreciation entailed in moving from Z_0 to Z_1 may be resisted, perhaps on the false grounds that it will also imply a real appreciation leading to a loss in competitiveness of the domestic traded-goods sector. Such a view is incorrect, of course, since the nominal appreciation is in response to a foreign price rise, and so is merely the process by which domestic competitiveness is kept in line. However, if the source of the fall in the nominal exchange rate is not clearly identified, the situation might be confused with one where a nominal appreciation does

[12] The new long-run equilibrium is attained instantaneously because in our model the only role for the exchange rate is to convert foreign prices into domestic currency units and hence only the product of E and the respective foreign prices matters. If the exchange rate played an additional role, for example in converting foreign denominated assets into domestic currency units which then influenced real spending, the results could be substantially different. See, for example, Calvo & Rodriguez (1977) or Purvis (1979).

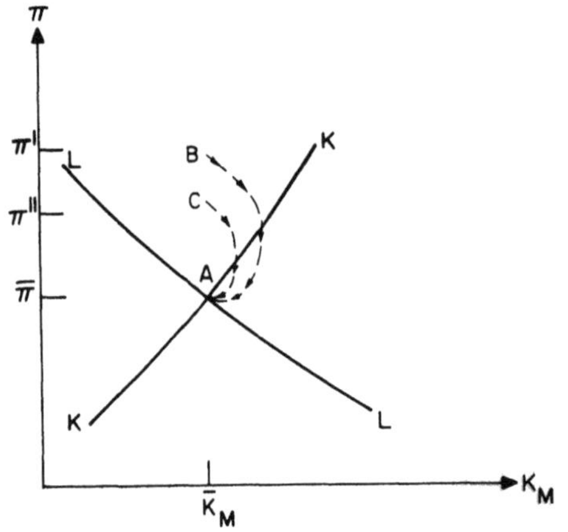

Fig. 7. Real adjustment to inappropriate monetary intervention.

harm the competitive position of the domestic export sector. Let us examine the implications of using monetary policy to "offset" the nominal appreciation.

Suppose first that the domestic money supply were raised in proportion to the foreign price rise. This would mean that the long-run equilibrium would remain at Z_0 in Fig. 6 and the long-run exchange rate would remain at E^0. But in the short run with P_S given, there would be an excess supply of money at Z_0. The MM curve shifts right to $M'M'$ and the short-run equilibrium moves to a point such as Z_2. Dynamic adjustment involves instantaneous increases in E *and* π followed by either continuous appreciation combined with increases in the price of domestic services (as depicted in Fig. 6) or by cyclical adjustment of all nominal variables. The policy mistake results in "importing" the foreign price increase since all domestic prices are higher at Z_0 than at Z_1 (where they were in fact unchanged), and in a misallocation of resources during the adjustment period since both nominal and real exchange rates differ from their long-run equilibrium values. The real adjustment is illustrated in Fig. 7; the initial and final equilibria are both at A and the short-run equilibrium immediately following the monetary intervention is at B. It is clear that there is at least one turning point in the adjustment of K_M, and in fact cyclical adjustment of both π and K_M is also possible.

An alternative form of monetary intervention would be to simply fix the nominal exchange rate at E_0 in Fig. 6. This would involve an instantaneous increase in the money supply proportionate to the impact on the price index of the rise in the traded-goods price (i.e., a less-than-proportionate change in M). There would then be excess demand for services leading to a continuous rise in P_S matched by a rise in the money supply sufficient to keep real balances constant. In terms of the nominal variables in Fig. 6

there are no dynamics as the economy remains at Z_0 throughout. However real adjustment still involves an instantaneous increase in the real exchange rate followed by either continuous real appreciation or a clockwise cyclical path. The former case is illustrated in Fig. 7 where the short-run equilibrium is at point C which involves a smaller real depreciation than when the money supply increases in proportion to the foreign price shock.

Inappropriate Policies and a Resource Boom

In the case of a foreign price disturbance just considered, the appropriate response on the part of the monetary authorities was to forego intervention and let the foreign-exchange market adjust completely to the shock. By contrast, in the case of a resource boom the sluggish adjustment of domestic prices provides a rationale for intervention: some of the transitional loss of output and employment could be avoided by a monetary expansion which would mitigate the initial rises in the real and nominal exchange rates.[13] This assumes however that the authorities correctly identify the source of the initial appreciation. If they fail to do so then by inaction they in effect tolerate the transitional unemployment attributable to the de-industrialisation effect of the boom. Worse still, if monetary policy is targeted towards exchange-rate stability rather than towards internal balance it may exacerbate the medium-run costs of the boom and delay the attainment of the new long-run equilibrium.[14]

These issues are illustrated in Fig. 8 which repeats the essential features of Fig. 3. Starting in initial equilibrium at A the boom leads to a new long-run equilibrium at C. With the sectoral allocation of capital and the nominal price of services fixed in the short run, speculative behaviour in the absence of intervention may induce a severe nominal appreciation which shifts the economy to point F, causing the real exchange rate to overshoot both its new long-run equilibrium level and the short-run equilibrium level which would obtain at B if commodity prices were flexible. The boom thus gives rise to a decline in competitiveness of the manufacturing sector accompanied by a rise in unemployment. Once again a cyclical adjustment path is possible, although for simplicity we concentrate on the case of monotonic adjustment.[15]

---

[13] In adopting this traditional Keynesian view of the desirability of intervention we are ignoring the possibility that the price adjustment equation (12) may embody a rational response to a changing economic environment, in which case it would not be independent of the policy rule adopted by the authorities.

[14] Throughout this section we assume that monetary policy takes the form of a relatively small number of once-and-for-all changes in the money supply, rather than a policy of continually changing the money supply.

[15] Still more complicated adjustment paths (without any jumps in the exchange rate) would ensue if speculators foresee such interventions. The effects of anticipated future disturbances on the adjustment paths of models with rational expectations have been studied by Wilson (1979) and Buiter & Purvis (1982).

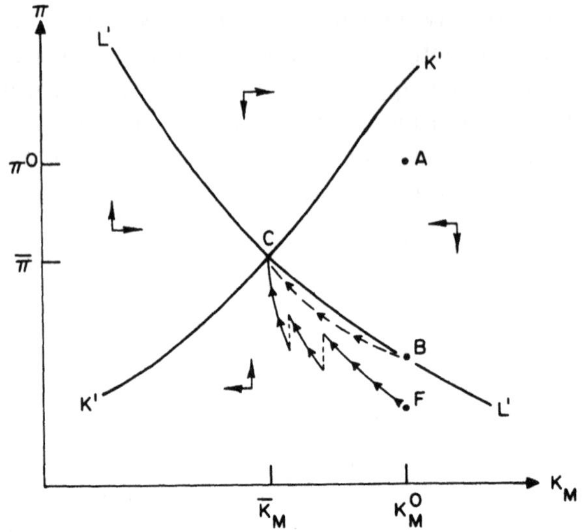

Fig. 8. Appropriate and inappropriate response to a resource boom.

One option open to the authorities in this case is to expand the money supply so as to partly offset the initial appreciation. Such a strategy could for example be targeted on the restoration of full employment in the short run, implying a move from *A* to *B*. At *B* foreign-exchange speculators would choose a path for the nominal exchange rate which would lead to a convergent movement towards the new long-run equilibrium *C*. Without further intervention some unemployment during the transition period is still inevitable, but its extent is less than along the no-intervention path starting at *F*.

However the high employment path through *B* will be attained only if the authorities correctly identify the source of the initial appreciation and recognize the desirability of responding to it with a policy which partly offsets the initial appreciation. Suppose instead that the authorities acquiesce in the initial appreciation and then subsequently attempt to counter the steady rise of the nominal and real exchange rates. One possible outcome is illustrated by the jagged path from *F* to *C* in Fig. 8 which assumes that the authorities, in the mistaken belief that the economy should be shielded from the steady nominal and real depreciation, twice intervene by reducing the money supply in an unanticipated manner. It is clear that the effect of this intervention is to delay the attainment of the long-run equilibrium and to lead to more transitional unemployment and loss of output than either the no-intervention path (implying a steady monotonic adjustment from *F* to *C*) or the high-employment path (from *B* to *C*).

VI. Conclusion

In this paper we have presented a model in which domestic prices do not respond instantaneously to imbalances between supply and demand. Without examining the micro foundations of this price-stickiness, we have assumed that it provides, in principle, a justification for government intervention. However because domestic factor markets do not adjust immediately to exogenous shocks, disturbances with similar short-run impacts may have very different long-run effects. Hence, as we have shown, an interventionist government which is unable to identify the source of a disturbance may respond in a manner which exacerbates the economy's performance and slows the return to long-run equilibrium.

In our view it is the risk of policy confusions of this sort rather than the undesirability of activist policy in itself which constitutes the major objection to a strategy of "fine-tuning" the macro-economy. This is not to deny that the authorities can and should take action to offset the effects of significant and clearly identifiable shocks. But they should be conscious of the need for different responses to shocks which have the same short-run effects. In particular, when international capital movements are volatile and exchange-rate expectations are formed in a rational manner, the authorities should not attempt to offset movements in the exchange rate which are an essential concomitant of the adjustment towards a new long-run real equilibrium. Finally, although we have concentrated in this paper on monetary intervention which can only affect the adjustment path, it is clear that the same principles also apply to fiscal intervention which can also influence the economy's long-run real equilibrium.[16]

Appendix

This appendix presents the principal equations of the model and sketches the derivation of the results. Further details on the flexible-price case may be found in Neary & Purvis (1981). Except where otherwise indicated, all variables are measured as natural logarithms, denoted by lower-case symbols (e.g., $e=\ln E$), and expressed in terms of deviations from their values in the initial equilibrium. (This is equivalent to choosing units of measurement such that the initial equilibrium levels of all variables are equal to unity.) Except where noted, all coefficients are defined to be positive.

[16] As noted by Dixit (1978) and Neary (1980) this is only the case if the intervention takes the form of government purchases of non-traded goods since, with exogenously given world prices of traded goods, intervention in traded goods markets effectively bypasses the domestic economy.

A.1. *The Real Model*

The demand for services, which is also that sector's demand for labour (since labour is the only factor used there), depends on prices and real income:

$$c_S = -\varepsilon_S p_S + \varepsilon_B p_B + \varepsilon_M p_M + \eta y \tag{A.1}$$

The compensated elasticities of demand ε_i obey the homogeneity restriction ($\varepsilon_B + \varepsilon_M = \varepsilon_S$), and the domestic prices of traded goods are related to their world prices by the nominal exchange rate e:

$$p_i = p_i^f + e \quad i = B, M \tag{A.2}$$

Real income, y, is defined as nominal income deflated by the consumer price index, p:

$$p = \beta_B p_B + \beta_M p_M + \beta_S p_S \tag{A.3}$$

where the β's are expenditure shares.

In the present paper we consider only two sources of change in real income: first, an increase in V, the endowment of the specific factor used in the benzine sector (whose impact depends on the share of that factor in national income θ_V); second, an increase in the world relative price of benzine which raises real income on the assumption that benzine is a net export (so that its share in national product, θ_B, exceeds its share in national expenditure, β_B):

$$y = \theta_V v + (\theta_B - \beta_B)\,\pi_B \tag{A.4}$$

We have introduced the symbol π_B to denote the terms of trade, and for later use we define π as the real exchange rate:

$$\pi_B \equiv p_B^f - p_M^f = p_B - p_M \tag{A.5}$$

$$\pi \equiv p_M - p_S = e + p_M^f - w \tag{A.6}$$

The demand for labour in manufacturing depends on the quantity of capital located there and on the real wage facing manufacturing firms:

$$l_M = k_M - \gamma_M (w - p_M) \tag{A.7}$$

where γ_M is the wage elasticity of the demand for labour in manufacturing. This in turn is related to the level of employment in the services sector by the full-employment constraint for labour:

$$\lambda_{LM} l_M + \lambda_{LS} l_S = 0 \tag{A.8}$$

where λ_{ij} is the proportion of factor i used in sector j. From equation (1) in the text the level of employment in the services sector may be identified with that sector's output. Hence equating demand and supply of services and substituting from earlier equations (recalling that $w = p_S$), we obtain an expression for the labour-market equilibrium locus, *LL* in Fig. 1, in terms of k_M, π and exogenous shocks:

$$\lambda_L k_M + \varepsilon\pi + \alpha_1 = 0 \tag{A.9}$$

where:

$$\varepsilon \equiv \lambda_L \gamma_M + \varepsilon_S > 0; \quad \lambda_L \equiv \lambda_{LM}/\lambda_{LS} \tag{A.10}$$

and

$$\alpha_1 \equiv \eta\theta_V v + \{\varepsilon_B + \eta(\theta_B - \beta_B)\}\, \pi_B \tag{A.11}$$

In the definition of the exogenous disturbance given by equation (A.11) the coefficient of π_B is the compensated cross-elasticity of demand for services with respect to the price of benzine, adjusted for the terms-of-trade effect on real income.

The capital-market equilibrium locus is found in a similar manner by relating the demands for capital from the benzine and manufacturing sectors by the full-employment constraint for capital:

$$\lambda_{KB} k_B + \lambda_{KM} k_M = 0 \tag{A.12}$$

The demand for capital in the benzine sector depends on the stock of the resource available there and the real rental facing the sector (where γ_B denotes the rental elasticity of capital demand):

$$k_B = v - \gamma_B(r_B - p_B) \tag{A.13}$$

In long-run equilibrium the rental in the benzine sector must equal that in manufacturing; the latter is related to the wage rate by the requirement that the price of manufactures must just cover unit costs:

$$p_M = \theta_{LM} w + \theta_{KM} r_M \tag{A.14}$$

where θ_{ij} is the share of factor i in the value of output in sector j. Setting $r_M = r_B$ and combining these equations with (A.2) yields the capital-market equilibrium locus:

$$\gamma_B^{-1} \lambda_K k_M - \theta_L \pi + \alpha_2 = 0; \quad \lambda_K \equiv \lambda_{KM}/\lambda_{KB}, \; \theta_L \equiv \theta_{LM}/\theta_{KM} \tag{A.15}$$

where:

$$\alpha_2 \equiv \gamma_B^{-1} v + \pi_B \tag{A.16}$$

This is depicted by the positively sloped *KK* curve in Fig. 1.

A.2. *Long-Run Comparative Statics and Disequilibrium Dynamics*

The long-run equilibrium values of k_M and π may be found by solving (A.9) and (A.15):

$$\Delta \cdot \bar{k}_M = -(\theta_L \alpha_1 + \varepsilon \alpha_2) \tag{A.17}$$

$$\Delta \cdot \bar{\pi} = -\gamma_B^{-1} \lambda_K \alpha_1 + \lambda_L \alpha_2 \tag{A.18}$$

where:

$$\Delta \equiv \lambda_L \theta_L + \gamma_B^{-1} \lambda_K \varepsilon > 0. \tag{A.19}$$

For given values of the exogenous variables, the attainment of long-run equilibrium is brought about by the dynamic adjustment equations (9) and (10) in the text. These may be written as a matrix differential equation, where φ and ψ denote the speeds of adjustment of the capital and labour markets, respectively:

$$\begin{bmatrix} \dot{k}_M \\ \dot{\pi} \end{bmatrix} = \begin{bmatrix} -\varphi\lambda_K/\gamma_B & \varphi\theta_L \\ -\psi\lambda_L & -\psi\varepsilon \end{bmatrix} \begin{bmatrix} k_M - \bar{k}_M \\ \pi - \bar{\pi} \end{bmatrix} \tag{A.20}$$

The determinant of the coefficient matrix in (A.20) is given by $\varphi\psi\gamma_B^{-1}\Delta > 0$ and the trace equals $-\{\psi\varepsilon + \varphi\lambda_K\gamma_B^{-1}\} < 0$. Since the trace and determinant conditions are satisfied, the system is globally stable.

During the adjustment period, there are further income effects that arise as capital is reallocated from less to more productive use; see Neary (1982). These second-order effects are neglected in our analysis. Alternatively one could consider these income effects as being anticipated so that their capitalized value augments the initial disturbance as measured by α_1.

A.3. *Money Demand and the Nominal Exchange Rate*

The money-market equilibrium condition (12) may be written as follows:

$$m - p = \xi y - \delta^{-1} i \tag{A.21}$$

(Note that *i* denotes the level, not the logarithm, of the interest rate.) Using (A.2), (A.5), and (A.6), the price index given in (A.3) can be rewritten:

$$p = e + p_M^f + \beta_B \pi_B - \beta_S \pi \tag{A.22}$$

Note that with π_B constant, a change in p_M^f implies a uniform change in the foreign prices of both traded goods. Equations (A.21) and (A.22) may now be combined to obtain a relationship linking the long-run values of *e* and π, substituting for y from (A.4) and recalling that i equals i^f in long-run equilibrium:

$$\bar{e}-\beta_S\bar{\pi}+\alpha_3=0 \tag{A.23}$$

where:

$$\alpha_3\equiv\xi\theta_V v+[\xi\theta_B+(1-\xi)\beta_B]\pi_B-m-\delta^{-1}i^f+p_M^f. \tag{A.24}$$

Combining this with (A.6) and (A.18) yields an expression for the long-run value of the nominal exchange rate:

$$\bar{e}=\beta_S\Delta^{-1}(-\gamma_B^{-1}\lambda_K\alpha_1+\lambda_L\alpha_2)-\alpha_3. \tag{A.25}$$

The three channels by which the nominal exchange rate is affected by exogenous shocks, α_1, α_2 and α_3, correspond respectively to the spending, resource-movement and liquidity effects discussed in the text.

A.4. *Exchange-Rate Expectations and Saddle-Point Stability*

Writing the exchange rate in logarithmic form, the uncovered interest parity condition (13) becomes:

$$i=i^f+\dot{e} \tag{A.26}$$

When combined with (A.21) this yields a third differential equation. The dynamic system may be written as follows:

$$\begin{bmatrix}\dot{k}_M\\ \dot{p}_S\\ \dot{e}\end{bmatrix}=\begin{bmatrix}-\phi\gamma_B^{-1}\lambda_K & -\phi\theta_L & \phi\theta_L\\ \psi\lambda_L & -\psi\varepsilon & \psi\varepsilon\\ 0 & \delta\beta_S & \delta(1-\beta_S)\end{bmatrix}\begin{bmatrix}k_M-\bar{k}_M\\ p_S-\bar{p}_S\\ e-\bar{e}\end{bmatrix} \tag{A.27}$$

Denoting the coefficient matrix in (A.27) by A, we wish to solve for its characteristic roots, which are the solutions to the characteristic equation:

$$f(\mu)=|-A+\mu I|=\mu^3-a_2\mu^2+a_1\mu-a_0=0 \tag{A.28}$$

where the coefficients are defined as follows:

$$a_0=|A|=\phi\psi\delta\Delta>0 \tag{A.29}$$

$$a_1=\phi\psi\Delta-\delta[\phi\gamma_B^{-1}\lambda_K(1-\beta_S)+\psi\varepsilon] \tag{A.30}$$

$$a_2=\operatorname{tr}A=\delta(1-\beta_S)-\phi\gamma_B^{-1}\lambda_K-\psi\varepsilon \tag{A.31}$$

Since the determinant is positive the system (A.27) must have either one or three positive roots. Since the trace of A (and so the sum of the roots) may be either positive or negative, we cannot rule out the unstable configuration of all three roots positive. We focus, however, on the more interesting case where only one root is positive. This gives rise to a typical saddle-point structure: the single positive root contributes a direction of instability, but exchange-rate speculators are assumed to choose an initial value of e (and hence of π) which ensures that the model converges towards a long-run equilibrium.

In order to solve (A.27) we use a technique suggested by Dixit (1980). He shows that if the solution paths for the three variables are to lie on the stable manifold they must satisfy the following equation:

$$e(t)-\bar{e} = u_1\{k_M(t)-\bar{k}_M\}+u_2\{p_S(t)-\bar{p}_S\} \tag{A.32}$$

where u_1 and u_2 are elements of the (normalized) left characteristic vector of A corresponding to the unstable positive characteristic root. They therefore satisfy the equation:

$$[u_1 \;\; u_2 \;\; -1][-A+\bar{\mu}I] = [0 \;\; 0 \;\; 0]. \tag{A.33}$$

where $\bar{\mu}$ is the positive root of (A.28). Equation (A.33) may be solved for u_1 and u_2 in terms of $\bar{\mu}$:

$$u_1 = \frac{\psi\lambda_L u_2}{\phi\gamma_B^{-1}\lambda_K+\bar{\mu}} \tag{A.34}$$

$$u_2 = \frac{\bar{\mu}-\delta}{\bar{\mu}} \tag{A.35}$$

By evaluating (A.28) for $\bar{\mu}=\delta$ it can be established that $f(\delta)$ is positive which implies that $\delta>\bar{\mu}$. Hence (A.34) and (A.35) show that both u_1 and u_2 are negative.

These results may be used to establish conditions under which an exogenous shock causes the nominal exchange rate to overshoot its long-run value. Since the values of k_M and p_S are fixed at their initial levels, (A.32) implies that:

$$e(0)-\bar{e} = u_1(k_M^0-\bar{k}_M)+u_2(p_S^0-\bar{p}_S). \tag{A.36}$$

where $e(0)$ is the value of the exchange rate immediately following the shock. The long-run value of k_M is lowered by a resource boom and that of p_S also falls unless the spending effect is dominant. Hence, as was asserted in the text, there is a presumption that $e(0)-\bar{e}$ is negative, implying (in the case where $\bar{e}<0$) that the nominal exchange rate overshoots. However it does not appear to be possible to establish that this is necessarily the case.

Using (A.32), the system (A.27) may be reduced to a system of two differential equations in k_M and p_S:

$$\begin{bmatrix} \dot{k}_M \\ \dot{p}_S \end{bmatrix} = \begin{bmatrix} -\phi(\gamma_B^{-1}\lambda_K - \theta_L u_1) & -\phi\theta_L(1-u_2) \\ \psi(\lambda_L + \varepsilon u_1) & -\psi\varepsilon(1-u_2) \end{bmatrix} \begin{bmatrix} k_M - \bar{k}_M \\ p_S - \bar{p}_S \end{bmatrix} \tag{A.37}$$

The trace and determinant conditions are both satisfied (the determinant of the coefficient matrix equals $\phi\psi\delta\varepsilon\Delta/\bar{\mu}$). Hence convergence towards long-run equilibrium is guaranteed: the system is globally stable, with the value of e changing continually to keep the system on the stable manifold. Just as with the system (A.19), a cyclical path is possible though not inevitable.

References

Bruno, Michael & Sachs, Jeffrey: Macroeconomic adjustment with import price shocks: Real and monetary aspects. Mimeo, 1979.

Buiter, Willem H. & Miller, Marcus: Monetary policy and international competitiveness: A story of smart speculators and sticky prices, set in a world of high-speed capital movements. *Oxford Economic Papers 33*, 143–175, 1981.

Buiter, Willem H. & Purvis, Douglas D.: Oil, disinflation, and export competitiveness: A model of the 'Dutch disease'. In J. Bhandari and B. Putnam (eds.), *The international transmission of economic disturbances under flexible exchange rates*. MIT Press, forthcoming, 1982.

Calvo, Guillermo & Rodriguez, Carlos: A model of exchange rate determination under currency substitution and rational expectations. *Journal of Political Economy 85*, 617–626, 1977.

Corden, W. Max & Neary, J. Peter: Booming sector and de-industrialization in a small open economy. *Economic Journal 92*, 1982.

Dixit, Avinash: The balance of trade in a model of temporary equilibrium with rationing. *Review of Economic Studies 45*, 393–404, 1978.

Dixit, Avinash: A solution technique for rational expectations models with applications to exchange rate and interest rate determination. Mimeo, 1980.

Djajic, Slobodan: Intermediate inputs and international trade: An analysis of real and monetary effects of an oil price shock. Mimeo, 1980.

Dornbusch, Rudiger: Expectations and exchange rate dynamics. *Journal of Political Economy 84*, 1161–1176, 1976.

Kouri, Pentti: Profitability and growth in a small open economy. In A. Lindbeck (ed.), *Inflation and employment in open economies*, pp. 129–142. North-Holland, Amsterdam.

Mayer, Wolfgang: Short-run and long-run equilibrium for a small open economy. *Journal of Political Economy 82*, 955–968, 1974.

Mussa, Michael: Tariffs and the distribution of income: The importance of factor specificity, substitutability, and intensity in the short and long run. *Journal of Political Economy 82*, 1191–1204, 1974.

Mussa, Michael: Dynamic adjustment to relative price changes in the Heckscher–Ohlin–Samuelson model. *Journal of Political Economy 86*, 775–791, 1978.

Neary, J. Peter: Short-run capital specificity and the pure theory of international trade. *Economic Journal 88*, 488–510, 1978.

Neary, J. Peter: Nontraded goods and the balance of trade in a neo-Keynesian temporary equilibrium. *Quarterly Journal of Economics 94*, 403–429, 1980.

Neary, J. Peter: Wage stickiness, intersectoral factor reallocation and the case for adjustment assistance. In J. Bhagwati (ed.), *Import competition and response*, forthcoming, 1982.

Neary, J. Peter & Purvis, Douglas D.: Real adjustment and exchange-rate dynamics. National Bureau of Economic Research conference paper, 1981.

Noman, Kamran & Jones, Ronald W.: A model of trade and unemployment. In J. Green and J. Scheinkman (eds.), *General equilibrium, growth and trade: Essays in honour of Lionel McKenzie*, pp. 297–322. Academic Press. New York, 1980.

Purvis, Douglas D.: Wage responsiveness and the insulation properties of a flexible exchange rate. In A. Lindbeck (ed.) (op. cit.), pp. 225–245, 1979.

Wilson, Charles A.: Anticipated shocks and exchange rate dynamics. *Journal of Political Economy 87*, 639–647, 1979.

Comment on J. P. Neary and D. D. Purvis, "Sectoral Shocks in a Dependent Economy: Long-run Adjustment and Short-run Accomodation"

John S. Flemming

Oxford University, Oxford, England

The results of this paper are plausible enough, but I have considerable reservations as to whether the model presented is well designed to illustrate the central proposition. Moreover there are a number of problems in the structure of the model and the details of its exposition. In this comment I take these points in turn.

The authors set up a model in which there are two sorts of stickiness: a sticky price and slow reallocation of capital between sectors. There are also two sources of real disturbance: the terms of trade and the level of (nondepletable!) resource reserves. There is one nominal disturbance, the foreign price level. No explicit model of the adjustment costs or other factors accounting for either stickiness is offered, yet one and not the other is assumed to represent an inefficiency. If sticky prices imply a role for intervention why do not sticky factors?

Unfortunately the model is nowhere specified in sufficient detail for welfare comparisons to be undertaken. This is true not only at the micro level but at the macro level too. Despite the references to "a transitional loss of output and employment", the corresponding dynamic equations appear neither in the text nor the Appendix.

The main implication of having two stickinesses is that second-best arguments apply. Policies in response to the price stickiness may have perverse results in the presence of low factor mobility. It is also the case that with several possible sources of disturbances, the appropriate policy depends not on the symptom of disequilibrium but the source of the disturbance. If governments respond to symptoms rather than causes they are liable to make mistakes. What is nowhere explained is why a government should behave so stupidly when the model does not make at all plausible their failure to distinguish between the types of shock. Models can be constructed in which the information structure makes the problem discussed here real—the present one does not.

The model is highly restrictive in its stylised description of the input–output structure. The least acceptable restriction is the exclusion of capital from any role in the production of nontradeable services. These include extremely capital-intensive public utilities (electricity generation and transport) as well as housing, so that empirically it is quite probable that the tradeable goods sector is *less* capital intensive.

In Sections II and III the model is kept "real" by fixing the exchange rate exogenously. However there is also no specified demand function for money and no role for real balances in the only specified demand function (for nontradeables). Thus at this stage, the asset structure and scope for a trade deficit are both obscure.

In Section III, the rate of change of the relative price of services, $\pi = P_M/P_S$, is specified as a function of the ratio of output and demand for *services*. It is suggested that as services are unaugmented labour services, this is equivalent to a wage adjustment function where the real wage W/P_M is not derived explicitly and indeed seems highly questionable. And if output of services is demand determined, as it should be, with a horizontal marginal cost curve, how can there be a deviation between output and demand? The problem is that we seem to be presented with a less than fully worked out hybrid. Admittedly equation (A.20) and the diagrammatical exposition in the text appear to be less objectionable, but the relationship to equation (10) is obscure. It is difficult to understand why an adjustment equation for the real wage is not stated explicitly in the conventional manner.

In Section IV the exchange rate and the nominal price level are made endogenous and the price adjustment equation (12) is respecified in terms of the *nominal* price of services P_S rather than the relative price $\pi(=P_M/P_S)$ in (10). The earlier stress on the equivalence with wage stickiness makes one wonder why there is no expectational term in this equation. The authors could argue that they only consider an unexpected step change in the exchange rate and that the relevant expectations term would always be zero. However this line of defence is vulnerable at three points. First, equation (12) is not stated to be of restricted generality. Second, consistent application of the argument would point to the exclusion of $\hat{E}$ (expected exchange rate changes) from the interest arbitrage condition (13). Finally, within the framework of the model, rational labour market participants would index their contracts to the exchange rate—again the information structure required to account for this failure is unspecified.

The argumentation leading up to Fig. 4 requires the (unstated) assumption that the foreign price level is constant. Only in this case does the equilibrium for given M and Y involve equality of nominal interest rates at home and abroad.

A recurring theme in these comments has been that the model is not completely specified. Among the omissions is any discussion of savings behaviour. We have domestic demand for services and a domestic supply function for manufacturers (and for "benzine" the supply of which is fixed in the short run) but we do not have the data needed to pin down the trade balance. This is necessary to keep track of the claims of residents on the rest of the world.

The impact effect of an exchange rate change (or monetary shock) depends on the net asset position and the currency in which the net claims are denominated. The omission might make one think that such claims were excluded but that that is not the case is made clear by the significance with which the authors invest the interest arbitrage condition.

Stabilization, Allocation and the 1970s Oil Price Shocks

*John F. Helliwell**

University of British Columbia, Vancouver, B.C., Canada

Paul M. Boothe

Bank of Canada, Ottawa, Ontario, Canada

Robert N. McRae

University of Calgary, Alberta, Canada

Abstract

The stabilization and allocation effects of two types of policy adopted by Canada in the 1970s to shelter the domestic economy from the 1973–74 and 1979–80 oil shocks are analyzed in this paper. After outlining the model, estimates of the effects of alternative Canadian energy pricing strategies are presented. The stabilization and allocation effects of the relatively expansionary public spending policies in Canada during the world industrial recession after the first oil shock are compared.

I. Introduction

The aim of this paper is to analyze the stabilization and allocation effects of two types of policy adopted by Canada in the 1970s to shelter the domestic economy from the 1973–74 and 1979–80 shocks in world oil prices. Throughout the post-1973 period, the Canadian federal government operated a two-price system that kept crude oil and natural gas prices for Canadian users well below world prices. In addition, during the 1974–75 industrial recession that followed the oil price shock of 1973–74, Canadian fiscal policies were generally less restrictive than those in other industrial countries. We propose to analyze the effects of these policies on allocation, and to see to what extent there could be said to have been a tradeoff

* In preparing and revising this paper, and in building the model on which it is based, we have had exceptionally dedicated research assistance from Ardo Hansson, Michael Margolick, Tim Padmore, Reg Plummer, and Murray Smith. The main financial support for the research is from the Social Sciences and Humanities Research Council of Canada. We are also grateful for assistance with data, computing, and travel expenses from the Bank of Canada, the University of Calgary, and the University of British Columbia.

between the allocation and stabilization effects of these policies. Regional distribution effects are also especially important in the Canadian case, as has been argued elsewhere by e.g. Helliwell (1981), because low energy prices have been, until recently, the primary means for distributing some of the benefits of Alberta's oil and gas wealth to Canadians outside Alberta.[1]

In executing our plan, we proceed in stages. In Section II, we present some brief background explanation of Canadian events and policies during the 1970s. In Section III we outline the modelling framework to be used. The equation structure of the macro block of our model is reproduced in Appendix B.

In Section IV we present our model-based estimates of the allocation and stabilization effects of three alternative Canadian energy pricing strategies: world prices for crude oil and natural gas; a phased movement toward world prices; and oil and natural gas prices kept constant, in real terms, at their 1973 levels. In Section V we compare the stabilization and allocation effects of the relatively expansionary public spending policies adopted in Canada during the world industrial recession following the 1973–74 oil shock. In our concluding section we summarize our results and point out some of the implications and shortcomings of our analysis.

II. Canada in the 1970s

Canada became an increasing net exporter of energy during the early 1970s, serving mainly the increasingly import-dependent U.S. economy. Thus the initial impact of rising world oil prices was to confer a relatively small terms-of-trade gain on Canada. From 1973 to 1974, the annual energy trade surplus fell from 0.8% to 0.6% of GNP in terms of constant 1971 Canadian dollars, but increased slightly in terms of current dollars. In both current and constant dollars, the energy trade surplus has been generally declining ever since, and even at its peak the overall surplus comprised offsetting surpluses and shortages that differed sharply by fuel and region.[2]

Only in the early 1970s was Canada a net exporter of crude oil. The

---

[1] In September 1981, the governments of Alberta (the province with 85% of Canada's oil and natural gas, and 10% of the population) and Canada signed an agreement that will move Canadian oil and natural gas prices much more rapidly toward world levels, with federal and provincial taxes collecting most of the surpluses on old oil, and the world price being paid for new discoveries of conventional oil and all production of synthetic oil. Parallel agreements with British Columbia and Saskatchewan, the other main producing provinces, were reached soon after. The effects of the new agreements are analyzed in Helliwell & McRae (1982). The results presented in this paper help to show why such an agreement was so long in coming, and why its achievement has important structural and allocational consequences for the Canadian economy.

[2] An overview of the general pattern of supplies, and the policies and institutions that gave rise to them, is given in Helliwell (1979).

pattern before and since has been for offshore crude imports to Quebec and the Atlantic provinces to exceed the exports of Western Canadian crude into the U.S. mid-west market. Canada was then, and remains, a major exporter of natural gas, with about 40% of total production being exported into U.S. markets. United States coal is imported into Ontario, and western coal is exported via British Columbia, in amounts that have come to exceed imports since the mid-1970s. Each province has a fairly autonomous electricity system, with surpluses (ranging from 3% to over 10% of production at the end of the decade) exported into U.S. markets.

Energy exports and imports have each ranged about 10% of merchandise trade, or about 2% of GNP. Since Canada's energy resources are rather diversified, and net energy trade rather small, the initial effect of the first oil price shock was modest. In fact, Canada was probably more affected by the unwinding of the 1971 to 1974 boom in other commodity prices than by the direct effects of the oil price shock.

Prior to 1973, prices for domestic oil in Canada were higher than for imported oil, and the domestic producers were protected by the 1961 National Oil Policy, which gave them the equivalent of all national markets from Ontario westward. In response to consumer complaints of rising prices, the Canadian federal government froze the wellhead price of crude oil at $3.80/bbl in mid-1973. This initial situation, coupled with the subsequent inability of Alberta and Ottawa to agree on a tax system that would collect and redistribute the revenues from much higher prices, have led to subsequent Canadian prices being set by political agreement or unilateral action by one government or another.

There were two separate oil price shocks in the 1970s, and they had rather different consequences for Canada. The 1973–74 increases led to countervailing claims by the producing industry, the federal government (with substantial overall tax powers, and powers to regulate international trade, and to a lesser extent inter-regional trade) and the governments of the producing provinces (with their powers of ownership and regulation of most natural resources within the provinces). After a year or more of budgets and negotiations, the federal and provincial governments agreed on a set of tax measures and a domestic pricing package for oil and natural gas. Domestic oil prices were to rise by $2 per barrel per year towards the world price. By mid-1979, domestic prices had reached 80% of world prices, just as the second oil price shock doubled world oil prices and created additional economic rents, and potential macroeconomic disturbances.

Soon after the first oil price shock, Canadian export prices for crude oil and natural gas were moved up, by federal regulation, close to world prices. For crude oil, the difference between the domestic and export prices was collected as a federal tax; for natural gas, the difference accrued to the producing firms and provincial governments. Access to export markets is set by federal regulation. Coal prices have never been regulated, for either domestic or trade purposes, while most electricity is sold at prices set by provincial crown corporations, and regulated by public utility boards.

Canada's macroeconomic experience during the mid-1970s was unusual among the larger OECD countries, although more similar to that of some of the Scandinavian countries. For the three years 1974–76, Canadian GNP grew in real terms about 4% per annum, faster than in any of the other six of the larger OECD economies. For all of the others, real output grew less than half as fast as in the eight years 1967–73, while in Canada the 1974–76 growth was three-quarters as great as in the earlier period. Only Canada, among these countries, grew faster in the 1974–76 period than in the subsequent three years. On the other side of the coin, Canadian inflation and balance-of-payments experience during the mid-1970s was correspondingly worse than that of most other industrial countries, although the comparisons here are less clear-cut than for GDP growth. After being more-or-less (and uncharacteristically) in balance from 1970 through 1973, the Canadian current account went into a deficit that averaged 2% of GNP from 1975 through 1979.

In contrast to the larger OECD countries, but in company with several of the smaller industrial countries, Canadian output growth was sheltered from the 1974–75 recession. Since the demand was fuelled by domestic absorption (and cheap oil) rather than by exports, there was a consequentially large net inflow of capital during the years between the OPEC price shocks. What we would like to know is the extent to which these differences can be explained by Canada's lower domestic energy prices, by a relatively easy fiscal policy, and by Canada's energy trade surplus. Even more ambitiously, we would also like to compare the actual policies to some alternatives, and assess their short and longer-term effects on the allocation of resources.

III. The Framework for Analysis

We make use of a model that highlights the major linkages between the energy sector and the rest of the economy, and between the domestic economy and world markets. This relatively small scale (about twenty stochastic equations) macro model is run as part of a much larger regionally disaggregated model of Canadian energy demand, supply, cost, taxation, and revenue sharing. The integration of these models gives us an unusually good opportunity to assess allocation, stabilization, and distribution effects of energy pricing and taxation. This was, of course, our intention, as we had become convinced that most earlier macro models built by ourselves and others were not able to disentangle the links between energy and the rest of the economy, and that these linkages are likely to be as important to an understanding of the 1980s as they have been in the 1970s.

Equally fundamental to our modelling strategy is the view, which was also central to the structure of the Canadian model RDX2,[3] that the factor-based modelling of aggregate supply is crucial to a realistic understanding of the consequences of policies and disturbances. In our new modelling efforts, we enriched the production structure, relative to RDX2, to include energy, as well as capital and labour, as separate factors, and we expanded our concept of gross output accordingly.

The broad theoretical structure we employ is that of a two sector national economy. The energy sector uses capital and a resource base to produce energy. The nonenergy sector has a weakly separable production function $Q=f((K,E),L)$, wherein capital and energy are combined in a vintage CES bundle of capital-plus-energy services, which is then combined with labour in a constant-returns Cobb-Douglas function for the gross output of the nonenergy sector.[4]

Like Neary & Purvis (1982), we follow the stylized facts of the Canadian case in ignoring the operating labour requirements of the energy production sector. However, we differ from them in the treatment of the capital employed in the energy sector. They assume that the capital used in energy production is perfectly tradeable. We treat energy investment, like other domestic absorption, as using domestic and imported content to a degree that varies with relative prices (with an estimated long-term elasticity of substitution of about 1.2) and capacity utilization. Thus our framework adds an important linkage (in addition to the capital inflow and export competition) between the energy and nonenergy sectors.

We do not follow the common practice of splitting the nonenergy sector further into tradeable and non-tradeable sectors. The Canadian data and trade linkages do not encourage such a distinction, since Canadian non-energy production competes against world markets, and especially U.S. markets, at all stages of production from the mine to the retail shelf. In addition, even to the extent that it is possible to segregate industries according to their export dependence, there is no corresponding difference in energy dependence. Thus we found it natural to treat the entire production of the nonenergy sector as derived from a single aggregate production function with cyclically variable factor utilization.

---

[3] Helliwell et al. (1971).

[4] Our nonenergy sector differs from the one-sector version of Bruno's (1982) model, which bundles capital and labour separably from raw materials, $Q=f(V(K,L),N)$. If the long-term real rate of return is set exogenously by capital mobility, as in his model and our experiments reported in this paper, then the real wage is independent of the raw materials price in his framework but not independent of the energy price in ours, assuming cost minimization and a fixed supply of labour in both cases.

Our production modelling for the nonenergy sector, described more fully in Helliwell & McRae (1981), embraces three main hypotheses:

1. Actual output varies in a cyclical manner about the level indicated by measured factor inputs. Such variation, whether due to supply or demand disturbances, sets in train a whole range of accommodating and offsetting changes in prices, wages, trade flows, factor demands, and income distribution.

2. Capital and energy are more freely substitutable ex ante than ex post, with empirical evidence used to determine the extent and speed of both types of substitution.

3. Factor demands are based on expectations of profitable and sustainable output levels, with the ex ante choice of factors based on cost minimization.

These hypotheses are all testable, to a greater or lesser degree, but even to pose them forces certain restrictions on our choice of functional form and estimation method. Since we are willing to suppose that our production constraints hold exactly on average, but not on a year-to-year basis, we tend to use sample averages rather than annual observations as a basis for some parameters, while our decision to use explicit vintage modelling of energy–capital substitution also forces us to keep the functional forms explicit and as simple as possible.

Our tentative choice has been of a three-level supply structure. Final utility of spending units is assumed to be a CES function of domestic output (q, eq. 1.11) and nonenergy imports (eq. 1.12). Entrepreneurs' desired level of domestic output (eq. 1.16) adjusts actual output for expected growth, for unintended inventory changes, and for a forward-looking estimate of the relative competitiveness of domestic output and imported goods. We have found that the properties of macroeconomic models depend less on the adjustments for inventory buffering and the lagged effects of other adjustments than on whether the long-term expected value of output is affected by the shocks or policies being assessed. The factor demand equations, however, show little empirical preference for using actual output adjusted for unintended inventory changes (eq. 1.15) or its trend value. We have therefore prepared, and shall discuss, two parallel sets of results, one using the actual value of output adjusted for unintended inventory changes, and the other its trend value, in the definition of expected output used in the derivation of factor demands.

Factor demand equations for investment, employment, and energy are based on partial adjustment towards cost-minimizing levels required to produce desired output. The energy demand equation (e, eq. 1.8) is used to estimate both the long-term elasticity of substitution (0.67) between capital and energy in the CES subfunction, and the parameter measuring the annual rate at which the energy-capital proportions in the energy–capital bundle KEV become malleable. The estimated rate of 0.60 for the latter parameter is at the high end of our subjective guesses. This means that more than half of the adjustment to higher energy prices can be made in the current year, and hence that the vintage and non-vintage measures of aggregate supply have quite similar properties.

The factor demand equations all fit much better if the cost-minimizing factor levels are derived using the sample average rather than the current year's value of the real supply price of capital to business. Monetary policy thus influences investment spending (eq. 1.1) not by interest rate sensitivity of the choice of long-run capital intensity, but by the use of Tobin's q (the ratio of the share market value to the replacement value of the business capital stock) as a determinant of the current rate of investment spending.

The output decision (q, eq. 1.11) is determined primarily by the factor-based synthetic supply measure, but is affected also by costs of production relative to the output price, abnormal changes in final sales, and deviations of inventory stocks from their target levels. This equation can equally well be interpreted as an equation for the change in inventories, since the change in inventories (eq. 1.13) is determined by the identity linking output and final sales.

Aside from investment spending (defined to include housing investment), the key elements of demand are consumption (c, eq. 2.1), non-energy exports (eq. 2.2) and government spending, with the latter treated as exogenous in real terms. Consumption is determined by a life-cycle model based on real disposable income and the market value of national wealth (not including, in our current version, the expected value of economic rents from energy resources). Government spending has both multiplier and crowding-out effects on consumption spending. The crowding-out effects appear through interest rate effects on the market value of wealth and through the impact of the utilization rate on wages and prices, to be described below.

Export demand depends primarily on foreign income and relative prices, with the export price (eq. 3.3) determined by world trade prices, the exchange rate, and the price of domestic output.

Turning to the wage–price block, the current rate of increase in average annual earnings (eq. 3.1) depends on the rate of increase in the absorption price, the change in the terms of trade, changes in the rate of capacity utilization, the ratio of the "natural"—using the series of Fortin & Newton (1981)—to the actual unemployment rate, the lagged change in wages, and separate dummy variables for each of the three years of Canada's 1976–78 system of wage and price controls. The three main equations of the wage–price block are jointly estimated by iterative three-stage least squares, with some key theoretical constraints imposed on the coefficients. The appendix shows the coefficients and the F-test on the imposed (but easily accepted) restriction on the wage equation that the coefficients on the absorption price change and on the lagged wage change should sum to 1.0. The equation suggests that a change in the terms of trade has a long-term effect of 0.26, about equal to the share of exports in GNP. Since the dynamics of this response are the same as those for the absorption price (almost two-thirds in the current year), this suggests that national real income gains or losses from changes in the terms of trade are translated fairly rapidly into corresponding changes in real wages.

The effects of unemployment and capacity utilization are also strong. In 1974, when the "natural" and actual unemployment rates were both just over 5%, a one percentage point reduction in the unemployment rate would directly increase the rate of wage inflation by 0.5% in the first year, with additional effects acting through induced changes in price expectations. A 1% increase in the level of gross output, relative to the level based on normal utilization in the vintage production function (eq. 1.17), has a 0.2% direct first-year impact on the rate of wage inflation.

As one would expect from our aggregation of tradeable and nontradeable output, the rate of inflation of the price of gross output (eq. 3.2) is determined by domestic cost changes (wages, energy prices, and interest rates), prices of competing foreign goods, and the extent to which the stock of inventories is above or below its normal value. The coefficients on the cost and foreign price variables are constrained to sum to 1.0, and the constraint is easily accepted by the data. The relatively small (0.04) but statistically important coefficient on the proportionate change in the interest rate shows the cost-increasing effect of higher nominal interest rates.

The inventory disequilibrium term has a theoretically and empirically important role in a model in which production is determined by the production function (augmented by factors influencing the desired rate of capacity utilization), and final sales are separately modelled as the result of spending decisions by domestic and foreign households and firms. The rate of capacity utilization provides one set of equilibrating forces through its influence on wages, imports, and factor demands, but the additional appearance of the inventory stock disequilibrium term in the output price equation assures that prices will continue to move until inventory stock and production flow equilibria are both regained. The role of the inventory stock term in the price equations is especially important in models, like ours, where the inventory stock disequilibrium term has a relatively small estimated direct impact on the production decision. The inventory term in the output price equation is strong, with a 10% stock discrepancy changing the annual rate of inflation by 1.4%, before accounting for any of the wage–price–wage feedbacks.

The final price equation, that for domestic absorption ($c+i+g$), is an estimated approximation to the identity that defines the prices of final spending in terms of the prices of its domestic and foreign content. The two driving variables are the rates of increase in the price of gross domestic output (which, of course, includes the effects of energy prices) and of non-energy imports of goods and services. The equation is forced to hold contemporaneously with coefficients constrained to sum to 1.0. The constraint is statistically rejected (the unconstrained sum is 0.87), but, given the definitional nature of the equation, we impose it anyway.

Another important feature of our model is the endogenous distinction between gross domestic product (q, eq. 1.11 is our closest approximation to GDP) and gross national income or product (eq. 3.6). Gross domestic product is the output of factors employed in Canada, while gross national product is the product of Canadian-owned factors wherever they are employed. The main difference between the two, in the Canadian case, is the income attributable to foreign-owned capital employed in Canada, since almost half of the business capital stock is owned abroad.

Expansionary domestic policies typically lead, with unchanged exchange rates, to trade account deficits. If capital is fairly easily mobile, small interest rate changes will bring in a matching capital inflow. If this situation is maintained, the mounting indebtedness will lead to increasing debt service payments and to GNP falling progressively far below GDP. To show this effect most clearly, the results reported in this paper employ the small open economy (SOE) assumption about capital mobility. This means that interest rates are effectively determined in the world economy, so that interest-rate and stock-market valuation effects can be ignored in our analysis of alternative energy-pricing and government spending policies. Our estimated equation (4.4) for the net foreign demand for Canadian assets implies a high enough interest elasticity that our current suppression of monetary policy and exchange-rate reaction functions is not likely to cause very large problems. Implicitly, what we are doing is to suppose that, for the given oil pricing and government spending policies, the accompanying monetary policy is to adjust the domestic interest rate sufficiently to finance the current account deficit at an unchanged exchange rate. The empirical SOE assumption is then that this policy leads to small enough changes in interest rates that their effects on domestic spending and prices can be ignored. We shall flag any results that suggest a large enough change in foreign indebtedness to imperil our SOE assumption.

The links between the macro block and the energy sectors are complex and highly simultaneous. Total energy expenditure is divided among fuels according to their relative prices, while the supply of oil and natural gas, and the rate of oil and gas investment, are determined chiefly by the relation between the wellhead prices, net of taxes and royalties, and marginal costs, which depend in turn on remaining geological potential and on the price of national output. In general, energy export prices and quantities

Table 1. *Economic rents to end-1980 from Canadian crude oil and natural gas (cumulated and reported in billion end-1980 dollars)*

	Total rents	Oil and gas industry	Users	(Waste)	Federal govern-ment	Provin-cial govern-ments	Canadian rents
Actual	117.2	− 0.3	50.0	(14.2)	− 3.0	63.0	105.4
Effects of world prices, relative to actual	+10.5	+14.8	−47.1	(−13.3)	+17.3	+23.4	− 2.1
Effects of constant real prices, relative to actual	−21.5	−12.4	+41.8	(+50.1)	−31.7	−18.6	−12.0

Note: The first row contains actual economic rents from 1950 through 1980, brought forward at a 7% real rate of interest. The other rows are differences from the actual, for pricing policies that differed from the actual over the 1974–80 period. All rents are computed using world prices as the opportunity values. The total rents in the first column are the sum of the industry, user, federal, and provincial rents shown, plus rents received by U.S. purchasers of Canadian natural gas. Total Canadian rents, shown in the right hand column, are the sum of user, federal, and provincial rents, plus the Canadian-owned share of oil and gas industry rents. The user rents shown are the areas under the compensated energy demand curves, between the simulated and world prices. They are thus net of the dead-weight losses noted as "waste". The details of the rent calculations are described more fully in Helliwell (1981).

are set exogenously, but in our world price cases we increase exports of natural gas and crude oil to make cumulative 1974–80 production about what it actually was.

The overall energy price index *Pe* is an endogenously weighted price index for total energy which therefore will rise more slowly than a fixed-weight index to the extent that users substitute against higher priced fuels. The economic rents reported in Table 1 relate only to crude oil and natural gas, and show cumulated rents from the 1950s (when the western Canadian petroleum industry became important) to the end of 1980. The total figures are the cumulative producers' and consumers' surpluses cumulated forward at a 7% real rate of interest. The figures noted under ("waste") are the dead-weight losses on the consumer side from pricing oil and natural gas for domestic use at less than their opportunity values.

IV. Effects of Oil Price Shocks

The best way of assessing the effects of the Canadian policy of gradual increases in domestic prices of oil and natural gas is to set up a control solution based on the actual prices, and to run the model again under the alternative policies.

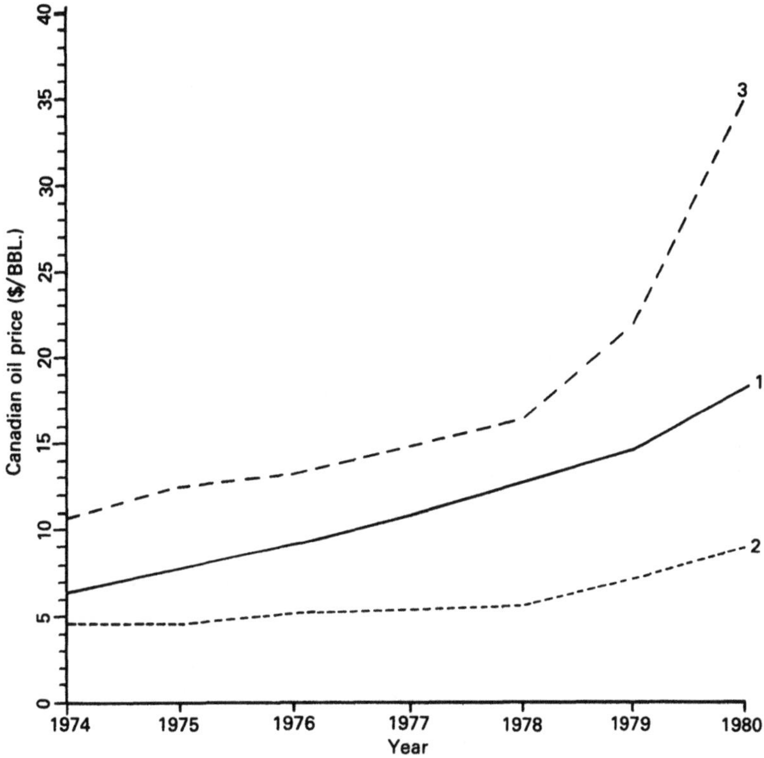

Fig. 1. Alternative Canadian crude oil prices. 1=historic price, 2=constant real price, 3=world price.

The two alternative policies are, on the one hand, to peg Canadian oil and natural gas prices at world levels, and, at the other extreme, to hold them constant, in real terms, at their pre-OPEC levels. Fig. 1 shows the actual Canadian crude oil prices 1974 to 1980 along with the ones used in our two policy alternatives. Figures 2 and 3 show the rates of real GNP growth and inflation corresponding to the three pricing cases. These results are from the version of the model with expected future output varying in response to changes in actual output. In the next section, we show for comparison some results in which expected future output (which is used to drive the factor demand equations) is set by a trend, and is hence unaffected by policy changes.

The actual pricing policy reduced the stagflationary effects of the OPEC oil price shocks. In 1976, for example, the domestic absorption price would have been 5% higher, and real GNP more than 2% lower, according to Figures 2 and 3, if Canada had adopted world-level energy prices after 1973. In the alternative version of the model, with expected output unchanged, the 1976 absorption price is 5% higher and real GNP 1.5% lower with

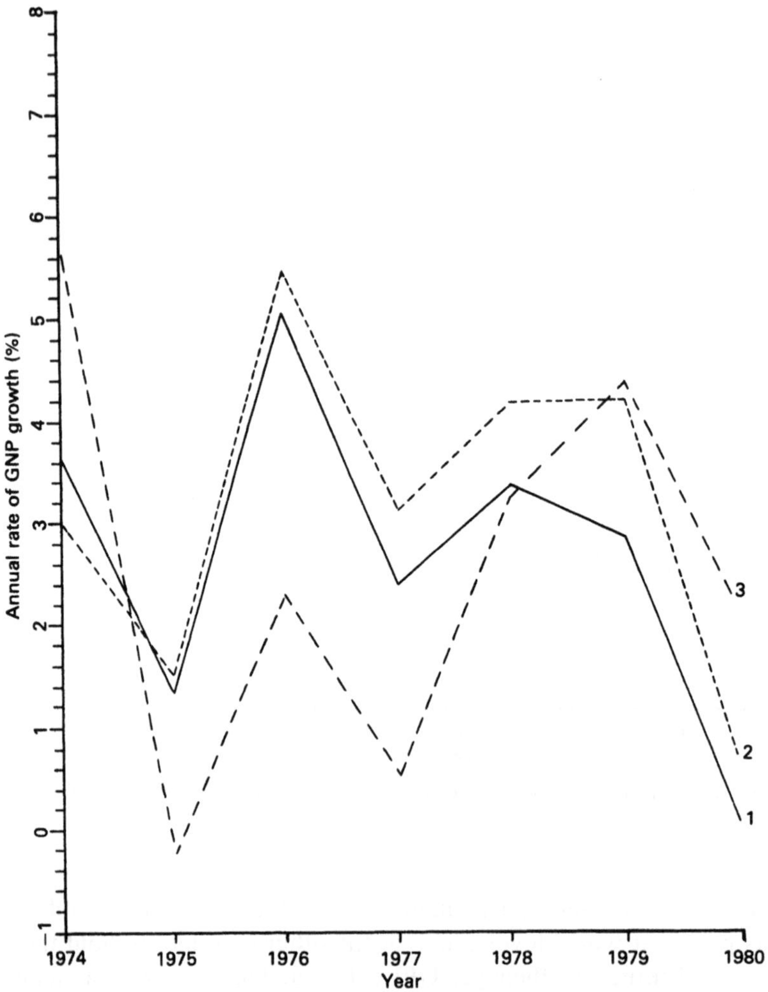

Fig. 2. Effect of oil pricing policies on real GNP growth. 1=historic price, 2=constant real price, 3=world price.

world oil prices than with the actual prices. A policy of constant real domestic energy prices would have led to lower inflation, to some extra output, but to little extra GNP, since much of the additional output would have been based on imported energy financed by foreign capital, thus driving an increasing wedge between domestic output and national income.

The longer term consequences of the alternative energy pricing strategies can be seen most vividly by examining their implications for energy use, and for the balance of trade and payments. In the constant-price case, energy use in 1980 would have been 50% higher than actual, while in the world price case it would have been 20% lower than actual. The annual

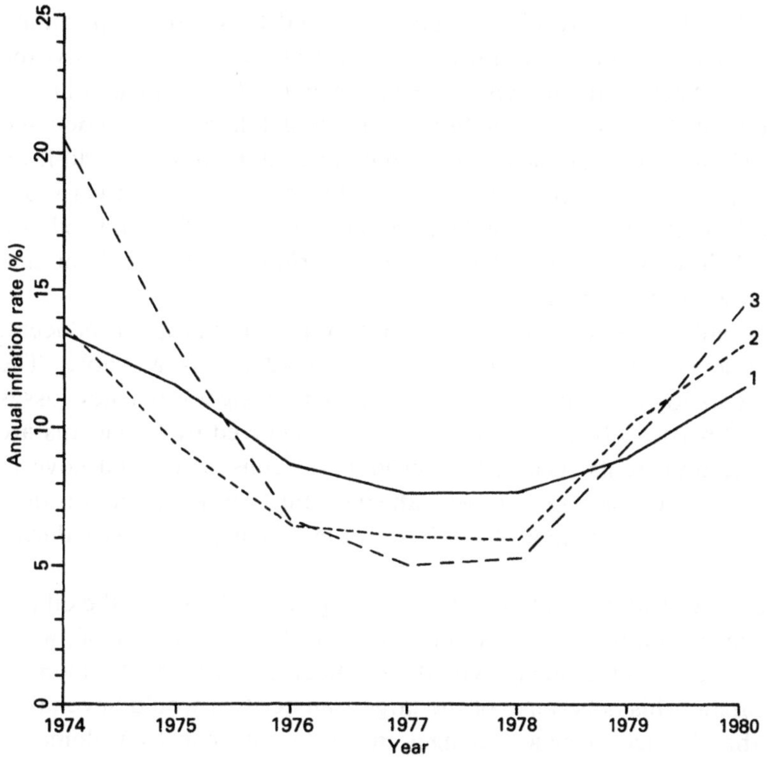

Fig. 3. Effect of oil pricing policies on inflation. 1=historic price, 2=constant real price, 3=world price.

balance of energy trade in 1980, which was about +\$2 billion with the actual energy prices, would have been +\$6 billion with world energy prices and −\$7 billion at constant energy prices. The overall balance on current account would have been −\$8 billion by 1980, and net foreign indebtedness at the end of 1980 would have been reduced by almost \$40 billion (or 20%) relative to its actual value if world oil prices had been adopted for domestic use throughout the 1970s, or increased by almost \$30 billion if domestic energy prices had been held constant, in real terms, at their 1973 levels.

The wage–price block includes strong links from the unemployment rate to wage inflation, and from inventory disequilibrium to price inflation. Thus the higher unemployment rate (up by 3% in 1978) and the drop in final demand (with a consequent build-up of inventories relative to desired levels) have strong effects in reversing the inflation caused by higher oil prices.

It is possible, using the detailed energy supply and demand structure, to compute the efficiency and distribution effects of alternative energy pricing strategies. In all cases, world oil prices are used to set the opportunity values for domestic oil and natural gas. Table 1 shows in the first row the present value of net economic rents received from crude oil and natural gas, up to the end of 1980, measured in billion end-1980 dollars. The second and third rows show how much these rents would have differed had world-level or constant prices been used for the pricing of Canadian oil and gas for use in Canada. Export prices for oil and gas, and import prices for crude oil, are all kept at their actual values, which were at world levels for crude oil and slightly below for natural gas.

The economic rents are reported separately for oil and gas producers, users, two levels of government, and for Canadians as a whole. The economic rents to energy users are net of the dead-weight efficiency losses reported as "waste". Note that the total rents received by Canadians are less than the total rents received by producers, consumers, and governments. This is because most of the industry rents accrue to nonresident shareholders, who owned more than 70% of the oil and gas industry during the 1970s.

If world prices had been adopted for oil and gas, total rents to the oil and gas resources would have been $10 billion higher by the end of 1980, while accumulated rents to Canadians would have been lower by $2.1 billion, or $900 per capita. This is because of the large transfer that would have taken place, in the absence of major changes in the tax system, from domestic energy users to foreign-owned producing firms. On the other hand, if Canadian oil and gas prices had been held constant at their 1973 levels, total rents to the resource would have been lower than actual by $21 billion and total rents to Canadians would have been reduced by $12 billion, or $500 per capita. The reason for this asymmetry is that most of the additional oil used with constant prices would have been imported, with the subsidy to refiners of imported oil being paid by taxpayers rather than by the producing firms.

With unchanged taxes and royalties, the typical Canadian was better off, after accounting for energy waste, but before accounting for stabilization and long-term allocation effects, with the actual pricing policy than with either a world price policy or a constant-price policy. Note, however, that the world price policy would have given much higher net benefits, over the 1973–80 period, than the constant-price policy.

Combining the evidence from Table 1 with that from the earlier analysis of inflation and real GNP growth, it appears that Canadians obtained at least short-term gains from the phased adjustment of domestic oil prices towards world levels. It is apparent, however, that the economic rent gains had a substantial efficiency cost, and could have been much larger and less costly had higher prices been combined with higher taxes, thus permitting more efficient use of energy. From the long-term allocation perspective, the speed with which energy prices are adjusted is less important than whether the adjustment takes place, and whether the chosen policy is sustainable. It is clear from the simulation results that a constant-price policy would not have been sustainable for long even if the world oil prices had not taken off for a second time in 1979–80. Similarly, the actual pricing policy, which was approaching a sustainable relation to world prices in 1978, was rendered unsustainable by the 1979–80 oil price increases. Given the complicated Canadian political structure, it is perhaps not surprising that it took two years to work out a new agreed price policy that would move domestic prices fairly rapidly towards world levels, in conjunction with several new federal taxes to provide an alternative mechanism for distributing economic rents from oil and natural gas to Canadians living outside Alberta.

Even if the tax and royalty system had been more flexible, the stagflationary effects of higher energy prices would have provided some incentive to delay the domestic price adjustments. Once again, it is necessary to distinguish the short-term and long-term effects of the pricing alternatives. The current version of the macro model suggests that moving immediately to world prices for oil and natural gas would have worsened the stagflation of the latter half of the 1970s, relative to a policy of phased adjustment.

V. Using Government Expenditures to Cushion the 1974 Oil Shock

To what extent did government expenditure policy offset or increase the Canadian stagflation of the late 1970s? To what extent could fiscal policy have been used to offset the stagflationary effects of even higher oil prices, had the Canadian prices been adjusted more rapidly to world levels? These are deep questions, to which the evidence from empirical macro models can provide only a partial answer. We shall focus primarily on the first question, by comparing the actual expenditure policy with a more restrictive policy based on average experience in other OECD countries.

The OECD (1976) reported that GDP or GNP growth in the seven larger OECD economies was −0.3% in 1974 and −1.5% in 1975. For Canada, the actual GNP growth was +3.6% in 1974 and +1.2% in 1975. The OECD (1976, p. 18) calculated that relatively expansionary public expenditure in Canada was an important factor in the different Canadian experience, contributing directly 1.7% and 1.1% to real GNP growth in 1974 and 1975, compared to 0.3% and 0.7% for the seven countries as a group. We approximated this differential growth of public expenditure by running a shock solution with real government spending cut by 1 billion 1971 $ in 1974, $1.5 billion in 1975, $1 billion in 1976, $0.5 billion in 1977, $0.25 billion in 1978 and returning to the control expenditure path in 1979. We are therefore assessing the effects of a presumed stabilization policy, and not of a continued change in the level of public spending. In 1974, a cut of $1

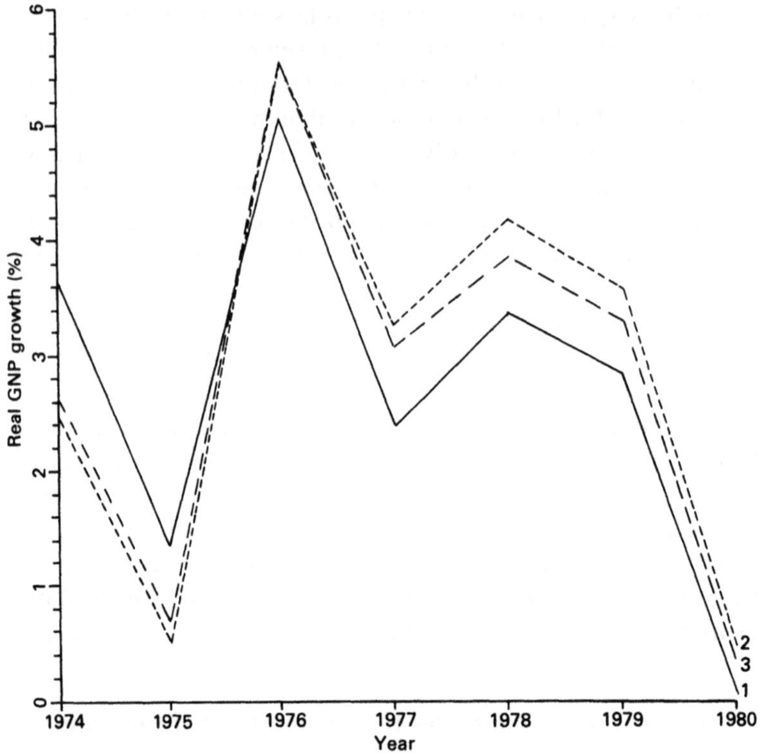

Fig. 4. Effect of government expenditure decrease on real GNP growth. 1=real GNP growth–control, 2=real GNP growth (with actual value of aggregate demand)–shock, 3=real GNP growth (with trend value of aggregate demand)–shock.

billion 1971 $ would have been 0.9% of GNP in that year, and would have made real government spending in 1974 equal to what it was in 1973.

The results of the experiment are shown in Figure 4 under two different assumptions about the impact of the fiscal policy on long-term expected output. The results in curve 2, with long-term expected output varying under the shock, indicate that the level of real GNP in Canada would have been 1.1% lower in 1974 and 2% lower in 1975 if Canada had adopted public expenditure growth policies similar to those in the other large countries. With long-term expected output invariant to the fiscal policy, as shown in curve 3 of Figure 4, the output effects of the spending policy are about one-quarter less in the first two years, and are cut more in later years. This can be seen more clearly if one assesses the effects of a sustained change in government spending. Such a simulation shows that the GNP effects of the spending change in the third and subsequent years are half as large if long-term expected output does not vary under the fiscal change.

What can be said about the longer-term effects of the counter-cyclical government spending policy of 1974–75? If we are correct in assuming that the policy was in fact a purely cyclical one, and if government spending returned to the long-term path that it would have taken without the policy, then our results suggest that the actual policy followed, relative to the OECD-average policy, increased output and employment by about 2% in 1975, with smaller and eventually reversed effects thereafter. The increases in real national income are initially of the same size as the changes in output, but become progressively more negative as debt service payments build up on the additional foreign indebtedness required to finance the expansionary policy. By the end of 1980, net foreign indebtedness is higher by about $11 billion, or 4% of GDP, meaning that about one-quarter of 1% of domestic output was being used to service the additional foreign debt (with a real cost of foreign borrowing of approximately 6%).

In broad terms, the effect of the actual fiscal policy relative to the more restrictive alternative was to make the 1975 drop in GNP growth smaller than it otherwise would have been, with some offsetting subsequent changes. It may also be useful to assess the effects of the expenditure policy over a longer horizon, and to illustrate the implied tradeoff between output and inflation. Figure 5 traces out the dynamic path of changes in the unemployment rate and the inflation rate in response to the temporarily reduced level of government spending. There is in most years a "contemporaneous tradeoff" between the inflation rate and the unemployment rate, in the sense that increases in the unemployment rate are associated with reductions in the inflation rate, although the dynamics are broadly those of a "Phillips circle" with the tradeoff curve shifting outward in years 3 to 8. There are several important non-linearities in the model, so the results can depend on the initial rates of inflation and unemployment, as well as on the size and sign of the fiscal shock. Figure 5 shows the effects of an expenditure cut, so the dynamic path goes counterclockwise, returning towards the original position at the end of the 13-year dynamic simulation. The results from the alternative version with expected output set equal to its trend value show much less change in inflation and unemployment, and no circular dynamics, with the year-by-year effects moving back and forth on a more-or-less unchanged "tradeoff" line.

We have not attempted to develop a hypothetical fiscal strategy that could have been used to dampen the cyclical effects that would have accompanied a much more rapid move toward world energy prices in the 1970s. This would have suggested more assurance than we have in the dynamic responses of a particular version of a particular model of the Canadian economy. The broad nature of our results is that of a fairly cyclical response to real shocks, whether they take the form of unexpected changes in government spending or of the terms of trade between the energy-producing and energy-using sectors of the economy. We have some

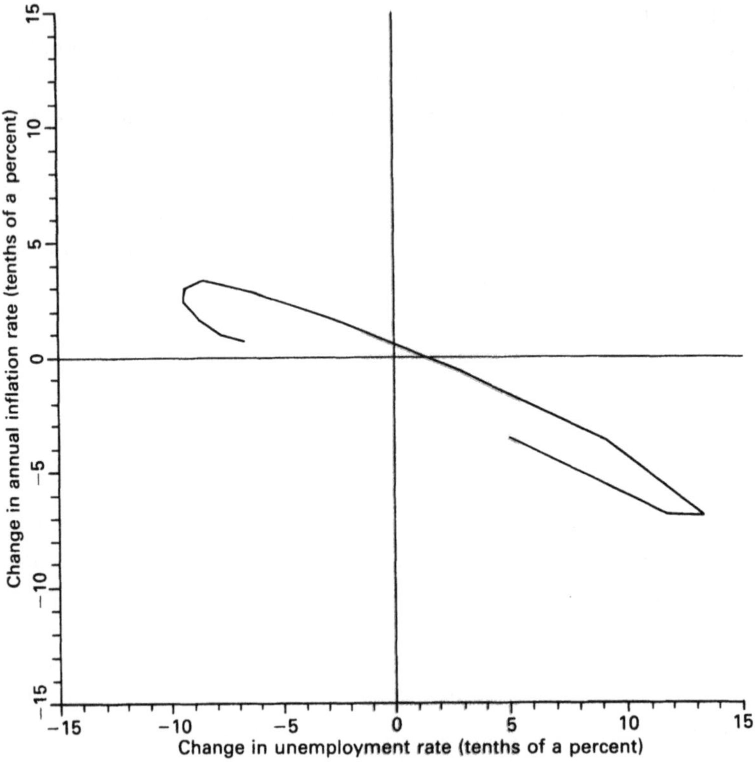

Fig. 5. Inflation and unemployment effects of a temporary cut in government spending.

evidence that the nature of these responses is affected rather importantly by the nature of expectations about future output, and by alternative specifications of the wage–price sector. The empirical evidence does not always provide strong grounds for choosing among these alternative specifications, so that our estimates of dynamic responses must be treated with some caution.

However, we can say that with most of the model alternatives we have tested the government expenditure policy followed by Canada in the 1974–76 period provided some temporary reduction in the domestic effects of the world stagflation, being partly responsible for Canada's relatively high GNP growth in 1974 and 1975, and relatively slower growth later in the decade, in comparison with the other major OECD countries.

The relatively unattractive tradeoff between extra growth and extra inflation in 1974–75 was in large measure due to the fact that the actual unemployment was at its estimated "natural" value in 1974. We have further tested the model by applying a similarly sized fiscal expansion in an environment with a much higher initial unemployment rate (almost twice its "natural" rate) and found that the peak reduction in the unemployment rate was almost 4%, compared to 1.5% in Figure 5. In addition, the temporary fiscal expansion left employment and output permanently higher (by over 1%), by generating new capital to combine with the unemployed labour on a continuing basis. In 1974, however, the labour market was fully enough stretched that the extra demand was crowded out, and left no lasting residue of increased potential output. This suggests that if higher energy prices had created a large pool of unemployed resources it would have been possible to design a fiscal policy to sustain aggregate demand and employment without inducing much further inflation.

VI. Conclusions

We have presented some preliminary results on the short-term and longer-term effects of Canadian stabilization policies related to the 1970s world oil price shocks. We assessed two main types of policy response: the gradual adjustment of domestic oil and natural gas prices toward world levels, and the adoption of a relatively expansionary public spending policy during the 1974–75 world industrial recession. The actual pricing policies were assessed relative to a world price policy and a constant real price policy, with primary attention paid to the five years between the two world oil price shocks. Estimates were made of the dead-weight efficiency losses and gains as well as of the macroeconomic effects. The policy of gradual price adjustment was seen to produce some stabilization gains, in terms of having less stagflation than in the world price case. From a Canadian national point of view, the moderated price increases provided, in the absence of tax changes that might not have been as acceptable to the producing provinces, a means of redistributing the rents within Canada, and for restricting the size of the windfall to foreign shareholders of the producing firms. Thus the Canadian rents per capita were higher in the historic pricing case than in the world price case, even after allowing for the dead-weight efficiency losses on both production and consumption.

The 1974–75 expansionary fiscal policy was estimated to have been responsible for about one-third of the difference between the Canadian and the average GNP growth rate for the seven larger OECD economies, with the 1976 price level being about 1.5% higher as a consequence. By the end of the decade, the residual effects of the policy were negative, with gross output slightly down, and GNP down further because of $500 million in service payments on the additional foreign debt.

Although the model we have used has been designed especially for analyzing in an integrated way the short-term and long-term effects of energy pricing and other stabilization policies, there are important qualifications to be made. Most of these apply to all assessments of the effects of policies. For one thing, we are still using a preliminary version of the model. It is possible, for example, that the perfect capital mobility assumption used may have suppressed some potentially important feedbacks operating through the domestic financial sector. Second, it is always important to remember, especially when assessing the effects of energy pricing policies, that the alternative policies may have different implications for the long-term efficiency of energy use. For example, the stabilization benefits of gradual adjustment of energy prices are felt immediately, while the longer-term allocation costs continue as long as the domestic price levels remain different from world levels.

Finally, we have shown by our use of two alternative versions of our model that, especially for an open economy with relatively easy access to world markets for capital, the output effects and, to a lesser extent, the real GNP effects, of stabilization policies depend heavily on the way in which producers form their expectations about the long-term level of domestic output. The empirical evidence available from factor demand equations does not allow us to distinguish the two cases very clearly, and yet the longer term consequences of stabilization policy, as depicted by the model, depend importantly on the expectational assumptions made. This is not, we emphasize, a distinction between a demand-determined and a supply-determined system, as both versions of the model constrain output, over the medium term, to what can be produced, at normal factor productivity, from the available capital, labour, and energy. In principle, and in practice, there are a number of feasible growth paths for an open economy. What is less clear is the extent to which alternative stabilization policies influence private expectations about future output. We have shown that making the long-term level of expected output invariant to policy changes substantially reduces even the short-term effects of policy changes. This tells us that the issue is important, but does not in itself help to decide which is the most relevant set of results to use in assessing the effects of stabilization policies. The most important conclusion may be that any estimates are subject to considerable uncertainty, with the amount of uncertainty increasing with the length of the assessment horizon.

Appendix A. List of Variables

Conventions

* denotes desired value, e.g., k^*_{ib}

~ denotes quantity given by a CES bundle, e.g., $\tilde{k}_e$

– denotes a two-period average, e.g., $\bar{k}_{ne} = \frac{1}{2}(k_{ne} + k_{ne-1})$

$-t$ denotes a lag of t years, e.g., q_{-1}

ˆ denotes equilibrium value at full capacity utilization after lags are worked out, e.g., $\hat{m}_{ne}$

· denotes one-period proportionate change in one period, e.g., $\dot{p}_a = (p_a - p_{a-1})/p_{a-1}$

Variable	Equation no.	Description
a	2.3	Real absorption, billion 1971 $
B	4.6	The balance of trade, billion $
B_e	4.9	The balance of trade in energy, billion $
c	2.1	Personal consumption expenditures, billion 1971 $
C_{ca}	Exogenous	Capital consumption allowance, billion $
c_q	1.10	Average unit costs of producing GDP
e	1.8	Energy expenditure, billion 1971 $
e_v	1.4	Vintage-based energy requirement, billion 1971 $
f_i	4.1	Net capital inflows excluding official monetary movements, billion $
F_{ireva}	4.7	Retained earnings and revaluation on foreign held domestic assets, billion $
F_{xo}	4.2	Official purchases of foreign exchange, billion U.S. $
g	Exogenous	Real government current and capital expenditures on goods and services, billion 1971 $
G_{misc}	Exogenous	Balancing item to link government National Accounts Balances to changes in government money and debt outstanding, including government transfers, billion $
G_{fsubo}	Link	Federal government subsidies to oil producers, million $
H	5.4	High powered money, billion $
i_e	Link	Energy investment, billion 1971 $
i_{ib}	1.13	Value of physical change in non-farm inventories, billion 1971 $
i_{ne}	1.1	Business fixed investment (excluding energy investment), billion 1971 $
i_{new}	1.3	Re-investment with energy use malleable in the current year, billion 1971 $
$\tilde{k}_{ev}$	1.3	Vintage measure of capital and energy, billion 1971 $
k_{ib}	1.14	Stock of non-farm inventories, billion 1971 $
k_{ne}	1.2	Business fixed capital stock (excluding energy), billion 1971 $

L_b	5.3	Net stock of government non-monetary liabilities, billion $
L_f	4.4	Net liabilities to non-residents (excluding official reserves), billion $
M_{car2}	Exogenous	Imports of cars from U.S., billion $
m_e	Link	Canadian imports of energy fuels, billion 1971 $
M_{id}	4.5	Interest and dividend payments to foreigners, billion $
m_{ne}	1.12	Imports of goods and services (excluding energy), billion 1971 $
N_e	1.6	Total employed (excluding armed forces), millions of persons
N_l	1.5	Total civilian labour force, millions of persons
N_p	Exogenous	Average population in each period, millions of persons
p_a	3.4	Implicit price of absorption, 1971=1.0
p_e	Link	Price of primary energy, 1971=1.0
p_{fx}	4.3	Spot price of foreign exchange, $CDN per $ U.S.
p_{me}	Link	Price index for imported energy, 1971=1.0
p_{mne}	3.5	Price of imports of goods and services (excluding energy), 1971=1.0
p_{mw}	Exogenous	Index of world price of Canadian imports (excluding energy), $p_{mw}=p_{mne}/p_{fx}$
p_q	3.2	Implicit price for gross domestic output, including imported energy, 1971=1.0
p_w	Exogenous	OECD real output deflator, 1971=1.0
p_{wxg}	Exogenous	Price index of world exports of goods, 1971=1.0
p_{xe}	Link	Price of energy exports, 1971=1.0
p_{xne}	3.3	Price of exports of goods and services (excluding energy), 1971=1.0
q	1.11	Real Gross Domestic Output plus energy at factor cost, billion 1971 $
q_a	1.15	Aggregate demand (output less unintended inventory accumulation), billion 1971 $
q^*	1.16	Desired level of profitable future output for investment demand, billion 1971 $
q_l^*	1.19	Desired level of profitable future output for labour demand, billion 1971 $
q_s	1.9	Synthetic supply variable, billion 1971 $
q_{sv}	1.17	Vintage-based synthetic supply, billion 1971 $
r_d	Exogenous	Ratio of Canadian bonds held by foreigners to total net liabilities to foreigners
r_{lf}	Exogenous	Fraction of population of labour force age

r_l	5.7	Average yield on Government of Canada bonds, 10 years and over, percent. Exogenous for SOE
r_{nat}	Exogenous	Natural rate of unemployment, percent
r_{nu}	1.7	Unemployment rate, percent
r_{part}	Exogenous	Participation rate in labour force
r_s	5.5	Average yield on Government of Canada bonds, 1–3 years, percent. Exogenous for SOE
r_{tb2}	Exogenous	Yield on 91-day U.S. Treasury bills converted to Canadian equivalence, percent
r_{tp}	Exogenous	Total personal income tax rate
r_{ti}	Exogenous	Indirect tax rate
r_{vb}	2.4	Proportion of business capital stock owned by foreigners
t		Time, 1900=0
T_d	5.2	Total direct taxes on corporations and persons, billion $
T_i	5.1	Indirect taxes less subsidies, billion $
V	Exogenous	Market value of private sector wealth, billion $
V_{kb}	Exogenous	Market value of year-end stock of business fixed capital and inventories in Canada, billion $
W	3.1	Wage rate, thousands of dollars per year per employed person
X_{car2}	Exogenous	Exports of cars to U.S., billion $
x_e	Link	Exports of primary energy, billion 1971 $
X_{id}	Exogenous	Interest and dividend receipts from nonresidents, billion $
x_{ne}	2.2	Exports of goods and services (excluding energy), billion 1971 $
X_{tr}	Exogenous	Net Transfers plus miscellaneous other items required to satisfy the Balance of Payments identity, billion $
y	3.6	Real gross national product, billion 1971 $
Y	3.7	Nominal gross national product, billion $
y_w	Exogenous	Real output in major OECD economies, billion 1975 U.S. $
δ_1	Exogenous	Annual rate at which energy/capital proportions become malleable in k_{ev}
δ_2	Exogenous	Depreciation rate. We set δ_2=0.05
Π	Exogenous	Labour productivity index for Harrod-neutral technical progress in Cobb-Douglas function for q
ϱ_r	Exogenous	Real supply price of capital, percent. We take ϱ_r=7.0

Appendix B. MACE Model Structure

1. *Supply and Factor Demands*

Fixed business investment:

$$i_{ne}/\bar{k}_{ne} = \underset{(3.70)}{0.38258}\, i_{ne-1}/\bar{k}_{ne-1} + \underset{(6.96)}{0.052500}\, (k^* - \bar{k}_{ne})/\bar{k}_{ne}$$

$$-\underset{(5.87)}{0.079159}\, c_q + \underset{(7.42)}{0.12167} \qquad (1.1)$$

2SLS 1954–1980: s.e.e.=0.00296; $\bar{R}^2$=0.823; Durbin-h=1.11

where

$$k^* = \frac{q^*}{3.5196}\left[\beta + \gamma^\sigma\left(\beta\frac{p_e}{p_k}\right)^{1-\sigma}\right]^{\sigma/1-\sigma}\left[\frac{\alpha W/\Pi}{(1-\alpha)\,(\beta^\sigma p_k{}^{1-\sigma} + \gamma^\sigma p_e{}^{1-\sigma})^{1/1-\sigma}}\right]^{1-\alpha}$$

is the desired long term level of capital and $p_k=(\delta_2+0.01\varrho_r)p_a$ is the price of capital services.

Business fixed capital stock:

$$k_{ne} = (1-\delta_2)\, k_{ne-1} + i_{ne} \qquad (1.2)$$

Vintage bundle of capital and energy ("energized capital"):

$$\bar{k}_{ev} = (1-\delta_1)\,\bar{k}_{ev-1} + i_{new}\left[\beta + \gamma\left(\frac{\gamma p_k}{\beta p_e}\right)^{\sigma-1}\right]^{(\sigma/\sigma-1)} \qquad (1.3)$$

where

$$i_{new} = i_{ne} + (\delta_1 - \delta_2)\, k_{ne-1}$$

is re-investment with energy use malleable in the current year.

Vintage-based energy requirement:

$$e_v = (1-\delta_1)\, e_{v-1} + \left(\frac{\gamma p_k}{\beta p_e}\right)^\sigma i_{new} \qquad (1.4)$$

Labour force:

$$N_l = r_{lf} r_{part} N_p \quad \text{(currently exogenous)} \qquad (1.5)$$

Employment:

$$N_e = \underset{(84.76)}{0.82100}\, N_{e-1} + \underset{(18.48)}{0.17900}\left(\frac{q_l^* \bar{k}_{ev}^{-\alpha}}{4.5336}\right)^{/(1-\alpha)} \qquad (1.6)$$

OLS = 1955–1978; s.e.e.=0.0559; $\bar{R}^2$=0.9984.

Unemployment rate:

$$r_{nu} = 100\frac{N_l - N_e}{N_l} \tag{1.7}$$

Energy demand:

$$\underset{(15.52)}{\ln e = 0.24484} + \underset{(18.77)}{1.1898 \ln \bar{k}_{ne}} \underset{(68.09)}{-0.67286} \frac{\sum_{i=0}^{3}(1-\delta_1)^{i+1} p_{e-i}/p_{k-i}}{\sum_{i=0}^{3}(1-\delta_1)^{i+1}} \tag{1.8}$$

OLS 1955–1978; s.e.e.=0.0158; $\bar{R}^2$=0.9989; D–W=1.54.

Synthetic supply variable:

$$q_s = 4.5336(\bar{k}_e)^{\alpha}(\Pi N_e)^{1-\alpha} \tag{1.9}$$

where

$$\bar{k}_e = (\beta k_{ne}^{(\sigma-1)/\sigma} + \gamma e^{(\sigma-1)/\sigma})^{(\sigma/(\sigma-1)}$$

is the CES bundle of capital and energy.

Average unit cost of producing GDP+net imported primary energy:

$$c_q = \frac{\grave{e}p_e + \bar{k}_{ne} p_k + N_e W}{q p_q} \tag{1.10}$$

Output equation:

$$\ln q = \underset{(5.75)}{-0.16676} + \underset{(146.47)}{0.99326 \ln q_{sv}} - \underset{(6.86)}{0.44012 \ln c_q} \tag{1.11}$$

$$+\underset{(0.618)}{0.48017} \ln \frac{a + x_{ne}}{q_{sv}} + \underset{(10.54)}{0.018998} \ln \frac{k_{ib}^*}{\bar{k}_{ib}}$$

OLS 1955–1978; s.e.e.=0.00454; $\bar{R}^2$=0.9998; D–W=1.59

where

$k_{ib}^* = 0.13357\, \bar{k}_{ne}$.

Non-energy imports:

$$\ln(m_{ne} - M_{car2}/p_{mne}) = \underset{(6.39)}{-1.2010} + \underset{(21.90)}{0.91363} \ln q \qquad (1.12)$$

$$\underset{(6.48)}{-1.2535} \ln\left(\tfrac{1}{3}\Sigma_{i=1}^{3} \frac{p_{mne-i}}{p_{q=i}}\right) + \underset{(3.13)}{1.3898} \ln\left(\frac{\bar{q}}{q_{sv}}\right)$$

OLS 1955–1978; s.e.e.=0.0288; $\bar{R}^2$=0.9944; D–W=2.16.

Change in non-farm business inventories:

$$i_{ib} = q + T_i/p_q - a - x_{ne} + m_{ne} \qquad (1.13)$$

Stock of non-farm business inventories:

$$k_{ib} = k_{ib-1} + i_{ib} \qquad (1.14)$$

Aggregate demand:

$$q_a = q - [i_{ib} - 0.08\,(k^*_{ib} - \bar{k}_{ib})] \qquad (1.15)$$

or, in cases where expected output is taken to be exogenous:

$$\ln q_a = 1.0277 + 0.047889t \qquad (1.15)'$$

Desired level of future output for investment demand:

$$q^* = 1.07^{3/4}\, q_a \left(\frac{q}{q_{-2}}\right)^{1/4} \qquad (1.16)$$

Vintage based synthetic supply:

$$q_{sv} = 4.5336(\bar{k}_{ev})^{\alpha} (\Pi N_e)^{1-\alpha} \qquad (1.17)$$

[(1.18) not used in this version.]

Desired level of future output for labour demand:

$$q^*_{\ell} = 1.07^{1/4}\, q_a [1 + 0.1(m_{ne} - \hat{m}_{ne})/q] \left(\frac{q}{q_{-2}}\right)^{3/4} \qquad (1.19)$$

where $\hat{m}_{ne}$ is the equilibrium level of imports at full capacity with lags worked out

$$\ln(\hat{m}_{ne} - M_{car2}/p_{mne}) = -1.2010 + 0.91363 \ln q_{sv} - 1.2535 \ln \frac{p_{mne}}{p_q}$$

2. *Personal and Foreign Expenditure on Goods and Services*

Personal expenditure:

$$c/y_d = \underset{(12.87)}{0.78957}c_{-1}/y_d - \underset{(3.94)}{0.36077}[0.01r_l(1-r_{tp}) - \dot{p}_a] \tag{2.1}$$

$$+\underset{(3.12)}{0.036267}\frac{V}{(Y-T_d)} + \underset{(2.76)}{0.12197}$$

where y_d = real disposable income = $(Y-T_d)/p_a$.

OLS 1955–1978; s.e.e.=0.0082; $\bar{R}^2$=0.9016; D–W=1.90.

Non-energy exports:

$$\ln(x_{ne} - X_{car2}/p_{xne} - X_{id}/p_{xne}) = -\underset{(17.48)}{6.9978} \tag{2.2}$$

$$+\underset{(24.87)}{1.2277}\ln y_w - \underset{(2.54)}{0.4284}\left(\frac{1}{3}\Sigma_{i=0}^{2}\frac{p_{xne-i}}{p_{fx-i}p_{w-i}}\right)$$

OLS 1955–1978; s.e.e.=0.0412; $\bar{R}^2$=0.9910; D–W=1.33.

Real absorption:

$$a = c + g + i_{ne} + i_e \tag{2.3}$$

Return to non-residents on Canadian business assets, as a fraction of the total return:

$$r_{vb} = \underset{(16.90)}{0.2404} + \underset{(19.03)}{0.6731}(1-r_d)\frac{L_f}{V_{kb}}$$

OLS 1954–1978; s.e.e.=0.0115; $\bar{R}^2$=0.9377; D–W=0.95.

3. *Prices, Wages and National Income*

Proportionate annual wage change:

$$\dot{W} = \underset{(0.25)}{0.0014817} + \underset{(4.39)}{0.36381}\dot{W}_{-1} + \underset{(7.67)}{0.63619}\dot{p}_a + \underset{(2.98)}{0.16984}\left(\frac{\dot{p}_{xne}}{p_{mne}}\right) \tag{3.1}$$

$$+\underset{(2.14)}{0.22425}\frac{\dot{\bar{q}}}{q_{sv}} + \underset{(3.24)}{0.023240}r_{nat}/r_{nu}$$

$$-\underset{(0.38)}{0.00221}D_{76} - \underset{(4.69)}{0.022570}D_{77} - \underset{(4.87)}{0.025765}D_{78}$$

with coefficients on $\dot{W}_{-1}$ and $\dot{p}_a$ constrained to sum to unity.

3SLS 1955–1978; s.e.e.=0.00544; $\bar{R}^2$=0.975; Durbin-h=−0.50; *F*-statistic for constraint=0.062.

Proportionate change in implicit price index for output:

$$\dot{p}_q = \underset{(12.40)}{-0.026725} + \underset{(25.78)}{0.80324}\dot{W} + \underset{(2.98)}{0.087383}\dot{p}_e + \underset{(3.52)}{0.066412}(p_{fx}p_{wxg}) \tag{3.2}$$

$$+\underset{(3.25)}{0.042967}\dot{r}_l + \underset{(4.03)}{0.13651}\frac{k^*_{ib}-\bar{k}_{ib}}{k^*_{ib}}$$

with cost shares constrained to add to unity.

3SLS 1955–1978; s.e.e.=0.0069; $\bar{R}^2$=0.968; D-W=1.98; *F*-statistic for constraint=0.047.

Price of non-energy exports:

$$\ln p_{xne} = \underset{(1.24)}{0.0062945} + \underset{(13.08)}{0.29941}\ln p_{wxg} + \underset{(19.47)}{0.52011}\ln p_q + \underset{(8.32)}{0.42717}\ln p_{fx} \tag{3.3}$$

OLS 1953–1978; s.e.e.=0.0105; $\bar{R}^2$=0.9986; D-W=1.38.

Proportionate change in absorption price index:

$$\dot{p}_a = \underset{(0.42)}{0.00067021} + \underset{(21.90)}{0.83163}\dot{p}_q + \underset{(4.43)}{0.16837}\dot{p}_{mne} \tag{3.4}$$

with domestic and import fractions constrained to sum to unity.

3SLS 1955–1978; s.e.e.=0.0078; $\bar{R}^2$=0.945; D-W=1.65; *F*-statistic for constraint=12.3.

Nonenergy imports:

$$p_{mne} = p_{fx}p_{mw} \tag{3.5}$$

Real GNP:

$$y = a + i_{ib} + x_{ne} + x_e - m_{ne} - m_e - M_{id}/p_{mne} \tag{3.6}$$

Nominal GNP:

$$Y = qp_q - M_{id} - m_e p_{me} + T_i \tag{3.7}$$

4. *Balance of Payments, Capital Movements*

Net capital inflows, excluding official monetary movements:

$$F_i = -B + p_{fx}F_{xo} \quad \text{(for the small open economy)} \tag{4.1}$$

Net foreign liabilities:

$$L_f = L_{f-1} + F_i + F_{ireva} \tag{4.4}$$

Interest and dividend payments to foreigners (BOP definition):

$$M_{id} = \underset{(0.41)}{0.0722} + \underset{(9.08)}{1.3186}\, r_d \frac{r_l}{100} \bar{L}_f + \underset{(1.45)}{0.010758} (1 - r_d) \bar{L}_f \tag{4.5}$$

OLS 1954–1978; s.e.e.=0.2476; $\bar{R}^2$=0.9646; D–W=1.21.

Balance of trade:

$$B = X_{tr} - M_{id} + x_{ne} p_{xne} - m_{ne} p_{mne} + B_e \tag{4.6}$$

Retained earnings and revaluation adjustments increasing liabilities to foreigners:

$$F_{ireva} = -\underset{(7.78)}{1.2471} + \underset{(69.20)}{1.0283}\bar{r}_{vb}(V_{kb} - V_{kb-1}) + \underset{(4.35)}{0.80392}(r_{vb} - r_{vb-1})\bar{V}_{kb} \tag{4.7}$$

OLS 1954–1978; s.e.e.=0.518; $\bar{R}^2$=0.9959; D–W=1..96.

Balance of trade in energy:

$$B_e = x_e p_{xe} - m_e p_{me} \tag{4.9}$$

5. *Government and Private Finance*

Indirect taxes:

$$T_i = r_{ti} a p_a - G_{fsubo}/1000 \tag{5.1}$$

Direct taxes:

$$T_d = \underset{(0.02)}{0.010735} + \underset{(2.57)}{0.15966}(Y - C_{ca} - T_i - WN_e) + \underset{(11.12)}{1.1722} r_{tp}(Y - C_{ca} - T_i) \tag{5.2}$$

OLS 1954–1978; s.e.e.=0.4806; $\bar{R}^2$=0.9978; D–W=1.03, where the capital consumption allowance is given by

$$\ln C_{ca} = -\underset{(41.76)}{2.6549} + \underset{(73.43)}{0.9971} \ln (k_{ne} p_a)$$

OLS 1952–1978; s.e.e.=0.0469; $\bar{R}^2$=0.9952; D–W=0.40.

Government bonds:

$$L_b = L_{b-1} + g p_a - T_i - T_d + p_{fx} F_{xo} + G_{misc} - H + H_{-1} \tag{5.3}$$

Demand for high powered money:

$$\ln H = -2.0472 + 0.89917 \ln Y - 0.093672 \ln r_s \qquad (5.4)$$
$$\quad (14.98) \quad (24.94) \qquad (3.01)$$

Cochrane-Orcutt 1952–1978; s.e.e.=0.0292; $\bar{R}^2$=0.9488; ϱ=0.837.

References

Bruno, M.: Adjustment and structural change under import price shocks. *Scandinavian Journal of Economics 84*, 1982.

Fortin, P. & Newton, K.: Labour market tightness and wage inflation in Canada. Cahier 8108, Groupe de Recherche en Politique Economique, Université Laval, Quebec, 1981.

Helliwell, J. F., Shapiro, H. T., Sparks, G. R., Stewart, I. A., Gorbet, F. W. & Stephenson, D. W.: *The Structure of RDX2.* Ottawa Bank of Canada, 1971.

Helliwell, J. F.: Canadian energy policy. *Annual Review of Energy 4*, 175–229, 1979.

Helliwell, J. F.: Canadian energy pricing. *Canadian Journal of Economics 14*(4), 579–95, 1981.

Helliwell, J. F. & McRae, R. N.: Output, potential output, and factor demands in an aggregate open economy model with energy and capital bundled together. Mimeo. 1981.

Helliwell, J. F. & McRae, R. N.: Resolving the national energy conflict: From the national energy program to the energy agreements. *Canadian Public Policy 8*(1), 1982.

Neary, J. P. & Purvis, D. D.: Sectoral shocks in a dependent economy: Long-run adjustment and short-run accommodation. *Scandinavian Journal of Economics 84*, 1982.

Organization for Economic Cooperation and Development. *Economic Outlook*, July 1976.

Comment on J. F. Helliwell, P. M. Boothe and R. N. McRae, "Stabilization, Allocation and the 1970s Oil Price Shocks"

Staffan Viotti

Stockholm School of Economics, Stockholm, Sweden

It is well known that the small open economy can protect itself from external shocks in various ways. In the 1970s, we have witnessed the attempts of a number of small countries (e.g. Canada, Australia and the Scandinavian countries) to cushion the effects of the oil price shocks. These attempts have met with varying degrees of success (or failure) from a stabilization point of view. The inflationary effects of the oil price rise have been allowed to reach the domestic economy only gradually through exchange rate adjustments or price control schemes; domestic aggregate demand and employment have been maintained through expansionary fiscal and monetary policy. Such stabilization is obviously bought at a cost. The oil price rises are generally considered to have caused a substantial permanent change in the relative price of energy in the world. For a small country to ignore and try to avoid this signal from the world market will sooner or later lead to serious losses in allocational efficiency. Although this trade-off between stabilization and efficiency is a simple and generally accepted truth, there are, to my knowledge, very few attempts to quantify it.

The paper by Helliwell, Boothe & McRae (H–B–M) is an attempt to analyze and measure stabilization and allocation effects of two types of policies adopted by Canada in the 1970s to shelter the domestic economy from the shocks in world oil prices. The analysis in the paper is based on the use of a macroeconometric model of a fairly small size (some twenty stochastic equations). This model is tied to a much larger model of the Canadian energy sector. The structure of the larger model and its connections with the macro model are, however, never spelled out in the paper.

The experiments performed by H–B–M are well designed and the results seem reasonable. As is usually the case with work based on experiments using econometric models, it is difficult for the reader to observe more than the top of the iceberg. Even with a fairly small econometric model such as the one H–B–M use, it is almost impossible for a reader who has not actually experimented with the model to get a clear picture of where all the rabbits come from on the basis of only a short presentation of the model structure and an appendix with the estimated equations. However, the fact that the model seems to be built on the Canadian RDX2 model—probably one of the most well-established econometric models in the world, at least for a small country—should be reassuring.

Basically the model is very simple. It is a one-sector model in the sense that there is only one good produced for final use in the economy. Private consumption is modeled according to a simple life-cycle hypothesis and its distribution between domestically produced and imported goods is basically determined by relative prices. The price–wage block is also very simple and conventional; wages are formed according to an expectations-augmented Phillips-curve mechanism and domestic prices (the GNP deflator) are mainly cost determined.

The financial sector is not very developed and seems to play a minor role. The main assumption stressed by the authors is the small-open-economy (SOE) assumption about capital mobility, which means that interest rates are determined in the world economy.

The only part of the model that goes beyond the simple, conventional macrostructure is the production side. It draws heavily on the approach taken in the RDX2 model, with the addition of explicit modeling of the energy sector. Space does not permit my going into any details; suffice it to say that the modeling of the production side is very interesting, with among other things its emphasis on the buffer role of inventories and the importance attached to expectations of profitable and sustainable output levels in determining factor demands. At the same time this has made the production sector much more complicated and impenetrable than other parts of the model. Although expectations about normal and sustainable output play such a strategic role, the modeling of these expectations is of a rather *ad hoc* nature. Needless to say, their connections with modern views on rational expectations are not spelled out. Although I do not think this is necessarily a serious matter, it illustrates a point made earlier. It is very difficult for the reader to see which assumptions on the production side are strategic and which are not.

Two experiments are carried out using the H–B–M model. First, Canada's actual energy pricing policy, which was a phased movement towards world prices through a two-price system, is compared with two extreme alternative policies: (1) an immediate adjustment of oil and gas prices to world prices; and (2) oil and gas prices are kept constant in real terms at 1973 levels.

Second, a less expansionary fiscal policy of the type prevalent in the major OECD countries is compared with the actual relatively expansionary policy in 1974–78, following the first oil price shock. We can be brief in regard to this experiment. The conclusion is simply that the expansionary fiscal policy actually followed seems to have worked well and kept the Canadian economy near its long-term equilibrium path. Let us instead focus on the first experiment.

The outcome of the first experiment is rather straightforward from a stabilization point of view. Policy (1), immediate adjustment to world prices, would have given rise to much higher volatility in inflation rates than the policy actually pursued. It would also have been stagflationary, with real domestic output falling 1–2 percent. Although the effects on the external balance are not clear, the experiment seems to show fairly clearly that the policy actually followed has definitely stabilized the economy as compared to a policy that would have let the oil price rises affect the domestic economy fully and immediately. Policy (2), the complete insulation policy, would give qualitatively the same results as policy (1) but, of course, with reversed signs. The dynamic patterns show some dissimilarities, however.

The allocational effects are more difficult to capture. H–B–M try to measure them by looking at changes in rentals from gas and oil. In other words, they seem to measure changes in consumers' and producers' surpluses caused by switching from the policy actually pursued to either of the two alternative pricing policies. The method for measuring these allocational effects is not spelled out in any detail in the paper and has to be accepted more or less at face value. The results, however, are intuitively reasonable. There is an efficiency gain from following world prices, but it is much smaller than the loss caused by the constant price policy.

As the authors point out, their results clearly indicate the existence of a trade-off between stabilization and efficiency for the Canadian economy. It is difficult not to agree on this point. The question is, however, how seriously the *quantitative* results can be taken. After all, the quantitative results must be the main purpose of an econometric exercise of this kind. The process of merely showing the *existence* of a trade-off could probably be achieved with a much smaller apparatus.

I think there are at least two important issues that should be dealt with before quantitative results concerning the trade-off between stabilization and allocation could really be taken seriously.

a) It is well known that measurement of efficiency gains (losses) by looking at welfare triangles the way H–B–M seem to do is a very static approach. Many studies indicate that static efficiency gains and losses are minor, as compared with dynamic, X-efficiency gains and losses. Obviously a constant price policy, if perceived to be more or less permanent, would give rise to structural changes over time that are not captured by welfare triangle analysis.

b) In order to measure the policy conflict between stabilization and allocation, there is a need for some index of successful or optimal stabilization policy. Without such an index it is impossible, for example, to rank two policies, one of which is relatively more successful in stabilizing prices, while the other is more successful in bringing about a stable development of the external balance.

In summary, the paper by H–B–M is a very interesting attempt to quantify the policy conflict between allocation and stabilization. But the reader is eager to see more of the submarine parts of the iceberg, the top of which the authors have presented in this paper.

Inflation, Tax Rules and the Accumulation of Residential and Nonresidential Capital

*Martin Feldstein**

Harvard University and National Bureau of Economic Research, Cambridge, Massachusetts, USA

Abstract

The present paper analyses the effect of the interaction between tax rules and inflation on the size and allocation of the capital stock with particular emphasis on the role of owner-occupied housing. The analysis is developed in the framework of an economy that is in equilibrium and in which a constant fraction of disposable income is saved. In this model, I show that, with current U.S. tax laws, an increase in the rate of inflation reduces the equilibrium amount of business capital employed in the economy and raises the amount of housing capital. The analysis also shows that a higher rate of inflation lowers the real net-of-tax rate of return to the provider of business capital. Another result is that accelerated depreciation increases the accumulation of business capital but that, unless firms are permitted to expense all investment immediately, an increase in inflation continues to depress the accumulation of business capital.

I. Introduction

For nearly two decades, the United States has pursued a series of short-run policies that have increased the rate of inflation and sustained it at a high level. The rate of increase of the general price level (as measured by the GNP deflator) rose from less than 2 percent a year in the early 1960s to more than 8 percent a year in the late 1970s. The expansionary monetary and fiscal policies began in the early 1960s as an attempt to lower the unemployment rate and expand the level of output. Easy money, lower tax rates on capital income, and specific incentives for business investment were combined with the aim of stimulating investment and thereby, through the traditional multiplier process, reducing unemployment. Although the rate of inflation began to rise, many economists argued that "moving up the Phillips curve" to higher inflation and lower unemployment represented a desirable trade off. Then came the decision by President Johnson to expand both the Vietnam War and his Great Society programs. He insisted on doing so without a tax increase but with an easy money policy aimed at

---

* This paper is part of the NBER study of Capital Formation. I am grateful to my colleagues at the NBER for numerous discussions of this subject and for comments on an earlier draft. Lars Calmfors also provided valuable editorial suggestions.

keeping interest rates from rising. This moved the inflation rate up sharply to more than five percent as the 1970s began.

In the 1970s, inflationary monetary and fiscal policies continued to be pursued despite a lack of agreement on the rationale for those policies even among the prevailing economists of that decade. In effect, these economists and the politicians agreed on the treatment of the economy even though they disagreed about the proper diagnosis of its economic condition. First, there were those who continued to believe in a long-run Phillips curve trade-off between inflation and unemployment. They advocated expansionary policy in the hope of reducing unemployment permanently even if that meant accepting a higher inflation rate. Second, there were those who recognized that no long-run trade-off exists but who misjudged how high the noninflationary unemployment rate had become because of changes in the demographic structure of the labor force and in the transfer programs that encouraged higher unemployment. They advocated expansionary monetary and fiscal policies because they believed that the economy was still operating with "too much unemployment". Finally, there were those who correctly perceived that the economy was at or below the noninflationary unemployment rate but who resisted a tightening of monetary and fiscal policy because they were unwilling to pay the price in higher unemployment for slowing the rise in inflation or reducing its level.

In this way the economy drifted to higher and higher rates of inflation.[1] Although some of the year to year changes in inflation were unexpected, the general level and even some of the upward drift clearly came to be anticipated. For more than a decade now, a major debate among American macroeconomists has been about whether such anticipated inflation has any effects on the real economy. At least since Milton Friedman's (1968) presidential address, economists have recognized that expected inflation is perfectly neutral in a simplified economy with flexible prices, inelastic money demand and no taxes. Subsequent research by Barro (1977), Lucas (1972), Sargent & Wallace (1975) and others has refined this idea and emphasized the corresponding neutrality of expected changes in the stock of money.[2]

The important question, however, is whether the neutrality of anticipated changes in money and in the price level is relevant to the actual economy in which we live. James Tobin (1965) emphasized that even fully anticipated inflation is not neutral because the demand for money balances varies inversely with the nominal interest rate and therefore with the expected rate

---

[1] The OPEC price shocks played a significant part in this process but do not alter the basic story that I have told above. For more extensive accounts, see Blinder (1979), Eckstein (1978), Feldstein (1981*a*), and Gordon (1981).

[2] See also the papers and discussion in Fischer (1979*a*).

of inflation. An increase in inflation caused by a more rapid growth of money would therefore raise the capital intensity of the economy by inducing households to substitute real capital for money in their portfolios. Stanley Fischer (1979*b*) has recently examined the lead and lag patterns by which expected changes in the money stock can alter the capital stock and real output through the Tobin money–capital substitution effect. Although this portfolio substitution process is analytically correct, it is generally agreed that the magnitude of the Tobin effect is extremely small.[3]

By contrast, the interaction of inflation and the tax rules can have very substantial effects on the incentive to save and on the relative returns to different types of investments. In Feldstein (1976) I examined the way in which the tax–inflation interaction could lower total capital formation by reducing the incentive to save. Then in Feldstein (1980*a*) I showed how the tax–inflation interaction would encourage individual investors to substitute interest bearing government debt for real capital in their portfolios and thereby reduce the real capital intensity of the economy. The present paper extends this analysis to examine how inflation diverts capital from plant and equipment to owner-occupied housing.[4]

The tax burden on business capital rises when there is inflation. Under existing U.S. tax rules,[5] inflation affects the taxation of business capital in three important ways. First, because of the "historic cost" approach to calculating the cost of production, a higher rate of inflation reduces the real value of depreciation allowances and understates the costs of replacing the goods withdrawn from inventory. Second, the owners of the equity of business firms pay capital gains tax on the rise in the nominal value of the capital stock. And, third, the firm gets to deduct nominal interest payments (thereby understating its taxable profits) but the creditors must pay tax on nominal interest receipts (thereby overstating their taxable income). Since the effective tax rate on the reduced corporate income is very close to the effective tax rate on the increased creditor income (Feldstein & Summers, 1980), this third effect is very small. On balance, inflation therefore raises the tax burden on the income from business investment.

Under present U.S. tax law, an individual who owns his own house may deduct the nominal interest payment in calculating taxable income and does not pay tax on the implicit rental income provided (in kind) by his house. In

---

[3] See Section II of this paper, especially page 301, for a discussion of why the Tobin effect is empirically too small to matter.

[4] I have previously discussed the way that inflation and tax rules combine to achieve this distortion in Feldstein (1980*b*, 1980*d*) but have not previously presented a formal model. For other analyses of the way that the tax-inflation interaction affects the demand for residential capital, see Hendershott (1979, 1980). Hendershott & Hu (1979), Hendershott & Shilling (1980), Poterba (1980) and Summers (1981).

[5] I.e., the tax rules as of July 1981.

addition, the capital gains on owner-occupied housing are virtually untaxed.

Since the stock of housing capital is about 74 percent of the stock of nonresidential capital[6] an incentive to shift capital from plant and equipment to housing can have a significant effect on the amount of plant and equipment in the economy. The ratio of net investment in residential capital to net investment in plant and equipment rose from 52 percent in the last half of the 1960s to 76 percent in the last half of the 1970s. In Feldstein (1980*e*), I presented econometric evidence that the interaction of tax rules and inflation reduced the incentive to invest in plant and equipment and that this can explain most of the variation in the share of GNP devoted to such investment during the past three decades.

The present paper analyses the effect of the interaction between tax rules and inflation on the size and allocation of the capital stock with particular emphasis on the role of owner-occupied housing. The analysis is developed in the framework of an economy that is in equilibrium and in which a constant fraction of disposable income is saved. In this model, I show that, with current U.S. tax laws, an increase in the rate of inflation reduces the equilibrium amount of business capital employed in the economy and raises the amount of housing capital. The analysis also shows that a higher rate of inflation lowers the real net-of-tax rate of return to the provider of business capital. In a richer model than the current one, i.e., in a model in which the rate of personal saving was an increasing function of the net rate of return, a higher inflation rate would therefore lower the rate of saving.

The present analysis also shows that permitting firms to depreciate investments more rapidly for tax purposes increases the accumulations of business capital but that, unless firms are permitted to expense all investment immediately, an increase in inflation continues to depress the accumulation of business capital.

The model considered in this paper is a very simple one. I ignore several issues that I have considered in earlier papers: changes in the saving rate; changes in the demand for money; government debt; and the mixture of debt and equity in corporate finance.[7] A model cannot be a complete picture of reality but should help to elucidate some particular aspect of reality.

One final point should be emphasized before turning to the formal analysis. Because the relation between inflation and capital formation depends on the fiscal structure of the economy, the specific distorting effect of

---

[6] This excludes land and includes inventories as well as fixed capital. Owner-occupied housing accounts for 42 percent of fixed capital alone. The data on capital stocks and inventories are from the Federal Reserve Board's *Balance Sheets of the U.S. Economy*.

[7] See Feldstein (1976, 1980) and Feldstein, Green & Sheshinski (1978).

inflation is not a universal constant but differs among countries and even within the same country from time to time.

II. A Growing Economy with Inflation and Housing

The simplest framework within which to examine the effect of inflation on the composition of the capital stock is an economy with two sectors. The corporate business sector produces a general good that can be used for both consumption and investment. The unincorporated household sector produces the services of the owner-occupied housing stock. The population grows exogenously in this economy at a constant rate (n) and the labor force is a fixed fraction of the population. Labor is employed only in the production of the general good; housing services are proportional to the stock of housing and are produced without labor.[8]

The Business Sector

If the general good is produced with constant returns to scale, the technology can be described by a production function that relates output per employee (y) to the capital stock per employee used in this sector (k):

$$y = f(k). \tag{1}$$

For simplicity, output is measured net of depreciation and all technical progress is ignored.

The pretax rate of return on corporate capital is f'. In the absence of inflation, corporations pay tax at rate τ on this return to capital. The net of tax returns on the marginal investment, $(1-\tau)f'$, must in equilibrium be equal to the firms' net cost of funds. The analysis is greatly simplified by assuming that all marginal investments are financed by debt.[9] On these funds, firms pay interest rate i. Since interest expenses are deducted in calculating a firm's taxable income, the net cost of borrowed funds is $(1-\tau)i$ and the firm's equilibrium condition is $(1-\tau)f'=(1-\tau)i$ or just $f'=i$.

If there is inflation and the price level rises at a constant rate, π, the

---

[8] The model also ignores the land used in housing. In the current framework, inflation would raise the relative price of land.

[9] The rationale for all "debt at the margin" finance is developed in Stiglitz (1973) and a model of growth equilibrium with such finance is presented in Feldstein (1976). More realistically, the costs of debt and equity funds depend on a firm's debt–equity ratio; see Gordon & Malkiel (1981) and Feldstein, Green & Sheshinski (1978, 1979). It is worth noting that the analysis of this paper could be done equally easily for an economy without any debt finance. In such an economy, firms would use only equity finance and homeowners would have no mortgages. The same basic results about the allocation of capital would be obtained, indicating that the fundamental issue is the inflation-induced rise in the relative taxation of business income and not the deductibility of nominal interest payments on mortgages.

nominal pretax rate of return on capital is $f'+\pi$. If inflation did not alter the measurement of real taxable profits, the tax liability per unit of capital (ignoring for a moment the tax treatment of debt) would be $\tau f'$ and the resulting nominal after-tax rate of return would be $(1-\tau)f'+\pi$. In fact, with the tax accounting rules that have prevailed in the United States, inflation causes taxable profits to increase relative to real profits. Both historic cost depreciation and the use of first-in-first-out inventory accounting cause an understatement of the true cost of production and therefore an overstatement of taxable profits.[10] As an approximation, the increase in taxable income per unit of capital can be written as a constant multiple of the inflation rate, $\lambda\pi$, per unit of capital.[11] The additional tax is thus $\tau\lambda\pi$. The nominal rate of return to the corporation net of tax is therefore $(1-\tau)f'+\pi-\tau\lambda\pi$.

Since the nominal interest rate is deducted in calculating taxable income, the net of tax cost of borrowed funds is $(1-\tau)i$. The equilibrium condition that requires equating the nominal net returns on the marginal unit of capital to the net cost of funds therefore implies

$$(1-\tau)f'+(1-\tau\lambda)\pi=(1-\tau)i. \tag{2}$$

Before proceeding to discuss the housing sector, it is interesting to note that equation (2) implies

$$i=f'+\frac{1-\tau\lambda}{1-\tau}\pi. \tag{3}$$

In contrast to the traditional conclusion of Irving Fisher that the nominal interest rate rises point for point with the rate of inflation, equation (3) shows that, *for a fixed real marginal product of capital,* the rise in the interest rate reflects the tax deductibility of nominal interest and the mismeasurement of depreciation and inventory profits. With economic depreciation and no artificial inventory profits, $\lambda=0$ and $di/d\pi=1/(1-\tau)$. With existing depreciation and inventory rules, $0<\lambda<1$ and $1<di/d\pi<1/(1-\tau)$.[12]

---

[10] If depreciation schedules permit tax depreciation that is faster than economic depreciation, taxable profits in the absence of inflation will be less than true profits. The increase in real taxable profits caused by inflation may leave taxable profits greater or less than true profits. What matters is the *change* in the size of this difference, i.e., profits relative to real profits, and not the sign of the difference.

[11] See Auerbach (1979) for an explicit derivation of the relation between π, f' n, the true rate of depreciation and the increase in taxable income caused by historic cost depreciation. Feldstein (1980*c*) discusses the additional contribution of FIFO inventory accounting. For the United States, a value of $\lambda=0.50$ is a reasonable approximation with the tax laws in effect in the late 1970s.

[12] The expression is more complex when firms use equity as well as debt in marginal finance. It is important to emphasize that these expressions for $di/d\pi$ are partial equilibrium relations that assume f' fixed.

If the individuals who provide capital to the business sector pay tax at rate θ on nominal interest income, the real net-of-tax interest that they earn is $(1-\theta)\,i-\pi$. From equation (3) it follows that

$$(1-\theta)\,i-\pi=(1-\theta)f'+\frac{[(\tau-\theta)-(1-\theta)\,\tau\lambda]}{1-\tau}\pi. \tag{4}$$

The impact of inflation on the real net return to lenders depends on two things. First, $\tau-\theta$ reflects the difference between the advantage of deducting nominal interest payments at the corporate level and the disadvantage of paying tax on nominal interest income at the personal level. Second, $(1-\theta)\,\tau\lambda$ reflects the additional tax paid at the corporate level because of the mismeasurement of depreciation and inventory costs. For any marginal personal income tax rate greater than 30 percent, i.e., for $\theta>0.30$, the coefficient of π is negative.[13]

The Housing Sector

The owner-occupied housing sector uses capital but no labor to produce housing services. Since in the long-run capital can move freely between the two sectors, the equilibrium price of a unit of housing capital is the same as the price of a unit of business capital which in turn is the price of a unit of the general good.[14] The price of housing services therefore depends on the cost of owning one unit of housing capital and of maintaining that capital.

More specifically, for each dollar of housing capital the individual pays or foregoes net interest of $(1-\theta)\,i$.[15] Local property tax, maintenance, depreciation and a standard risk premium add an additional net cost of z per unit of housing capital.[16] Since the value of net housing capital rises at the rate of inflation, the real net cost of owning and maintaining a unit of housing capital is:

$$r=(1-\theta)\,i+z-\pi. \tag{5}$$

Note that r is thus the implicit rental cost of a unit of owner-occupied housing capital.

---

[13] The corporate tax rate τ is 0.46 and, as noted above, λ has been estimated to be 0.50; Feldstein (1980*c*).

[14] By contrast, in the short run the stocks of housing capital and business capital are given and equilibrium must be achieved by changes in the prices of these capital stocks; see Poterba (1980) and Summers (1981).

[15] This assumes that individuals borrow and lend at the same interest rate. It also reflects the U.S. tax rule that permits individuals to deduct mortgage interest payments in the calculation of taxable income.

[16] I say "net" cost because local property taxes are a deductible expense in calculating individual taxable income. By "standard risk premium" I mean the premium for a "standard" or "basic" amount of housing capital; the risk premium may be a function of the amount of housing capital in a way specified below.

The demand for housing capital by individual home owners reflects both the demand for housing services and the demand for housing capital as a portfolio asset. Since I have assumed that the amount of housing service is proportional to the housing stock, it is not necessary to distinguish the demand for services from the demand for a portfolio asset. Instead, the demand for housing capital can be considered directly with its determinants reflecting both the portfolio and service characteristics. The simplest such specification is equation (6) where h is the housing capital stock per employee and $\phi'<0$. This equation implies that the relative demand for housing services and for other goods varies inversely with the implicit rental price of housing.[17]

$$h=\phi(r). \tag{6}$$

Even in the restricted form of equation (6), the demand for housing capital as an asset influences the form of the demand function, ϕ. In particular, since each individual must own the housing capital that produces his housing services, an increase in the consumption of housing services beyond some level involves increasing portfolio risk.[18] This implies that, for high values of h, the demand for housing capital is less responsive to the implicit rental price than would be true if individuals did not have to own their housing capital.[19] Even when the implicit rental price would otherwise be zero or negative, risk considerations limit the demand for housing capital.[20]

---

[17] Since the other goods represent the numeraire, r is also the rental price of housing relative to the price of other goods. A more general specification would make the demand for housing a function of real income and of wealth. Within the current paper, however, the equilibrium values of real income and wealth remain constant except for changes in the efficiency of resource allocation. If the initial condition of the economy is regarded as one of optimal resource allocation, the changes in resource allocation that result from a small increase in the rate of inflation do not change real income to a first order approximation. A large change in inflation would, however, reduce real income. Similarly, a small increase in inflation would reduce real income if, in the initial condition, non-neutral tax rules cause there to be too much housing capital. A reduction in real income would cause individuals to consume less housing and this would partially offset the inflation-induced transfer of capital from the business sector to housing. Shifting one unit of capital from the business sector to housing reduces real income by the difference between the real marginal products of capital in the two sections and this income effect reduces the demand for housing capital by the marginal propensity to own housing capital as a function of real income. The real marginal product difference is less than f' which is approximately 0.12 in the United States. The marginal housing-to-income ratio is less than three. Thus this real income effect offsets at most about one-third of any shift of capital from the business to housing sectors.

[18] This is particularly true when the acquisition of housing capital is financed by borrowing.

[19] The model assumes that all housing is owner-occupied when in reality about 75 percent of the housing capital stock is owner-occupied. The tax advantages and other aspects of home ownership probably outweigh risk considerations at most income levels. The tax advantage of home ownership is increased by inflation since rental property is adversely affected by historic cost depreciation rules.

[20] This was probably the case in the 1970s.

The Demand for Money

Money plays two quite distinct roles in a model of equilibrium growth. First, the exogenously given rate of growth of the nominal money stock determines the rate of inflation. This follows directly from the fact that the stock of real money balances per employee must remain constant in equilibrium growth since real income per employee, real assets per employee and the rate of interest are all constant.[21] If real money balances per employee are to remain constant, the rate of growth of the nominal money stock ($\dot{M}/M$) must equal the rate of growth of prices plus the rate of growth of the labor force:

$$\frac{\dot{M}}{M} = \pi + n. \tag{7}$$

The second role of money is as an asset that absorbs savings and thereby reduces the equilibrium size of the real capital stock, $k+h$. As mentioned above, Tobin (1965) has emphasized that an increase in inflation, by increasing the real cost of holding money balances, encourages households to economize on real money balances and therefore to devote a larger share of their wealth to real capital formation. The importance of this substitution effect depends on the size of the stock of "outside money" (i.e., money that does not represent a liability of any private entity) relative to total wealth and on the elasticity of money demand with respect to the nominal rate of interest. The monetary base, a reasonable measure of the stock of outside money,[22] was only \$160 billion in 1980 or less than 3 percent of the total stock of private wealth. Since all estimates of the interest elasticity of money demand are substantially less than one, it is clear that even major changes in the nominal rate of interest would have very little effect on the fraction of savings devoted to real capital formation. I shall therefore ignore the interest elasticity of demand completely and write the demand for real money balances per employee (m) as a constant fraction (μ) of the corresponding real capital assets:

$$m = \mu(k+h). \tag{8}$$

Public and Private Consumption

The government consumes a fraction (γ) of real national income and households consume a fraction ($1-\sigma$) of real disposable income. National income

---

[21] If there is technical progress, the statement is true with "employee" interpreted as "effective employee".

[22] It would be wrong to include in the measure of outside money any interest bearing government debt since the market interest rate would adjust with inflation. Tobin's procedure of combining money and government debt is therefore misleading; see Feldstein (1980*a*) for a model that distinguishes money, government debt, and private real capital.

consists of the output of the business sector plus the output of the owner-occupied housing sector.[23] To combine these two products, I assume a constant relative price of housing services, i.e., an implicit rental of ϱ per unit of housing capital; national income per employee is thus $y+\varrho h$.[24] Real government spending per employee is

$$g=\gamma(y+\varrho h). \tag{9}$$

Disposable income may be defined as national income minus both taxes paid (t) and the loss in real money balances caused by inflation (πm).[25] Thus consumption per employee is

$$c=(1-\sigma)(y+\varrho h-t-\pi m). \tag{10}$$

Since the government deficit equals the increase in the stock of money balances i.e., $g-t=(\pi+n)m$, equation (10) can be rewritten:

$$c=(1-\sigma)(y+\varrho h-g+nm). \tag{11}$$

This formulation, which is essentially due to Tobin (1965), assumes that households regard their increase in real balances as a component of disposable income even though the real resources available to households (i.e., the maximum feasible consumption) are only $y+\varrho h-g$.[26] The amount that households save, including the amount that is saved in the form of increased real money balances is therefore

$$s=\sigma(y+\varrho h-g+nm) \tag{12}$$

or, using (9) to substitute for g,

$$s=\sigma[(1-\gamma)(y+\varrho h)+nm]. \tag{13}$$

---

[23] This ignores the value of the services of the stock of money, an omission that has no qualitative effect on the results of this analysis.

[24] The value of ϱ is the initial rental price of housing services. A small change in the rental price changes real income to the extent that (*a*) it reallocates capital between h and k and (*b*) the marginal product of business capital differs from ϱ. That is, the change in real income is $f'\,dk+\varrho\,dh$. It would be incorrect to include a term of the form hdr in evaluating the change in real income since dr represents either a change in the implicit price that individuals pay themselves on housing or a change in the tax consequences of home ownership that would merely be offset by a change in other taxes.

[25] Taxes include the taxes on capital income from corporations and industries and an additional nondistorting tax. Changes in tax revenue that result from changes in inflation are offset by changes in the nondistorting tax to keep total tax revenue unchanged. If the offsetting change in other sources of tax revenue were in a distortionary tax, the effect of inflation on real income would be more complex than the current analysis indicates. See Feldstein (1976) for a discussion of this issue.

[26] Ignoring nm in (11) or πm in (10) would not change any of the qualitative results.

Growth Equilibrium

Real savings per employee are divided into the increase of real business capital per employee ($\dot{K}/N$), the increase of real housing capital per employee ($\dot{H}/N$), and the increase of real money balances per employee ($(\dot{M/p})/N$). Denoting total real wealth by A and total real wealth per employee by a, we have

$$s=\frac{\dot{A}}{N}=\frac{\dot{K}}{N}+\frac{\dot{H}}{N}+\frac{(\dot{M/p})}{N}=\frac{\dot{K}}{K}k+\frac{\dot{H}}{H}h+\frac{(\dot{M/p})}{M/p}m. \tag{14}$$

In steady-state equilibrium, all three stocks grow at the same rate as the population, implying that

$$s=na=n(k+h+m). \tag{15}$$

Combining (13) and (15) gives the basic equation of growth equilibrium:

$$\sigma[(1-\gamma)(y+\varrho h)+nm]=n[k+h+m]. \tag{16}$$

Using (8) to substitute for m, (6) to substitute for h, and (1) to substitute for y, equation (16) can be rewritten

$$\sigma[(1-\gamma)(f+\varrho\phi)+n\mu(k+\phi)]=n[k+\phi+\mu(k+\phi)]. \tag{17}$$

Recall that ϕ is a function of r and that equation (5) shows this implicit rental price to be $r=(1-\theta)i+z+\pi$. Equation (4) shows that the households' real net interest rate is given by $(1-\theta)i-\pi=(1-\theta)f'+x\pi$ where $x=[\tau-\theta-(1-\theta)\tau\lambda]/(1-\tau)$. Thus

$$\phi=\phi[(1-\theta)f'+x\pi+z]. \tag{18}$$

If (18) is used to substitute for ϕ in (17), it provides an equation that determines the stock of business capital as a function of the inflation rate and the tax rules.

Disequilibrium Adjustments

The next section uses equations (17) and (18) to examine the equilibrium effects of changes in the rate of inflation and the tax rules. The complex expressions that result are readily interpreted in terms of the disequilibrium adjustments of the capital stock. This permits determining the directions of equilibrium change without having to specify numerical values for individual parameters.

Two very plausible disequilibrium adjustment assumptions will be made. The first is labelled the Net Adjustment Assumption: an increase in either type of capital stock per employee above its equilibrium value causes total wealth per employee to decline:

$$\frac{d\dot{a}}{dk} < 0 \tag{19}$$

and

$$\frac{d\dot{a}}{dh} < 0. \tag{20}$$

Equation (19) is satisfied if, when k exceeds its equilibrium value, k falls and the other types of wealth (housing plus real money balances) do not increase by an even greater amount. A similar interpretation holds for equation (20).

The second assumption is labelled the Partial Adjustment Assumption: when the stock of business capital per employee exceeds its equilibrium value, the total wealth per employee will decline even if housing wealth per employee is held constant:

$$\left.\frac{\partial \dot{a}}{\partial k}\right|_h < 0. \tag{21}$$

Since the fall in k is likely to raise the housing stock, holding housing constant should make it easier to satisfy the condition that a positive perturbation of k causes total wealth to decline. In this sense, (21) is a weaker assumption than (19) and (20).

III. Effects of Changes in Inflation

We are now in a position to examine the effect of inflation on the capital intensity of the business sector, on the consumption of housing services, and on the real net return to savers. Before beginning the formal derivations it is useful to consider the general logic of the process.

A higher rate of inflation reduces the after tax profitability of investment because the tax accounting procedures for dealing with depreciation and inventories raise the effective tax rate. This lower after-tax profitability means that firms can pay only a lower real net rate of return to the creditors who supply their capital.

The net return to the suppliers of business capital is also affected by the fact that firms deduct *nominal* interest payments and that lenders pay tax on *nominal* interest receipts. This matters, however, only to the extent that the tax rates of borrowers and lenders are different.

On balance, inflation lowers the real net rate of return and therefore reduces the implicit rental cost of housing. This in turn raises the consumption of housing services relative to the output of other goods. The present section will now show explicitly that this reduces the equilibrium amount of business capital per employee and therefore the productivity of the labor force. The decrease in productivity and the reallocation of production to housing also lowers the real income per capita.[27]

Substituting equation (18) into (17) and totally differentiating with respect to k and π yields:

$$Q_1\,dk+Q_2\,\phi'x\,d\pi=0 \tag{22}$$

and thus

$$\frac{dk}{d\pi}=-\frac{Q_2\,\phi'x}{Q_1} \tag{23}$$

where the expressions for Q_1 and Q_2, derived in the Appendix, are shown to satisfy $Q_1=d\dot{a}/dk$ and $Q_2=d\dot{a}/dh$. From equations (19) and (20) we have $Q_1<0$ and $Q_2<0$. Consequently, since $\phi'<0$, the sign of $dk/d\pi$ is the same as the sign of $x=[\tau-\theta-(1-\theta)\,\tau\lambda]/(1-\tau)$. As I noted above, with realistic values of λ and τ, $x<0$ for any $\theta>0.30$ and therefore $dk/d\pi<0$.

Since a higher rate of inflation unambiguously reduces the real equilibrium capital intensity of the business sector it increases the pretax real rate of return (f'). The net of tax real rate of return and the rental cost of housing nevertheless declines. To see this, note that since $(1-\theta)\,i-\pi=(1-\theta)f'+\pi x$,

$$\frac{d[(1-\theta)\,i-\pi]}{d\pi}=\frac{d[(1-\theta)f'+\pi x]}{d\pi}=(1-\theta)f''\frac{dk}{d\pi}+x. \tag{24}$$

Since f'', $dk/d\pi$ and x are all negative, it seems at first as if the effect of inflation on the real net return is ambiguous. However, substituting (23) for $dk/d\pi$ yields

$$\frac{d[(1-\theta)\,i-\pi]}{d\pi}=[Q_1-(1-\theta)f''\phi'Q_2]\,x/Q_1. \tag{25}$$

Using the expressions for Q_1 and Q_2 in the Appendix gives

$$\frac{d[(1-\theta)\,i-\pi]}{d\pi}=[\sigma(1-\gamma)f'+\sigma n\mu-n(1+\mu)]\,x/Q_1. \tag{26}$$

Since both x and Q_1 are negative, the sign of $d[(1-\theta)\,i-\pi]/d\pi$ is the same as the sign of

$$Q_3=\sigma(1-\gamma)f'+\sigma n\mu-n(1+\mu). \tag{27}$$

The Appendix shows that

---

[27] Although the analysis takes the saving rate (σ) as fixed, the reduction in the real net rate of return implies that the saving rate in a more general model would probably also be reduced, thereby further decreasing the capital intensity of production.

$$Q_3 = \left.\frac{\partial \dot{a}}{\partial k}\right|_h.$$

The Partial Adjustment Assumption implies $Q_3<0$ and therefore, from (26), $d[(1-\theta)\,i-\pi]/d\pi<0$.[28]

Since the demand for housing is a function of the real interest rate, an increase in inflation unambiguously increases the equilibrium stock of housing capital:[29]

$$\frac{dh}{d\pi} = \phi'\frac{dr}{d\pi} = \phi'\frac{d[(1-\theta)\,i-\pi+z]}{d\pi} = \frac{\phi' Q_3 x}{Q_1} > 0. \tag{28}$$

Since all four terms are negative, $dh/d\pi>0$.

The final effect of inflation that I wish to examine is on total real income, $y+\varrho h$. If the initial allocation of capital between business and housing were optimal, a small increase in inflation would leave real income unchanged, since any small change from an optimum involves no loss to a first order approximation. But if taxes and inflation make the initial condition suboptimal, the reallocation of capital caused by an increase in inflation will have a first order effect on real income. More specifically, the very favorable tax treatment of owner-occupied housing implies that even in the absence of inflation the real return to marginal housing capital (ϱ) is less than the return to business capital (f'). A positive inflation rate widens the gap. This implies that a reallocation of capital from the business sector causes a loss of real income. More formally the change in real income induced by an inflation-induced change in the allocation of capital is

$$\frac{d(y+\varrho h)}{d\pi} = f'\frac{dk}{d\pi} + \varrho\frac{dh}{d\pi}. \tag{29}$$

Substituting from (23) and (28) implies

$$\frac{d(y+\varrho h)}{d\pi} = (\varrho Q_3 - f' Q_2)\frac{\phi' x}{Q_1}. \tag{30}$$

Substituting for Q_2 and Q_3 from the Appendix yields,

---

[28] An alternative suggested by Kouri is a model in which saving is optimized in a Ramsey model by individuals who live forever. In this case, the real net rate of return, $(1-\theta)\,i-\pi$, is fixed. This in turn means that r and therefore h are not influenced by inflation. It follows, however, from equation (4) that f' must rise to keep the right hand side constant; since $f''<0$, $dk/d\pi<0$. In words, to earn the same real net return when inflation raises the effective tax rate, the pretax return would have to increase and therefore the business capital stock would have to decrease.

[29] Note again that, to the extent that housing is also a function of real income and real income declines, this will partially offset the value of $dh/d\pi$ derived in (28).

$$\frac{d(y+\varrho h)}{d\pi} = [\varrho(\sigma(1-\gamma)f'+\sigma n\mu-n(1+\mu))-f'(\sigma(1-\gamma)\varrho+\sigma n\mu-n(1+\mu))]\,\phi' x/Q_1$$

$$= (f'-\varrho)\,n[1+(1-\sigma)\mu]\,\phi' x/Q_1. \tag{31}$$

Thus with $f'>\varrho$, real income falls since $\phi'<0$, $x<0$ and $Q_1<0$.

IV. Indexing the Tax Rules

Inflation causes a misallocation of capital between the business and housing sectors because the tax laws mismeasure capital income and expenses. A complete indexing of the tax laws would eliminate this source of the distortion caused by inflation. Complete indexing has three aspects (1) eliminating the mismeasurement of depreciation and inventory profits that causes business operating profits to be overstated, (2) limiting the deductions for business interest to real interest payments only; and (3) limiting the taxation of household interest income and expenses to the real interest rate. This section shows the neutrality of inflation when all three of the features are present and examines non-neutrality when there is only partial indexing.[30]

Consider a general tax indexing rule under which firms pay tax at rate τ_1 on operating profits net of real interest expenses but deduct the inflation component against their tax liability at rate τ_2; under existing law $\tau_1=\tau_2$ while with complete indexing $\tau_2=0$. With these rules, the firms' equilibrium condition, analogous to equation (2), is

$$(1-\tau_1)f'+(1-\tau_1\lambda)\pi = i-\tau_1(i-\pi)-\tau_2\pi. \tag{32}$$

If households are taxed on real interest receipts at rate θ_1 and on the inflation component of interest payments at rate θ_2, the real net rate of interest is $i-\theta_1(i-\pi)-\theta_2\pi-\pi=(1-\theta_1)i+(\theta_1-\theta_2)\pi-\pi$. Since the implicit rental cost of housing is the real net rate of interest plus the "other costs per unit of housing capital" (z), the rental cost of housing is

$$r = (1-\theta_1)i+(\theta_1-\theta_2)\pi-\pi+z \tag{33}$$

and, using (32) to eliminate i,

$$r = (1-\theta_1)f'+\frac{1-\theta_1}{1-\tau_1}(1-\tau_1\lambda)\pi-\frac{1-\theta_1}{1-\tau_1}(\tau_1-\tau_2)\pi+(\theta_1-\theta_2)\pi-\pi+z. \tag{34}$$

---

[30] These three forms of indexing are discussed in Feldstein, Green and Sheshinski (1978) but there is no housing sector in that model and all of the distortions are in financial returns.

When there is no indexing ($\tau_1=\tau_2$ and $\theta_1=\theta_2$), equation (34) reduces to the same implicit rental cost that has already been analyzed. With complete indexing ($\theta_2=\tau_2=\lambda=0$), equation (34) reduces to

$$r=(1-\theta_1)f'+z. \tag{35}$$

Here the implicit rental price is independent of inflation.[31]

It is sometimes proposed that the elimination of historic cost depreciation be coupled with limiting the business interest deduction to the real cost of funds. In terms of equation (34), this implies $\lambda=\tau_2=0$ but $\theta_1=\theta_2$. The resulting implicit rental cost of housing is then:

$$r=(1-\theta)f'+z+\left[\frac{1-\theta}{1-\tau_1}-\frac{1-\theta}{1-\tau_1}\tau_1-1\right]\pi=(1-\theta)f'+z-(1-\tau_1)\,\theta\pi. \tag{36}$$

An increase in inflation reduces the implicit rental cost because the firm is denied a deduction for the inflation premium in the interest rate but the household pays tax on that premium. An increase in the rate of inflation thus reduces the real net return to households on business capital and thereby lowers the cost of funds that enters the housing rental cost. Thus a partial indexing approach that focuses only on the firm may exacerbate the bias in favor of housing that is caused by inflation and clearly does not leave an inflation-neutral allocation of capital. More specifically, comparing (36) and (18) shows that the partial indexing rule causes a lower value of r than the existing unindexed tax law if $(1-\tau_1)\,\theta>-x$; with $\tau=0.46$ and $\lambda=0.5$, this is satisfied for all values of $\theta<0.48$.[32]

Most countries have dealt with inflation by accelerating the rate of depreciation used for calculating taxable profits but without changing the tax treatment of interest income and expenses. Accelerating depreciation has two distinct effects. First, at any rate of inflation (including zero), this lowers the effective tax rate on operating profits. In the notation of equation (32), it is equivalent to increasing f'; note that it is not equivalent to lowering τ_1 since that would also affect the tax treatment of interest. Second, more rapid depreciation reduces the sensitivity of the tax to the rate of inflation, i.e., it lowers λ. To see the effects of these changes on the implicit rental cost of housing, set $\tau_2=\tau_1$ and $\theta_2=\theta_1$ in equation (34) and evaluate the total differential of r with respect to f' and λ:

$$dr=(1-\theta)\,df'-\frac{(1-\theta)}{(1-\tau_1)}\tau_1\pi\,d\lambda. \tag{37}$$

[31] The allocation of capital still favors housing because the net services of housing are not taxed while interest income is taxable and the mortgage interest payments are deductible ($\theta_1>0$) but this is a separate matter.

[32] Note that correcting the depreciation and inventory rules (i.e., making $\lambda=0$) is sufficient to achieve inflation neutrality if $\tau=\theta$.

The decrease in λ raises the implicit rental cost of housing since it reduces the excess tax on business capital caused by historic cost accounting methods. Similarly the rise in f' raises the return on business investment and thus directly increases the implicit rental cost of owner occupied housing. Although full indexing avoids all of the tax induced distortions associated with inflation, any specific acceleration of depreciation can achieve the same effect only for one particular rate of inflation.

V. Conclusion

It is ironic that an easy money policy aimed at stimulating investment in plant and equipment is likely to have just the opposite effect: reducing the long-run capital intensity of production. Whatever the short-run virtue of expansionary policies, the long-run consequence of inflation under existing U.S. tax laws is to reduce investors' demand for business capital and to increase it for owner-occupied housing.

The simple model developed in this paper shows more generally how the expectation of further inflation of the sort that resulted from the inflationary experience of the 1960s and 1970s can have very substantial effects on the real economy. The notion that a fully-anticipated monetary expansion or inflation has no effect on the real economy is not plausible in a modern economy with a complex set of tax rules. The specific effect of inflation will, moreover, vary from country to country and from time to time as a function of the particular features of the country's fiscal structure.

It would be useful to extend the current analysis in a variety of ways. Of particular interest would be replacing the debt-only assumption of corporate finance with a mixture of debt and equity. This would bring out the more limited significance of the corporate deductibility of nominal interest payments and would show the relevance of the taxation of nominal capital gains. A further (or alternative) extension to include interest bearing government debt as well as money would permit the government to vary the real interest rate through its debt management policy and would show the effect of inflation on residential investment when low-risk government debt is an alternative asset. Finally, since the analysis here is limited to U.S. tax rules, it would be quite interesting to see it altered to describe the tax rules of other countries and used to analyze the effect of inflation in these settings.

The present model, either in its current form or with the extensions described above, could be the basis for a more explicit dynamic analysis of the transition path when the expected rate of inflation changes. This in turn would provide a sounder foundation for the empirical analysis of the effect of inflation on the accumulation of residential and nonresidential capital.

Appendix

This appendix discusses the relation of Q_1, Q_2 and Q_3 of Section III to the disequilibrium adjustment process.

Combining equations (13) and (14) yields

$$\sigma[(1-\gamma)(y-\varrho h)+nm]=\frac{\dot{A}}{N}. \tag{A.1}$$

It follows directly from differentiating a with respect to time that

$$\frac{\dot{A}}{N}=\dot{a}+na. \tag{A.2}$$

Thus (A.1) can be rewritten

$$\sigma[(1-\gamma)(y+\varrho h)+nm]=na+\dot{a}. \tag{A.3}$$

Along a balanced growth path, $\dot{a}=\dot{k}=\dot{h}=\dot{m}=0$. This condition was imposed for the analysis in the text. But when k, h or m are not at their equilibrium values, these ratios will change to bring about equilibrium.

By substituting $h=\phi$ and $m=\mu(k+h)$, equation (A.3) can be rewritten:

$$\sigma[(1-\gamma)(f+\varrho\phi)+n\mu(k+\phi)]-n(1+\mu)(k+\phi)=\dot{a}. \tag{A.4}$$

Taking the derivative of both sides with respect to k yields:

$$\begin{aligned}Q_1&=\sigma(1-\gamma)f'+\sigma n\mu-n(1+\mu)+(\sigma[(1-\gamma)\varrho+n\mu]-n(1+\mu))\phi'(1-\theta)f''\\&=d\dot{a}/dk.\end{aligned} \tag{A.5}$$

Similarly the derivative of (A.4) with respect to h yields

$$Q_2=\sigma[(1-\gamma)\varrho+n\mu]-n(1+\mu)=d\dot{a}/dh. \tag{A.6}$$

The net adjustment assumptions (19) and (20) imply directly that $Q_1<0$ and $Q_2<0$.

To derive the interpretation of Q_3 of equation (27), take the partial derivative of both sides of equation (A.4) with respect to k holding h (i.e., ϕ) constant:

$$Q_3=\sigma[(1-\gamma)f'+n\mu-n(1+\mu)]=\left.\frac{\partial\dot{a}}{\partial k}\right|_h. \tag{A.7}$$

References

Auerbach, Alan: Appendix to "Inflation and taxes in a growing economy with debt and equity finance" by M. Feldstein, J. Green & E. Sheshinski, *Journal of Political Economy 86*, S68–70, 1979.

Barro, Robert J.: Unanticipated money growth and unemployment in the U.S. *American Economic Review 67*, 101–115, 1977.

Blinder, Alan S.: *Economic policy and the great stagflation*. Academic Press, New York, 1979.

Eckstein, Otto: *The great recession*. North Holland, Amsterdam, 1978.

Feldstein, Martin: Inflation, income taxes, and the rate of interest: A theoretical analysis. *The American Economic Review 66*, 809–820, 1976.

— Fiscal policies, inflation and capital formation. *American Economic Review 70*, 636–650, 1980*a*.

— Inflation, capital taxation and monetary policy in R. Hall (ed.), *Inflation*. NBER Conference Volume, forthcoming, 1980*b*.

— Inflation, tax rules and the stock market. *Journal of Monetary Economics 6*, 309–331, 1980*c*.

— Tax rules and the mismanagement of monetary policy. *The American Economic Review 70*, 182–186, 1980*d*.

— Inflation, tax rules, and investment: Some econometric evidence. The Fisher-Schultz Lecture at the Fourth World Congress of Econometric Society, August 1980 and *Econometrica*, forthcoming.

— Inflation in the American economy. The Joseph Schumpeter Lecture at the University of Vienna, March 1981, *Empirica*, forthcoming. (A revised version will also appear in the *Public Interest*, 1982.)

— with Jerry Green and Eytan Sheshinski: Inflation and taxes in a growing economy with debt and equity finance. *Journal of Political Economy 86*, S53–70, 1978.

— with Jerry Green and Eytan Sheshinski: Corporate financial policy and taxation in a growing economy. *The Quarterly Journal of Economics*, 411–432, 1979.

— with Lawrence Summers: Inflation and the taxation of capital income in the corporate sector. *National Tax Journal 32*, 445–70, 1980.

Friedman, Milton: The role of monetary policy. *American Economic Review 59*, 1–17, 1968.

Fischer, Stanley: Anticipations and the nonneutrality of money. *Journal of Political Economy 87*, 225–53, 1979*a*.

— *Rational expectations and economic policy*. University of Chicago Press, 1979*b*.

Gordon, Roger H. & Malkiel, Burton G.: Corporation finance. In *How taxes affect economic behavior* (ed. H. Aaron and J. Pechman), pp. 131–198. The Brookings Institution, 1981.

Hendershott, Patric & Shilling, James D.: The economics of tenure choice: 1955–79. NBER Working Paper No. 543, 1980.

Hendershott, Patric H.: The decline in aggregate share values: Inflation and taxation of the returns from equities and owner-occupied housing. NBER Working Paper No. 370, 1979.

Hendershott, Patric & Hu, Sheng Cheng: Inflation and the benefits from owner-occupied housing. NBER Working Paper No. 383, 1979.

Lucas, Robert E.: Expectations and the neutrality of money. *Journal of Economic Theory 4*, 103–124, 1972.

Musgrave, John: Fixed nonresidential business and residential capital in the United States, 1929–75. *Survey of Current Business*, April 1976.

Polinsky, A. M.: The demand for housing: A study in specification and grouping. *Econometrica 45*, 1977.

Poterba, James: Inflation, income taxes and owner-occupied housing. NBER Working Paper No. 553, 1980.

Sargent, T. J. & Wallace, N.: Rational expectations, the optimal monetary instrument, and the optimal money supply rule. *Journal of Political Economy 84*, 207–54, 1975.

Stiglitz, Joseph: Taxation, corporate financial policy, and the cost of capital. *Journal of Public Economics*, 1–34, 1973.

Summers, Lawrence: Inflation and the tax system. *American Economic Review 71*, 429–434, 1981.

Tobin, James: Money and economic growth. *Econometrica 33*, 1965.

Comment on M. Feldstein, "Inflation, Tax Rules and the Accumulation of Residential and Nonresidential Capital"

R. C. O. Matthews

Clare College, Cambridge, England

It is a familiar point that investment in dwellings is encouraged, relative to other investment, by the nonimputation for tax purposes of the rental of owner-occupied dwellings. The possible source of bias in favour of residential investment indicated by Feldstein is entirely separate from this. It arises because inflation affects differently the tax liability on the return from the two different types of investment, on two accounts: the allowance made for inflation in measuring depreciation and inventory costs for corporate tax is incomplete; and the personal tax rate may not be the same as the corporate tax rate. In practice, Feldstein suggests, the first of these is the one that matters.

The model, as presented, relates to steady state growth. It also assumes a perfect capital market. These assumptions are made in order to make clear the underlying properties of the tax system. How far do the assumptions limit the applicability of the model to reality?

The *first* point about the steady state assumption is obvious. It is natural that nonresidential investment should be discouraged if tax arrangements do not take proper account of the effects of inflation on depreciation and inventory-holding. But it is only because the level of unemployment and the propensity to save are assumed constant that a corresponding positive effect on residential investment appears in the model. Otherwise the result might simply be a reduction in total investment.

A *second* point about the steady state assumption concerns the rate of interest. Very many owner-occupiers are conscious that inflation has caused their housing investment to have turned out extremely profitable. Most of these would, I guess, be rather surprised to learn that the reason why they have done so well is that corporate taxation makes insufficient allowance for the effects of inflation on depreciation and inventory-holding. The logic of this contention in the model is made clear by equation 1.3. In a system where taxes are assessed on *nominal* interest payments and the effects of inflation on depreciation and inventory-holding are properly allowed for, inflation will, in a steady state, raise the interest rate by *more* than point for point. If this really happened, investment in dwellings would not be abnormally profitable. In fact, so the argument runs, interest rates do not rise by the full extent because tax laws do not treat depreciation and inventory-holding properly. The resulting relatively low interest rates make for high returns from owner-occupation. However, in history as opposed to the steady state, this is surely not the only reason why interest rates did not rise by enough to prevent owner-occupation from being a very good bargain. Another reason was that for much of the postwar period the extent of the imminent inflation was underestimated. The profitability of owner-occupation was the reward for high gearing in a period when inflation was faster than had been expected.

Reference to the level of interest rates also raises questions concerning the imperfection of this capital market. These are institutional questions; but tax systems are institutional too, so no improper change in the level of discourse is involved. One reason for relatively low mortgage interest rates in many countries was simply that governments wanted them to be low, for political reasons, and they were able to give at least some effect to their wishes because the institutions for mortgage finance were in some degree separate from the corporate capital market.

Now that high rates of inflation have come to be foreseen, it is not entirely clear that their effects *are* favourable to residential investment, given the institutional arrangements. This is because of the front-loading phenomenon. With high inflation and high interest rates, interest payments are a very high proportion of the borrower's income initially; the loan in real terms is repaid over less then its nominal period. With a perfect capital market the loan could be rescheduled continuously and there would be no problems; but with actual mortgage institutions front-loading acts as a serious deterrent to first-time buyers and to owner-occupiers seeking to trade-up. This affects residential investment more than nonresidential investment, because the equivalent of equity financing does not normally exist in the mortgage market.

Feldstein invites comments on the extent to which his model may be applicable to countries other than the U.S. In the U.K. many of the relevant tax provisions are broadly similar, but, whether because of front-loading or some other reason, residential investment as a proportion of total investment has fallen, not risen, as the rate of inflation has increased (this applies both to residential investment as a whole and to the owner-occupied part of it). When other countries are brought into the comparison, it is important to note that Feldstein's model applies only to owner-occupied dwellings. The magnitude of the effects he analyses will therefore depend on the extent of owner-occupation. Countries differ greatly in this, with the principal division being, apparently, between English-speaking countries, where the proportion is generally around 60 percent, as in the U.S., and other OECD countries, where it is generally less than 50 percent and often much less, probably largely because of differing tax arrangements. It would, incidentally, be an interesting extension of Feldstein's model to analyse how far the distortions he describes may be responsible for changes over time in the owner-occupied proportion, though this analysis could not, of course, be done within the steady-state framework.

While Feldstein's model does not apply to rented dwellings, investment in that sector of the housing market may also be affected by inflation. For example, in the U.K., local authorities seek to break even on the historic cost of their housing stock and consequently the low nominal costs of old houses have served to keep down the average level of rents and so have made for a high demand for house-room. A characteristic of many countries, however, particularly in Continental Europe, has been complicated systems of subsidies to rented dwellings. These systems have been subject to numerous changes over time, both in their amount and form, and the changes could not sensibly be described as a regular function of the rate of inflation. In many countries, moreover, the forms and rates of tax on corporate profits have changed frequently and businesses have learnt that there is no presumption that existing arrangements will be permanent. The steady state properties of any particular set of arrangements is thus hardly likely to be observed in actual events, even in the owner-occupied sector.

To conclude. Nontaxation of the imputed rental of owner-occupied dwellings has undoubtedly made for over-investment in many countries. Has inflation been a further source of distortion? Feldstein has put forward a set of possible reasons why it may have been. His suggestions are to be taken seriously. Whether they amount to the most important of the effects that inflation has had on residential investment is less clear. The answer may well differ between countries. Not all the effects, moreover, work in the same direction.

Profitability and Growth

*Pentti J. K. Kouri**

Helsinki University, Finland, New York University
and the National Bureau of Economic Research, Cambridge, MA, USA

Abstract

The link between profitability and growth is explored by means of an alternative explanation suggested by standard neoclassical theory of the firm. The growth model developed clarifies the relationships between the real wage rate, the rate of profit, taxation and savings behavior and the rate of growth.

I. Introduction

The importance of "profitability" for capital accumulation and growth is often emphasized in policy debates, but there are very few theoretical models which link the rate of profit to the rate of growth in an explicit way. One way to formalize this relationship is to assume, along with Kaldor and other exponents of Cambridge growth theory, that the propensity to save out of profits is greater than the propensity to save out of wage income. In such cases a shift in the distribution of income from wages to profits increases the propensity to save and thereby the rate of investment and growth. There is, however, no convincing theoretical argument as to why the propensity to save out of capital income should be higher than the propensity to save out of wage income. On the contrary, the life-cycle model suggests that the reverse is true.

An alternative explanation of the link between profitability and growth is explored in this paper. It is suggested by standard neoclassical theory of the firm as developed, in particular, by Lucas (1967), Treadway (1969) and Uzawa (1969), and surveyed by Söderström (1976).[1] As is shown by Uzawa (1969), a firm's rate of growth is a function of the rate of profit and the rate of interest when the firm is not constrained in either the labor market or the output market. Thus profitability is a determinant of the propensity to invest, rather than of the propensity to save.[2]

---

* I wish to thank Hans Söderström for his critical comments, and Alain Nairay and participants in the conference for helpful discussions.

[1] See also Williamson (1966) and Ylä-Liedenpohja (1976).

[2] In a recent monograph, Malinvaud (1980) analyzes the role of profitability in different types of disequilibrium situations and is, in part, concerned with the same issues as this paper.

The Uzawa model of the firm is reexamined in Section II and interpreted as a model of a small open economy suffering from "classical unemployment". Alternatively, the model could be interpreted as a model of growth in the modern sector in a labor surplus economy à la Lewis; see Marglin (1966). It is shown that such an economy cannot grow unless the rate of profit is above a critical minimum which depends on the rate of interest. It is also shown that, *ceteris paribus*, an increase in the real wage rate not only reduces output and employment, but also reduces the rate of growth in output, a point emphasized in Kouri (1978).

The model is closed in Section III. The rate of interest is determined simultaneously with the rate of growth, as in Uzawa (1969) and Abel & Blanchard (1980). It is shown that fixity of the real wage rate implies a steady-growth Solution, provided that the rate of profit exceeds a critical minimum. The equilibrium rate of growth in the economy is an increasing function of the rate of profit and of the "propensity to save". It is also shown that taxation of capital income lowers the rate of capital formation and growth of output.

The growth model developed in this paper is a special case of a standard neoclassical growth model as developed by Uzawa (1969) in particular. It is highly simplified, but does serve to clarify the relationships between the real wage rate, the rate of profit, taxation and savings behavior, and the rate of growth.

The model suggests that under conditions of classical unemployment, restoration of growth and full employment requires an increase in the rate of profit, an increase in the rate of saving and elimination of tax distortions that discourage saving and capital formation. These policy implications are quite different from those of Keynesian models that emphasize aggregate demand and the accelerator mechanism as the driving forces of growth.

The policy implications of the model are further discussed in the concluding section.

II. The Rate of Profit and the Rate of Growth: Exogenous Interest Rate

We begin by examining the relationship between the rate of profit and the rate of growth at the firm level, assuming that firms are not constrained in either the labor market or the output market. The model is the same as in Uzawa (1969), but it is analyzed in a slightly different way in anticipation of the general equilibrium analysis in Section III. As shown by Uzawa, the optimal solution implies steady growth at a rate which is an increasing function of the rate of profit and a decreasing function of the rate of interest. This result is derived in a slightly different way, and it is also shown that there is a minimum rate of profit at which growth becomes negative. The model of the firm is then interpreted as a model of a small open economy consisting of many such firms.

Optimal Investment and Growth of Firms

All firms are assumed to be identical. At each point in time they maximize gross profit subject to a standard neoclassical production function, a fixed stock of capital, and an exogenously given real wage rate. It is assumed that there is no demand constraint in the output market, and no shortage of labor in the labor market. In short, the economy suffers from "classical unemployment" in terms of the Barro–Grossman–Malinvaud classification of disequilibria. Excess supply of labor is assumed to be large enough so that even if employment grows faster than the supply of labor, it will take a "long time" before full employment is reached.

Profit-maximizing levels of output, employment and real gross profit are proportional to the stock of capital for each firm and for the economy as a whole.

$$Q=\sigma(w)K, \quad N=n(w)K, \quad V=v(w)K, \tag{1}$$

where Q = output, K = stock of capital, N = employment in terms of effective labor input, V = real gross profit, w = real unit labor cost, and $\sigma'(w)$, $n'(w)$ and $v'(w)$ are all negative.

Firms seek to maximize the present discounted value of profits net of investment costs.

$$E=\max \int_0^{\infty} (vK-H(I,K))\, e^{-\varrho(\tau)}\, d\tau, \tag{2}$$

where

E = market value of the firm,
$H(I,K)$ = investment cost function,
$\varrho(\tau)=\int_0^{\tau} r(t)\, dt$ = τ-period discount factor,
$r(\tau)$ = instantaneous rate of interest at time τ.

The investment cost function incorporates the actual cost of investment goods as well as the costs of installation, which are assumed to be internal to each firm; see Mussa (1977) and Söderström (1976). The investment cost function is assumed to be homogeneous of degree one in I and K, so that it can be written as:

$$H(I,K)=H(I/K)\,K, \tag{3}$$

where the h function is assumed to be twice continuously differentiable and to satisfy the following restrictions:

$$h(0)=0, \quad h'(x)>0, \quad h''(x)>0, \quad \forall x \tag{4}$$

These restrictions imply that $vK-H(I,K)$ is concave in (I,K).

Because of the time dependency of the discount factor there are two state variables in the control problem: the stock of capital and the rate of discount. Their motions are governed by differential equations (5) and (6):

$$\dot{K}=I-\alpha K, \tag{5}$$

where α=rate of depreciation of capital;

$$\dot{\varrho}=r(\tau), \tag{6}$$

where $r(\tau)$=instantaneous rate of interest.

Gross investment must always be nonnegative so that α is the maximum rate of decline:

$$I \geqslant 0. \tag{7}$$

Equations (2)–(7) define a standard problem in dynamic control except for the fact that the discount rate is time dependent. By changing the time scale, however, the problem can be reduced into one with only one state variable; see Uzawa (1968) and Nairay (1981). Using the fact that $d\varrho=r(\tau)\,d\tau$, we can rewrite the control problem as:

$$E=\max\int_0^\infty \frac{vK-H(I,K)}{r}e^{-\varrho}\,d\varrho \tag{8}$$

$$\frac{dK}{d\varrho}=\frac{I-\alpha K}{r}. \tag{9}$$

Maximization of (8) subject to (9) and the nonnegativity constraint on investment yields the following first-order conditions:

$$h'(I/K)=\lambda, \quad \text{for } \lambda>h'(0), \quad \text{and} \quad I=0, \quad \text{for } \lambda\leqslant h'(0) \tag{10}$$

$$\dot{\lambda}=[\alpha+r(\tau)]\lambda-v+h(I/K)-h'(I/K)\,I/K \tag{11}$$

$$\dot{K}=I-\alpha K, \tag{12}$$

where we have reverted back to the original time scale. λ is the shadow price of installed capital, or Tobin's q, or Keynes' demand price of capital, while $h'(I/K)$ is the marginal supply price of capital. Gross investment is positive if the shadow price of capital exceeds the marginal cost of investment at zero level of investment. Since $h''(I/K)$ is positive everywhere, I/K is an increasing function of λ for all λ greater than $\boldsymbol{\lambda}=h'(0)$:

$$I/K=\phi(\lambda), \quad \text{for } \lambda>h'(0)=\boldsymbol{\lambda}, \quad \text{and} \quad I/K=0, \quad \text{for } \lambda\leqslant h'(0), \tag{13}$$

where $\phi(\lambda)$ is the inverse function of h' and $\phi'(\lambda)>0$, and $\phi''(\lambda)<0$.

Substituting this in equations (11) and (12) we have:

$$\dot{\lambda} = [\alpha + r(\tau)]\lambda - v + h(\phi(\lambda)) - \lambda\phi(\lambda) \quad \text{for } \lambda > \boldsymbol{\lambda} = h'(0) \tag{14a}$$

$$\dot{\lambda} = [\alpha + r(\tau)]\lambda - v, \quad \text{for } \lambda \leqslant \boldsymbol{\lambda} = h'(0) \tag{14b}$$

$$g = \dot{K}/K = \phi(\lambda) - \alpha \quad \text{for } \lambda < \boldsymbol{\lambda} = h'(0) \tag{15a}$$

$$g = -\alpha, \quad \text{for } \lambda \leqslant \boldsymbol{\lambda} = h'(0). \tag{15b}$$

In this section we assume that the interest rate is constant and return to the variable interest rate case in the subsequent general equilibrium analysis.

It is shown in Appendix I that if an optimal solution exists, it is given by the stationary solutions of equations (14) and (15):

$$\lambda^* = \frac{v}{r+\alpha} \quad \text{if} \quad \frac{v}{r+\alpha} \leqslant h'(0) \tag{16a}$$

$$(\alpha + r)\lambda^* = v - h(\phi(\lambda^*)) + \lambda^*\phi(\lambda^*), \quad \text{if} \quad \frac{v}{r+\alpha} > h'(0). \tag{16b}$$

It is shown in the Appendix that a necessary and sufficient condition for the existence and uniqueness of the optimal stationary solution is that the maximal rate of growth (the limit of $\phi(\lambda)-\alpha$ as λ approaches infinity) is less than the rate of interest. It is intuitively clear why this is a necessary condition, for otherwise the discounted value of profits could be made infinite; from equation (16b) the present discounted value of profits is equal to $(v-h)/(r+\alpha-\phi)$ which becomes infinite as $(\phi-\alpha)$ approaches r.

Determinants of the Rates of Investment and Growth

We now demonstrate that the rate of growth depends in an expected way on the rate of interest, the rate of profit and the cost of investment. The analysis can be interpreted as applying to an open economy facing an exogenously given interest rate in the world capital market.

The basic diagram is developed in Figure 1. The $0X$ schedule plots the value of the l.h.s. of equation (16) as a function of λ, and its slope is equal to $\alpha+r$. The $0Y$ schedule plots the r.h.s. of equation (16) and it starts at $y=v$ for values of λ below $\boldsymbol{\lambda}=h'(0)$. Provided that the boundary condition for the rate of growth holds, the $0X$ and $0Y$ schedules have a unique intersection, represented by A_0 in Figure 1. This intersection determines the shadow price of capital.

If the value of capital in existence $v/(\alpha+r)$ is greater than the marginal replacement cost $h'(0)$, gross investment is positive, and the rate of invest-

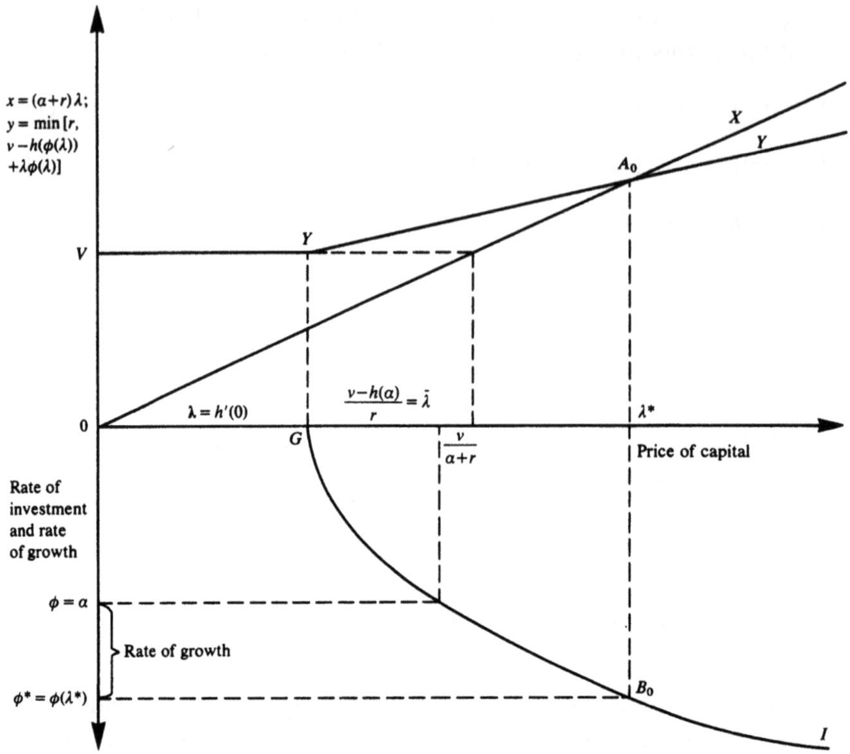

Fig. 1

ment is given by the *GI* schedule in the lower quadrant of Figure 1. Net investment and, therefore, the rate of growth, are positive when λ is equal to $[v-h(\alpha)]/r$ which is the market value of the firm when it invests just enough to keep its capital stock constant. $(v-h(\alpha))/r$ can be either less than or greater than the market value of the firm with zero investment, $v/(\alpha+r)$. For the most part, we assume that the equilibrium value of λ exceeds both $\boldsymbol{\lambda}$ and $\tilde{\lambda}$, so that both gross and net investment are positive.

Figure 2 illustrates the effects of an increase in the rate of interest. The economy is initially in equilibrium at (A_0, B_0) with λ equal to λ_0 and the rate of growth equal to $\phi(\lambda_0)-\alpha$. An increase in the interest rate tilts the $0X$ schedule to the left to $0X'$. New equilibrium obtains at (A_1, B_1) with a lower price of capital, λ_1, a lower rate of investment, $\phi(\lambda_1)$, and a lower rate of growth, $\phi(\lambda_1)-\alpha$.

The effects of an increase in the rate of profit are shown in Figure 3, where the economy is initially in equilibrium at (A_0, B_0) with λ equal to λ_0 and the rate of growth equal to $\phi(\lambda_0)-\alpha$. An increase in the rate of profit shifts the *YY* schedule up to $Y'Y'$. New equilibrium obtains at (A_1, B_1) with a higher price of capital, λ_1, and an increased rate of growth $\phi(\lambda_1)-\alpha$.

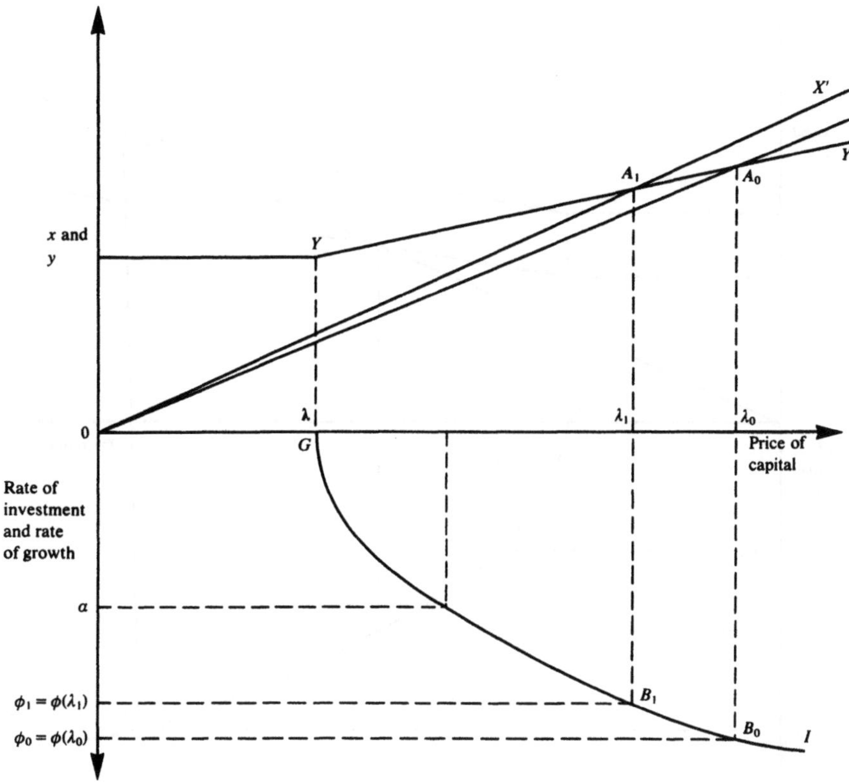

Fig. 2

The effect of a decline in the cost of investment would be to shift the *YY* schedule up and the *GI* schedule down, and thus increase the price of capital and the rate of growth.

A decline in the rate of interest, an increase in the rate of profit and a decline in the cost of investment represent three alternative strategies for stimulating capital formation and growth.

The Effects of Anticipated Policies and Disturbances

Forward-looking firms respond not only to their current environment but also to all anticipated changes in the rate of interest, the rate of profit or the cost of investment. When an increase in profitability is anticipated some time in the future, the analysis in the preceding subsection is no longer sufficient. Figure 3 still determines the price of capital from time (T) when the rate of profit has increased. In order to determine the behavior of λ between time t and time T, we have to go back to differential equation (14)

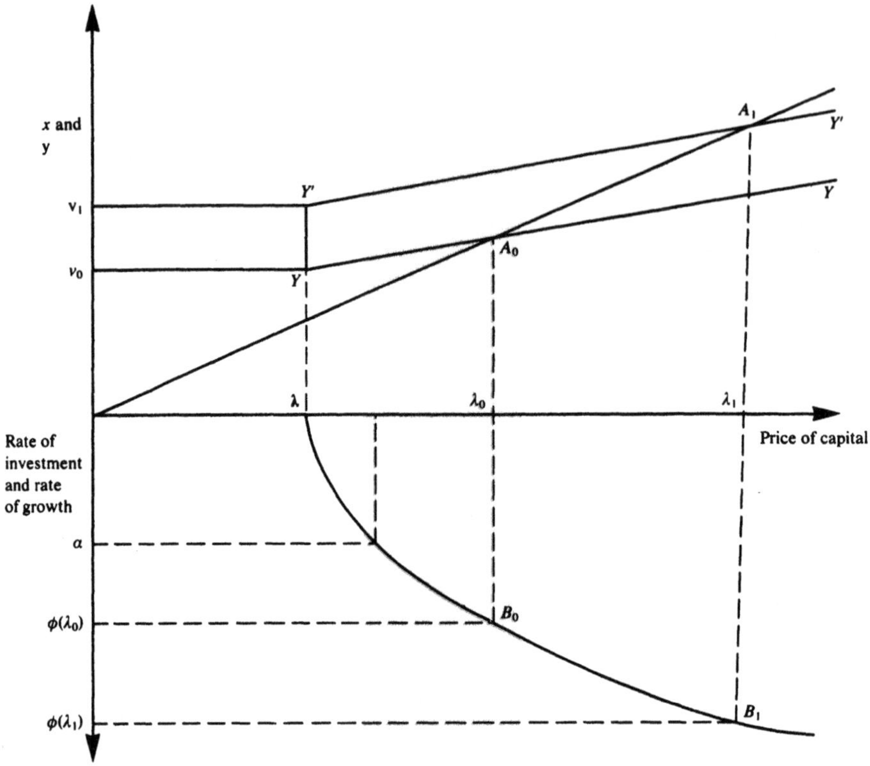

Fig. 3

and find a solution $\lambda^*(t)$ which satisfies $\lambda^*(T)=\lambda_1$, where λ_1 is the constant equilibrium value of λ after time T. There cannot be any jump in λ at time T because, by assumption, the increase in the rate of profit is fully anticipated; a jump must occur immediately on the receipt of the information about higher future profit to rule out certain speculative profit.

Figure 4 illustrates the adjustment of λ to an anticipated change in the rate of profit at time T. The economy is initially in equilibrium with λ to λ_0 and the rate of investment equal to $\phi(\lambda_0)$. At time 0, firms and the market come to expect an increase in the rate of profit at time T. The shadow price of capital and the price of equity immediately jump to λ_0', and, as shown in the left-hand quadrant, the rate of investment increases to $\phi(\lambda_0')$ and B_0'. From then on the price of capital continues to increase at an accelerating pace, reaching λ_1—the new long-run equilibrium value consistent with the higher profit rate—at time T. When the change in the rate of profit actually occurs at time T, there is no change in either λ or the rate of investment because the event has been fully "discounted" in advance.

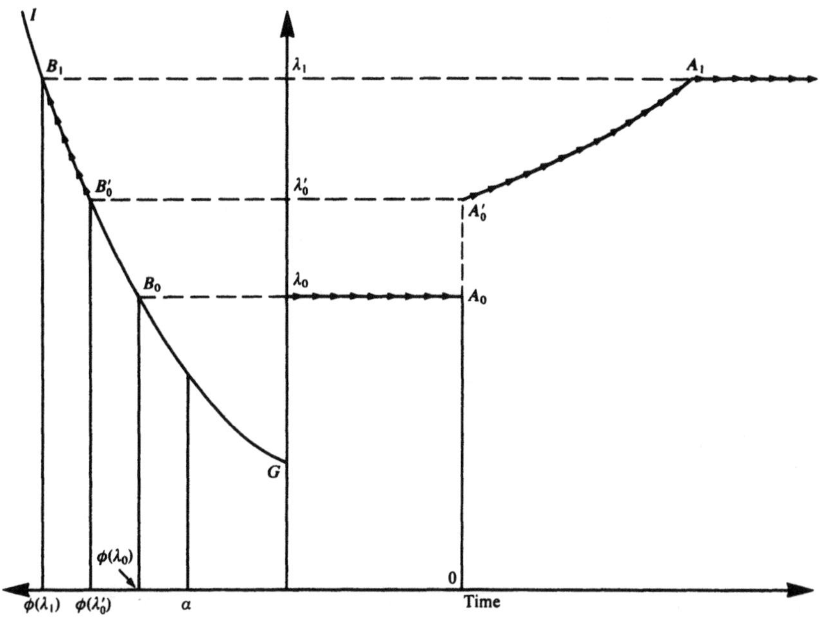

Fig. 4

The effects of anticipated changes in other variables can be analyzed in exactly the same way.

The Effects of Transitory Changes

The effects of changes in the rate of profit, the rate of interest and other variables are weakened if the changes are perceived to be transitory.

Figure 5 illustrates the response to a transitory increase in the interest rate. The economy is initially in equilibrium with λ equal to λ_0 and the rate of investment equal to $\phi(\lambda_0)$. At time 0, the rate of interest is increased. Firms, however, expect the interest rate to return to its initial level at time T, and stay constant from then on.

We know that λ must equal λ_0 at time T. Therefore at time 0, after the change in the rate of interest, its value must be greater than λ_1—the steady-state value consistent with the higher interest rate. For only then can λ increase and reach λ_0 at time T. Thus the initial jump is to a value of λ greater than λ_1, such as λ'_0 in the figure. After the jump, λ increases steadily back to its initial level. The effect on the rates of investment and growth can be read from the left-hand quadrant. There is initially a "sharp" decline and then a recovery of investment and growth as λ jumps to λ'_0 and then moves back to λ_0.

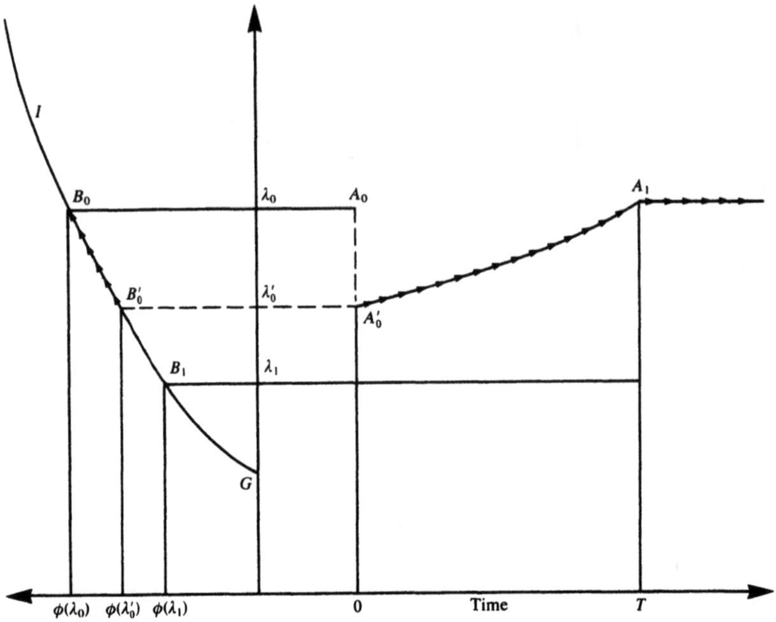

Fig. 5

Output, Employment and the Real Wage Rate

It is shown in Kouri (1978) that an increase in the real wage rate not only causes classical unemployment in the short run,[3] but it also reduces the rate of growth in output and employment by lowering the rate of profit. Above, we established the fact that a reduction in the rate of profit, whatever its cause, lowers the rate of growth in output. We now examine the implications of this result more carefully.

Figure 6 illustrates the economy growing steadily before time 0, with output growing at the same rate as labor supply in terms of effective labor input. At time 0, there is an increase in the real wage rate, and the level of output immediately declines to A_1. But the story does not end here. From A_1 on the rate of investment will be less and therefore the rate of growth will also be less; the gap between "potential output" and actual output grows wider and wider. There is nothing that aggregate demand policy can do, however, to get the economy back to its trend growth path unless inflation succeeds in reducing the real wage rate and in increasing the rate of profit. Even then, inflation may be counterproductive from the viewpoint of growth and capital formation once the distortionary effects of taxes in the presence of inflation are taken into account; see Feldstein (1980).

[3] See Barro & Grossman (1971), Malinvaud (1977), Bruno & Sachs (1981).

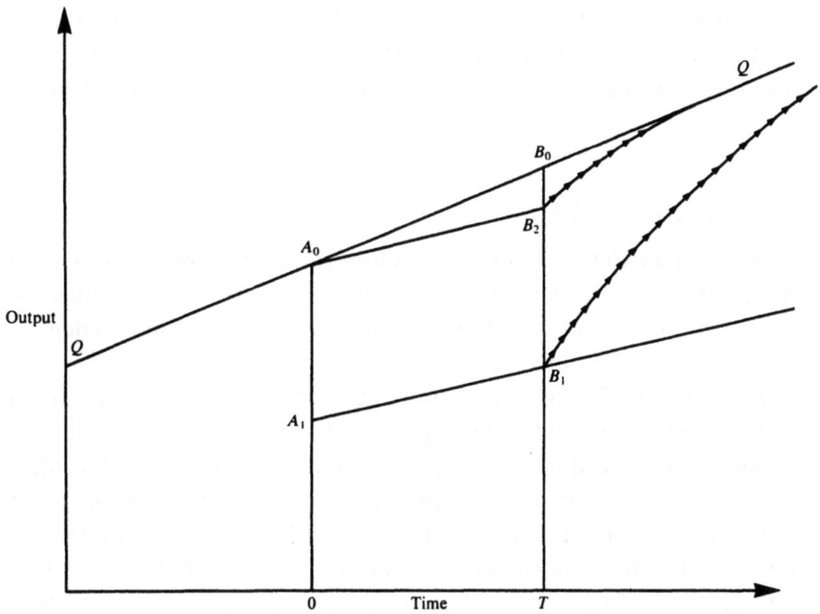

Fig. 6

Even if real wages become completely flexible after some time, for example at time T, output could not be restored to its trend growth path (B_0 in the figure) immediately because of the shortfall in capital formation in the intervening period. The maximum feasible level of output is the full employment level, B_2 in Figure 6. The fastest way to get the economy back to its trend growth path, if it were feasible, would be to restore full employment immediately by lowering the real wage rate and, from then on, to grow at full employment. This alternative is indicated by the arrows going from B_2. Any other recovery program, such as the one going from B_1, implies a slower return to the trend growth path because of a lower rate of profit, and hence a lower rate of investment.

Anticipation of Labor Shortage

If the rate of growth in output exceeds the "natural growth rate" determined by the rate of growth in labor input in effective units, full employment will eventually be reached and at that point, the analysis thus far no longer applies without modifications. If firms anticipate that full employment will eventually be reached, this, too, will have an effect on the shadow price of capital and hence on the rate of investment today. The more distant the prospective labor shortage is, however, the less effect it has on current investment decisions—for a long time the steady growth path is a reasonable approximation of the fully optimal plan. Because of a considerable gain in terms of clarity of certain key economic relationships, we have chosen to ignore the effect of a prospective future labor shortage on current investment.

III. The Complete Model

We now close the model developed in Section II as far as the rate of interest is concerned. The rate of interest and the rate of growth are simultaneously determined by the rate of profit on the one hand, and "impatience" or savings behavior on the other.

A necessary and sufficient condition for the existence of a unique steady-growth equilibrium is derived and it is proven that it is the only equilibrium.

The model is then applied to study the effects of changes in the rate of profit and in the propensity to save on the rate of interest and the rate of growth. In the concluding section, the effect of capital income taxes is analyzed. It is shown that a wedge between the rate of interest received by savers and the rate of interest paid by investors lowers the price of capital and the rate of capital formation and growth.

Optimal Saving and Consumption

It is assumed that society consists of Ramsey families with infinite lifetime who seek to maximize an additive intertemporal utility function of the form:

$$J = \max \int_0^\infty U(C)\, e^{-\delta\tau}\, \delta\tau, \tag{17}$$

where U is the instantaneous utility function, C is consumption and δ is the rate of time preference. The U function is assumed to be twice continuously differentiable, strictly concave, increasing and positive:

$$U(C) > 0, \quad U'(C) > 0, \quad U''(C) < 0. \tag{18}$$

For future reference we define the elasticity of the U function as:

$$\eta = \eta(C) = -\frac{U''(C)\,C}{U'(C)} > 0. \tag{19}$$

In this paper we assume that η is constant. Population is assumed to be constant and is set equal to one so that all variables are in *per capita* terms.

Each family receives an equal share of labor income (and unemployment) and capital income. Labor income is perfectly substitutable with capital income in the sense that receipt of one unit of wage income at time τ has the same present value as a τ period discount bond. Therefore, we can lump capital and labor income together and study the savings–consumption choice in terms of accumulation of one asset yielding a time varying instantaneous rate of return equal to $r(\tau)$, and income equal to $r(\tau)A(\tau)$, where $A(\tau)$ is the real value of total wealth at time τ. Ignoring taxes and the government, we have the asset accumulation equation:

$$\dot{A} = r(\tau)A - C. \tag{20}$$

Maximization of (17) subject to (20) yields the first order conditions:

$$U'(C) = \mu \tag{21 a}$$

$$\dot{\mu} = [\delta - r(\tau)]\mu \tag{21 b}$$

where μ is the marginal opportunity cost of one extra unit of current consumption.

The optimal saving problem is familiar and we need not discuss it any further, except to note that from equations (21), the optimal consumption plan satisfies the differential equation:

$$\eta\dot{C}/C = r(\tau) - \delta. \tag{22}$$

This enables us to go directly to the analysis of market equilibrium.

Market Equilibrium

In equilibrium the demand for consumer goods must equal the supply of consumer goods. The supply of consumer goods, in turn, is equal to the difference between total output and the demand for investment goods.

$$C^s = Q - H(I, K) \tag{23}$$

Substituting from Section II.1 we obtain:

$$C^s = \sigma K - h(\phi(\lambda))K = [\sigma - h(\phi(\lambda))]K, \quad \text{for } \lambda > h'(0) \tag{24 a}$$

$$C^s = (\sigma - \alpha)K, \quad \text{for } \lambda \leqslant h'(C). \tag{24 b}$$

Assuming continuous equilibrium between the demand for and the supply of consumer goods, we can substitute $\dot{C}^s/C^s$ for $\dot{C}/C$. Using the fact that $\dot{K}/K = \phi(\lambda) - \alpha$ for $\lambda > h'(0)$, and $\dot{K}/K = -\alpha$ for $\lambda \leqslant h'(0)$, we obtain

$$r(\tau) = \delta + \eta(\phi(\lambda) - \alpha) - \frac{\eta\lambda\phi'(\lambda)}{\sigma - h(\phi(\lambda))}\dot{\lambda}, \quad \text{for } \lambda > h'(0); \tag{25 a}$$

$$r(\tau) = \delta - \eta\alpha, \quad \text{for } \lambda \leqslant h'(0). \tag{25 b}$$

In (25 a) we used the fact that $h'(\phi(\lambda)) = \lambda$.

It is shown in Appendix II that if an equilibrium solution exists—with

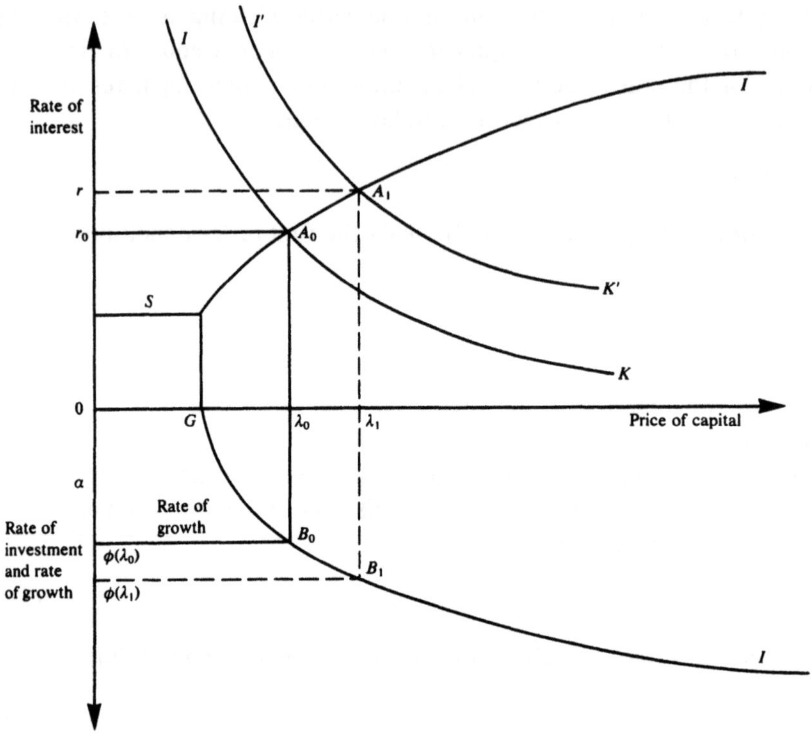

Fig. 7

firms and households implementing their optimal plans—it is given by the stationary solution:

$$(\alpha+r)\lambda = v-h(\phi(\lambda))+\lambda\phi(\lambda) \tag{26a}$$

$$r=\delta+\eta(\phi(\lambda)-\alpha); \quad \text{for } \lambda>h'(0) \tag{26b}$$

$$r=\delta-\eta\alpha \tag{27a}$$

$$\lambda=\frac{v}{r+\alpha}; \quad \text{for } \lambda\leqslant h'(0). \tag{27b}$$

It is shown further that a necessary and sufficient condition for the existence of a unique steady-growth equilibrium is that

$$\delta>(1-\eta)(\bar{\phi}\lambda-\alpha), \tag{28}$$

where δ = the rate of time preference, y = elasticity of substitution between "today's" and "tomorrow's" consumption, and $\bar{\phi}\lambda-\alpha$ = maximal rate of growth.

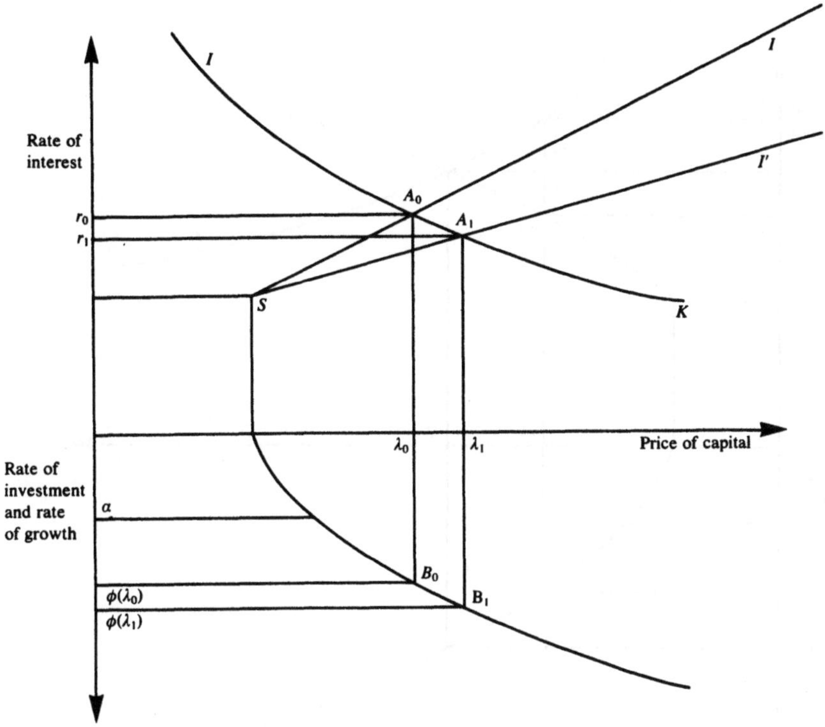

Fig. 8

Fundamental Determinants of the Rate of Interest and the Rate of Growth

We now analyze how the rate of interest and the rate of growth depend on savings behavior and the rate of profit. Figure 7 illustrates the determination of the equilibrium rate of interest, the equilibrium price of capital and the equilibrium rate of growth. The *SI* schedule plots the interest rate as a function of the price of capital, and it is defined by setting $\dot{\lambda}$ equal to zero in equation (25 a) for values of λ greater than $h'(0)$. For smaller values of λ, the rate of interest is equal to $\delta - y\alpha$, which can be positive or negative. As λ increases, r also increases because $\phi'(\lambda)$ is positive. In the limit r approaches $\delta + \eta(\bar{\phi} - \alpha)$.

The downward sloping *IK* schedule plots the relationship between the value of capital and the interest rate. It can also be interpreted as an equilibrium condition for the equity market. The *IK* schedule also has a discontinuity at $\lambda = h'(0)$ when gross investment becomes zero.

As shown in the Appendix, provided that condition 26 holds, the *IK* and the *SI* schedules have a unique intersection, represented by A_0 in Figure 7.

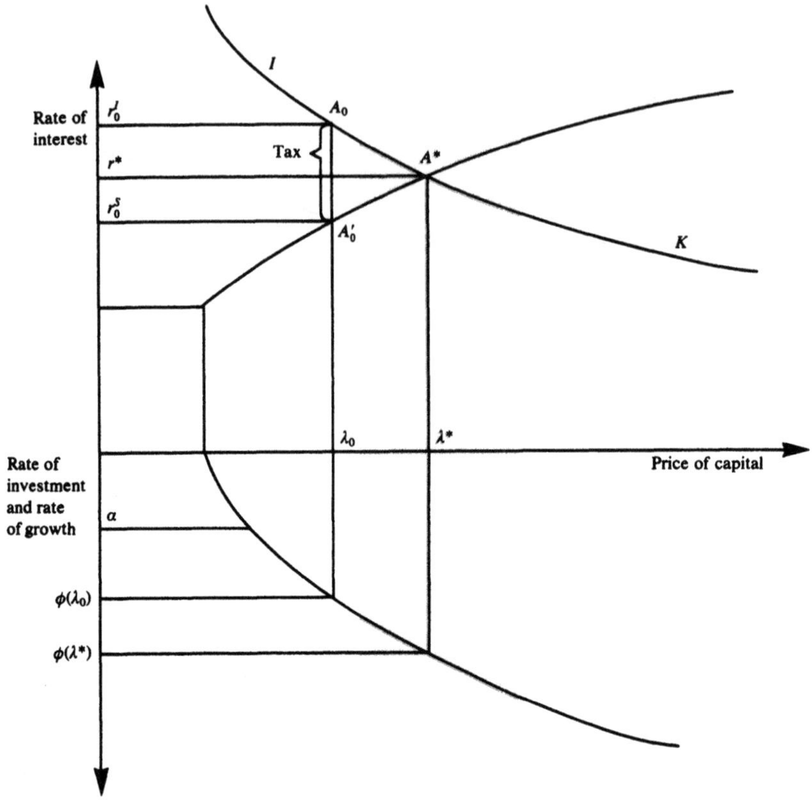

Fig. 9

This intersection determines the equilibrium rate of interest and the equilibrium price of capital.

The rate of investment can be read from the lower quadrant in Figure 7. At the initial equilibrium position, the rate of investment is equal to $\phi(\lambda_0)$ and the rate of growth is equal to $\phi(\lambda_0)-\alpha$.

An increase in the rate of profit shifts the IK schedule to the right, to $I'K'$ in the figure. New equilibrium obtains at (A_1, B_1) with a higher interest rate and a higher rate of investment and growth ($\phi(\lambda_1)$ and $\phi(\lambda_1)-\alpha$, respectively).

Figure 8 illustrates the effects of an increase in "savings propensity" interpreted as a decline in the rate of time preference. The economy is initially in equilibrium at (A_0, B_0) with interest rate r_0, price of capital λ_0 and rate of investment $\phi(\lambda_0)$. A decline in δ tilts the SI schedule down. New equilibrium obtains at (A_1, B_1) with a lower interest rate (r_0), higher price of capital (λ_1), and higher rate of investment ($\phi(\lambda_1)$) and growth ($\phi(\lambda_1-\alpha)$).

We conclude by illustrating the effects of capital income taxation, leaving a more detailed analysis of tax policies for another paper.

With taxation of capital income, the cost of capital to firms is higher than the interest rate obtained by savers on their savings. This wedge reduces the price of capital, the rate of investment and the rate of growth in the economy as is shown in Figure 9. With taxation the economy is in equilibrium at (A_0, A_0', B_0), with price of capital λ_0 and rate of investment $\phi(\lambda_0)$. Elimination of the tax distortion would lower the cost of capital and increase the rate of interest to savers to r^*, increase the price of capital and equity to λ^*, increase the rate of investment to $\phi(\lambda^*)$, and the rate of growth to $\phi(\lambda^*) - \alpha$.

IV. Conclusion

The relationship between the rate of profit and the rate of growth has been examined in an economy where firms are not constrained by either aggregate demand or supply of labor. The model provides one perspective on the slowing-down of growth in the industrialized countries in the presence of high and increasing unemployment, as well as on the continuation of rapid growth in the newly-industrialized countries. In the industrial countries the rate of profit, relative to the cost of capital, is too low to justify a sufficiently rapid rate of capital formation; in the NICs the rate of profit is high and consequently the center of growth in the world economy is gravitating towards these countries.

From the perspective of the model developed in this paper, restoration of growth at full employment requires a reduction in the real wage rate and/or policies that stimulate capital formation and growth.

Recent events in Finland are illuminating in this respect. In the 1970s, Finland experienced a severe recession that lasted from 1975 to 1978 with virtually no growth in output. Rather than attempting to stimulate domestic demand, economic policy aimed to restore profitability in the tradable sector by means of devaluations, wage restraint and tax policies supportive of capital formation. These policies succeeded in restoring profitability and led to a vigorous export and investment-led boom in 1979/80.

I do not want to conclude by implying that this is what other countries should do, nor do I want to suggest that we can ignore the aggregate demand side. However, in a capitalist economy, growth is the result of capital formation undertaken by profit-seeking firms and individuals. Whatever else is done in the field of economic policy, growth at full employment is not possible unless it is profitable for firms to invest at a sufficiently high rate. Maintenance of "sufficient" profitability requires not only that aggregate demand be sufficient, but also that the real wage rate be appropriate. The increase in the real cost of energy and increasing competition from low-cost developing countries are two examples of real changes that require adjustments in the labor market; the failure of recent years is, at least in part, the failure of real wages to adjust to these changes. As a result, profitability has been squeezed and the rate of capital formation and growth has slowed down below a level that is consistent with full employment.

Finally, the analysis in this paper brings out the importance of profitability in the process of structural adjustment. Suppose that there is a reduction in the price of a tradable good with no change in other prices. The domestic industry producing this good will experience a decline in the rate of profit, and therefore a decline in its rate of growth. In order for full employment to be maintained, there has to be an increase in the rate of profit in other industries. Thus, there has to be a decline in the product real wage in these industries. Without such adjustment, the relative price change will lead to increased, and growing, unemployment.

Appendix I

We first derive a necessary and sufficient condition for the existence of a unique steady-state growth (or decline) solution for the model in Section II and then argue that if it exists, it is also the optimal solution. If the steady-growth solution is not unique, or if it does not exist, there is no optimal solution.

To study the existence of a solution to $\dot{\lambda}=0$, we rewrite equations (14a) and (14b) as

$$(\alpha+r)\lambda = v-h(\phi(\lambda))+\lambda\phi(\lambda), \quad \text{for } \lambda > \boldsymbol{\lambda} = \eta'(0), \tag{A 1}$$

$$(\alpha+r)\lambda = v, \quad \text{for } \lambda \leqslant \boldsymbol{\lambda} = h'(0). \tag{A 2}$$

Figure 10 plots the values of both sides of equations (A 1) and (A 2) as functions of λ. The $0X$ ray represents the l.h.s. and it has slope $(\alpha+r)$. The r.h.s. is represented by a schedule that starts at $y=v$ for values of λ below $\boldsymbol{\lambda}=h'(0)$. Consider first the case where $\boldsymbol{\lambda}_0$ is less than the value of the firm at zero level of investment ($v/(\alpha+r)$). As λ increases beyond $\lambda=\lambda_0$ investment picks up and the r.h.s. becomes equal to $v-h(\phi(\lambda))+\lambda\phi(\lambda)$. From then on there are two possibilities. One is that the y-schedule intersects the $0X$ ray and the other is that it does not. The slope of the y-schedule is $-h'(\phi(\lambda))\,\phi'(\lambda)+\phi\lambda'(\lambda)+\phi(\lambda)=\phi(\lambda)$ because by the first-order condition, $h'(\phi(\lambda))=\lambda$. Thus the y-schedule increases and at an increasing rate because $\phi'(\lambda)>0$. A necessary condition for the y-schedule to intersect the $0X$-ray is that $\phi(\lambda)$ is less than $r+\alpha$, or that the rate of growth $\phi(\lambda)-\alpha$ is less than the rate of interest for "small" values of λ, that is for values of λ close to $\boldsymbol{\lambda}$.

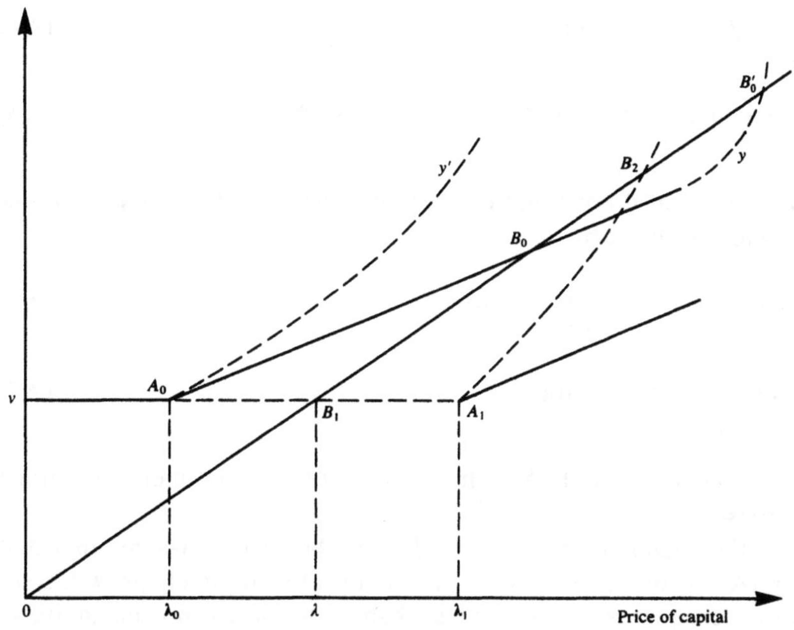

Fig. 10

This is necessary because if the slope of the y-schedule at A_0 is greater than that of the $0X$ ray, there can never be an intersection, as is illustrated by the broken y' line. Suppose that $r+\alpha$ is greater than $\phi(\lambda)$ for "small" values of λ so that the y-schedule intersects the $0X$ ray at B_0. Is this a unique equilibrium? Not necessarily because $\phi(\lambda)$ increases with λ and thus the y-schedule could intersect the $0X$ once more, as illustrated by the broken line going through B_0', but only once more. If, however, $\phi(\lambda)$ is less than $r+\alpha$ as λ increases without limit, the y-line must intersect the $0X$ ray and only once.

Consider next the possibility that the critical value of λ is greater than $v/(\alpha+r)$, such as λ_1 in Figure 10. Then $\lambda=v/(\alpha+r)$ is a rest point of the system but there can still be another rest point. If $\phi(\lambda)$ exceeds $(r+\alpha)$ for large values of λ, the y-schedule can intersect the $0X$ ray for the second time as is illustrated by the broken line going from A_1 to B_2. A sufficient and necessary condition for this not to occur is that $\lim \phi(\lambda)$ is less than $\alpha+r$ as λ goes to infinity.

We have therefore established that a necessary and sufficient condition for the existence of a unique solution of equations (A 1) and (A 2) is that

$$\lim_{\lambda\to\infty} \phi(\lambda) = \bar{\phi} < r+\alpha. \qquad \text{(A 3)}$$

The stationary solution is given by:

$$\lambda^* = \frac{v}{r+\alpha} \quad \text{if} \quad \frac{v}{r+\alpha} \leqslant h'(0) \tag{A 4}$$

$$(\alpha+r)\lambda^* = v - h(\phi(\lambda^*)) + \lambda^*\phi(\lambda^*), \quad \text{if} \quad \frac{v}{r+\alpha} > h'(0). \tag{A 5}$$

Next we argue that if condition (A 3) is met, there exists a unique optimal solution and it is given by:

$$I = 0, \quad \dot{K}/K = -\alpha, \quad \text{if} \quad \frac{v}{r+\alpha} \leqslant h'(0) \tag{A 6}$$

$$I/K = \phi(\lambda^*) \quad \text{if} \quad \frac{v}{r+\alpha} > h'(0) \tag{A 7}$$

where λ^* is the solution of (A 5). If condition (A 3) is not met, no optimal solution exists.

Leaving the details of the argument for another paper, assume first that condition (A 3) is met and consider alternatives to the steady-growth solution. For the case where $v/(r+\alpha)$ is less than $h'(0)$, there is no ambiguity, so assume that $v/(r+\alpha)$ is greater than $h'(0)$. Suppose that λ is initially set either greater or less than λ^*. In the second case λ must increase without limit because $\partial\dot{\lambda}/\partial\lambda = \alpha + r - \phi(\lambda) > 0$.

Asymptotically λ then increases at rate $\alpha + r - \bar{\phi}$ where $\bar{\phi} = \lim \phi(\lambda)$, while K would in that case asymptotically grow at the maximal rate $\bar{\phi} - \alpha$. Therefore $\lim K(\phi) e^{-rt} \lambda(\phi) = \lim e^{\alpha t}$ and thus the transversality condition is violated. If, on the other hand, $\lambda(0)$ is set below λ^*, λ decreases at rate $\alpha + r - \phi(\lambda)$ and reaches the critical value $h'(0)$ in a finite time. At that point it is no longer optimal to follow the program which means, according to Bellman's principle, that the program was not optimal in the first place.

Thus equations (A 6) and (A 7) indeed define the optimal solution for the case where condition (A 3) holds. If condition (A 3) does not hold, firms can always increase profits without limit by growing faster since the growth rate can be made greater than the interest rate. Therefore, no optimal finite solution exists. In market equilibrium the interest rate becomes an endogenous variable and can never be less than the rate of growth.

We also note that along the optimal growth path the market value of the firm satisfies:

$$E = \int_0^\infty [vK^* - H(I^*, K^*)]\, e^{-r\tau}\, d\tau = L^* K^* \tag{A 8}$$

where λ^* is given by equations (A 6) and (A 7) and $(I^*(\tau), K^*(\tau))$ is the associated optimal investment program. Thus, if the firm issues only equity to finance its investment program, and if the market knows the firm's

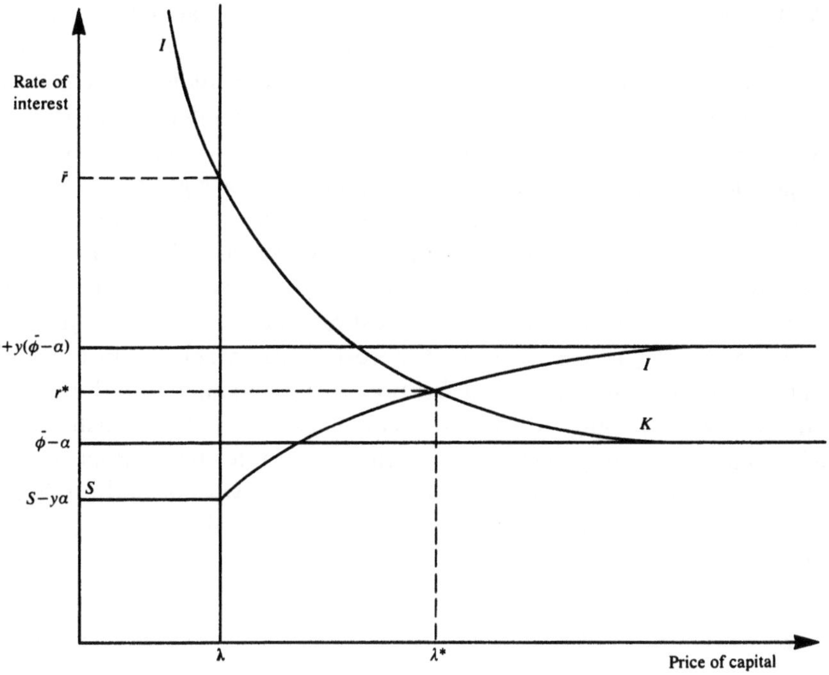

Fig. 11

investment program, the equilibrium price of equity is equal to the shadow price of capital λ^*.

Appendix II

In this appendix we analyze the existence of an equilibrium in the model of Section III.

Any equilibrium solution must satisfy differential equations (25) and (14). As in Section II, we show that the only equilibrium solution is a steady-growth solution defined by setting $\dot{\lambda}$ equal to zero in (14) and (25). If there is a steady-growth solution, it must be unique; if there is none, no equilibrium exists.

Figure 11 enables us to analyze the existence of equilibrium. We continue to assume that the rate of growth is bounded from above:

$$\lim_{\lambda \to \infty} \phi(\lambda) = \bar{\phi}. \tag{A 9}$$

The *SI* schedule plots the interest rate as a function of the price of capital defined by setting $\dot{\lambda}$ equal to zero in (25a). For λ less than or equal to

$\lambda = h'(0)$, the interest rate is equal to $\delta - \eta\alpha$, which can be positive or negative. As λ increases, r also increases because $\phi'(\lambda)$ is positive. As λ approaches infinity, r approaches $\delta + \eta(\bar{\phi} - \alpha)$. η is the elasticity of the U function and from equation (19) it can be interpreted as the interest elasticity of the consumption schedule. If η is equal to one (the Bernoulli case), a one percentage point increase in the rate of growth increases the equilibrium interest rate by the same amount. In this case a necessary and sufficient condition for the existence of a steady-growth solution is that the rate of time preference be positive. If η is greater than one (interest inelastic case), the rate of time preference need not be positive; the interest rate increases by more than the rate of growth. If η is less than one (interest elastic case), the rate of time preference must be greater than a fraction of the maximal growth rate.

The downward sloping *IK* schedule is the locus of r and λ consistent with equilibrium in the equity market. For high interest rates ($r \geqslant \bar{r}$), gross investment is zero and the price of capital is given by $\lambda = v/(r - \alpha)$ and obviously goes to zero as r goes to infinity. Fro r less than $\bar{r}$ we have, from equation (14):

$$r = -\alpha + \phi(\lambda) + \frac{v}{\lambda} - \frac{h(\phi(\lambda))}{\lambda}.$$

Therefore r is a decreasing function of λ since $\partial r/\partial\lambda = -(v - h)/\lambda^2$. As λ increases without limit, r approaches $-\alpha + \bar{\phi}$. Since both the *SI* and *IK* schedules are monotonic, they can intersect only once. A necessary and sufficient condition for the existence of a unique intersection is that $\delta + \eta(\bar{\phi} - \alpha) > \bar{\phi} - \alpha$ or

$$\delta > (1 - \eta)(\bar{\phi} - \alpha). \tag{A 10}$$

Another possibility, implicitly ruled out by the way Figure 11 is drawn, is the zero-investment solution with negative growth rate $-\alpha$. This solution obtains if the critical interest rate $\bar{r}$, which makes gross investment zero, is less than $\delta - \eta\alpha$. In this case the *IK* schedule intersects the straight line segment of the *IS* schedule. This possibility can occur if the rate of profit is very low.

It can be shown that $\partial\dot{\lambda}/\partial\lambda$ is positive around the stationary solution. Therefore, $\lambda = \lambda^*$ is an unstable equilibrium.

If λ is set initially below λ^*, it continues to decline at an accelerating pace and therefore must reach the critical value $\boldsymbol{\lambda}$ in a finite time. At that point it is no longer optimal to continue along such a path, which means that it could not have been optimal in the first place. On the other hand, if λ is greater than λ^* initially, it increases at an accelerating pace thereafter. The rate of growth converges asymptotically to $\bar{\phi} - \alpha$ while, from equation

(14a), $\dot{\lambda}/\lambda$ converges to $\alpha+r-\bar{\phi}$. This violates the transversality condition for the firms and therefore investment cannot be optimal along such a path.

We conclude then that condition (A 10) is a necessary and sufficient condition for the existence of a unique steady-growth equilibrium. The equilibrium solution is given by:

$$(\alpha+r)\lambda = \nu - h(\phi(\lambda)) + \lambda\phi(\lambda) \tag{A 11}$$

$$r = \delta + \eta(\phi(\lambda) - \alpha) \quad \text{for } \lambda > \frac{\nu}{r+\alpha} \tag{A 12}$$

$$r = \delta - \eta\alpha, \tag{A 13}$$

$$\lambda = \frac{\nu}{r+\alpha}. \tag{A 14}$$

References

Abel, Andrew, B. & Blanchard, Olivier J.: An intertemporal equilibrium model of saving and investment. Report 8006, University of Chicago, Center for Mathematical Studies, Business and Economics, February 1980. Forthcoming in *Econometrica*.

Barro, R. J. & Grossman, H. L.: A general disequilibrium model of income and employment. *American Economic Review*, March 1971.

Bruno, M. & Sachs, J.: Supply versus demand approaches to the problem of stagflation. In *Macroeconomic policies for growth and price stability: The European perspective* (ed. J. C. B. Mohr). Paul Steinbeck, Tübingen, 1981.

Feldstein, M.: Fiscal policies, inflation and capital formation. *American Economic Review*, 1980.

Kouri, P. J. K.: Profitability and growth in a small open economy. In *Inflation and employment in open economies*, (ed. Assar Lindbeck). North Holland, Amsterdam, 1979.

Lucas, R. E.: Adjustment costs and the theory of supply. *The Journal of Political Economy*, V. 75, No. 4, 1967.

Malinvaud, E.: *The theory of unemployment reconsidered*. Basil Blackwell, Oxford, 1977.

Malinvaud, E.: *Profitability and unemployment*. Cambridge University Press, London, 1980.

Marglin, S. A.: The rate of interest and the value of capital with unlimited supplies of labor. In *Essays on the theory of optimal economic growth* (ed. K. Shell). MIT Press, Cambridge, 1967.

Mussa, M.: Market value and the investment decision in an adjustment cost model of firm behavior. Department of Economics, University of Rochester, Discussion Paper 74-15, July 1974.

Nairay, A.: Consumption–investment decisions under uncertainty and variable time preferences. Unpublished Ph.D. Dissertation, Yale University, June 1981.

Söderström, Hans Tson: Production and investment under costs of adjustment: A survey. *Zeitschrift für Nationalökonomie 36*, 1976.

Treadway, A. B.: On rational entrepreneurial behavior and the demand for investment. *Review of Economic Studies 36*, 1969.

Uzawa, H.: Time preference and the Penrose effect in a two class model of economic growth. *The Journal of Political Economy 77*, 1969.

Williamson, J.: Profit, growth and sales maximization. *Economica 33*, 1966.

Yla-Liedenpohja, T.: On optimal financing, dividends, and investment of the firm. Ph.D. Dissertation, The Helsinki School of Economics, Helsinki, 1976.

Comment on P. J. K. Kouri, "Profitability and Growth"

Thorvaldur Gylfason

Institute for International Economic Studies, Stockholm, Sweden

The purpose of Kouri's paper is to establish an explicit link between profitability and growth in an economy characterized by capital shortage and excess supply of labor. This link is derived from the effect of the rate of profit on the investment behavior of intertemporally profit-maximizing firms which, in the second part of the paper, is taken to interact with the saving behavior of intertemporally utility-maximizing households.

The paper is divided into two parts. First, the author presents a dynamic model of investment in which the interest rate is exogenous and develops some propositions about the effects of changes in the interest rate, the rate of profit and the cost of investment on the optimal rate of investment and hence growth. In the second part, an intertemporal optimization model of saving is added and the interest rate becomes endogenous. From this "complete model", Kouri derives further propositions about the effects of exogenous changes in saving behavior, profitability and the cost of investment on the interest rate, investment and growth as well as on the shadow price of capital.

As the author acknowledges, the two major ingredients of the analysis, the investment model and the saving model, are well known and widely accepted. In fact, the same applies to the main propositions derived from the analysis. Thus, hardly any economist is unfamiliar with the basic conclusion of Section II that a "decline in the rate of interest, an increase in the rate of profit and a decline in the cost of investment represent three alternative strategies for stimulating capital formation and growth" (p. 323). Nor is it likely that the main result of the second part of the paper would take anyone by surprise, i.e., that an "increase in the rate of profit [results in] a higher interest rate and a higher rate of investment and growth, [while] an increase in "savings propensity" [produces] a lower interest rate, higher price of capital and higher rate of investment and growth" (p. 332). These propositions are well known and have long been an integral part of the conventional wisdom of mainstream macroeconomics.

As the derivation of these propositions presented in the paper is somewhat esoteric, it may be helpful to sketch the essence of the argument here

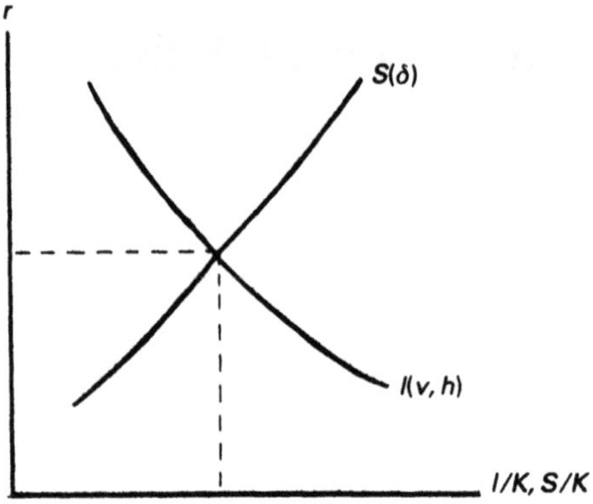

Fig. 1

in order to demonstrate the elementary character of the conclusions that are drawn from the analysis. In Section II, a dynamic theory of profit-maximizing firms is used to derive an investment function:

$$I/K = \phi(\lambda), \tag{1}$$

where I/K is the ratio of (gross) investment to the capital stock ("the investment rate"), λ is the shadow price of installed capital, and $\phi' > 0$. The first-order conditions of the solution to the dynamic optimal control problem of the firm are shown to imply that the price of capital varies inversely with the interest rate, r, and directly with the rate of profit, v, from which it follows that the investment function may be written in the following standard form:

$$I/K = f(r, v), \tag{2}$$

where the signs of the partial derivatives, $f_r < 0$ and $f_v > 0$, imply two of the key propositions mentioned above. The author then proceeds to discuss the effects of anticipated and transitory changes in r and v. Assuming real wage rigidity and unemployment, he then uses the model to show that a rise in the real wage lowers the rate of profit and hence the investment rate and the rate of growth, and increases unemployment.

In Section III, an intertemporal theory of utility-maximizing households is used to derive a standard saving function consistent with an optimal consumption path that satisfies the differential equation

$$\dot{C}/C = (r - \delta)/\eta, \tag{3}$$

where C is consumption, δ is the rate of time preference, and η is the elasticity of marginal utility with respect to C. Then, as consumption is

Table 1

On	Effects of an increase in Propensity to save	Profit-ability	Cost of investment	Taxes on capital
Interest rate	−	+	−	...
Investment rate	+	+	−	−
Growth rate	+	+	−	−
Price of capital	+	+	−	−

proportional to the capital stock in equilibrium, so that $\dot{C}/C$ equals $\dot{K}/K = I/K$, and saving S equals investment, equation (3) may be converted into a (quasi-reduced-form) saving function:

$$S/K = (r - \delta)/\eta. \tag{4}$$

The essence of the analysis can now be illustrated in an elementary diagram (Figure 1) where the interest rate is shown on the vertical axis and investment and saving are shown on the horizontal axis. Equation (2) is shown as a negatively sloped investment schedule which shifts to the right when profitability rises (and to the left when the cost of investment h rises). Equation (4) is shown as a positively sloped saving schedule which shifts to the left when the rate of time preference rises (i.e., when the propensity to save falls). The diagram therefore implies the sign pattern shown in Table 1, which summarizes the main propositions presented in the paper. The signs shown in the bottom line of the table are implied by equation (1), while those shown in the last column follow from the obvious fact, as pointed out by the author, that taxation of capital income drives a wedge between the cost of capital to firms and the rate of return on savings, thus reducing incentives to save and invest.

To recapitulate, the main conclusion of the paper is that in order to stimulate investment and growth in the industrial countries it is necessary to (1) encourage saving, (2) raise profitability, (3) reduce the cost of investment, and (4) reduce capital taxation. Kouri develops these propositions rigorously and in detail, and pays considerable attention to the derivation of conditions for the existence, uniqueness and stability of equilibria. But the fact remains that the ingredients, methods and conclusions of the analysis are all familiar and undisputed,[1] although some details differ. Thus, as a true connoisseur, Kouri serves old wine in old bottles; but this

[1] See, e.g., Karl Shell (ed.), *Essays on the Theory of Optimal Economic Growth*, MIT Press, Cambridge, Mass., 1967.

vintage, one might add, improves with age, for a clear understanding of the conventional wisdom about the crucial link between interest rates, profits and the incentives to save and invest is of great importance, and increasingly so in view of the slowdown in productivity growth, and hence in economic growth in general, in our part of the world since the early 1970s.

Finally, two comments or qualifications are in order. In the first place, a clear distinction should be made between medium-term growth and the rate of growth in the economy as it moves along a long-run steady-state growth path. For the neoclassical growth models developed over the last quarter of a century have taught us that while the long-run rate of growth is determined by the growth rates of the labor force and labor productivity, the medium-term growth rate (i.e., the rate of growth as the economy moves from one long-run steady-state path to another) also depends on saving and investment behavior. Thus, by stimulating saving and investment, public authorities can lift the economy onto a higher growth path and thus raise the rate of growth in the medium term. But for increased saving and investment to raise the rate of growth in the long run, it is necessary that they create conditions for more rapid growth in labor productivity (i.e., more rapid labor-augmenting technical progress); otherwise, increased capital formation cannot increase the long-run rate of growth in the economy as suggested by Kouri.

In the second place, it is essential in any analysis of saving, investment, interest and growth in the inflation-ridden industrial countries at present to distinguish between real and nominal rates of interest (and profit). By not making this distinction (and by leaving money matters out of the analysis), Kouri ignores an important issue that concerns the relationship between inflation and real interest rates (as well as real wages and profits). In view of the variability of real interest rates in the industrial countries over the last decade and of old and new evidence of an inverse relationship between real interest rates and the expected rate of inflation over this period and even longer, it would seem that a theory of profitability and growth performance in the industrial countries in our times should take inflation into account.

Employment Policies, Wage Formation and Trade Union Behavior in a Small Open Economy

*Lars Calmfors**

Institute for International Economic Studies, Stockholm, Sweden

Abstract

A model of trade-union determined wages is developed which provides an explanation of underemployment based on optimizing behavior. It is shown that fiscal policy will in general affect employment under perfect foresight and immediate wage flexibility. Future consequences of short-run stabilization policies are discussed. Ratchet effects with respect to government expenditure and game-theoretic interdependence between government and trade union behavior are emphasized. If the trade union takes short-run policy measures in order to increase employment as an indication of an employment stabilization rule, the future behavior of the trade union changes and the result may be a decrease in long-run employment.

I. Introduction

The purpose of this paper is to examine the role of stabilization policy in small open economies. The background is the growing scepticism about traditional Keynesian employment policies in the recent macroeconomic discussion, which has stressed the risks of long-run adverse effects on inflation and resource allocation.[1] These risks are clearly illustrated by the recent experiences of many small open economies, such as Belgium, Norway and Sweden, where the countercyclical policies adhered to in the mid-1970s seem to have prevented wage adjustments and contributed to a declining tradables sector and a growing public sector.

On the theoretical level, the criticism against Keynesian policies has come mainly from the *rational-expectations school,* according to which demand policies can change employment only to the extent that private agents base their decisions on incorrect expectations.[2] With perfect fore-

---

* I would like to thank Lars E. O. Svensson for helpful discussions on the technical parts of the paper. I have also benefited from comments by M. June Flanders, Thorvaldur Gylfason, Michael Hoel, Henrik Horn, Assar Lindbeck, Felix Nordström, Andrew J. Oswald, Torsten Persson, Assaf Razin and Hans Tson Söderström. I am grateful to Gunnel Löfberg for typing the manuscript with great care and patience.

[1] Cf. e.g. The McCracken Report (1977).

[2] Cf. e.g. Lucas (1975) or Sargent & Wallace (1975 and 1976).

sight, stabilization policy loses its effect on employment and instead only affects the price level. But although the importance of endogenizing expectations is now widely recognized, these conclusions can be questioned. Perfect price–wage flexibility and market clearing are usually assumed and variations in employment are regarded as *voluntary*. In contrast to this, a more Keynesian tradition still stresses how various kinds of wage stickiness give rise to *involuntary* unemployment, thereby creating a role for active employment policies.[3] But this literature usually fails to give convincing reasons for the assumed wage stickiness.

This analysis stresses the importance of *trade unions* for wage formation. Indeed, in view of the important role played by trade unions in most small European economies, it is surprising that so little attention has been devoted to them in the literature.[4] This neglect is particularly serious for the Scandinavian economies, where wage bargaining is highly centralized.

The purpose of the analysis is to discuss the interaction between employment policies and wage formation. A wage explosion of the type that occurred in 1975/76 in Sweden will be taken as a point of reference. The aim is to provide a *general* discussion of alternative policy responses in such a situation. To simplify, it is assumed that there exists only *one* trade union which organizes all labor and that this trade union is powerful enough to set the wage rate. The trade union maximizes a utility function with the real wage and employment as arguments; see Oswald (1979 and 1980). The fact that the trade union acts as a monopolist makes it possible to explain the existence of underemployment without resorting to various arbitrary assumptions on wage stickiness.

Our approach fails to take into account factors such as the bargaining process and employers' resistance to union wage demands, competition between various groups of wage earners and market-determined "wage drift" beyond the control of centralized bargaining. Instead the focus is on the interaction between government and trade union behavior. The analysis stresses how short-run stabilization policies that accomodate past wage increases may give rise to long-run effects, *either* because of ratchet effects with respect to government expenditure, *or* because the trade union learns about the government's reaction function (policy rule).

The results can be compared with the rational-expectations literature. Here, demand policies will have real effects under perfect foresight and wage flexibility. But these effects need not work in the expected direction. A key conclusion is that Keynesian employment policies may have per-

---

[3] Cf. e.g. Buiter (1980), Modigliani (1977) or Solow (1979).

[4] Although a literature in labor economics, originating with Dunlop (1944), does exist, this tradition has never had a large impact on macroeconomics. For a recent exposition, see Mulvey (1978).

verse employment effects once the trade union takes government policy rules into account.

The paper is structured as follows. The basic analytical framework is given in Section II. It combines a model of a small open economy with the assumption of a utility-maximizing trade union that acts under perfect foresight and without constraints on the speed of wage adjustments. The model is reformulated in Section III to allow the trade union to make expectational errors. A wage disturbance is assumed to occur because the trade union overestimates international price increases and alternative government policy responses are discussed. The analysis is extended in Section IV by assuming ratchet effects for government expenditure. Game-theoretic considerations are introduced in Section V.

II. The Model Structure

In this section the determination of output and employment as well as trade union behavior are discussed. The effects of government policy changes are analyzed.

The Output-employment Bloc

Our economy produces two goods: tradables and nontradables. Tradables are produced according to a constant-returns-to-scale production function with both capital and labor as inputs. The stock of capital in the sector is assumed to be fixed, so that output and employment there depends only on the product real wage in the sector. The price of tradables in foreign currency is exogenously determined in the world market. Nontradables are also produced with capital and labor as inputs, but according to a production function with both constant returns to scale and fixed factor proportions. Since the capital stock is assumed to be fixed here as well, output of nontradables is proportional to employment below the point of full utilization of capital. This asymmetrical treatment of tradables and nontradables is not necessary but greatly facilitates our analysis of trade union behavior. It also conforms to the assumptions in the Scandinavian model.[5]

Private demand for each good depends on total private expenditure and the relative price between the two goods. Using the symbols listed below, the markets for tradables and nontradables can be described as follows:

$$X = S_T(w_T) - D_T(\bar{p}_N, \bar{Z}) \tag{1}$$

---

[5] Cf. Lindbeck (1978). An alternative possibility which gives the same structure is to assume that labor is the only input in the nontradables sector.

$$aE_N - D_N(\tilde{p}_N, \tilde{Z}) = 0 \tag{2}$$

$$P_N = \frac{W}{a}. \tag{3}$$

List of symbols

D_T = private demand for tradables
D_N = private demand for nontradables
P_N = money price of nontradables
P_T = money price of tradables in domestic currency
P_T^* = money price of tradables in foreign currency
e = exchange rate (units of domestic currency per unit of foreign currency)
$\tilde{p}_N$ = P_N/P_T = relative price between nontradables and tradables
$\tilde{Z}$ = total private expenditure measured in terms of tradables
X = trade balance measured in terms of tradables
S_T = private supply of tradables
W = money wage
w_T = W/P_T = product real wage in the tradables sector
w_N = W/P_N = product real wage in the nontradables sector
G_L = government purchases of labor in hours
t = marginal (and average) tax rate
$\tilde{Y}$ = value of private sector output measured in terms of tradables
E = total employment in hours
E_T = employment in hours in the tradables sector
E_N = employment in hours in the nontradables sector
P = $P(P_T, P_N)$ = an overall price index
$\tilde{w}$ = W/P = before-tax real wage
w^* = $\tilde{w}(1-t)$ = after-tax real wage
N = number of workers employed
h = an individual worker's supply of labor.

Partial derivatives are indicated by a subscript. D_{N1} for example is the partial derivative of demand for nontradables with respect to the first argument in the function (the relative price).

Equation (1) defines the trade balance as the difference between domestic supply and domestic demand for tradables. Equation (2) is the market-equilibrium condition for nontradables. The supply of nontradables is proportional to labor input. Equation (3) states that the price of nontradables equals marginal (and average) cost.

Provided that the wage rate is set above or at the market-clearing level, total employment (in hours) must equal total demand for labor (also measured in hours). Total demand for labor is obtained by adding the demands of the tradables sector, the nontradables sector and government. As in Söderström & Viotti (1978), government expenditures are confined to direct purchases of labor. This labor does not produce any marketed output during the time period studied.[6]

$$E = E_T(w_T) + E_N + G_L. \tag{4}$$

The private sector spends all its disposable income and holds no wealth. Private disposable income equals the sum of the production value of the private sector and the wage bill in the government sector minus total taxes. Measuring in terms of tradables we have:

$$\tilde{Z} = (1-t)(\tilde{Y} + w_T G_L) = (1-t)(S_T + \tilde{p}_N aE_N + w_T G_L). \tag{5}$$

The expression for the trade balance from equation (1) can be rewritten as the difference between government receipts and expenditures by adding the expression for excess supply of nontradables (equal to zero) from equation (2).

$$\begin{aligned} X &= S_T - D_T = (S_T - D_T) + \tilde{p}_N(aE_N - D_N) = (S_T + \tilde{p}_N aE_N) - (D_T + \tilde{p}_N D_N) \\ &= \tilde{Y} - \tilde{Z} = \tilde{Y} - (1-t)(\tilde{Y} + w_T G_L) = t\tilde{Y} - (1-t)\, w_T G_L. \end{aligned} \tag{6}$$

Although private saving or dissaving has been ruled out, the country as a whole may thus accumulate or decumulate wealth, since the government is not required to balance its budget. If there is a government budget deficit, the government will issue debt, but since the domestic private sector does not hold wealth, this debt must be issued abroad.

After choosing units of measurement so that $a=1$, we note that $w_N = W/P_N = 1$ and that $\tilde{p}_N = P_N/P_T = w_T/w_N = w_T$. Using this and making appropriate substitutions, the complete system can be written:

$$E_N - D_N[w_T, (1-t)\{S_T(w_T) + w_T E_N + w_T G_L\}] = 0 \tag{2'}$$

$$E = E_T(w_T) + E_N + G_L \tag{4}$$

$$X = t[S_T(w_T) + w_T E_N] - (1-t)\, w_T G_L. \tag{6'}$$

The solution to this system depends on the assumptions about wage and

---

[6] Adding government as a producer of tradables and nontradables does not change the qualitative conclusions, provided that the supply effects of changes in government production are dominated by the demand effects arising from the accompanying changes in the government wage bill. With our formulation, the labor employed by the government can be regarded as producing goods for government stocks. Likewise all qualitative results are unchanged if government expenditures are confined to purchases of nontradables.

exchange rate determination. We assume that the exchange rate e is fixed (or rather exogenous), so that the domestic-currency price of tradables $P_T = P_T^* e$ can also be treated as exogenous. At this stage we assume an exogenously determined money wage W. It then follows that the product real wage in the tradables sector $w_T = W/P_T$ can be treated as an exogenous variable too. Our three equations can then be solved for the endogenous variables: employment in the nontradables sector (E_N), total employment (E) and the trade balance (X). With the assumptions in the Appendix we get (the signs of the partial derivatives are indicated in parentheses):

$$E_N = E_N(\overset{(-)}{w_T}, \overset{(+)}{G_L}, \overset{(-)}{t}) \tag{7}$$

$$E = E(\overset{(-)}{w_T}, \overset{(+)}{G_L}, \overset{(-)}{t}) \tag{8}$$

$$X = X(\overset{(-)}{w_T}, \overset{(-)}{G_L}, \overset{(+)}{t}) \tag{9}$$

An increase in the product real wage in the tradables sector reduces output and employment there. This causes a fall in income that, along with the rise in the relative price of nontradables, reduces demand for nontradables. Consequently output and employment in the nontradables sector fall as well. The fall in output in the two sectors reduces tax income and therefore has a negative effect on the government budget and thus also on the trade balance.

An increase in government purchases of labor directly increases employment. In addition, the increase in the government wage bill increases demand for nontradables so that output and employment in this sector increases. Although the output expansion increases tax income, the net effect on the government budget and the trade balance is always negative.

An increase in the tax rate works only via the nontradables market and reduces output and employment there. The extra tax income generated by a tax rate increase will always outweigh the loss in tax income due to decreased output, so that there is a positive net effect on the government budget and the trade balance.

Determination of the Real Wage and Trade Union Behavior

The next step is to introduce a mechanism for the determination of wages. It is assumed that all workers are organized in *one* trade union, which tries to set the money wage in such a way that a desired overall real wage is reached. In this subsection we assume perfect foresight and no restrictions on the speed of wage adjustments, so the real wage objective of the trade union is always reached. The overall real wage is defined in terms of a price index, $P=P(P_T, P_N)$, which is homogeneous of degree one in the two prices so that:

$$\bar{w} = \frac{W}{P(P_T, P_N)} = \frac{W}{P_N P\left(\frac{P_T}{P_N}, 1\right)} = \frac{1}{P\left(\frac{1}{w_T}, 1\right)}. \tag{10}$$

How does the trade union attain its real wage goal when it can only control the money wage? It can proceed by a simple two-step method. If it knows the price index and the price equation (3) for nontradables, then in the first step it can use equation (10) and compute the product real wage in the tradables sector that corresponds to a certain overall real wage. Provided that the trade union knows the exchange rate and the world market price of tradables, in the second step it can compute the money wage necessary to achieve this product real wage.

How does the trade union determine the desired overall real wage? It is assumed that the trade union has a *stable* utility function which it tries to maximize. In the Appendix we derive such a utility function with the current after-tax real wage and the current number of employed workers as arguments, as in Oswald (1981). The intuitive appeal of this type of utility function is that it captures the trade-off between after-tax real wages and employment which plays a central role in applied policy discussions.[7]

The trade union thus maximizes:

$$U = U[\bar{w}(1-t), N] \qquad 0 \leqslant N \leqslant M. \tag{11}$$

Since the number of workers (= the number of members of the trade union) is assumed to be fixed at M, the utility function is only defined for $0 \leqslant N \leqslant M$. It is shown in the Appendix that the utility function is quasi-concave.

In order to solve the maximization problem, an equation for the number of employed workers must be derived. We assume that when employment (in hours) is below the Walrasian market-clearing level, it is rationed in such a way that an individual is *either* unemployed *or* employed and that those employed work exactly the amount of hours they want. To simplify, we assume here that the individual worker's supply of labor h is constant.[8] Then the number of employed workers is:

$$N = \frac{E[w_T(\bar{w}), G_L, t]}{h} = N(\overset{(-)}{\bar{w}}, \overset{(+)}{G_L}, \overset{(-)}{t}). \tag{12}$$

---

[7] What our formulation does not capture, however, is the possibility of intertemporal considerations on the part of the trade union. The utility maximization is strictly atemporal.

[8] The Appendix treats the general case where h is a function of the after-tax real wage.

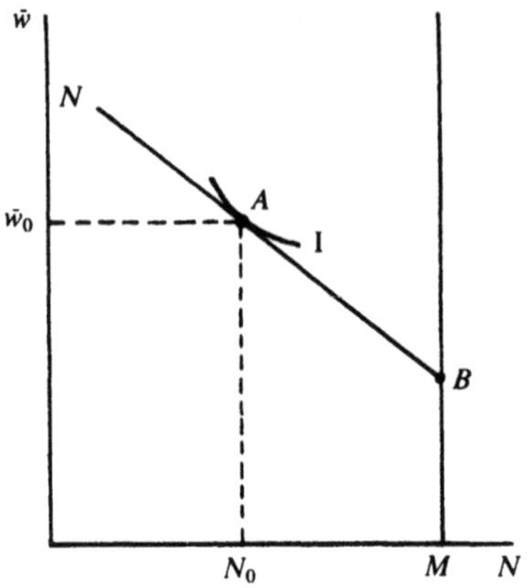

Fig. 1 a

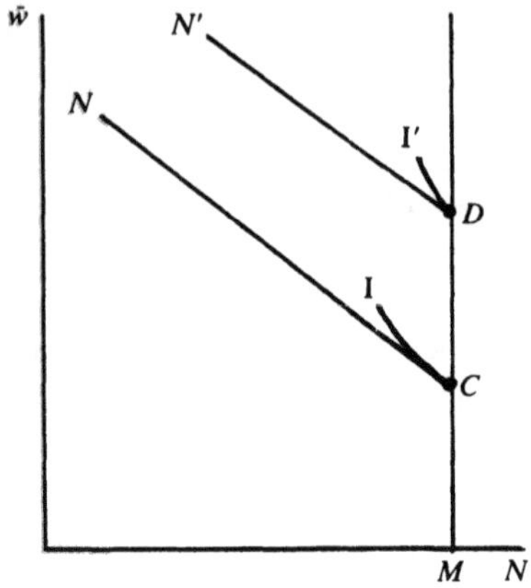

Fig. 1 b

The trade union is assumed to have full knowledge of the model, so that it is able to compute the reduced-form equation (12). The trade union thus sees beyond the first-round effects of changes in the real wage and understands their full implications. Provided that the trade union regards the values of the government parameters as independent of its own actions (a Cournot–Nash case), its decision problem is therefore to select a real wage that maximizes equation (11) subject to the employment constraint (12).

The maximization problem is solved by calculus in the Appendix. The solution is illustrated here by means of a simple graph in the $\bar{w}$, N-plane, showing indifference curves and the employment function. Provided that the indifference curves are more convex than the employment curve, the trade union maximizes utility by choosing a real wage $\bar{w}$ that equates its marginal rate of substitution with the slope of the employment curve. In Figure 1 *a*, this is achieved at the tangency point A, at which the real wage is larger and consequently employment lower than in the Walrasian competitive equilibrium at B, where the employment curve intersects the vertical supply curve.[9]

[9] We rule out the case where the real wage is set so high that the tradables sector is driven out of existence. Since government employment is exogenous, the trade union would, without this restriction, maximize utility by choosing an infinitely high real wage. We assume that the government is not willing to accomodate such a devdelopment. Government employment is thus assumed to be exogenous and independent of the real wage only within the range of real wage rates that permit production in both the tradables and nontradables sectors.

In the diagrams the employment curves are drawn as straight lines, i.e. as if $N_{11}=0$. The curves may, however, be curved, i.e. $N_{11} \neq 0$, but they must obey the constraints imposed. The employment curves are cut off in the diagrams at the point where $N=M$, since this point represents maximum employment. But a negatively sloped reduced-form labor-demand curve could also be constructed for $N>M$, once it is specified how labor is allocated between the sectors in situations of excess demand.

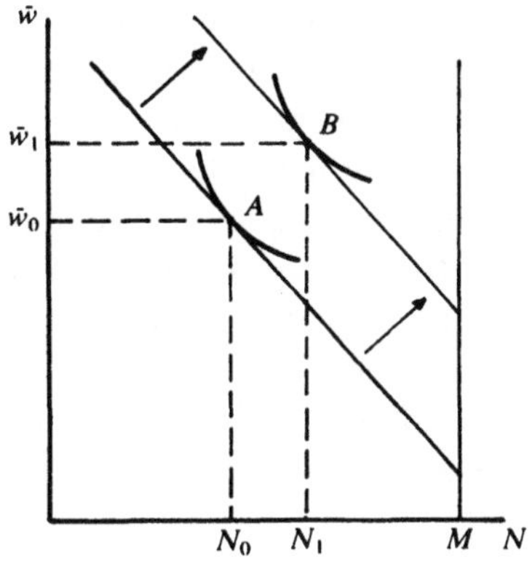

Fig. 2

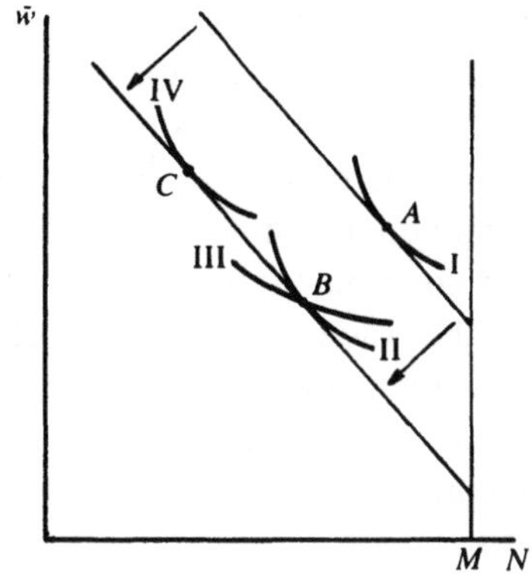

Fig. 3

But it could well be that this tangency point is on the full-employment line as at *C* in Figure 1 *b* (as shown in the Appendix, the indifference curves intersect the full-employment line with finite negative slopes). It could also be that there is a corner solution such as *D* in Figure 1 *b*, where the marginal rate of substitution is larger than the slope of the employment curve. In these two cases the optima chosen by the trade union coincide with the Walrasian competitive ones, i.e. the demand for workers equals the fixed supply. Later on, however, we focus on the more interesting case where the initial situation is an underemployment equilibrium.

The Effects of Government Policy Changes

We start by examining an increase in *government purchases of labor* in Figure 2. The effect can in general be decomposed into two components analogous to the income and substitution effects in ordinary demand theory (cf. the Appendix). The *first* is a parallel rightward shift of the employment curve (an "income effect"), since an increase in government purchases of labor increases employment at each real wage. The *second* effect is a change in the slope of the employment curve (a "substitution effect").

Provided that the real wage and employment are "normal goods"—i.e. that the marginal rate of substitution decreases when we move horizontally to the right and increases when we move vertically upwards in the indifference curve diagram—*and* that the employment function is not too convex, the *parallel-shift effect* will increase both the real wage and employment (cf. the Appendix). The effect on the slope of the employment curve cannot, however, be signed without more restrictions on the functions in the model. But the parallel-shift effect is assumed to dominate the effects on both the real wage and employment. In this case the trade union splits the increase in labor demand caused by the increased government purchases of labor into both a real wage and an employment increase.

Apart from raising both employment and the real wage, increased government purchases of labor also raise the product real wage in the tradables sector as seen from equation (10). Output and employment in the tradables sector must therefore fall. From equation (9) we then have that the trade balance must deteriorate. Thus, the expansion of total employment due to increased government purchases of labor cannot take place without deterioration of the trade balance and a crowding-out effect on production in the tradables sector that arises from the induced wage increase.[10]

The analysis of a *tax rate change* is somewhat different.[11] In this case we can distinguish between a *demand* effect and a *cost-push* effect; cf. the Appendix.

The *demand effect* measures the effect which works via the employment function (12).[12] In the same way as above, this demand effect can be decomposed into a parallel-shift effect and a slope effect. The parallel-shift effect of a tax rate increase moves the employment curve to the left in Figure 3, whereas the slope effect cannot in general be signed. As before, we assume that the parallel-shift effect dominates. Then the demand effect of a tax rate increase tends to reduce both the real wage and the number of employed workers, thus moving the economy from *A* to *B* in Figure 3.

The *cost-push effect* of a tax rate increase measures the effect which works via the real-wage argument in the utility function.[13] It can be illustrated as a change in the slope of the indifference curves. Somewhat surprisingly, the direction in which this cost-push effect works is not clear (cf. the Appendix). On the one hand a tax rate increase tends to reduce the after-tax real wage and thus raise the marginal utility of wages. On the other hand an increased tax rate reduces the utility gain from a wage increase, since more of the wage increase is now taxed away. These effects work in opposite directions; the first tends to lower the marginal rate of substitution between $\bar{w}$ and N, the second to raise it. We assume that the first effect dominates. In this case the indifference curves become less sloped (absolutely). This also holds for the indifference curve passing through *B*. With

---

[10] The above analysis presupposes that the economy starts in an underemployment equilibrium. The conclusions change, of course, if we instead start at full employment. In this case increased government purchases will only increase the real wage, whereas employment will not change. The same conclusions as above, however, hold with respect to output in the tradables sector and the trade balance.

[11] A sufficient (though not necessary) condition for a zero slope effect as assumed in Figure 2 is constant expenditure shares for the two goods and an inelastic individual labor supply (cf. the Appendix).

[12] The demand effect thus measures the effect of a tax rate change that would result if the before-tax real wage rather than the after-tax real wage entered as an argument in the utility function.

[13] The cost-push effect thus measures the effect of a tax rate change that would arise if the tax rate did *not* enter as an argument in the employment function.

our assumptions on marginal rates of substitution, the new tangency point *C* must therefore lie to the northwest of *B*. This means that the cost-push effect works in the "right" direction by tending to increase the real wage and lower employment.

Hence we cannot in general conclude what happens to the real wage when the tax rate increases, since the demand effect and the cost-push effect then work in opposite directions. Consequently, the effect on the product real wage in the tradables sector and thus on output and employment in this sector as well as on the trade balance are also unclear. What is clear, however, is that *total* employment falls, since both the demand effect and the cost-push effect here work in the same direction.

Nothing has been said so far about *exchange rate changes*. This case is easily treated. As the model has been formulated, a change in the exchange rate can have *no* effect on *real* variables. The optimum real wage for the trade union is independent of the exchange rate. Therefore, as long as there is perfect foresight and immediate wage flexibility, exchange rate changes will only affect nominal variables. A devaluation will e.g. raise the domestic-currency price of tradables, the wage rate and the price of nontradables equiproportionally.[14]

The general conclusion of our trade union model is thus that fiscal policies will have real effects under perfect foresight and immediate wage flexibility, whereas exchange rate policies will not. But the results with respect to fiscal policies should be interpreted with caution. A crucial assumption has been that the trade union regards fiscal policy action as independent of its own behavior. Therefore it does *not* necessarily follow that policymakers can choose an employment target and then use the model backwards to compute values of the policy parameters that achieve this goal. The reason is that once government policy becomes endogenous in this way, the trade union is likely to change its behavior. This case is analyzed later.

III. Stabilization Policy and Trade Union Behavior under Imperfect Information

In this section the assumptions of perfect information and immediate wage flexibility are relaxed.

It is assumed that the trade union fixes the money wage for a certain period of time. Once the money wage has been set, it is not changed during the period of the wage contract. Since the wage is set in advance, the trade

---

[14] Needless to say, these conclusions depend crucially on the absence of real-wealth effects. If such effects were present, a devaluation would have a contractionary effect tending to reduce both the overall real wage and employment.

union's decision is in general based on imperfect information, i.e. the trade union has to guess the value of the foreign-currency price of tradables and the values of the government policy parameters in the next period.

Government on the other hand is free to act whenever it likes. In order to keep the model simple, we assume that the government determines the values of its policy parameters after the trade union has set the money wage. The government thus knows the money wage when making its decisions. Moreover, at this point in time, it is assumed that the government knows the foreign-currency price of tradables which the trade union had to guess.

These assumptions are exaggerated, but they do reflect important institutional features. Money wages *are* usually determined in advance for long periods (1–2 years in the Scandinavian economies), whereas the government has the possibility of changing its policy parameters throughout the period of the wage contracts. This asymmetry creates an important role for stabilization policy, as has been argued by Fischer (1977).

The sequence of events analyzed below is very specific. The starting point is an expectational error by the trade union. The trade union overestimates price increases for tradables in the world market. The consequence is a wage disturbance; the trade union chooses a money wage that *ex post* results in a higher product real wage in the tradables sector and thus also a higher overall real wage than it regards as optimal.[15] This is illustrated in Figure 4, where the real wage increases from $\bar{w}_0$ to $\bar{w}_1$.

We now discuss the consequences of various policy strategies in this situation. We make the simplifying assumption that the expectational error is a one-shot event and that expectations will be correct again in the next period. The following policy alternatives are analyzed.

1. *Unchanged government policies.* In this case the economy moves from the original optimum *A* along the employment curve to *B* in Figure 4. Since a higher overall real wage corresponds to a higher product real wage in the tradables sector, employment falls in both sectors and the trade balance deteriorates. This situation prevails during the period of the wage contract. But with correct price expectations in the *next* period, the real wage will then be adjusted downwards and the economy returns to the trade union optimum at *A*. The consequence of the one-period expectational error is thus only a *temporary* decrease in employment—affecting both sectors—and a *temporary* deficit in the trade balance.

2. A *devaluation* would again reduce the real wage and could instantaneously move the economy back to the trade union optimum at *A* (or to

---

[15] This sequence of events is motivated by the Swedish wage explosion in 1975/76 discussed in the introduction. One of the major causes of this seems to have been a serious overestimation of price increases in the world market. Cf. Calmfors (1979).

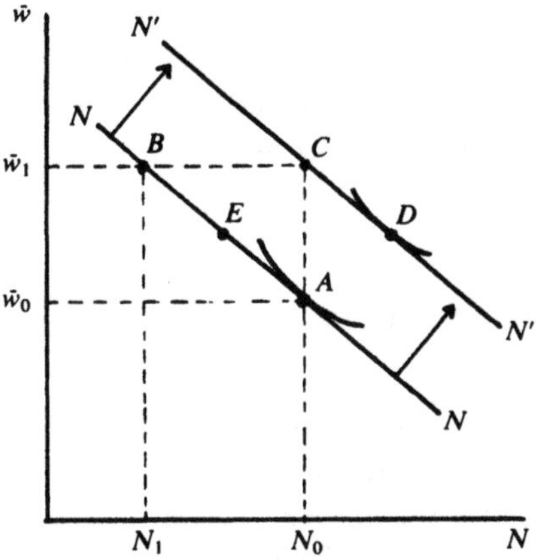

Fig. 4

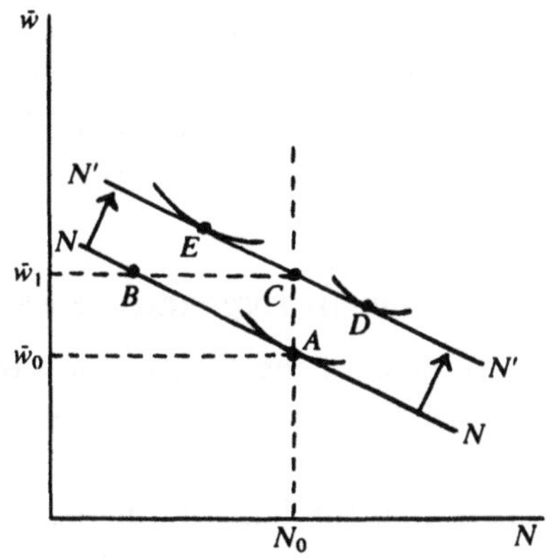

Fig. 5

some point such as *E* along the employment curve between *B* and *A*). The temporary increase in unemployment and deficit in the trade balance are then avoided (or reduced), but at the cost of additional price increases.

3. *Increased goverment purchases of labor* would shift the employment curve to the right.[16] If the curve is shifted to $N'N'$, the increased government purchases of labor compensate fully for the fall in employment due to the increased real wage and move the economy to point *C* in Figure 4. The effect on the trade balance depends on whether the increase in government expenditure is tax financed or not. If the tax rate is held constant, the trade balance must deteriorate. But if the increased expenditure is financed by raising the tax rate, the trade balance can be held in equilibrium.[17] The sectoral distribution of employment, however, is affected in both cases; employment falls in the tradables sector and increases in the government sector (in the nontradables sector the outcome is unclear). But these effects are temporary, provided that the expansionary measures are withdrawn in the next period *and* provided that the trade union anticipates this.

The diagrams are drawn so that the initial trade union optimum is an underemployment equilibrium. The role of stabilization policy is thus to prevent the expectational error of the trade union from causing a further fall in employment. The rest of the discussion is devoted to *future* consequences of these policies. However, all of the basic conclusions are the same if the initial situation which the government tries to maintain is one of

---

[16] An alternative expenditure-increasing policy would be to lower the tax rate. Our analysis is confined to increases in government expenditure, which according to both empirical experience and public choice theory seems the most likely to occur. Cf. e.g. Meltzer (1977).
[17] This is the case emphasized by Söderström & Viotti (1978).

full employment. Two problems are dealt with: 1) ratchet effects with respect to government expenditure and 2) the possibility that the trade union "learns" about government behavior, i.e. that it takes the government responses as an indication of a policy rule to be considered when the wage rate for future periods is set.

IV. Government Expenditure and Ratchet Effects

We now discuss the future consequences of increased government purchases of labor if policymakers are unable to reduce government expenditure again. According to public choice theory, the rationale for such ratchet effects is that the benefits of the increased expenditure accrue to a well-specified group whose costs of organizing efficient pressure groups capable of preventing expenditure cuts are low.[18]

We have to take into account whether the increased government purchases of labor are tax financed or not. In both cases the trade union is assumed to have perfect foresight, i.e. it understands that government purchases of labor and the tax rate in the next period will remain fixed at first-period levels. Thus the values of the government policy parameters in the next period are still assumed to be independent of the trade union's own actions in this period.

Consider first the case where the increased government purchases of labor have not been tax financed. Employment in the first period has been restored to N_0 despite the higher real wage $\bar{w}_1$ (point C). But if the increase in government expenditure persists in the next period, it follows from our earlier analysis that point C cannot represent a trade union optimum. Nor can the original position A. Since the labor demand schedule has shifted to the right, the new trade union optimum is a point such as D. Both the real wage and employment are *higher* at D than in the original position at A. But the real wage at D is *lower* than the "incorrect" real wage at C in the preceding period with an expectational error. The permanent increase in government purchases of labor does not completely eliminate the trade union's incentive to reduce the real wage again, but the end result is still a rise in the real wage as compared with the initial position.[19] Consequently, as shown earlier, there is also a rise in the product real wage and thus a fall in output and employment in the tradables sector, and a deterioration of the trade balance in comparison with the initial position.

---

[18] Cf. e.g. Meltzer (1977).

[19] This conclusion presupposes that the initial trade union optimum is an underemployment equilibrium. Had the initial optimum been at full employment, there would be no incentive for the trade union to lower the real wage again, so the "incorrect" first-period real wage $\bar{w}_1$ would persist in the next period.

Consider next the case of a tax-financed increase in government purchases of labor. If the increase in both government expenditure and the tax rate remain in effect in the next period when expectations are correct again, there is both a *demand* and a *cost-push* effect. The demand effect can be illustrated by a rightward shift of the employment curve and the cost-push effect by lowered (absolute) slopes of the indifference curves.

Provided that the parallel-shift effect dominates any slope effect, the demand effect tends, as before, to raise the real wage above the earlier optimum *A* in Figure 5.[20] This rise is reinforced by the cost-push effect, which has been assumed to work in the "right" direction. Although the optimal real wage must then rise, it is not clear whether the new optimal real wage in period two will be above or below the real wage based on incorrect expectations in period one (point *C*) and whether employment will rise or fall. If the demand effect dominates, it will be below and the economy ends up at a point such as *D*, where employment exceeds initial employment at point *A*. Since the combination of increased government expenditure and taxes equilibrated the trade balance at point *C*, it follows from equations (11) and (9) that the trade balance at point *D* shows a surplus. If the cost-push effect dominates instead, the second-period real wage rises above the "incorrect" first-period real wage; the economy ends up at a point such as *E* with lower employment than initially at point *A*. For the same reasons as above it then follows that the trade balance at point *E* shows a deficit.

To summarize, we have shown that an overestimation of price increases by the trade union may trigger an expansion of the public sector which permanently accomodates a higher real wage. If the increased government expenditure is not tax financed, a partial downward adjustment of the real wage may take place. But with tax financing there may be a further real wage increase, with the consequence that unemployment and external-balance problems are only moved from the first to the second period.

V. Wage Determination and Learning about Government Responses

We now abstract from ratchet effects and assume that policy parameters are completely flexible. The trade union is assumed to regard the policy action of government in the first period as an indication of a *policy rule* to be taken into account when setting the wage for future periods. The trade union thus no longer regards the future values of the government policy parameters as independent of its own actions. In the terminology of game theory, the trade union instead adheres to a Stackelberg strategy, i.e. it

---

[20] As before, the diagram is drawn as if there were a zero slope effect.

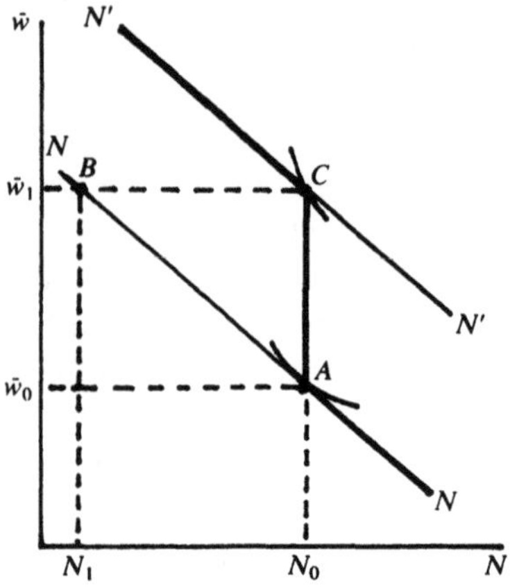

Fig. 6

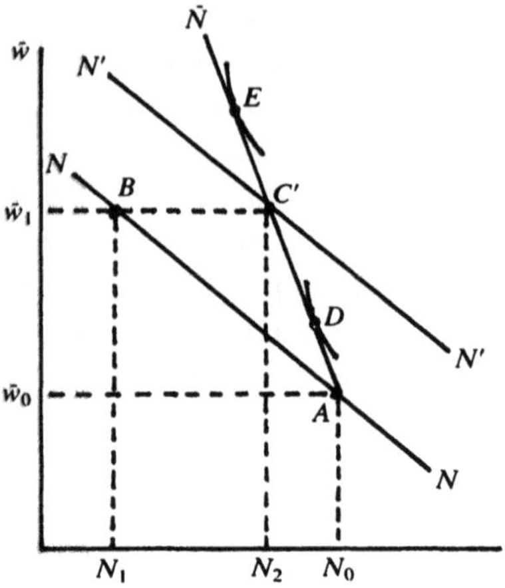

Fig. 7

learns to optimize against a perceived reaction function of the government.[21] The analysis is confined to 1) increased government purchases of labor without tax financing and 2) a devaluation.

Learning and Demand Policies

Consider first the case where the government has held employment constant during the period of the expectational error through increased government purchases of labor, shifting the labor demand schedule from *NN* to *N'N'* in Figure 6. If this causes the trade union to believe that the government will prevent *any* rise in the real wage from causing increased unemployment, there is no longer a trade-off for the trade union between the real wage and employment. Nothing in this atemporal model would then stop the trade union from pushing up the real wage without limit.[22] But this is not likely to occur, since the trade union probably realizes that the government's willingness to accomodate real wage increases is limited.

A more realistic picture is that the trade union tries to guess the real wage at which the government stops accommodating real wage increases. As before, we let *A* represent an original optimum (without expectations of accommodation policies) in Figure 6. Suppose now that the trade union regards the policy action during the period of the expectational error as an indication that any increase in unemployment will be prevented as long as the real wage does not exceed $\bar{w}_1$. More precisely, government purchases

[21] Cf. e.g. Varian (1978) for a brief discussion of Stackelberg equilibria.

[22] This result would not hold in an intertemporal model, if the trade union expects present employment policies to cause future decreases in government expenditure (or future tax increases).

of labor are believed to be varied in such a way that employment is pegged at the initial level N_0 when the real wage is between $\bar{w}_0$ and $\bar{w}_1$. If so, the reduced-form labor demand curve, taking the expected government policies into account, will be the double-kinked schedule $N'CAN$. Then the trade union maximizes utility by choosing the real wage $\bar{w}_1$. If this is done, the government has to choose between following the expected accomodation policy and thus increase its purchases of labor permanently (in which case point C is reached) or accepting that the rise in the real wage causes unemployment along the initial employment curve (point B).

Instead of assuming that *any* increase in unemployment is prevented in the first period, it could be assumed that the tendencies towards a reduction of employment below the initial level N_0 are only *partially* offset. Without any policy measures, employment would have fallen to N_1 in Figure 7. Suppose now that government purchases of labor were increased only to the extent that the economy ended up at C' in the period of the expectational error. Assume furthermore that the trade union takes this policy action as an indication that government adheres to a rule of partial accommodation.

We now let N denote the employment that would result if no stabilization policy measures were taken, i.e. if government purchases of labor and the tax rate were held constant at certain long-run values G_L^0 and t^0. Letting N_g denote the employment created by government stabilization policy measures, which are assumed to be confined to variations in government purchases of labor in relation to the long-run value G_L^0, the perceived policy rule of the government can be formulated:

$$N_g = \gamma[N_0 - N] = \gamma[N_0 - N(\bar{w}, G_L^0, t^0)] \quad N \leq N_0 \leq M,\ 0 < \gamma < 1. \tag{13}$$

Now the trade union can estimate the government reaction function by computing γ from its experiences in period one. γ can be computed as $(N_2 - N_1)/(N_0 - N_1)$ in Figure 7. Having computed γ, the trade union can estimate a new employment function for $N \leq N_0$, taking the perceived policy rule of the government into account. Calling this employment function $\bar{N}$ we have:

$$\begin{aligned}\bar{N} &= N + N_g = N + \gamma[N_0 - N] = N_0 + (1-\gamma)\, N(\bar{w}, G_L^0, t^0) \\ &= \bar{N}(\bar{w}, G_L^0, t^0, \gamma, N_0) \qquad N \leq N_0 \leq M.\end{aligned} \tag{14}$$

Since $\bar{N}_1 = (1-\gamma)\, N_1$, it follows that expected employment becomes less responsive to changes in the real wage when anticipated government reactions are taken into account. In terms of Figure 7, the new employment function is steeper than the one without government responses for $N \leq N_0$. It must pass through points A and C'.

It then follows directly from our assumptions on the utility function that when government responses are taken into account, the trade union will aim for a higher real wage and lower employment than at *A*.[23] The reason is that the "price" of a higher real wage in terms of lower employment is reduced. At *A* the marginal utility of an increase in the real wage was exactly equal to the marginal disutility of the resulting fall in employment along the initial *NN*-line. But the perceived government policy rule reduces the expected fall in employment due to an increase in the real wage. Hence the marginal disutility arising from the effects of a given increase in the real wage on employment is reduced. The new real wage in period two, however, may be lower (point *D*) or higher (point *E*) than the suboptimal real wage in period one.

As before, what happens to actual employment in the second period depends on whether or not the government follows the perceived policy rule. If it does, the economy ends up at *D* or *E*. If government purchases of labor in period two are again cut back to their original level, employment falls even more.

The conclusion is that total employment in period two would have been larger without the employment policies in period one, since it would then have been optimal for the trade union to choose point *A* again. Although the employment policy studied *increases* employment in periods where price increases are overestimated, it thus has *perverse* employment effects in future periods with correct anticipations.[24]

Policy Rules and Devaluations

We now turn to the case where policy makers instead respond to the threatening unemployment in period one with a devaluation. Suppose that this devaluation instantaneously moves the economy back to full employment and that this is taken by the trade union to reflect a policy rule, according to which exchange rate changes are used to prevent all variations in employment. How is learning about such a policy rule likely to affect future trade union behavior?

The major difference between the demand policies discussed above and a devaluation is that the former accomodate a higher *real* wage, whereas a devaluation accomodates only a higher *nominal* wage by reducing the real wage again. The behavior of the trade union is therefore affected differently in the devaluation case, where no incentive to attain a higher future real wage is created. But accomodation through devaluations may have profound effects of another type.

---

[23] This result remains unchanged if the initial equilibrium (= the employment goal of government) is at full employment and is a tangency point.

[24] Cf. also the Appendix for a generalization of these results.

The devaluation policy may change the trade union's perception of the decision problem if it is felt that the decision about the real wage is moved from the trade union to the government. If government is expected to determine the real wage through its exchange rate policy *after* wage bargains have been made, the trade union no longer has to trade off the real wage against employment. In principle this makes the nominal wage rate indeterminate. The trade union can choose any nominal wage rate, if policymakers are anyway expected to adjust the exchange rate so as to achieve the real wage desired by both the government and the trade union. It is then impossible to predict what will happen to money wages in our model.

Perhaps it could be concluded that there is likely to be a lower limit to money wage increases in the next period, since a perceived policy rule involving devaluations when the real wage is considered excessively high does not imply that there will be revaluations in the opposite case. Perhaps there is also an upper limit to money wage increases, if policymakers are believed to have an upper limit on the inflation they will accept. Perhaps it could be maintained that the trade union's "safest" strategy would be to choose the money wage expected to give the optimal real wage without exchange rate changes, since it can never be *certain* of the government policy rule.[25] These are, however, *ad hoc* considerations. In a more elaborate analysis, the rate of inflation should also be included as an argument in both the trade union preference function and the government reaction function.

What would happen in the above analysis if the government reduced only part of the suboptimal real wage increase in the first period (the economy was moved from, say, *B* to *E* in Figure 4)? Suppose that the trade union takes this as evidence that the government follows a policy rule according to which tendencies toward unemployment are *partially* offset through devaluations? Such a policy rule is not likely to affect the future behavior of the trade union. The trade unon still has an incentive to choose the money wage that results in the optimal real wage at a constant exchange rate. Only by doing this can it reach the optimum *A*, since exchange rate changes in this case are used only to reduce—but not eliminate—deviations from this optimum.

The conclusion is therefore that it seems possible to *reduce* unemployment caused by an expectational error through a devaluation policy without adverse effects on future trade union behavior. However, this conclusion

---

[25] The argument that the trade union is likely to follow this policy would be strengthened if real-wealth effects were introduced. A devaluation, by reducing real wealth, would then have a contractionary effect shifting the employment curve to the left, which is to the disadvantage of the trade union.

depends crucially on our assumption that employment at the trade union optimum A coincides with the government employment goal.[26]

VI. Conclusions and Possible Extensions

The main conclusions of our trade union model are:

1. The real wage set by the trade union may or may not coincide with the Walrasian full-employment real wage. If not, the analytical framework provides an explanation of underemployment equilibria based on optimizing behavior.
2. Changes in government expenditure and tax rates which the trade union regards as independent of its own actions will affect employment when there is perfect foresight and immediate wage flexibility.
3. If wages are set in advance for longer periods and the decisions of the trade union are based on imperfect information, government policies can offset the effects of expectational errors by the trade union on employment. We analyze a case where the trade union overestimates international price increases and therefore chooses an excessively high real wage.
4. With ratchet effects for government expenditure, an expenditure increase in order to stabilize employment during the period of an expectational error will permanently accommodate a higher real wage and shift employment from the tradables to the government sector.
5. If the trade union takes a government expenditure increase in the period of an expectational error as an indication of a Keynesian policy rule, the future behavior of the trade union will change. The trade union is likely to aim for a higher real wage and lower employment.
6. Learning may also take place when employment is stabilized through a devaluation. If the trade union believes that exchange rate changes will be used to prevent *all* employment variations, the *money* wage may become indeterminate. But with only a *partial* accommodation, trade union behavior is not likely to be affected.

The most important results concern the role of Keynesian demand policies. Although it is recognized that a one-shot policy change affects employment under perfect foresight and that demand policies have a further role to play under long-term wage contracts, an employment stabilization rule may actually *lower* long-run employment. This result should be contrasted with the ordinary rational-expectations conclusion that automatic feedback rules, according to which present policies respond to *earlier*

---

[26] An attempt to reach an employment level higher than the one consistent with the trade union optimum through a devaluation policy is, of course, bound to fail in the long run, since the trade union would learn to take expected exchange rate changes into account when setting future wages or resort to formal indexation.

disturbances, have *no* effect on employment when policy makers and price setters have the same information.[27] Here it may be optimal for the trade union to choose such a high real wage that employment is lowered because of game theoretic interdependence; an anticipated government policy response in the same period lowers the expected cost of real wage increases in terms of lost employment.

Further work in this area could extend the simple framework used here.

1. *Money* could be introduced in the way suggested in some of the footnotes, which would modify the conclusions on devaluations. This would also allow an analysis of the case with a perfectly flexible market-determined exchange rate.

2. *Intertemporal aspects* should be given greater weight. A rational trade union should care about future as well as current real wage and employment levels. It should realize that current trade balance deficits impose burdens on the future and would therefore be likely to show greater restraint when the trade balance deteriorates than in our analysis. It should also realize that the future relation between real wages and employment is affected by present real wages via their effects on investment.

3. *An underlying utility function* for government could be specified. This would enrich the game-theoretic analysis and make it possible to analyze various cooperative equilibria (social contracts). It would also make it necessary to address the fundamental question of why the government pursues other goals than the all-encompassing trade union.

Appendix

1. *The Output-employment Bloc*

Differentiation of equation (2′) gives:

$$dE_N = A_1\, dw_T + A_2\, dG_L - A_3\, dt \tag{A 1}$$

where:

$$A_1 = \frac{\overbrace{D_{N1} + D_{N2}(1-t)(S_{T1} + E_N + G_L)}^{(?)}}{\underbrace{1 - D_{N2}(1-t)\, w_T}_{(+)}}$$

$$A_2 = \frac{\overbrace{D_{N2}(1-t)\, w_T}^{(+)}}{\underbrace{1 - D_{N2}(1-t)\, w_T}_{(+)}} > 0$$

[27] Cf. e.g. Fischer (1977), Lucas (1975) or Sargent & Wallace (1975 and 1976).

$$A_3 = \frac{\overbrace{D_{N2}(\bar{Y}+w_T G_L)}^{(+)}}{\underbrace{1-D_{N2}(1-t)\,w_T}_{(+)}} > 0.$$

It is immediately seen that $dE_N/dG_L>0$ and $dE/dt<0$. Assuming the two goods to be gross substitutes, i.e. that $D_{N1}+D_{N2}(1-t)(S_{T1}+E_N+G_L)<0$, we also have $dE_N/dw_T<0$.

Differentiation of equation (4) and substituting from above gives:

$$dE = \left[\overset{(-)}{E_{T1}}+\overset{(-)}{A_1}\right]dw_T + \left[1+\overset{(+)}{A_2}\right]dG_L - \overset{(+)}{A_3}\,dt. \qquad (A\,2)$$

It is immediately seen that $dE/dw_T<0$, $dE/dG_L>0$ and $dE/dt<0$.

Differentiation of equation (6′) and substituting from above gives:

$$dX = \left[\overset{(-)}{tS_{T1}}+\overset{(-)}{tw_T A_1}-\overset{(+)}{(1-t)\,G_L}+\overset{(+)}{tE_N}\right]dw_T - \frac{\overset{(+)}{A_2}\left(\overset{(+)}{1-D_{N2}w_T}\right)}{\underset{(+)}{D_{N2}}}dG_L + \frac{\overset{(+)}{A_3}\left(\overset{(+)}{1-D_{N2}w_T}\right)}{\underset{(+)}{D_{N2}}} \qquad (A\,3)$$

It is immediately seen that $dX/dt>0$ and $dX/dG_L<0$. Provided that

$$tS_{T1}+tw_T\frac{\{D_{N1}+D_{N2}(1-t)(S_{T1}+E_N+G_L)\}}{1-D_{N2}(1-t)\,w_T}-(1-t)\,G_L+tE_N<0,$$

it also follows that $dX/dw_T<0$.

2. *The Behavior of the Trade Union*

The trade union utility function used can be derived as follows. Assume that all individual members of the trade union have identical preferences that can be represented by the following weakly separable utility function:

$$u = u(d_N, d_T, -h) = \mathcal{U}[f(d_N, d_T), -h] \qquad (A\,4)$$

where u = utility, d_N = consumption of nontradables, d_T = consumption of tradables, h = supply of labor.

Assume further that the f-function is linearly homogeneous. We can then define a true cost-of-living index $P(P_T, P_N)$, which is homogeneous of degree one in the two prices, and solve the individual's maximization problem in two steps. Defining real consumption measured in terms of this price index as Z, we can determine real consumption and the supply of labor in a *first* step and then, given the real consumption, determine the composition of consumption in a *second* step. Here we need only the first step, which is to maximize:

$$u = \mathcal{U}[Z, -h] \tag{A 5}$$

subject to the constraint:

$$P(P_N, P_T)\, Z - W(1-t)\, h = 0. \tag{A 6}$$

The maximization gives the following indirect utility function:

$$V = V[P, W(1-t)]. \tag{A 7}$$

Since the indirect utility function is homogeneous of degree zero in the price index and the after-tax wage, we can write

$$V = V\left[1, \frac{W(1-t)}{P}\right] = v[\bar{w}(1-t)] = v(w^*). \tag{A 8}$$

Now, suppose that the government guarantees a certain utility level $\bar{v}$ to those who become unemployed by distributing goods from government stocks.[28] If the number of employed workers is N and the total membership of the union is M, the expected utility of an individual member can be written as in equation (A 9). The trade union is assumed to maximize this function, which can also be regarded as a social welfare function with equal weights for all members.

$$U = \frac{N}{M} v(w^*) + \left[1 - \frac{N}{M}\right] \bar{v}. \tag{A 9}$$

Assuming a fixed utility for the unemployed and a fixed number of members, we can write:

$$U = U(w^*, N) = U[\bar{w}(1-t), N] \tag{A 10}$$

where

$$U_1 = \frac{N}{M} v_1(w^*) > 0$$

$$U_2 = \frac{1}{M}[v(w^*) - \bar{v}] > 0$$

[28] The goods in these stocks can have been produced by the labor employed by the government. In order for us to write the supply and demand equations for tradables and nontradables as in the text, the composition of the transfer received by the unemployed must conform to individual preferences, so that no market transactions are induced. It is necessary that $\bar{v} < v(\bar{w}^*)$, since otherwise everyone would prefer being unemployed.

$$U_{11}=\frac{N}{M}v_{11}(w^*)\gtreqless 0$$

$$U_{22}=0$$

$$U_{12}=U_{21}=\frac{1}{M}v_1(w^*)>0.$$

The only ambiguous sign is for U_{11}, the sign of which depends on whether $v_{11}(w^*)$ is positive or negative. We assume that $v_{11}(w^*)<0$, i.e. that individuals are indirectly risk averse, which makes $U_{11}<0$.

The trade union utility function can be illustrated by a map of indifference curves in the $\bar{w}$, N-plane as in Figure 1 in the text. The trade union utility function has the following properties:

(1) The indifference curves are negatively sloped, since:

$$\left.\frac{d\bar{w}}{dN}\right|_{\bar{U}}=-\frac{U_2}{U_1(1-t)}=-\frac{\frac{1}{M}[v(w^*)-\bar{v}]}{\frac{N}{M}v_1(w^*)(1-t)}=-\frac{v(w^*)-\bar{v}}{Nv_1(w^*)(1-t)}<0. \quad \text{(A 11)}$$

(2) The indifference curves are convex (and the utility function thus quasi-concave), since:

$$\left.\frac{d\left(\frac{d\bar{w}}{dN}\right)}{dN}\right|_{\bar{U}}=-\frac{U_2^2}{U_1^3(1-t)^3}\left[U_{11}(1-t)^2-2U_{12}\frac{U_1}{U_2}(1-t)^2+U_{22}\left(\frac{U_1}{U_2}\right)^2(1-t)^2\right]$$

$$=-\frac{[v(w^*)-\bar{v}]^2}{(1-t)N^2[v_1(w^*)]^3}\left[v_{11}(w^*)-\frac{2[v_1(w^*)]^2}{v(w^*)-\bar{v}}\right]>0. \quad \text{(A 12)}$$

(3) The marginal rate of substitution between $\bar{w}$ and N (the absolute value of the slope of the indifference curves) decreases when N increases at a constant $\bar{w}$, i.e. when we move horizontally to the right in the indifference curve diagram, since:

$$\frac{\partial\left(\frac{dw}{dN}\right)}{\partial N}=\frac{U_2U_{12}-U_1U_{22}}{U_1^2(1-t)}=\frac{1}{N^2}\cdot\frac{1}{1-t}\cdot\frac{v(w^*)-\bar{v}}{v_1(w^*)}>0. \quad \text{(A 13)}$$

(4) The marginal rate of substitution between $\bar{w}$ and N increases when $\bar{w}$ increases at a constant N, i.e. when we move vertically upwards in the indifference curve diagram, since:

$$\frac{\partial\left(\frac{d\bar{w}}{dN}\right)}{\partial\bar{w}}=\frac{U_2U_{11}-U_1U_{21}}{U_1^2}=-\frac{1}{N}\cdot\frac{[v_1(w^*)]^2-v_{11}(w^*)[v(w^*)-\bar{v}]}{[v_1(w^*)]^2}<0. \quad \text{(A 14)}$$

(5) The utility function is defined only for $N \leqslant M$. When $N=M$, we have, from equation (A 9), $U=v(w^*)$, i.e. the expected utility of a member equals the utility of an employed worker. The slopes of the indifference curves have finite negative values for $N=M$, in which case we have:

$$\left.\frac{d\bar{w}}{dN}\right|_{\bar{U}} = -\frac{v(w^*)-\bar{v}}{M(1-t)\,v_1(w^*)}<0. \tag{A 15}$$

2.1. *The number of employed workers*. In order to solve the maximization problem of the trade union, an expression for the number of employed workers must be derived. This can be done in two steps. First, by differentiating equation (10) in the text we have:

$$dw_T = \frac{w_T}{w}\cdot\frac{1}{\alpha}\,d\bar{w} \qquad \alpha = P_1\cdot\frac{P_T}{P} = \frac{\partial P}{\partial P_T}\cdot\frac{P_T}{P}. \tag{A 16}$$

Second, since $N=E/h(w^*)$, it follows from differentiation of this equation and from equations (A 2) and (A 16) that:

$$dN = \left\{\frac{w_T}{\bar{w}}\cdot\frac{1}{\alpha}\cdot\frac{1}{h}\left[\overset{(-)}{E_{T1}}+\overset{(-)}{A_1}\right] - \frac{\overset{(+)}{E}\overset{(?)}{h_1}\overset{(+)}{(1-t)}}{h^2}\right\}d\bar{w}$$
$$+\frac{1}{h}\left[1+\overset{(+)}{A_2}\right]dG_L+\frac{1}{h}\left[\frac{\overset{(+)}{E}\overset{(?)}{h_1}\overset{(+)}{\bar{w}}}{h}-\overset{(-)}{A_3}\right]dt. \tag{A 17}$$

From equation (A 17) we have directly that $dN/dG_L>0$. Provided that h_1 is not too negative, we have $dN/d\bar{w}<0$. Provided that h_1 is not too positive, we have $dN/dt<0$.

2.2. *The utility maximization of the trade union*. The trade union maximizes its utility function subject to the employment constraint (12). The conditions for an interior maximum are:

$$\frac{dU}{d\bar{w}} = U_1(1-t)+U_2N_1 = 0 \tag{A 18}$$

$$\frac{d^2U}{d\bar{w}^2} = \phi_1 = U_{11}(1-t)^2+2U_{12}N_1(1-t)+U_{22}N_1^2+U_2N_{11} =$$
$$=U_{11}(1-t)^2-2U_{12}\frac{U_1}{U_2}(1-t)^2+U_{22}\left(\frac{U_1}{U_2}\right)^2(1-t)^2+U_2N_{11}<0. \tag{A 19}$$

2.3. *The effect of a change in government purchases of labor*. By differentiating equating (A 18) totally, holding t constant, we get:

$$\frac{d\bar{w}}{dG_L} = -\frac{\overset{(+)}{N_2}\overset{(+)}{(1-t)}\overbrace{\left\{U_{12}-\frac{U_1}{U_2}U_{22}\right\}}^{(+)}}{\underset{(-)}{\phi_1}} - \frac{\overset{(?)}{N_{12}}\overset{(+)}{U_2}}{\underset{(-)}{\phi_1}}. \tag{A 20}$$

Substitution into equation (A 17) gives:

$$\frac{dN}{dG_L} = N_1\frac{d\bar{w}}{dG_L}+N_2 = \frac{\overset{(+)}{N_2}\left[\overset{(+)}{(1-t)^2}\overbrace{\left\{U_{11}-\frac{U_1}{U_2}U_{12}\right\}}^{(-)}+\overset{(+)}{U_2}\overset{(?)}{N_{11}}\right]}{\underset{(-)}{\phi_1}}+\frac{\overset{(?)}{N_{12}}\overset{(+)}{U_1}\overset{(+)}{(1-t)}}{\underset{(-)}{\phi_1}}. \tag{A 21}$$

The effect of an increase in government purchases of labor can thus be decomposed into a "parallel-shift effect" and a "slope effect" analogous to the income and substitution effects in the theory of demand. The parallel-shift effect is measured by the first and the slope effect by the second term in equations (A 20) and (A 21). Equations (A 13), (A 17) and (A 19) establish that the parallel-shift effect on $\bar{w}$ is positive. Provided that

$$(1-t)^2\left(U_{11}-\frac{U_1}{U_2}U_{12}\right)<-U_2N_{11},$$

equations (A 14), (A 19) and (12) establish that the parallel-shift effect on N is positive as well.

The slope effects cannot be signed unless we know the sign of N_{12}, which cannot be determined without specifying the functions in the model more exactly. In order to see this, assume e.g. that the expenditure shares of the two goods are independent of income, i.e. that

$$P_N D_N = \alpha\left(\frac{P_N}{P_T}\right)(1-t)(P_T\tilde{Y}+wG_L) = \alpha(w_T)(1-t)(P_T\tilde{Y}+wG_L). \tag{A 22}$$

We then obtain:

$$N_1 = \frac{\partial N}{\partial \bar{w}} = \frac{1}{h}\cdot\frac{1}{\alpha}\cdot\frac{w_T}{\bar{w}}\left[E_{T1}+\frac{\alpha(1-t)S_{T1}}{w_T}-\frac{S_T}{w_T^2}+\alpha_1(1-t)\left\{\frac{S_T}{w_T}+E_N+G_L\right\}\right] - \frac{E(1-t)h_1}{h^2}. \tag{A 23}$$

Consequently:

$$N_{12} = \frac{\partial\left(\frac{\partial N}{\partial \bar{w}}\right)}{\partial G_L} = \overset{(+)}{\frac{1}{h}}\cdot\overset{(+)}{\frac{1}{\alpha}}\cdot\overset{(+)}{\frac{w_T}{\bar{w}}}\cdot\overset{(?)}{\alpha_1}\,\overset{(+)}{(1-t)}\,\overbrace{[E_{N2}+1]}^{(+)} - \frac{\overset{(?)}{h_1}\,\overset{(+)}{(1-t)}\,\overset{(+)}{E_2}}{h^2}. \tag{A 24}$$

Equation (A 24) shows that the sign of N_{12} is not clear. However, a sufficient—but not *necessary*—condition for $N_{12}=0$ is *constant* expenditure shares, i.e. $a_1=0$, and an inelastic individual supply of labor, i.e. $h_1=0$.

2.4. *The effect of a change in the tax rate.* The effect of a change in the tax rate is obtained by differentiating equation (A 18) totally while holding G_L constant.

$$\frac{d\bar{w}}{dt} = -\frac{\overset{(-)}{N_3}\,\overset{(+)}{(1-t)}\,\overbrace{\left[U_{12}-\frac{U_1}{U_2}U_{22}\right]}^{(+)}}{\underset{(-)}{\phi_1}} - \frac{\overset{(?)}{N_{13}}\,\overset{(+)}{U_2}}{\underset{(-)}{\phi_1}} + \frac{\overset{(+)}{\bar{w}}\,\overset{(+)}{(1-t)}\,\overbrace{\left[U_{11}-\frac{U_1}{U_2}U_{12}\right]}^{(-)}}{\underset{(-)}{\phi_1}} + \frac{\overset{(+)}{U_1}}{\underset{(-)}{\phi_1}}. \qquad \text{(A 25)}$$

Substituting into equation (A 17) gives:

$$\frac{dN}{dt} = N_1\frac{d\bar{w}}{dt} + N_3 = \frac{\overset{(-)}{N_3}\left[\overset{(+)}{(1-t)^2}\overbrace{\left(U_{11}-\frac{U_1}{U_2}U_{12}\right)}^{(-)} + \overset{(+)}{U_2}\,\overset{(?)}{N_{11}}\right]}{\underset{(-)}{\phi_1}}$$

$$+\frac{\overset{(+)}{U_1}\,\overset{(+)}{(1-t)}\,\overset{(?)}{N_{13}}}{\underset{(-)}{\phi_1}} + \frac{\overset{(-)}{N_1}\,\overset{(+)}{\bar{w}}\,\overset{(+)}{(1-t)}\overbrace{\left(U_{11}-\frac{U_1}{U_2}U_{12}\right)}^{(-)}}{\underset{(-)}{\phi_1}} + \frac{\overset{(-)}{N_1}\,\overset{(+)}{U_1}}{\underset{(-)}{\phi_1}}. \qquad \text{(A 26)}$$

The effects of a tax rate change can thus be decomposed into four terms. The first term in the two equations is a parallel-shift effect and the second a slope-effect of the same type as before. The sum of these two effects are labelled the *demand effect* in the text. The last two terms in the equations are labelled the "cost-push effect". The third term indicates that a tax rate increase tends to reduce the after-tax real wage and thus to raise the marginal utility of wages. The fourth term indicates that an increased tax rate reduces the utility gain from a wage increase, since more of the wage increase is now taxed away.

The cost-push effect is illustrated in the text as changing the slopes of the indifference curves. A lowered (absolute) slope of the indifference curves in the case of a tax rate increase is equivalent to a positive net impact of the cost-push effect on $\bar{w}$ in equation (A 25).

3. *The Effect of Perceived Policy Rules*

If the employment target of the government is N_0 and the government policy rule is perceived to be $N_g=\gamma[N_0-N]$, the perceived employment $\bar{N}$ taking the policy rule into account is:

$$\bar{N}=\gamma N_0+(1-\gamma)N(\bar{w},G_L^0,t^0)=\bar{N}(\bar{w},G_L^0,t^0,\gamma,N_0). \tag{A 27}$$

Below it is assumed that the government employment stabilization rule is symmetric, i.e. that it applies for $N>N_0$ as well as $N\leqslant N_0$. Then the first-order condition for a trade union maximum becomes:

$$U_1(1-t)+U_2\bar{N}_1=U_1(1-t)+U_2(1-\gamma)N_1=0. \tag{A 28}$$

Differentiating totally while holding N_0, G_L^0 and t_0 constant gives:

$$\frac{d\bar{w}}{d\gamma}=-\frac{\bar{N}_4(1-t)\left\{U_{12}-\dfrac{U_1}{U_2}U_{22}\right\}}{\phi_2}-\frac{\bar{N}_{14}U_2}{\phi_2}=$$

$$=-\frac{\underset{(+)}{(N_0-N)}(1-t)\overbrace{\left(U_{12}-\dfrac{U_1}{U_2}U_{22}\right)}^{(+)}}{\underset{(-)}{\phi_2}}+\frac{\underset{(-)}{N_1}\,\underset{(+)}{U_2}}{\underset{(-)}{\phi_2}}. \tag{A 29}$$

$$\phi_2=U_{11}(1-t)^2+2U_{12}\bar{N}_1(1-t)+U_{22}\bar{N}_1^2+U_2\bar{N}_{11}<0$$

is required as the second-order condition for a maximum. Consequently, it follows that a sufficient condition for $d\bar{w}/d\gamma>0$ is that $N_0=N$, i.e. that the economy is initially at the perceived employment target.

The effect on perceived employment is given by:

$$\frac{d\bar{N}}{d\gamma}=\frac{\bar{N}_4\left[(1-t)^2\left\{U_{11}-\dfrac{U_1}{U_2}U_{12}\right\}+U_2\bar{N}_{11}\right]}{\phi_2}+\frac{\bar{N}_{14}U_1(1-t)}{\phi_2}$$

$$=-\frac{(N_0-N)\overbrace{\left[(1-t)^2\left\{U_{11}-\dfrac{U_1}{U_2}U_{12}\right\}+U_2(1-\gamma)N_{11}\right]}^{(-)}}{\underset{(-)}{\phi_2}}-\frac{\underset{(-)}{N_1}\,\underset{(+)}{U_1}\underset{(+)}{(1-t)}}{\underset{(-)}{\phi_2}}. \tag{A 30}$$

Again it is seen that $N_0=N$ is a sufficient condition for $d\bar{N}/d\gamma<0$.[29]

[29] In the case discussed in the text, γ was increased from zero to a positive number between zero and one, and the employment stabilization rule was assumed to be asymmetric, i.e. to apply only to $N\leqslant N_0$. The above results are, of course, compatible with those derived diagrammatically in the text, since the economy there was also initially at $N=N_0$, and since the change in the trade union optimum is then only affected by the steeper slope of the employment function for the interval $N\leqslant N_0$.

References

Buiter, W. H.: The macroeconomics of Dr Pangloss: A critical survey of the new classical macroeconomics. *Economic Journal,* March 1980.

Calmfors, L.: Lärdomar av kostnadskrisen. *Ekonomisk debatt,* No 8., 1979.

Dunlop, J. T.: *Wage determination under trade unions.* Macmillan, New York, 1944.

Fischer, S.: Long-term contracts, rational expectations and the optimal money supply rule. *Journal of Political Economy,* February 1979.

Lindbeck, A.: Imported and structural inflation and aggregate demand: The Scandinavian model reconstructed. In *Inflation and employment in open economies* (ed. A. Lindbeck). North-Holland, 1978.

Lucas, R. E.: An equilibrium model of the business cycle. *Journal of Political Economy,* December 1978.

Meltzer, A.: The decline of the liberal economy. *Vie et sciences economiques,* January 1977.

Modigliani, F.: The monetarist controversy or should we forsake stabilization policies? *American Economic Review,* March 1977.

Mulvey, C.: *The economic analysis of trade unions.* Martin Robertson, Oxford, 1978.

Oswald, A. J.: Wage determination in an economy with many trade unions. *Oxford Economic Papers,* No 3, 1979.

Oswald, A. J.: The microeconomic theory of the trade union. Forthcoming in the *Economic Journal,* 1982.

Sargent, T. J. & Wallace, N.: Rational expectations, the optimal monetary instrument, and the optimal money supply rule. *Journal of Political Economy,* April 1975.

Sargent, T. J. & Wallace, N.: Rational expectations and the theory of economic policy. *Journal of Monetary Economies,* April 1976.

Solow, R.: Alternative approaches to macroeconomic theory: a partial view. *Canadian Journal of Economics,* August 1979.

Söderström H. & Viotti, S.: Money wage disturbances and the endogeneity of the public sector in an open economy. In *Inflation and employment in open economies* (ed. A. Lindbeck). North-Holland, 1978.

Towards full employment and price stability: A report to the OECD by a group of independent experts (The McCracken Report), 1977.

Varian, H. R.: *Microeconomic analysis.* Norten & Company, New York, 1978.

Comment on L. Calmfors, "Employment Policies, Wage Formation and Trade Union Behavior in a Small Open Economy"

Michael Hoel

University of Oslo, Norway

Calmfors describes an open economy with a strong trade union and highly centralized wage negotiations. These are features which on the whole fit both Sweden and Norway very well, although a few objections will be raised below. The paper is therefore a valuable contribution to our understanding of the functioning of economies such as Norway and Sweden, and probably several other European countries. Although Calmfors' analysis is carried out within the context of a particular macroeconomic model, most of his conclusions are valid for a wide range of specifications of an open economy.

One possible exception to the relevance of the assumptions mentioned above concerns the assumption that wage changes are determined only through centralized wage negotiations. At least in Norway, a large part of the wage increases in the last decade have *not* been a direct consequence of central wage negotiations. This part of the wage increases has often been called "wage drift", and is determined partly by market forces and partly by local wage settlements. In his introduction, Calmfors also admits that his approach fails to take these factors into account.

Another question concerns Calmfors' assumption of a proportional tax. This is clearly unrealistic for an economy such as Norway, which has a very progressive nonindexed tax system. One consequence of introducing a progressive nonindexed tax function of the Norwegian type would be that the model's homogeneity in nominal variables will no longer hold.[1] Another consequence, which is more important in Calmfors' context, would be as follows. In Calmfors' model, and most other open economy models with a proportional tax rate, a higher nominal wage rate will lead to a higher after-tax real wage. With a strongly progressive income tax, this need not be the case. Since after-tax nominal wages in this instance will increase propor-

---

[1] A discussion of the effect of a progressive tax function in an open economy is given by Rødseth (1981 *a*).

tionately less than the pretax nominal wage, the after-tax nominal wage increase may be proportionately less than the price rise caused by the wage increase. In an article in 1977, Calmfors himself pointed out that with plausible numbers for Sweden, we will actually find such a negative relation between a change in the pretax nominal wage and the resulting change in the posttax real wage in the absence of indexed taxes.[2] A similar point has been made by Rødseth (1981 *b*) for the Norwegian economy.

The implications of such a negative relationship between pretax nominal wages and posttax real wages are the following. Since employment is higher, the lower the nominal wage rate is, the trade union will obviously wish to set a *low* nominal wage rate, thereby obtaining both a high after-tax real wage and a high level of employment.

Clearly, trade unions in Norway or Sweden have never been observed pushing for lower nominal wages. There are at least *two* reasons for this. In the *first* place, wage settlements are in reality not as centralized as assumed in Calmfors' model. With several trade unions, we may get a prisoners' dilemma solution with a high nominal wage, even if all trade unions taken together would benefit from a reduction in the nominal wage rate. This effect will of course be strengthened if unions care about relative wages in addition to their own after-tax real wage.

A *second* reason why unions do not push for lower nominal wages could be that in addition to their after-tax real wage, they have preferences regarding the income distribution between wage income and capital income. This will be the case if unions consider the "fairness" of the income distribution as a separate variable entering their utility functions in addition to their disposable real income and unemployment rate. None of these aspects of union behavior are incorporated in Calmfors' paper.

There is also a third implication of a negative relationship between pretax nominal wage changes and posttax real wage changes. Such a relationship implies that tax rates will cause trade unions considerable concern. We would therefore expect an important part of the union's activity to be directed towards influencing government policies. In this context it is clearly unrealistic to consider government policy as exogenous.

In Calmfors' Section III, the decision sequence is important for the results. Calmfors assumes that the trade union makes its decision for a future period first, after which the government makes its decisions for the same period. In a game theoretical context, the trade union is a Stackelberg leader, while the government is a Stackelberg follower. In Section V,

---

[2] Today, however, taxes in Sweden are indexed (with a one-year lag), so the assumption of a proportional tax rate suits Sweden better, although *real* wage increases will, of course, be hit by progressive taxation.

Calmfors lets the trade union's decisions be influenced by the fact that the government's policy depends on the trade union's decisions.

The decision sequence assumed by Calmfors is obviously not then only possible one. Calmfors' assumption probably gives a reasonable description of the facts in Norway up to the beginning of the 1970s. Until then, most wage settlements took place in April and often lasted for two years, except for revisions after one year which were closely related to the past rate of inflation. During this two-year period, the government was free to change tax rates and other policy instruments without this affecting the wage settlement. In the last ten years, however, things have changed slightly due to the government's attempt to pursue a more active income policy. In recent years, wage settlements have lasted for only one year. Furthermore, at least some government policy instruments, such as various tax rates, have been explicitly or implicitly determined as part of the wage settlements. In some years, wages and tax rates have been determined simultaneously. In other years, tax rates have been decided on before the wage negotiations, but with the provision that tax rates would be kept unchanged if and only if the wage settlement reached satisfied certain conditions set by the government.

An analysis of different types of decision sequences could be made within the framework of Calmfors' model. The results of such an analysis would no doubt be of interest to a government trying to find an effective incomes policy.

Calmfors mentions among possible extensions of his paper that trade unions should care about current account deficits, since such deficits impose burdens on the future. With trade unions taking the current account deficit into consideration, we could actually assume an endogenous government policy ensuring full employment. The trade union's behavior in this case could be described as maximizing a utility function containing the after-tax real wage and the current account balance. Current account deficits affect the utility level negatively, since a large deficit might lead to higher future taxes or even to abandonment of the full employment policy in the future. The analysis of an economy where a trade union maximizes a utility function as just described, would be very similar to Calmfors' analysis. However, in several cases, the effects of policy changes and external events would differ substantially from the results which would follow from Calmfors' model.

Calmfors also mentions that the future relation between real wages and employment in a richer model would be affected by present real wages via their effects on investment. In the long run, the capital stock in each sector must therefore be determined endogenously. If the production function in each sector is homogeneous of degree one in capital and labor, and the long-run rate of return on capital is exogenously given by the world market rate of interest, the real wage rate will also be fixed in the long run. In the long run, the trade union can therefore not affect the real wage rate. It may thus be in the interest of the trade union to push for a policy that would restrict international capital mobility, thereby avoiding the rate of return on capital and the real wage rate being fixed in the long run.

References

Calmfors, L.: Inflation in Sweden. In *World-wide inflation* (ed. L. Krause and W. Salant). Brookings, Washington D.C., 1977.

Rødseth, A.: Progressive taxes and automatic stabilization in an open economy. Memorandum from the Institute of economy, University of Oslo, 15th of October, 1981 *a*.

Rødseth, A.: Om prisforventningar i Phillips-kurva. Abeidsnotater nr. 3, Finansdepartementet, Oslo, 1981 *b*.

General Discussion: What Have We Learned?

Edited by Nils Gottfries, University of Stockholm and Torsten Persson, Institute for International Economic Studies, Stockholm, Sweden

Assar Lindbeck: The purpose of this conference has been to analyze the consequences of short-term stabilization policy for the allocation of resources. The idea behind this final discussion is an attempt to summarize what we have learned. However, before we try to answer this question, it may be useful to try to answer a somewhat easier question: what have been the main themes of the conference?

One theme, found in most of the papers, has been the consequences of short-term shocks and short-term policies for the *"static" allocation of resources among sectors* in a long-term perspective. Various papers have emphasized how the allocation of resources between production sectors, such as tradables versus nontradables or manufacturing versus natural resource sectors, is affected. Others have stressed the effects on the distribution of resources between alternative end uses, such as private and public use. It has become particularly clear that temporary shocks and short-term policies often have permanent effects on this type of "static" allocation of resources at a given point in time.

Another theme has been the consequences of short-term shocks and policies for the *allocation of resources over time*. Some papers have emphasized the effects on investment and growth, others the effects on the current account of the balance of payments. It has been shown that *both* individual life-cycle consumption plans *and* intergenerational aspects have to be taken into account, particularly when studying the role of deficits in the current account. Otherwise, stabilization policy discussions about deficits of this type tend to be quite superficial.

Another way of classifying the themes of the conference is to distinguish between the *different types of disturbances*. A rather rich spectrum of disturbances has been discussed on the demand as well as the supply side. Most of the authors have also been eager to distinguish between monetary and real disturbances and between temporary and permanent disturbances. Policy mistakes, due for instance, to incorrect expectations, have also been emphasized in several papers.

There have been some attempts to *endogenize the behavior of governments and unions* and study the interactions between these organizations.

Even though most papers emphasize issues of positive economics, normative aspects, such as *criteria for evaluating policies* which change the allocation of resources, have also been discussed. The motivation for policy intervention is a related issue. Economists are always creative in finding rationales for policy interventions. It is interesting to note that at this conference, arguments for policy intervention have been expressed if prices adjust immediately to the new momentary, or short-run, equilibrium position (sometimes called "overshooting") *and* if prices do not adjust to such momentary, or short-term, equilibria because of various rigidities, thereby creating market disequilibria. However, it is probably fair to say that the conference has not been characterized by a naive belief in the ability of governments to improve on the decisions taken by markets. Rather the conference has been characterized by considerable scepticism towards the information, ability and incentives of politicians to make rational interventions.

Peter Neary: I want to begin by noting that at this conference, as at any conference, we not only learn from what is said but also from what is not said. One set of arguments, in particular, has been conspicuous by its absence from this conference. I am speaking, of course, of the critique of *anticipated policy rules* associated with the so-called new classical macroeconomics, particularly with the work of Robert Lucas. This sort of argument did appear on just one occasion, in Lars Calmfors's paper. In his model, with a rational wage-setting trade union, if the union anticipated government action to offset a deflationary shock, then it might respond in a manner which would actually give rise to more unemployment in the long run than would have ensued from a policy of nonintervention. But with this exception, I think most of the papers have accepted that there may indeed be some role for intervention in principle. And instead they proceeded to examine what we might call the by-product distortions of intervention.

What can we conclude from this difference between our discussions and recent theoretical debates in the journals—or at least in some of the journals? One could argue that it simply reflects the tastes of the conference organizers in choosing whom to invite and whom not to invite! But I think that one can perhaps go somewhat deeper and suggest that it reflects a failure of the new classical macroeconomic school to convince a majority in the profession that policy rules should be avoided in principle. And I can think of two reasons for this.

First despite all that has been said here and elsewhere, many of us still believe that there are many *rationales for intervention*—even intervention of a systematic and foreseeable kind. Some of these rationales are more persuasive than others, and we have debated this during the conference. One rationale which was criticized was the assumption that individuals have short horizons, as compared to governments which have foresight and are concerned with intergenerational equity, and so intervene to overcome this. I would agree that this particular combination of assumptions (which, as John Flemming pointed out, follows a long tradition in English welfare economics) is not very persuasive in itself. However, it may very well be that individual agents have a shorter horizon than the government, not because of different perceptions, but because of capital-market imperfections which give rise to differential access to capital markets. Many people would argue that the presence of substantial moral hazard problems adequately explains why capital-market imperfections are endemic. And to the extent that this is so, there is a strong case for intervention in order to smooth consumption streams even with respect to foreseeable shocks. Rationales of this and other kinds still appear to be generally accepted as justifying short-run intervention.

A second reason which is extremely relevant to the topic of this conference is the *problem which faces a decision-maker*. Consider a hypothetical policy-maker with two advisers, one a dyed-in-the-wool new classical macroeconomist who argues that nothing systematic should ever be done at any time, and the other a traditional Rip van Winkle Keynesian who argues for systematic (and so, predictable) policy rules. Quite apart from the political economy incentives which we know will arise, if the policy-maker has no clear basis for choosing in principle between his two advisers, it would be rational for him to follow a course of action which lies between their two extreme prescriptions. In other words, any weighted average of no intervention and extensive intervention will imply that systematic and in principle predictable intervention will sometimes appear to be justified.

So, for these two general sets of reasons, it has been accepted at this conference—and I think it is still widely accepted—that intervention in principle may frequently be justified. Of course this is not at all to say that the tone of the conference has been favorable toward intervention. On the contrary, we have quite specifically taken intervention as perhaps justified in the short run, but looked critically at its longer-run consequences.

One issue relevant to these consequences, which has been referred to, is the question of *policy mistakes*. I think we recognize that it is difficult to model policy mistakes persuasively, especially if the model is already so complicated that the explicit incorporation of uncertainty would make it totally unwieldy. So, some of the papers have ended up treating this sort of issue in a rather *ad hoc* way. But it is interesting nonetheless that they have taken rather similar approaches. I am thinking of my own paper with Douglas Purvis, which looked at misperceptions by government stemming from a confusion between real and monetary shocks, and the paper by Lars Calmfors which considered misperceptions by a trade union in mistaking a rise in world prices and therefore setting the wage rate on the basis of imperfect information. Another possibility is that a state of classical unemployment is mistaken for a state of Keynesian unemployment. One theme of the conference, and one thing we can say we have learned, is that it is mistakes of this kind, rather than any objection to intervention in principle, which give rise to the real risks that are involved in an activist stabilization program.

The point about classical versus Keynesian unemployment brings me to a general question which has been raised as to whether the present recession is mainly of a classical or a Keynesian kind, using the now standard Malinvaud terminology. Perhaps one of the reasons why stabilization policy is not working as successfully at the moment is a change in the *nature of the shocks*. This is something which has been around for some time, but we have seen a number of more clearly defined studies of problems which can arise in this situation, where the economy is subjected to a supply-side shock but the response to it is more appropriate to a shock emanating from the demand side. Perhaps this is something we knew already, but to have it reinforced does not necessarily mean that we have not learned anything.

John Helliwell: The exchange of views at this conference has been unusually free and the group has been very diverse. Thus the amount of learning has been much greater than I would normally expect in a conference of specialists who are often very much aware of what the others are going to say; they may either agree or disagree, but they will not learn. The variety of ideas received has made it very hard for me to summarize my impressions. But let me try.

This conference has focused on different ways of viewing the role and longer-term consequences of stabilization policy. Some different analytical styles and approaches have appeared, or reappeared, and it will take quite a while before I—and probably others—will be able to decide whether the individual papers represent temporary disturbances, parts of a recurring cycle or an emerging trend. In methodology there is the same uncertainty as there is in the world of events, and for many of the same reasons.

Our various methods of analyzing stabilization policy are the result of an interplay of supply and demand forces. The main demand pull comes from the organizers, who asked us all to focus our attention on the allocational effects of stabilization policy. On the supply side, we authors all tried to employ our comparative advantages, while attempting to minimize the amount of obsolescence that was thereby created in our existing stocks of intellectual capital. The temporary balancing of supply and demand forces was also, I am glad to say, influenced by what has been happening in our various economies over the past decade. Thus there was, among other things, emphasis on supply shocks and sectoral imbalances, and also on the distinction between temporary and permanent shocks. Although many of the papers had a monetary sector, most of the shocks studied were real shocks, and most of the analytical emphasis was on the real consequences of those shocks and any accompanying stabilization policies.

Supply shocks that take the form of an unanticipated but permanent change in the imported raw material price cause an immediate drop in conventionally measured productivity and require time-consuming changes in the factor mix. Depending on the nature of the fixity of the real wage and the coincident effects of the shock on world absorption and national income, the stagflation may be exacerbated by deficient demand, even in relation to the shrunken capacity to produce. Some papers extended this analysis of the effects of supply shocks to situations where there are two domestic sectors that differ in their exposure to foreign markets. The results of the supply shock in these cases depend rather importantly on how much each sector depends on capital, labor and raw material. The emphasis on two or more sectors whose short and long-term competitiveness is differentially affected naturally raises the question of what sort of stabilization policy, if any, should be adopted and what its effects are, especially on long-term allocation.

Now at this stage—and here I am somewhat uncertain—there is some kind of contrast in several of the papers because the full-blown intertemporal optimization frameworks do not in general leave any scope under perfect information for stabilization policy, or indeed any need for it. So as to make the models usable for an analysis of the effects of such policy, *some fixity of relative prices* is introduced and policy subsequently analyzed. A possible conclusion of the analysis must be, of course, that the most efficient policy is to remove the arbitrarily imposed fixity and recover full optimality. This narrow lesson is so narrowly derived from its often implausible assumptions that it does not teach us anything. However, looking on the bright side, an analysis in this sort of framework does have two very clear implications that probably extend into the real world of events.

First, when *stabilization policy* imposes *a new rigidity*—for example a target balance for the current account in the short run in the face of a supply shock such as the first oil price shock—costs are clearly raised in the adjustment of the system to the full equilibrium. This follows from the kind of investment/saving explanation of the current account that was presented.

Second, conventional *stabilization targets and instruments* have to be *rethought* very carefully under a supply-side shock. The notion that a supply shock is exogenous to the system may be suitable for a small open economy, but it was generalized in several papers to a situation where the supply shock in fact comes from elsewhere in the world or elsewhere in the economy. There are two types of issues here and two types of models were used to deal with them.

One is the economics of countries, and this could be regions rather than countries, where there are important resource sectors and where the shock, which is effectively an increase in the price of the resources, can be interpreted as a potential for a resource investment boom in the other sector. Now if the sectors compete in factor markets and are in a common currency area facing world prices, then the change in resource price starts a whole chain of complicated interactions. And here the boom-town or bonanza era in the resource sector (or country) raises the *costs of an unstabilized adjustment* in the declining sectors when they face competition from the booming sector in both input and output markets. These costs are probably higher than the kind that were dealt with in the papers—especially when there are elements of common property and insecure tenure. The same kind of issue can be posed in a world model with OPEC as a booming sector and other countries as producing differentiated tradable goods and with differing energy intensities. There was less of this at the conference. But I would argue that a good number of the single-country models used can be reinterpreted reasonably handily and extended into a world framework.

Let me see what conclusions we could draw from this. What are the implications for the national economy and its aggregate demand, labor/capital substitution and the sectoral allocation of activity? As you might guess, the policies that have the best allocative and welfare effects turn out to be those that do not slow down the private sector's response unduly, where unduly has to be defined in terms of the costs of adjusting at different speeds. Now, the implication of this general rule is that policies with a good allocational effect are those aimed at removing precisely the rigidities that were assumed in order to get the analysis off the ground, as I mentioned before. And if the *stickiness* is reasonably realistic, then it has a *counterpart in real policy analysis*. Thus, for example, when the real absorption wage is sticky, then a change in the exchange rate can help to adjust profitability in the tradable sector; if the real wage is sticky in the output price, then changes in payroll packages or similar measures turn out to be the instrument of choice.

Well, this is all relevant stuff and it has a real-world counterpart. But in its application it relies rather heavily on the ability to *identify* instances where there are *rigidities* in the real economy and on being sure that the rigidities do not have a function. It was pointed out, directly or indirectly, in some of the conference papers how the ability of the economy to adjust relatively costlessly depends rather crucially on when the shock in question is expected to arise—in the present or in the future—and whether it is permanent or temporary.

In a world where adjustments are costly and sometimes irreversible, many of what may seem to be *rigidities* or sluggish responses *may* therefore be *rational responses* to relative price changes and other shocks whose likely duration, importance and macroeconomic significance are simply unknown to private decision-makers. Whether they are any better known or understood by policy-makers is another important issue that obviously must be settled in one way or another before one can decide what role there is for stabilization policy. This issue was addressed chiefly by assumption rather than by evidence or analysis in most of the papers.

The final lesson that I have learned—or at least had repeatedly and forcefully stressed to me—is that policy-makers, like scholars, ought to design their stabilization policies with the allocational effects clearly in view. To be precise, only by way of example, if a policy is intended to smooth an adjustment path to a new pattern of capital/labor use in a sector, or the transformation from one industrial structure to another, then the impermanence of the support must be spelled out clearly if it is not to cause costly delay and risks of never completing the move towards the more efficient new situation.

Michael Bruno: My comments concern intertemporal aspects and government/trade union interaction.

Starting with the *intertemporal aspects,* we have left a phase where there were two distinct avenues of analysis: short-run stabilization policy, which was usually made within a one-period context; and the separate literature that dealt with growth problems, usually in real terms, with no money. Structural change problems came under the latter heading of either growth or development. The novelty of the kind of discussion we are conducting here is the attempt to combine both spans of time so as to elucidate the long-run implications of short-run policy.

Looking at some of the models that were presented, one might be led to think that anything done today affects the future in such an overriding manner that there is simply no way of considering only the short run. One example of this in the discussion was the idea that government cannot really do anything effectively by taxing today because the long run will not be affected.

Now, I think it is important to get a perspective on the way our thinking goes; it tends to move in waves. Let me take the *current account* as an example. The trade and development literature of the early 1960s was full of what were at the time called two-gap models—where the current account was regarded as constrained either by the difference between imports and exports, or by the difference between investment and savings along with a long-run view of the current account deficit as borrowing over time. However, this literature did not take short-run stabilization issues into account. Then came another phase which developed at the end of the 1960s and the beginning of the 1970s. That was the literature on stabilization in open economies, to which many contributions were made in this country, and where there was no regard for long-run structural change issues.

Now we are coming back to a combination of both and also returning to some of the issues that were relevant in the 1960s. And it is interesting to ask what makes for this. One argument, for instance, that might be advanced for the renewed interest in optimal borrowing now is the *emergence of a private capital market* where countries can borrow freely. It is this institutional change which has also brought back the alternative view of the current amount.

But it is important to state some institutional *limitations on the superrationality* of intertemporal substitution that were expressed in the discussions. First of all, *households* have finite lifetimes. We also know that capital markets are imperfect and we know that the permanent income model does not explain fully consumption behavior if we look at empirical research. Nor is it explained by Keynesian consumption functions. It is some kind of combination of the two.

Governments too have a finite lifetime—they have to be reelected. And this severely limits the kind of conclusions that can be drawn. Let me just give an example from the discussion. It might be a reasonable policy to try and drive down money at whatever cost in unemployment if the next election is, say, only six years from now. But as you approach the election date and if you worry about the chance of being reelected—and the individuals in the economy know it—then your policy becomes less and less credible over time. These considerations then become an important input into the kind of model that can sensibly be constructed.

As to *firms'* investment functions, we write them down as rational-expectations type investment demand. But we know empirically that investment demand is heavily weighted by current profits, much more than you would expect from a simple rational expectations model. Now this may have to do with uncertainty or liquidity constraints, which obviously limit the applicability of this type of model.

And the last example in the same field is the fact that governments worry about the current account. Is this irrational? I would say no. There is a good chance that what governments do has some sense in it. We should not merely tell them to stop worrying about the current account—that is a point which came up in the discussion. One could think of arguments for not making extreme statements, such as the imperfections of capital markets. The private capital market may also disappear again. Most loans are not taken on a long-run basis, but are *revolving loans*. You have to renew a loan on an annual basis, the interest rate changes and the lender can simply tell you that it will not be renewed. So the long-run borrowing that we have in stylized models is not a true reflection of how the real world works.

Now, all this is not to minimize the importance of taking simple theoretical extremes and learning what they look like. But I think it is also important to stress the limitations and try and improve the models in that light.

The second, and last, issue I would like to take up is *government versus trade union interaction*. Lars Calmfors's paper was really the only one that directly addressed this problem. My question here is whether the technique with which we normally analyze these models, that is, using mathematical analysis, is the relevant one. Perhaps game theory, empirical research and research on institutional behavior may in due course throw more light on this issue than the kind of models we are used to working with. The signals that a government conveys in its actions are a very important input into the bargaining process with trade unions. Take a recent example: the U.S. air controllers' strike this year (1981). In my interpretation, this is similar to something I would advise the government in my own country to do, that is, choose a public-sector union and try and signal by means of the bargain you strike with it so as to affect the wage bargaining process for the rest of the economy. It's a question of signalling and credibility.

This can be linked to the first subject—the intertemporal aspects—by two last points. One is a suggestion made by Lars Svensson in a previous discussion that you can incorporate trade union behavior into a two-period model and allow for some intertemporal substitution between rigid real wages now and unemployment in the future. Variations in the rate of time preference would then indicate the degree of trade-union myopia. The other point that leads back to the intertemporal aspect is the question of learning from past mistakes. A proper way of looking at two-period models is not as a once-and-for-all decision, but as a revolving plan—tomorrow you will again look at the two-period model, in which you will embed the learning from the mistakes you have made today.

Johan Myhrman: I would like to start by disagreeing with a statement made by Peter Neary. He said that "it has been accepted at this conference—and I think it is still widely accepted—that intervention in principle may frequently be justified." I do not agree with this statement in general and I do not think it can be interpreted as a conclusion of the papers in this conference.

In particular, I disagree with the word "frequently". In my view there are not many clear-cut cases for intervention and I think the experience of the least decade is *strong evidence against frequent intervention*. As a rule, the governments in most Western economies have frequently misunderstood the problem, intervened at the wrong time and by measures of inappropriate size. I think it is about time for us as economists to recognize the enormous information problems which confront decision-makers. After having been involved in decision-making for some years, I can only stress the problem of uncertainty. I cannot recommend a certain policy today unless I have a clear picture of the development of the economy one or two or three years from now without any action. The opinion about such a prediction usually varies by several percentage points in GDP growth rates. To this we have to add the public choice problem of different politicians' private aims.

With reference to the papers in this conference, it is clear that most of the models do not introduce uncertainty explicitly. This is all right as long as we stick to pure theory and positive economics. Uncertainty makes it difficult to handle the problem in a fruitful way in terms of theoretical analysis. But we have to be careful about the policy conclusions which we are allowed to draw from such analysis.

It is interesting to note the difference between this conference and the previous conference in Stockholm about flexible exchange rates in 1975.[1] The problem then was the effects of some disturbances on the economy in a system with flexible exchange rates. Most papers concentrated on monetary disturbances, although I also discussed some real disturbances in my article. At this conference, most of the disturbances discussed are real disturbances. In particular, the problem is often the difference between a temporary and a permanent disturbance or, in one case, the difference between a monetary and a real disturbance.

Mostly, these problems are analyzed using a general equilibrium approach. This gives very valuable insight into the nature of the adjustment problem from a more long-run perspective. It is also noteworthy, however, that these models usually lack a specification of the policy sector. Therefore, the policy problems of, for example, distinguishing a permanent from a temporary shock and a monetary from a real shock are not highlighted. My conclusion from all this is that the conference has been extremely valuable in stating the long-run consequences of different shocks but that *no obvious policy conclusions* can be drawn. This may hopefully be an answer to Peter Neary's statement about one set of arguments "which has been conspicuous by its absence from this conference."

Hans Tson Söderström: I felt very sympathetic towards Börje Kragh in our policy discussion yesterday when he stood up and said something like: "Well, here you sit and talk—but *what should we do,* those of us who are responsible for policy?" I think Peter Neary's distinction between the interventionist and noninterventionist positions is very useful in this context. Most of us here would not throw away systematic policy intervention simply by reference to the rationality of individual agents, as would representatives of the new classical macroeconomic standpoint. On the other

[1] Flexible Exchange Rates and Stabilization Policy, *Scand. J. Econ. 78* (2), 1976.

hand, we do have a critical attitude towards intervention. And when you add up all the points about which you have to be critical towards intervention, the question is whether they do not amount to the same conclusion as that of the new classical economics.

If we tried to use all the papers presented here to advise the government on what to do in a specific stabilization policy situation, then I guess we would have to say: Well, first you have to try and find out what type of shock we have just been subjected to; is it a real shock or a monetary shock, is it a temporary shock or a permanent shock? Then the government must ask itself: To what extent will individual agents—households and firms—be able to cushion this shock by themselves? Now, if they cannot do this to a full extent, then there is an *a priori* case for policy intervention. In forming the policy, we would ask the government to take into account what the allocational, intertemporal and long-run effects of the intervention would be. How will the intervention affect the future behavior not only of individuals, households and firms, but also of trade unions and perhaps even other governments? And when they have considered all these various aspects of the policy intervention, there should be some kind of welfare weighting of the benefit of the intervention relative to its potential costs. Such costs may include the risk of misjudgement as to the type of shock, the long-run effects of intervention (even when the shock is correctly perceived) on allocation, distribution and the future effectiveness of policy and so on. When you add all these problems together, the question is how far from the new classical position do we end up. This brings me back to Johan Myhrman's question: What *policy rule* should we recommend when we take all the complications of stabilization policy that have been discussed at this conference into account?

Robin Matthews: I would like to develop a point that has already been made a little further—it concerns the difficulty of identifying the shocks that the economy has been subjected to. As both an economist and an economic historian, I have always been struck by the way we are far more ready to discuss the present and the future than we are to give firm reasons why things happened in the past. I find the greatest difficulty in explaining real trends in the past. After long study, I tend to draw up lists and say: Well, maybe it was a bit of each and I do not quite know how much, what proportion and so on. So, I remain more agnostic than some other people about the extent to which we have had novel changes in the last ten years. Maybe we have—very likely we have—but I think we have seen changes to some degree all the time. And I would not wish to chastise governments too much for not interpreting the nature of shocks correctly.

Peter Neary listed various kinds of shocks we may have been subjected to. One could add a couple of others. The first is *world industrialization* over the last thirty years—enormous increases in output of manufactured products entering the world market from countries which formerly supplied far less of them—principally Japan. This represents a change in the relative output of manufactures and other things which must certainly make a difference for the rest of the world. Second, we have not talked very much about the *cycle* at all. But there may surely have been an element of a super boom in the twenty-year period of the 1950s and 1960s. And the reaction may be an element of what has occurred in the 1970s, so that the situation is different from what it would have been if we had started out from an equilibrium position and then subjected it to shock.

Now, if you say that there is great uncertainty in interpreting the shocks, this may appear to strengthen the case for governments not trying to do anything about them. And I think there is considerable force in that argument—a great deal of force. Unfortunately, the policy seems to me to be not feasible because government inaction constitutes action in some cases. The government has to decide *how to do nothing*. This is familiar in elementary macroeconomics: does doing nothing mean keeping the money supply constant, or does it mean keeping the interest rate constant? Does it mean keeping the tax rate constant, or does it mean keeping tax revenues in a constant proportion of national income? You have to decide. The larger the public sector, the more the government is involved willy-nilly in decisions with macroeconomic consequences.

Another reason why governments which do not want to do anything find that they are doing something is that, following a period of what they consider to be inappropriate stabilization, the very act of not stabilizing involves huge policy shifts. We have seen this in the zealous attempts of Mrs Thatcher and President Reagan to do nothing, which have meant absolutely revolutionary changes in policies.

Some of the things I have said at this conference may have suggested that I am a Rip van Winkle unreformed Keynesian. In fact, I would like to make clear that I am not a great believer in government action. I think the various constraints which government is inevitably subject to by virtue of its nature as government make good decisions extremely difficult. And therefore it would be nice if governments did not have to do much. Unfortunately, they have to do much. And they have to use discretion in dealing with these things—try and take them all into account. My main hope is that they would not be too ambitious in trying to do this. New governments, on entering office, would perform better than most governments have done if they set as their objective not to make matters any worse than they would otherwise have been. Quite a difficult thing to do.

Assaf Razin: I would like to talk about four points which were all discussed during the conference. The first is concerned with the current account, the second with wage formation, the third with the notion of stabilization policies and the fourth with the question of unemployment and growth.

As for the question of whether we should worry about the *current account* situation, it is clear that there is Pareto optimal intergenerational allocation of resources when an optimizing private sector is left to itself in a competitive framework with perfect foresight, provided that there are tradable assets. The role of the government is simply to transfer income across generations according to social norms. However, I still think that the current account is a real-world problem and that it is so particularly due to government behavior and government-induced changes in the current account. As mentioned by many others, decision-making on public spending tends to be myopic and often leads to excess government spending, which in turn gives rise to some of the phenomena that we see today in many countries—large current account deficits, a large service sector, a large government sector and low investment. There is therefore some bias in government behavior that tends to lay the burden on future generations.

I do not think that imperfections in the world capital market could be a rationale, or justification, for government intervention in the current account. I am talking now about small countries. In such a country the government, as well as the private sector, cannot affect the terms of borrowing and lendning to any large extent, so there is no great advantage for the government to be directly involved in these activities. I see a few exceptions, of course. For example, the government can be situated in an area where there is considerable political disorder. This means that through its political influence in the area, the government can sometimes have better borrowing terms than the private sector—Israel is a case in point.

The second issue is about *wage formation*. It seems, and I think Michael Bruno pointed this out, that the main reasons for relatively high wages, in reverse causation to the Scandinavian model, are government accomodations. Accommodating policies are often reflected in high wage settlements. And this, of course, leads to the phenomena I just mentioned, that is low growth and a large government sector. So I think we should at least partly abandon the notion that wages explode out of the blue; instead the wage explosion should be tied to the behavior of the government. This was the approach that Lars Calmfors took.

The third point is about the notion of *stabilization policies*. To me this notion is still very vague, although it is part of the title of this conference. Torsten Persson and Jeff Sachs dealt with explicit welfare evaluations of the effects of disturbances (especially Persson, who looked at monetary disturbances), but others were more or less satisfied with a rather vague notion of stabilization. But it should be kept in mind that stabilizing output or consumption can many times lead to bad situations, such as severe restrictions on intertemporal consumption choice, for example.

Finally, with respect to *unemployment and growth*, several papers were concerned with the negative effects of excessive and sticky wages on economic growth. The issue was raised by Pentti Kouri, who suggested a growth-oriented policy in order to increase employment. This particular recommendation should be thought about a little more carefully. It seems that if excessive and sticky wages are the problem, a more direct and seemingly more efficient tool would be a wage policy, specifically payroll tax policy. But this also requires a change in the government accommodation policies which led to high wages.

Michael Hoel: I have a couple of comments regarding the analysis in some of the papers. The papers I have in mind are those which treated intertemporal aspects of supply-side shocks, not only the immediate consequences but also gradual adjustment through the capital stock.

Real wage rigidity has been stressed in several of these papers. As some of the other conference participants have already mentioned, the wage setting process is a very important part of the analysis in these papers. I think it is fair to say that we do not know enough about wage setting in economies with strong trade unions, so that this is an important area for future research.

My second point regarding these papers concerns the *description of the production side* in the economy. Most of the papers rely on the simple neoclassical production function. We know that for very long-run purposes, for example steady-state growth, etc., results based on a neoclassical production function do not differ very much from those which would be obtained with a more realistic putty-clay production function. We also know that for the very short run, the neoclassical production function may be used at the sectoral level, even if we have fixed factor proportions at the individual firm level. However, regarding the more intermediate phase when we are adjusting from a shock towards a new equilibrium, I think the implications of the putty-clay production structure are quite important. For instance, after an energy price rise, some of the old capital units will go out of production, as will the labor force associated with them. If there are rigid wages and therefore a declining capital stock due to reduced profitability, this decline will come about through lower investment in new production units than that which would have occurred in the absence of the energy price rise. Thus, the change in the capital stock will usually have implications for the age structure of the production units, which may be of importance. It is difficult to analyze this aspect of changes in the capital stock with a neoclassical production function.

For these reasons, I believe that the analysis of the intermediate run requires improvements in the description of the production side of the economy. Personally, I think it is more useful to try to model this aspect of the economy, than it is to attempt to model highly sophisticated expectations formation and intertemporal behavior of firms and households.

Thorvaldur Gylfason: In my view, there has been considerable preaching to the converted around this table over the last couple of days. I think this atmosphere reflects an emerging consensus among mainstream neo-Keynesian economists, on both sides of the Atlantic, that the present crisis of the industrial countries is one of classical unemployment in the sense that wage costs are too high, rather than Keynesian unemployment due to deficient demand. Hence, we have had *stagflation* since the mid-1970s, not the old kind of unemployment with deflation as before.

Two questions arise in this context. First, how did this come about? And second, what can be done about it? I think these are really the questions that have been addressed by most of the papers presented at this conference.

The answer to the first question—*how did this come about?*—is obviously that we have had a series of supply shocks in the 1970s. Part of the explanation can be traced to the increase in oil and raw material prices, as was stressed in the papers by Michael Bruno, Peter Neary and Douglas Purvis, and John Helliwell. Another reason is the partly exogenous, partly endogenous wage-push behavior of organized labor, as was emphasized in the paper by Lars Calmfors.

The answer to the second question is also obvious: something must be done to *stimulate the supply side* of the economy. In this vein, Martin Feldstein's paper dealt with the necessity of changing capital taxation to stimulate business investment in plant and equipment, while Pennti Kouri's paper treated the need to raise profitability, by lowering real wages or by other means.

The question of what can be done about supply shocks is, of course, fundamental. Should governments try to stimulate aggregate supply by attempting to lower real wages, and if so, how? Or, should governments accept real wage rigidity as an inevitable fact of life and try to get at the supply side by encouraging capital formation and thereby stimulate employment?

Let me look at each of these strategies in turn. If *real wages* need to be *lowered,* how can this be done? Three possibilities may be considered. The first is monetary and fiscal contraction with ensuing unemployment. The British example, which has been cited repeatedly at this conference, is not very promising in this respect, because real wages have been rising persistently over the last two years in England despite mounting unemployment, although some think they may be stagnating now.

The second alternative is devaluation. Unfortunately, it appears to me uncertain whether labor unions or nonunionized workers would go along. It seems to me that from the point of view of rational labor unions, it may be desirable—even optimal—to have high real wages combined with some unemployment. This is because there may be a conflict of interest between, say, strong members of a union who elect the leadership and find it to their advantage to keep real wages high and weaker members who will be thrown out of their jobs as a result of excessive real wage demands. In the light of this possibility, it might be worthwhile to reexamine the concept of the natural or full-employment rate of unemployment and the related distinction between voluntary and involuntary unemployment. In this perspective, the question of real wage rigidity becomes very closely related to income distribution problems and economic conflict in general.

The third way of reducing real wages would be through reduced payroll taxes and employment subsidies. These policies may reduce unemployment, but the financing issue remains. Somehow, some day, somebody would have to pay for these kinds of measures.

As for the second option, in which real wages would have to be regarded as untouchable so that the only way to stimulate employment and output growth would be by *encouraging capital formation,* it is not clear how this could be effected within the time constraint imposed on policy-makers in democratic societies. As Martin Feldstein pointed out, it may require a great deal of capital formation, and hence take a long time, to stimulate investment enough to return the economy to full employment along this route. And the fact that investment is also a component of aggregate demand should not be overlooked. Increased capital formation may thus lead to excess demand and inflation in the short run and it may take a long time for the supply effects to be felt in the form of reduced pressure on prices.

In conclusion, I do not think we know yet how supply management policies could be used effectively to engineer a noninflationary economic recovery in the industrial countries. The question remains unanswered. As I see it, the essence of the problem is that the key determinant of aggregate supply and the cost of production in these countries, that is, wages, is largely beyond the control of the government. Other things being equal, I do not think we can expect relief from present stagflationary tendencies until those who are responsible for wage decisions—primarily labor unions —are brought into the political process and held accountable to the public at large in approximately the same way as the government in a democracy.

Assar Lindbeck: Before we continue, I would like to throw in a comment on the real wage issue, because I wonder if we are really specifying the problem correctly. Many models assume constant real wage rates. But if you look at the data, what you see is really not rigid real wages but rather disturbing *fluctuations in the real wage.* The typical features for most countries often seem to be two or three years of rapidly rising real wages. Many countries experienced this in the period 1972–75, when the increase in some countries was as large as 15–20 per cent. Later on, during 1976–80, many countries have no doubt been able to reduce the growth rate of wages again, although this process has without doubt often been quite painful. Thus, perhaps the problem is rather cyclical fluctuations in real wage rates that are not conducive to macroeconomic stability.

It was said in the discussion that in the United States there is considerable flexibility in the real wage rate due to long-term contracts in money terms, combined with a relatively flexible price level. What is also different, I think, is that in the U.S. the real wage rate does not tend to be excessively *high* to the same extent as in several other countries.

Lars Calmfors: I want to make a rather specific point about the possibilities of successful *nonaccommodation policies* in a democracy. It seems to me that the key question is as follows. How can nonaccommodation policies be made to appear credible? How can we avoid ending up in a British noncooperative game situation with heavy unemployment, where the government waits for the trade union to lower real wages, while the trade union waits for the government to abandon its nonaccommodation policies.

I think that the British situation is also a very unfortunate one from the point of view of fighting inflation. When nonaccommodation policies produce heavy unemployment, as in Great Britain, the rational expectations of trade unions must be that the nonaccommodation policies are soon likely to be abandoned—either because the present government will lose the next election to a political opposition willing to pursue traditional Keynesian employment policies *or* because the present government will change its policies in order to avoid defeat in the next election.

This leads to the conclusion that the approach taken by the political opposition may be as important as the policies followed by the government for the success of nonaccomodation policies. Only if the political opposition also supports the nonaccommodation policies, will it be rational for the trade unions to expect these policies to be lasting ones.

It is interesting to note that the countries where nonaccommodation policies seem to have worked well have all had a broad *consensus* about these policies. Austria, Finland, Germany and Switzerland are examples. In contrast, Great Britain is a case where the opposition has been very much against the nonaccommodation policies tried, and where these policies also seem to have failed. France may be another less drastic case; the nonaccommodation policies of the conservative government seem to have contributed to the loss of power this year (1981) to socialist parties, which are now opting for traditional Keynesian employment policies.

The point that I am trying to make is thus that the success of nonaccommodation policies really depends on a consensus among all the political parties that could conceivably come into power.

Assar Lindbeck: A coalition government?

Lars Calmfors: No, I am not necessarily saying that. There was no coalition in Germany. The point is, successful nonaccommodation policies seem to require that a shift of power from one political block to another is not expected to involve a radical change in stabilization policies.

Assar Lindbeck: Well, let us now listen to a German voice.

Harmen Lehment: Yes, but I would like to take a wider look, not limited to the German perspective. The target of stabilization policy was initially to cushion demand instabilities originating in the private sector. Little is heard of this any more. When we speak about stabilization policy today, we mean a reaction to either current or previous policy mistakes, or a reaction to a supply shock. This view is also taken in many of the papers at this conference, where raw material price shocks or wage shocks represent the starting point. In the case of a demand shock, you could take action and stabilize both prices and employment. In the case of a supply shock, you can go towards either price or employment-oriented stabilization policies, so there is a trade-off.

If I may focus on *employment stabilization,* I think this conference has brought out quite clearly that employment-oriented stabilization policies may have important allocational effects by reducing economic growth. Let me mention three channels. One is the increase in the size of the public sector. The second is the increase in the public debt which tends to have a negative effect on private capital formation. And the third, stressed by Martin Feldstein, is the increase in inflation, which under present tax laws also tends to reduce capital formation in the business sector. Thus, when the benefits and costs of employment-oriented stabilization policies are compared, the discussion should not be limited to Okun gaps versus Harberger triangles, to use James Tobin's famous phrase, but should also consider the long-term allocation effects of these policies.

I would also like to make a few remarks about the *current account.* Michael Bruno mentioned that governments worry about the current account. The question is: what should we do as economists? There has been a proposal by Jürg Niehans to solve the problem by burning account statistics.

Ephraim Kleiman: Does he also suggest getting rid of the unemployed?

Harmen Lehment: Well, his idea was that nobody worries about the current account of Bavaria or Texas, because you have no figures. I think that would be going a bit too far, but I would like to stress the view which goes back at least to Haberler and recently emphasized by Corden and McKinnon, that the current account is simply the sum of the current accounts of the individuals of a country, including the government. Insofar as the current account deficit represents net private borrowing, there is in general no reason for the public to step in. In my view, a policy problem arises only when the current account reflects a budget deficit. So, what the government should worry about is its own budget deficit rather than the current account deficit. I think this is important because of the policy implications. Suppose you say that we have to remove the current account deficit. Then you easily come to capital restrictions, trade restrictions, and all kinds of interventions. If you instead say that the real problem behind the current account deficit is the budget deficit, I think you arrive at more suitable policy reactions.

Ephraim Kleiman: I ought to point out that my remark about doing away with the unemployed rather than with unemployment was a throwback to H. G. Wells—I think it was "The First People on the Moon"—where the unemployed were put out to hibernate until they were needed again for work.

If, in the years to come, somebody would make a textual analysis of the proceedings of this conference, he would find that one of the key words was *rigidity*. Another one was, probably, *overshooting*.

I was glad to hear Assar Lindbeck's comment on that a few minutes ago, because I think rigidity is not a state of nature, except in death—rigor mortis. But otherwise, things are not rigid in nature. I think we are really using the word as shorthand for *real wage resistance*.

Let us say wages do not react to changes in other variables the way you would expect them to in order to bring about equilibrium, but instead there is some real wage resistance because people try to protect their real wage. They do not keep it at the same level all the time, but things are sticky—it goes down too slowly. These are all synonyms, really. As John Helliwell put it, the optimal thing to do would be to remove this rigidity or, as I would say, to lower this resistance. The question is how this can be done. As economists, we advocate a very strong medicine, which ultimately has a large element of unemployment in it. Now, this is really a policy prescription. If I may make a dubious, perhaps semantic distinction, I would distinguish between *policy,* which is steps taken given the existing institutional structure and *politics,* which is changing the structure itself.

So, one suggestion is a policy which is a rather painful one, and I would state more strongly what Michael Bruno said before: we may be in the wrong discipline for making prescriptions. It may be that lowering wage resistance is really the job of labor relations people, psychologists, God knows whom. I do not know how good they are at it, but we are offering the only alternative we can take from our discipline, and that alternative may be unnecessarily harsh.

The other alternative is in the realm of politics—changing the structure. It has been pointed out that in the United States, where unions are weak, there is very little real wage rigidity. So, presumably, doing away with the unions may be the solution.

Now, I apologize, I am being slow-witted. Perhaps I should have made my last remark in the discussion of Lars Calmfors's paper. But one possible line of investigation I was thinking about is an attempt to investigate alternative institutional arrangements and see what their effect would be on wage rigidity. One such thing has already been mentioned, the effects of learning-by-doing on union behavior. Another would be to investigate the effect of politics which would shift the burden of unemployment benefits from the state to the unions, so that the unions would have to maximize the total real wage bill, including unemployment benefits.

There are probably many other alternative institutional arrangements. I think it might be fruitful to try and investigate what economists could contribute by analysing the consequences of such institutional changes.

Hans Genberg: I would like to comment on the relationship between what has been said at this conference and the analysis of the *new classical macroeconomics* as a reaction to Peter Neary's discussion of the differences between the two. In fact, I would argue that there are several *similarities* between the frameworks used here and in the new classical macroeconomics. One of these is the intertemporal framework in many of the papers, and the implication that future policies will have strong effects on current events. Another, also due to the intertemporal framework, is the important role played by expectations in various markets. A third similarity is the explicit incorporation of maximizing behavior of individual agents and unions in several conference papers. These features are all part of the classical framework and do not differentiate the conference papers from that body of literature. What then are the *differences*? I think there are at least three.

One difference stems from the kinds of policies that have been analyzed. We have been looking mainly at *relative price policies*, for instance policies aimed at wedges between what workers receive and what employers pay. These kinds of policies would be expected to have real effects, regardless of whether they are anticipated or not. The classical macroeconomists would not arrive at different conclusions in this respect. We have not talked much about purely monetary disturbances, and anticipated ones in particular.

A second difference is that we have not really been talking about *policy rules*. We have analyzed unanticipated policy measures, as Assaf Razin mentioned in the context of Torsten Persson's paper. But most other papers have also considered mainly unanticipated policies, and not policy rules which have been incorporated into the behavior of the agents we model.

A final difference is that several papers have *imposed rigidities* on the system, real and nominal wage rigidities, without considering how these rigidities might be related to the policy behavior of the government. I suspect that, if an attempt were made to look behind the reasons for the rigidities by, for instance, relating them to policy rules, then many of the conclusions of the classical macroeconomics literature—such as the inability of anticipated monetary policy to affect output—would also come through in the models used here.

Peter Neary: The only response I will make to Hans Genberg's points is to reiterate my belief that some, although certainly not all, rigidities in real and nominal variables do provide grounds for intervention. I would like to come back to the issues raised by Thorvaldur Gylfason, that is to say not so much what have *we* learned, but what a *policy-maker might have learned* from this conference. I sympathize with his analysis, but I do not really share his pessimism.

I can think of at least three fairly specific policy prescriptions on which most of us might agree after this conference. The first is some change in the tax treatment of saving and investment along the lines described by Martin Feldstein. The second is a cut in payroll taxes financed by almost anything. And the third is for the government to make a greater effort than some governments have to resist wage demands by its own employees. These are all relatively marginal changes, "tinkering with the system" if you like, which are unlikely to bring about major improvements in macroeconomic performance in the short run. But they are steps in the right direction, which the governments of many European countries could profitably take.

This brings me to a final point of a methodological kind that has been made in earlier sessions, especially by Robin Matthews, that is, the question of the *behavior of the government* as an economic agent. I think the government has been a very shadowy presence in all our papers, it has been G or T, or whatever—something in the background. In this respect our models are not very different from most macroeconomic models. It is a fact that we know very little about government behavior and I am not quite sure how far we want to go in the direction of modelling governments explicitly. But there are at least two levels where we might try. First the information question. We have talked about how difficult it is for economists to identify different shocks; so, clearly, it is crucial that we should try and have some views on how the government manages (or fails) to do so. The second is the choice of policy instruments. How exactly do actual governments choose among policy instruments? I am not sure whether formal modelling is the route we should take here to try to understand more. But it remains an area in which we are extremely ignorant.

Michael Bruno: Let me just repeat a point that I think has already been made on the question of real wage rigidity. If you look at the end point of a period and compare it with the initial point, then you find much fewer differences among countries than those Assar Lindbeck talked about. The main difference is in the phasing, but that makes for a great deal of difference in behavior.

I would also like to stress one aspect of what Peter Neary said in response to Thorvaldur Gylfason. I do not really share Gylfason's pessimism, as Neary does not. Pessimism would be justified if all countries did consistently badly over the whole period. But some of the countries did better than others. Now you might argue that maybe the institutional system is so much better in these countries. But then I would say that sometimes the same country has done badly over part of the period, and better over other parts of the period. And governments change, so there is sufficient scope for thinking that things can be run better than they sometimes seem to be.

Assar Lindbeck: Well, I do not want to summarize the summary. But to a person who contributed to formulating the topic of the conference, it is clear that several of the problems which we had in mind have been highlighted. One problem that has come out very clearly in many papers is the *permanent* effect of temporary shocks and temporary policies, by way of the influence on, for example, investment, the size of the public sector and the market for shares. Another thing that has been brought out clearly is the importance of considering *intertemporal* aspects. The main risk with current account deficits is perhaps that the government pleases the present generation of voters by expropriating income from future generations, and maybe this is the reason why many people are worried about the deficits.

Third, a conflict between short-run and long-run considerations has also emerged. The most pronounced example is probably the *accommodation* problem, because here we are all completely schizophrenic. We all say that governments have to announce that they cannot accommodate indefinitely. But the next minute we say that the product real wage rates have to be reduced by government intervention. Let us start our nonaccommodation policy with a big accommodation, for instance by reducing payroll taxes or by devaluing. Do we create confidence in a nonaccommodation strategy by starting with a big accommodation? I admit my own ambivalence on this issue.

Finally, some asserted policy effects which we believed in earlier may not occur if the analysis is widened to encompass additional long-run aspects. This point comes out well in Martin Feldstein's paper. We have learned from Tobin and others that the *policy mix* to pursue, if we want growth, is easy money and a strict fiscal policy. Now Feldstein argues that exactly this combination in fact has the opposite effect! It leads to inflation and, through the nonneutral tax system, discriminates against investment in plant and equipment. Instead, he says, we have to do the opposite: restrictive monetary policy to avoid inflation in combination with fiscal incentives for investment. Thus, he reverses the assignment of Tobin, by considering something which was not considered to any large extent before: that inflation, because of the tax-system, is highly nonneutral towards the allocation of investment.

Let me end with a final reflection. Many of us realize that in highly open economies we have to rely heavily on stabilization policy instruments that change relative prices rather than domestic aggregate demand. However, exactly the policies that influence relative prices also have domestic allocational effects. So in an open economy, stabilization policies automatically have considerable allocational effects.

Michael Bruno: It may be remarked in passing that we started in sunshine and ended in sunshine.

Assar Lindbeck: But in between there was a long, dark tunnel!

MIX
Papier aus verantwortungsvollen Quellen
Paper from responsible sources
FSC® C105338

If you have any concerns about our products,
you can contact us on
ProductSafety@springernature.com

In case Publisher is established outside the EU,
the EU authorized representative is:
Springer Nature Customer Service Center GmbH
Europaplatz 3, 69115 Heidelberg, Germany

Printed by Libri Plureos GmbH
in Hamburg, Germany